The King of Brilliance

James Lomas – A Rugby League Superstar

Graham Morris

London League Publications Ltd

The King of Brilliance
James Lomas – A Rugby League Superstar

© Graham Morris. Foreword © Pat Clancy

Cover design © Stephen McCarthy.

Front cover: Top: James Lomas in an England jersey. The dog is probably a Salford club mascot as it also appears with club players and officials in another photograph.
Bottom: A rare action shot of James as he is about to pass to a colleague during the Oldham versus Runcorn game on 11 February 1911. A large crowd was present to watch his home debut for the Roughyeds.
Back cover: A meeting of legends as James, then aged 43, and 19-year-old Jim Sullivan pose for the camera. The occasion was the Salford versus Wigan match at The Willows on 10 March 1923. Sullivan would, in the years ahead, overtake the Cumbrian's record as rugby league highest ever points-scorer.

A CIP catalogue record for this book is available from the British Library.

First published in Great Britain in September 2011 by:
London League Publications Ltd, P.O. Box 65784, London NW2 9NS

ISBN: 978-1903659-57-1

Cover design by: Stephen McCarthy Graphic Design
                              46, Clarence Road, London N15 5BB

Layout: Peter Lush

Printed and bound in Great Britain by Charlesworth Press, Wakefield

Foreword

I lived with my grandparents, James and Annie Lomas, for almost 15 years from the time when I was just a toddler in the 1940s. I knew then that my grandfather had been a rugby player, but I had no idea that he was such a famous one. To me he was just my granddad, who was a lovely, kind man. But as the years have gone by I have come to realise just how much he achieved during his rugby career and grown to feel very proud of him.

He used to work at the docks, which was near where we lived in Byrom Street in Salford, and I can remember when I was about eight or nine years old that I would walk to Broadway, just outside the docks, to meet him after he finished in the early evening. He had a hook on the end of a wooden handle which he kept at home and took to work with him. He must have used it to grab cargo as it was unloaded at the dockside. He worked until he was about 72 and it must have been hard for him as he got older. I can remember in later years that he used to rub liniment into his legs each evening to ease the stiffness he must have felt in his joints.

On Sundays he used to take me for walks through Ordsall Park, which was always very busy in those days, particularly if the weather was good. We would often call in at a friend of his to say hello and have a chat. Sometimes one of my aunties would visit us – two lived in Belfast and another near London – so there would be other grandchildren as well, but he would take us all with him. It never bothered him. He was not really what you would call a Church-goer, but when I was little he would say prayers with me when it was my bedtime. I suppose he thought it was the right thing to do. When I was about 12 or 13 I would go to the nearby Central Mission some evenings where they held 'tea dances', waltzing and that type of thing, and granddad would always meet me after it finished at 9pm to walk me home. He had a very caring, protective nature.

My grandfather was a quiet man. He had his favourite chair where he would sit and smoke his pipe. In his later years he would smoke woodbines instead. My grandma used to get the *Daily Express* delivered each morning. She would read its Rupert Bear cartoon strip to me when I was young and I suppose granddad must have read the paper in the evening. I remember that he never wanted a television in the house, not everybody had one in those days, but when I was about 14 I kept asking if I could have a radio because I wanted to listen to the pop music on Radio Luxembourg. He finally gave in and he got me a Rediffusion set. It was wonderful. We never did get a television set, though, and my grandma used to go round the corner to my brother, Billy Mahaffy's, house to watch his sometimes.

Granddad used to go to a pub in Cross Lane on Sunday lunchtime, but did not drink a lot. I think he only had one drink and he did not bother at all during the week. My grandparents used to take me to the cinema quite often. There was plenty to choose from in those days and we would go as many as three times a week. Normally, it was The Empire on Trafford Road on a Monday, the Borough near Ordsall Park on Tuesday, and the Carlton at Cross Lane on Wednesday.

My grandparents also used to visit some friends. I am not sure where they lived, but I remember thinking at the time that they must have had a garden because they always brought gooseberries back with them. Granddad would sometimes get dressed up in a suit and tie and go to rugby reunions at the Midland Hotel in Manchester. I think it must have been when he was a member of the British Lions Association. He never had any medals or anything on display at home. He had a lot of caps that he kept in a cupboard. There was a lad next door called Peter Sullivan and granddad would sometimes get a cap out of the cupboard and put it on his head and then Peter would go out into the street wearing it.

All my grandfather's friends knew him as Jim or Jimmy, but my mother and her three sisters always called him Da, probably because they had spent much of their lives in Belfast and that was how the Irish would address their father. My Auntie Olive, when she visited from Belfast, got grandma and granddad to change from gas lighting – which a lot of people still had then – to electricity. She also arranged to get rid of an old black range iron fireplace, which we could cook on, and replace it with a proper tiled fireplace. At Christmas she would post a large chicken and granddad's older sister Sarah always sent a big Christmas cake from Maryport. Granddad also received a food hamper from New Zealand every year. I cannot remember now who it was from, but it always said 'With Thanks' so it must have been because of his visit there in 1910. I remember it used to include sugared almonds which I loved.

Grandma and granddad were very close. They were a nice loving couple who never had an argument. I have a lot to be grateful for. I had a lovely childhood with them.

Pat Clancy
Granddaughter of James Lomas

Bibliography

Newspapers: *The Athletic News* (Manchester), *The Guardian* (Barrow), *Leeds Mercury, Manchester Courier, Manchester Guardian, Oldham Evening Chronicle, Oldham Standard, Salford Chronicle, Salford Reporter, The News* (Barrow), *West Cumberland Times, Yorkshire Evening Press* (York), *Yorkshire Herald* (York) and *Yorkshire Post* (Leeds).

Publications: Rugby League Record Keepers' Club publications (editor Irvin Saxton, 1972 to 1994), *Code 13* (editor Trevor Delaney, 1986 to 1991), *100 Greats: Cumberland Rugby League* (Robert Gate, 2002), *Best In the Northern Union* (Tom Mather, 2010), *The British Rugby League Records Book* (Graham Williams. Peter Lush and Dave Farrar, 2009), *The Encyclopaedia of Rugby League Players* (Alan Whiticker and Glen Hudson, 1999), *The Grounds of Rugby League* (Trevor Delaney, 1991), *Guinness Rugby League Fact Book* (Robert Gate, 1991), *The International Grounds of Rugby League* (Trevor Delaney, 1995), *Keeping The Dream Alive* (Dave Huitson, Keith Nutter and Steve Andrews, 2008), *Oldham RLFC: The Complete History* (Michael Turner, 1997), *Rugby League in Twentieth Century Britain* (Tony Collins, 2006), *Rugby League Lions* (Robert Gate, 2008), *Those Who Played* (Bruce Montgomerie, 2004).

'James' or 'Jimmy'

In modern times, we know him as 'James Lomas', but many of the newspaper reports at the time used 'Jimmy'. The text of the book uses 'James', or occasionally 'James Lomas', but we have not changed any quotes from the time, which usually use 'Jimmy'.

Introduction

James Lomas was one of the first superstars of rugby league or, to be more precise, the Northern Union as it was known in his day. Many historians have described him as the code's outstanding performer through the opening decade of the 20th century, a period that climaxed for him in 1910 when he led his countrymen in the first ever Northern Union tour of Australia and New Zealand. Plying his rugby trade for hometown Maryport, Bramley, Salford, Oldham and York, he was twice the subject of a world record transfer fee.

Short in stature, he possessed a solid looking, almost square build, reminiscent of the silhouette associated with many of the modern-day hookers. What he lacked in inches he made up for in sheer power with a capability to hand off the meanest of defenders as he charged for the try-line. His defensive qualities too were unshakable. It is a common tactic today for a club to target one of the opposition's smaller players – usually a half back – by launching some giant back-row forward in his direction. In the case of James Lomas it was a ploy unlikely to succeed.

James, or 'Jimmy' as he was usually referred to in the press at the time, was also known as 'Jumbo'. There was even a suggestion (not by the publisher I might add!) that the title of this book should be 'Jumbo', an idea I resisted. One hundred years ago it was a well meant term of endearment, one that related to his frame and incredible strength. Presented to a modern audience it sounds less complimentary, implying he was overweight and unfit but, as you will discover in the pages that follow, nothing could be further from the truth.

A match winner without equal, he began as a stand-off before settling into the centre threequarter berth where he spent two-thirds of his senior career. Such was his influence on proceedings that one sports journalist was moved to write "when Lomas was on the field you never noticed anybody else". But it was not just his physical presence that provided inspiration for his colleagues. His scoring exploits too were something to behold. He was a human points-machine that notched tries and goals in vast quantities, whatever the occasion or opposition. This at a time when scoring was significantly lower than in subsequent eras and when – until 1906 – there were still 15 opponents to contend with.

James was the leading points scorer for Bramley in 1900–01, Oldham in 1911–12 and York in 1914–15. At Salford, he led the scoring chart through nine consecutive seasons from 1901–02. He was also the Northern Union's top scorer on five occasions, twice setting a new high for the code. His career harvest of 2,312 points remained unsurpassed until Wigan's great Welsh full-back Jim Sullivan appeared on the scene during the inter-war years. But, whereas Sullivan compiled his massive points tally through his phenomenal goalkicking, Lomas was equally adept at claiming tries and, to this day remains one of a handful of players to register in excess of 300 tries and 300 goals.

James was unexpectedly and magically restored to life on our television screens in 2005 when a BBC2 series was shown based on recently discovered film reels shot in the early-1900s by the Mitchell & Kenyon Film Company. It included footage of several Northern Union matches, one of the most prominent being the Salford versus Batley contest from November 1901, James's seventh appearance for the Reds. It captures him emerging with colleagues on to their former New Barnes pitch before the start, clearly showing off the muscular physique so often referred to during his playing days. Even better was the remarkable sight of him scoring his second half try and goal.

Alf Beecroft covered the affairs of the Salford club in the *Salford City Reporter* during the 1920s and early 1930s, using the name of 'Ajax'. On the occasion of the club's official

Centenary in 1979 he interrupted his retirement to write "I still maintain that Salford, in their history, have had three legends – the great Jimmie (sic) Lomas of the First World War era, Gus Risman, and David Watkins of more modern times." The latter two have, quite justifiably, been the subject of biographies, whereas the story of the mercurial James has, thus far, not been committed to immortality in print. It was an omission in the code's literature that I had often thought of rectifying – an ambition stimulated through seeing the Mitchell-Kenyon footage – but it always felt like a daunting task given the long time-lapse since he played.

I would respectfully add a fourth name to Alf's list, that of 1974 Lions tour captain Chris Hesketh with whom I had the pleasure of working with on his autobiography, published in 2006. The major and obvious difference between the creation of Chris's biography and that of James's is that the former is still very much alive and kicking and therefore we were able to sit down together at regular periods to record his thoughts and reminiscences. With James – who was born in 1879 – that was clearly not an option. Certainly I could research all of the matches he participated in, but how could I get inside the mind of a man who is now only with us in spirit? It was a situation exacerbated by the fact that I had no contact with, or indeed any knowledge of family descendants.

Enter Tom Mather! Tom, a good friend over many years, was working on his book about the 1910 Northern Union tour, *Best in the Northern Union*, when, in March 2009, he was contacted by a gentleman called Andy Dellar. Andy's father Rob Dellar, based in Essex, is a grandson of James Lomas. In fact, Rob's full name is actually Robin James Lomas Dellar, his mother Evelyn was the second eldest of James's four daughters. Like so many things in life Andy's approach to Tom was the culmination of a series of events. He had 'surfed' the internet looking for tit-bits about his illustrious forebear and came upon *The Master*, an Australian publication about the great Dally Messenger, a contemporary of James's. Andy contacted joint-author Sean Fagan, who mentioned to him that Tom was working on the aforementioned book and provided contact details.

From my point of view the 'discovery' of Rob and Andy Dellar provided the impetus to finally attempt a biography of James. Since that moment there have been other areas of encouragement. Rob had in his possession eight handwritten pages by James in which he sets out his thoughts on his career. Written in the late 1930s (a date calculated from the address James obligingly wrote in the top corner of the first page) I refer to them as the James Lomas 'memoirs' whenever I quote from them within the text of this book. A further invaluable insight into his opinions – that Tom came across – appeared in a lengthy interview featured in a 1924 New Zealand newspaper. Since then, I have uncovered other snippets, through my own research or the invaluable help of members of the Lomas family.

Through my contact with the Dellars, I subsequently was put in touch with, and received help from Carol McConnell, James's granddaughter and one of several descendants living in Belfast. This was followed by another stroke of good fortune during August 2010 when Steve Clancy took his young son to the new Museum of Museums at the Trafford Centre complex. Within its walls they discovered that the Salford City Reds had a display section and, not only that, there was a picture of James Lomas on the wall. Although not rugby fans they recognized the face. Steve's mother Pat Clancy is also a granddaughter of James and another valuable link was forged. I am grateful to John Blackburn (the driving force behind Salford's museum display) who passed on my contact details to Steve. Having subsequently met Steve on several occasions I am sure I am not the only person struck by the uncanny resemblance to his famous predecessor.

The majority of James's rugby career took place while the infant Northern Union game was slowly but surely maturing into a fully grown adult, incorporating along the way many of the features of the code that are still with us today. Its continuing rule changes at that time steered a course that, while taking it further from the old rugby union laws, provided a challenge for its players in adapting to them, including James. The advent of the Northern Union also mirrored a period of great social changes and unrest, particularly for the working classes from whom the fledgling code drew most of its support.

Transport too was on the increase to the benefit of the masses and, while the new motor vehicles were still beyond the pocket of most Northern Union fans, the railway network continued to grow in popularity. Apart from enabling families to visit the seaside for the first time, it was the main form of transport for teams and their supporters to away matches. The phenomenal growth in the sport was also given an official stamp of approval through being absorbed into the school curriculum in 1906.

We can now look back on the Edwardian period as an exciting time in the development of rugby league as the initial shoots of the 1895 breakaway began to flower. The early isolation of a sport that was based only in the northern counties of England ended almost unexpectedly through the ground breaking visits of the New Zealanders in 1907 and Australian's in 1908. It gave the code a new feeling of justification and self-belief. It also introduced exciting new heroes from the opposite side of the planet, such as Lance Todd and Albert Rosenfeld, who remained in England to play against and alongside the pioneering home-based stars such as Billy Batten, Albert Goldthorpe and, of course, James.

There have been many rugby league biographies written, particularly over the past 30 years, but mostly they are of current or recently retired players. To my knowledge, James's story is the first to have as its subject someone who played through that fascinating Edwardian period of the code's history. It was not a claim I had intended and, indeed, such a thought had not occurred to me at the outset. However, despite the huge task of reaching back through the generations to his playing days, researching James's story has been as fascinating and interesting as it has been challenging. It was also enlightening. I knew before I began this book that James was seen as a great player. What I had not realised was just how great he was and how highly he was valued during his time as a performer.

In James's day, there were no radio broadcasts or television. The only way the public kept abreast of their heroes' deeds was through the newspapers which, at that time, provided very detailed 'blow-by-blow' accounts of the games, usually followed by a summary of the performances of the players. Thankfully, many of these reports still survive via microfilm in the various local history libraries, providing us with the opportunity to step back in time. In James's case, particularly during the decade he spent with Salford, it is clear he was the stand-out performer in virtually every game he played, tales of his exploits included one superlative after another, and he was amazingly consistent over a long period.

I thought long and hard about an appropriate title for this book, one that summed up the great esteem in which James was held during his playing career. My answer came when I read the words of a contributor to the *Salford Reporter* who, in 1908, was so inspired by James's heroics that he put his thoughts into verse (reproduced elsewhere in this publication). He concluded his adulation with the words "A King of brilliance, dash and pluck, play up, Jim, my boy". I could not have said it better! It therefore remains for me to invite you to read on about 'A King of Brilliance'.

Graham Morris
Worsley, August 2011

Note on research

In compiling James Lomas's story and as stated in the introduction, most of my research has been accomplished through referencing the newspapers of the day. James was of such standing that his performances were scrutinized in virtually every match report ranging from superlative pros to cutting comments whenever he fell below the level of expectation placed upon him. James rarely had a 'poor' game but, in my endeavour to provide an honest account of his playing career, I have tried to accurately reflect the observations of the journalists that saw him play, whether or not it placed him in a good light. However, in order to strike a correct balance in the mind of the reader, I should point out that many of the negative quotes can look out of context when taking into account the full match report. During his pomp James was, like all great sportsmen and women, invariably the outstanding player even when he fell below his own exacting standards.

Acknowledgements

I could not have written this biography if it was not for the kind help of others. Firstly I have to thank Tom Mather because, as explained in the Introduction, if it had not been for my many conversations with Tom, the idea of attempting this book would not have presented itself to me. I must similarly express gratitude to Peter Lush and Dave Farrar of London League Publications Ltd for sharing my enthusiasm for this work. Without their support you would not now be reading these notes.

Those who have provided welcome assistance along the way include Mavis Blackburn, Ron and Doreen Burrow, Tony Capstick, Steve Fox, Robert Gate, David Gronow, Andrew Hardcastle, Mick Harrop, Steve Haslam, Roy Holdman, Ian Jones, Mike Turner, Brian Walker and Terry Williams (Australia). I must also give a special mention to Sarah Moriarty and Susan Shaw who went to a great deal of trouble to produce a Lomas family tree. It proved invaluable to my work and is a gesture greatly appreciated by myself. Another important contributor to my research was Trish Milner who is the great, great-granddaughter of John Smith, who is mentioned in the opening chapter.

My thanks also to the staff of Salford Local History Library (particularly Trish Nuttall and Duncan McCormick), Manchester Central Library, Oldham Local Studies Library, Leeds Central Library, York Minster Library, Maryport Library, Workington Library (Mary Hart, Jean Griffiths), Cumbria Archive Service in Barrow (Kate Pearson), Belfast Central Library (Suzanne Drake), Birkenhead Central Library, St Helens Central Library, Warrington Library, Wigan Local History Library and the University of Huddersfield Archive (Hilary Haigh and colleagues). I would also like to acknowledge the feature on the Maryport Maritime Museum by Malcolm Bobbitt (2001) which I came across via the internet.

And last but by no means least, a big thank you to James's descendants who all enthusiastically supplied me with information and photographs in addition to patiently answering my many questions with good humour. They are Pat Clancy (granddaughter) and her husband Graham, Steve Clancy (great-grandson), Rob Dellar (grandson), Andy Dellar (great-grandson) and Carol McConnell (granddaughter). I know that all of them were excitedly awaiting the finished product. I sincerely hope that they will not be disappointed!

Graham Morris

London League Publications Ltd would like to thank Steve McCarthy for designing the cover, and the staff of Charlesworth Press for printing the book.

Contents

Jimmy Lomas – A King of Brilliance, Dash and Pluck

He's a captain worthy of the name,
Salford's pride and joy,
A player known only to fame,
Play up, Jim, my boy.

In the game he puts both heart and soul,
And always plays to win;
To score a try, to kick a goal,
Is the one aim of Jim.

It is a matter for regret,
And with you we sympathise,
For opponents always have you "set",
Such tactics we despise.

But you seldom give them tit for tat,
And your pluck we all admire,
Such patience makes one raise one's hat
To you, most worthy sire.

If every player played like him
What honours ours would be;
Then every match Salford would win,
As easy as A B C.

Your equal in the football world
Is difficult to find;
Long may your banner be unfurled
And floating on the wind.

All "Reds" wish you the best of luck,
Of health, and fame, and joy;
A King of brilliance, dash and pluck,
Play up, Jim, my boy.

By A.S. (*Salford Reporter*, October 1908)

1. Life in a seafaring town

Maryport, situated on the West Cumbrian coast, has reinvented itself in recent years as a popular tourist resort after emerging from a long era of depression that began biting hard during the 1920s after the collapse of its core industries. Today, its picturesque harbour, watched over by a small lighthouse that has attended its gateway since 1796, is the magnet that attracts visitors. With the Northern Fells providing a perfect backdrop, its vigorous past is much in evidence, reflected through the many old taverns and fishermen's quayside cottages that still abound. Indeed, it's long established fishing tradition continues although with far fewer vessels and at a more modest pace than before. This delightful maritime setting bursts into life each year when the 11,000 residents welcome visitors to such events as the Maryport Blues Festival.

The seafaring town sprang up around the River Ellen and can trace its roots back to Roman times, the harbour providing shelter from the worst excesses of the Irish Sea. Previously known as Ellenfoot, it became Maryport in 1749 when the then Lord of the Manor, Humphrey Senhouse, renamed it after his wife Mary. It became the busiest port on the Cumbrian coastline, creating wealth through the local coal trade, the produce of which found its way to the pier on railway wagons and thence by sea to Ireland. There was also a prosperous shipbuilding industry, Maryport's first shipyard being opened in 1765. By the mid–1800s it was a bustling trading port, the Elizabeth Dock being opened in 1857 and the Senhouse Dock during 1884. This growth was reflected in a population surge and from 8,126 residents in 1881 it had shot up to 12,526 by the time of the 1891 census.

It was into this thriving environment that James Lomas was born on 26 August 1879 at the Curzon Street address of his parent's James (senior) and Sarah. Apart from being the birth year of the Northern Union's first tour captain, 1879 has its place in history through the battle for survival of 104 British troops at an old mission station on Rorke's Drift. On 22 January, in what was then known as Zululand in southern Africa, they repelled a reported 4,000 Zulu warriors, an encounter immortalized in the dramatic 1964 movie *Zulu*. Indeed, the Northern Union dubbed the decisive 1914 test victory in Australia as 'The Rorke's Drift Test' having been reduced to ten men during the match. 1879 was also when Thomas Edison developed the light bulb and the year that the club with which James would build his reputation became known as Salford, having begun life as Cavendish in Manchester's Hulme district six years earlier.

Within two years of James's birth, the 1881 census reveals that the family had transferred to a four-bedroomed end-terraced house in nearby Lawson Street, built as recently as 1878. Occupying two floors with a small attic built into the roof, the move was possibly to accommodate an ever-expanding family. Initial research suggested that James was the couple's third child and only son, preceded by Sarah and Mary and followed by Hannah and Rebecca, all born in Maryport. There were also several step-brothers and stepsisters to take into account. His mother had previously been married to the late John Smith and between them they had, apparently, produced five children; Barbara, followed, in turn, by William Tyson, Annie, Isabella and Thomas (Tom), again all Maryport-born.

However, a book called *Maritime Maryport* by Annie Robinson, published in 1978, says that John Smith was one of six men – from a crew of 10 – lost at sea following a shipwreck near Formosa (now Taiwan) in October 1870, having hit a rock. The vessel was a 350 ton barque called the Humberstone and used for trading, with probable commodities including silk and tea. There is a suggestion that Smith – who was also the captain – and his father-in-law William Tyson had money invested in the venture. Smith's first four children with Sarah were born in the 1860s – twins Annie and Isabella were the last during July 1868 – whereas Tom did not arrive until the mid–1870s and was clearly not his.

The clue to solving this mystery lies in the fact that maritime law dictated if a person was lost at sea and their body not recovered, they could not officially be declared dead until several years had elapsed. With Sarah subsequently meeting James Lomas senior they were, therefore, unable to marry until June 1875. It is highly probable that Tom was their first child and, because they were not then wed, he inherited his mother's surname.

Tom (full name Thomas McGraa Smith) was born on 26 November 1874 and no father is named on his birth certificate. He was destined to become a well-known footballer. An outside right, he played for Preston North End from 1895 until 1897 before moving to London to join Tottenham Hotspur. He subsequently returned to Preston in 1903, and concluded his career with Carlisle United, where he was also the trainer, and hometown Maryport Tradesmen. However, before excelling in the round ball game, he played rugby for the Maryport club, following the footsteps of older brother William Tyson who was referred to in the press at that time as 'W.T.'.

The revelation that Tom Smith – the footballer – and James Lomas – the rugby player – probably shared the same parents goes against everything ever written about the pair, the perceived wisdom was that they were step-brothers. Tom had three sons who distinguished themselves in sport. The eldest, Francis Sidney Smith – born in Tottenham in 1902 – became a half-back for Workington AFC and subsequently moved to the United States. Arthur Edward Smith was a rugby league centre for Warrington in the mid–1920s and later chairman of Maryport Urban District Council. The youngest, Ernest Donald Smith, became secretary of the Cumberland Football Association.

James's father, James senior, was born around 1844 in a village called Holme Low, two miles inland from the coastal town of Silloth and approximately 12 miles north of Maryport. His father was William Lomas, but details of his parentage have proved elusive although he was known to have had, at least, two younger siblings – a sister and brother. At the time of his death – around 1929 – it was reported he came from 'farming stock' and at the age of six was 'taken' from Great Broughton, where he had been living, to Silloth. Quite how he was relocated from his place of birth to Great Broughton, which is about four miles south-east of Maryport, and then north back to Silloth is not recorded. What is known is that it was a tough time for any working class youngster to be growing up. Most fell into the category of 'child labourers' and were expected to supplement the income of their often starving families. Education was not on the agenda in the mid–19th century, but long tiring hours of employment certainly were.

True, he was not sent down a coalmine or put to work in a factory like so many others, but he was away from home performing manual tasks. The 1851 census, when he would have been aged six, describes him as a lodger and agricultural labourer for the Bendle family at Greenrow, near Silloth, which was possibly his destination when 'taken' from Great Broughton. In the 1861 census he is shown as one of two servants employed by the family of 'card winder' Thomas Bell in a place called Calvo, again not too far from Silloth.

Showing initiative, he became an ironmonger and then shoemaker, and arrived in Maryport in the mid–1870s where he established himself at a shop in Crosby Street making seamen's boots. He was by all accounts a colourful character and a local personality in the town. Described as a short man "lightly but symmetrically made" with a powerful physique he was, in his younger years, a wrestler "of no small repute in the county". It was a description that could almost fit his illustrious son who was also to dabble in the art of wrestling. A photograph of James Lomas senior as a young man in modest wrestling attire shows a muscular build that was probably developed during his early exertions in Greenrow. Described as being of "a peaceful, unselfish disposition," it suggests a similar temperament to that of his rugby playing offspring. He was still a familiar sight in Maryport's streets when he reached his early 80s – he lived to be 85 – walking "with the light step and upright carriage of a much younger man."

James's mother had been born in about 1840 as Sarah Scott Tyson in Maryport, the second eldest of seven children produced by the previously mentioned William Tyson, who was a mariner born during 1814 in Allanby, Cumberland, and Ann – formerly Robinson, born 1812 in Maryport. Several years older than her second husband, Sarah was destined to pass away some 17 years before him.

It seems, though, that life for James Lomas senior was not without problems. In March 1888, the *West Cumberland Times* reported that he appeared at Cockermouth County Court claiming he had 600 debtors despite "between 2,500 and 3,000 circulars [having been] sent out applying for debts [to be settled]". He said the postage had cost between £10 and £13 "while the labour had been immense". Apparently, his objective was not to make a complaint, but rather to point out to the court "the great difficulty there was in getting debts in."

Business must have been good, however, because by 1891 the Lomas family had moved into an impressive looking three-storey terraced house in Fleming Square. By this time the headcount was 14 people, including three lodgers, thereby increasing the household purse. Like at Curzon Street and Lawson Street, and typical of Maryport, the Fleming Square address was a narrow, but tall, building, reminiscent of those surrounding Amsterdam's many canals. It seems that land space was used sparingly in Maryport in the 1800s. They did not stay in the Square, though, and at the time of the 1901 census the couple were living in Catherine Street along with four other family members. James junior was not among them, having left Maryport in 1900 to pursue his rugby career. However, it may well have been the last address he lived at in Maryport with his parents.

In later years, James Lomas recalled that the first rugby match he witnessed was Cumberland against the Maoris, played at Maryport on 17 November 1888. Apart from the fact that it was staged on the local cricket ground, nine-year-old James would have been drawn by the appearance of his 21-year-old step-brother 'W.T.' in Cumberland's pack. In all probability he would have accompanied the remainder of the Lomas family on what was a special day in their lives as well as for the whole community.

The *West Cumberland Times* described the scene: "The largest concourse of persons which was ever known to witness a football match in Maryport or, in fact, any of the neighbouring towns, was the one which assembled on the cricket field of that place." It was suggested that, but for the rain of the preceding days and the showers before kick-off, the attendance, around 2,000, could have been even higher. Played over two 35-minute periods on a slippery pitch, the tourists won 10–2 by virtue of scoring six tries to two, at a time when a try was worth one point and converted try three points.

Although dubbed by the press as the 'Maoris' (a term now considered inaccurate with 'Maori' used to describe both singular and plural) they were officially called the New Zealand Native Football Team. An original plan to tour as the New Zealand Maori was scrapped after the late addition of several Pakeha (a reference to European settlers who had integrated with the Maori). Their visit to Maryport was match number 17 in a punishing 74-game schedule that began during October 1888. Incidentally, the concluding month of the tour – March 1889 – included fixtures against James's future clubs: Salford, Oldham and York.

Whether James returned home disappointed with the loss we will never know. He could, though, console himself in future years knowing he had witnessed a piece of sporting history after watching the first overseas rugby tourists to visit the British Isles. Maybe he drew some inspiration from his experience or perhaps it was already in his blood given his father's grappling skills and the sporting prowess of his older brothers but, either way, James took up rugby with the school team.

Unlike his father, James junior received a formal education, benefitting from the introduction of the Forster's Education Act in 1870 that ensured 'less privileged' children attended school from the age of five to 10, extended to 13 by 1899. His schooling would have been at the British School in North Street or the National School on Eaglesfield Street, both being close to his home. There is no record to confirm which he attended.

Having completed his education he joined Ritson & Sons, a local shipbuilding company where he served his apprenticeship as a ship riveter. It was a company that mirrored the rise and fall of Maryport as a commercial seaport. In the 1820s John Ritson had started to build ships alongside the River Ellen. Joined by his two sons he eventually created Ritson and Sons, their first iron ship – as opposed to timber – was launched in 1885. But Maryport's shipbuilding industry became a casualty of progress. The last ship launched there was in 1914. Its decline was due to the new steamships having to be towed to the Clyde or Tyne to have boilers and engines installed. Competition from rivals that had such facilities on site was Maryport's downfall and what was once the busiest port on Cumbria's coast could offer its soldiers, returning from the Great War of 1914–18, little or no work. Ritson & Sons built their last vessel in 1902 prior to the company being sold although the name survives today through 'Ritson's Wharf', a residential complex which occupies the old site.

Walking around Maryport's waterfront today – particularly in midweek – there is a relaxed, tranquil feel. There are quayside cafes and bars, a marina, an information centre, maritime museum and the obligatory crazy golf. A short stroll away is a promenade and Roman museum that overlooks the Irish Sea and, at the spot where Ritson's once launched ships into the River Ellen, stands a modern leisure complex that incorporates a theatre. Looking around the surrounding quayside and its harbours one cannot help but imagine how it must have been when James was living and working there in the late–1800s; the general hubbub of the place, the pounding of machinery in shipbuilders' yards, the rumble of railway trucks transporting coal for shipment to Ireland, the seagulls pursuing the herring boats into the harbour and the early evening rush as men rewarded a day's toil by converging on the many inns dotted around the water's edge.

James left Maryport in 1900 at the age of 21 to continue his emerging rugby career in west Yorkshire. Thereafter he never became a stranger in his birthplace, and returned on many occasions to spend periods of time with relatives, even into his later years. Except for one particular short-lived occasion, he never set up home there again. Nonetheless, Cumberland, and Maryport in particular, always remained close to his heart.

A dashing, youthful James resplendent in jacket and tie.
(Photo: Courtesy Rob Dellar)

James Lomas senior was a well-known personality in Maryport. He was a prominent wrestler in the area and clearly an influence on his more famous offspring.
(Photo: Courtesy Rob Dellar)

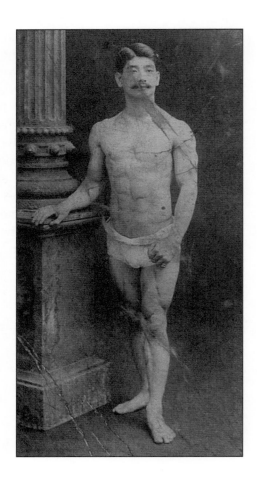

2. Like father, like son

It was once said that James Lomas inherited his father's "strong heart and activity". There was also a physical likeness; at five feet seven inches tall he had a similarly short stature and, like his parent, possessed great strength. Throughout his career his weight was quoted as over 13 stone, the 1910 tour brochure, produced by the *Athletic News*, was more specific at 13 stone three pounds. One observer said he had "a heavy, powerful frame so heavily coated with muscle that no tackle hurt him, while his strength was such that he was feared on the field and men would quickly pass the ball when they saw him coming for them." Throw in his speed, awareness, and ability to kick the ball with unerring accuracy during loose play, and you have all the attributes of a near-perfect rugby player.

Like his father, James indulged in wrestling – an extremely popular sporting pastime in Cumberland at that time – and was also something of an athlete. In the 'Prominent Salford Sportsmen' series, published in the *Salford Reporter* in 1926, 'Ajax' – who would almost certainly have conferred with James – wrote "In his younger days Lomas won several valuable prizes for foot-racing, and what is more, won his races in excellent times." Another account referred to him taking part in, and winning "foot-racing handicaps". He was also a strong swimmer, a skill that would save several people from drowning.

'Ajax' went on to say that "after figuring in school teams he became associated with the Maryport [rugby union] club when only 16 years of age." With two older brothers in William Tyson Smith and Tom Smith already wearing the maroon of Maryport, it would have been a natural progression for a sports-loving, competitive young man such as James. As previously stated, 'W.T.' was in the Cumberland county side that met the Maoris in 1888. He was also a member of the Maryport team that captured the Cumberland Challenge Cup in 1893, beating Cummersdale Hornets 4–3 in the final. On occasions he captained the side and remained a cornerstone of the Maryport pack throughout the time that James played for the team, including the club's earliest years in the Northern Union.

Tom's career, on the other hand, was more varied. By all accounts he was a speedy and agile character and excelled at both codes of football; association and rugby. He first played for the Maryport rugby club as a wing threequarter at the start of the 1893–94 season, a couple of months before his 19th birthday. It was a campaign that ended with the two Smith brothers sharing in a second Cumberland Challenge Cup success. Maryport retained their prize with an 8–4 triumph over Egremont. Tom continued patrolling the Maryport flank throughout 1894–95 in a team that also included in its back division John Timoney and Billy Hannah, who would move on to Wigan and Hunslet respectively. In January 1895, Tom took advantage of a gap in the rugby fixtures to turn out for Maryport's association football club, "the well-known Maryport threequarter flyer" was in the side beaten 5–3 by Moss Bay Exchange reserves and, apparently, gave a good account of himself.

When the 1895–96 campaign got under way, Tom's future seemed uncertain. On the first football weekend of the season – Saturday 7 September – he again turned out for the town's association football club. He played at centre-forward against Wigton Harriers and created another positive impression. The *West Cumberland Times* said: "If Smith would only stick to this game he couldn't help getting county honours." Over the next two months he continued to play for Maryport's football club although he did make a couple of rugby appearances with 'W.T.'. He played for the Maryport team that won 5–0 at Whitehaven Recreation on 5 October and in a Cumberland county trial at Workington on 12 October. Seven days after the latter he was, indeed, included in a Cumberland representative team, but at football, playing against the Northumberland Football Association at Benwell, Newcastle-upon-Tyne. Preston North End were alerted to his talent and quickly moved in for his signature, a meteoric rise in his round-ball career. Establishing himself on the right wing, he was transferred to Tottenham Hotspur two years later.

As one brother departed the local rugby scene, another arrived. James appeared in the Maryport reserve team on 4 April 1896. Aged 16 years, seven months, he scored a try in his team's 23–0 success. Whether he played in any other reserve matches that season is difficult to confirm because match reports for the second XV were basic. It seems fairly certain he did not play much before that, if at all, because, on the odd occasions that the Maryport reserve line-up is listed by the *West Cumberland Times*, his name is not included. Seven days after that first confirmed appearance, his step-brother, 'W.T.', was in the Maryport senior side defeated 13–4 by Aspatria in the Cumberland Challenge Cup Final at Workington's Lonsdale Park.

James began the 1896–97 season by appearing at outside-half for the reserves against Aspatria Hornets. Played on Maryport's ground at Sandy Lonning on a Saturday afternoon, 19 September, he made several breaks but did not get on the score sheet in a 23–0 victory. As already mentioned, match reports for the reserves were very sketchy and although he probably continued his development with the second-string over the next few weeks, it is difficult to verify. What can be confirmed, though, is that he played in the first team beaten 3–0 at Millom on 14 November and this may well have been his debut at that level. Unable to raise a full XV – a problem occurring several times that season – Maryport put out a XIV-man side that included 'six shield men', a reference to their reserves, the Cumbrian second teams having their own Cumberland Shield knock-out competition. James was one of the 'shield men' and partnered J. Bell at half-back.

He must have impressed because he kept his place and contributed to the three consecutive home wins that followed; against Whitehaven 3–0, Workington 10–3, and Aspatria 7–0. The match reports show that he was dangerous in attack and came close to scoring on several occasions. At that time the fixtures were mostly friendlies and usually against West Cumbrian clubs. The furthest south the side ventured was to Barrow and Millom. The only competitive element to the season was the Cumberland Challenge Cup in which Maryport – with James still in their side – met Aspatria in the first round. Played at

Sandy Lonning on 27 February 1897, Maryport were unable to replicate their earlier home success and went down 22–3. The Maryport line-up for James's first ever 'competition' game read: J. Hayton; A. Tweedie, J. Dakin, J. Steel, T. Semple; J. Lomas, J. Bell; W.T. Smith, W. Orr, R. Barnes, W. Bell, H. Graham. J. Osmotherley, J. Morton, E. Doran.

The 1897–98 season saw the Cumberland Senior League make its bow; Maryport were one of nine clubs taking part. Possibly its introduction was a response to the creation of the breakaway Northern Union code in August 1895 with its attendant league structure and ability to entice leading Cumbrian players to Lancashire and Yorkshire. The new code had also recently attracted its first Cumbrian club with Millom joining north Lancashire outpost Barrow in defecting from the Rugby Football Union. If the loss of Millom fired the Cumberland Rugby Union's desire for a league competition as a means of retaining its remaining members, it would ultimately prove unsuccessful. In short, 1897–98 was to be a landmark season in the history of Cumbrian rugby with Maryport at the forefront of its revolution.

For Maryport – and James – the season began serenely enough; its members held a pre-season meeting at the Old Court Room in Fleming Square on 20 August. The annual statement of accounts was discussed and the decision taken to submit entries for the Cumberland Challenge Cup for the first team and Cumberland Shield for the second team. It was also decided that the club's headquarters would be the Butcher's Arms in Crosby Street. Another change was that home matches would be played on the Cricket Field next to the railway station.

Their campaign opened with two wins and a draw in the new league competition; Penrith 4–0, at home, 4–0 at Whitehaven, and 3–3 at home to Aspatria. James proved to be something of a livewire in the latter game – played on 2 October. He broke down a "rush" by Aspatria and caused panic when he raced into opposition territory before slipping. The visitors took a 3–0 lead after the interval, and he rescued matters after securing the ball from a scrum near the Aspatria 25-yard flag. Racing down the touchline he went over in the corner to claim his first ever points for the senior side to level the score, Hayton just missed with the goal attempt. James was also in a scoring vein for the next fixture two weeks later, a friendly at Wath Brow. Three points down at half-time, he again took possession from a scrum to score the equalising try, his conversion – and debut goal in Maryport's first team – clinched a 5–3 victory.

The next match was a curiosity by today's standards. Maryport entertained Aspatria again on 30 October to replay their drawn league game from a few weeks earlier. Despite a couple of promising first half runs by James, one of which almost produced a touchdown, it was Aspatria who clinched victory with a second half try. However, the *West Cumberland Times* did not include the result in their latest league table as the match still had to be sanctioned as a league fixture by the Cumberland authorities. It seemed that the two clubs had not read the fine print because an endorsement was not forthcoming and the rerun was relegated to friendly status. Maryport retained their one point from the original draw.

During one match – at home to local rivals Brookland Rovers in the League on 27 November – James was moved into the centre to cover for an injured colleague, one of the forwards took over his out-half slot. In later years he played a vast number of matches in that position but, on this particular occasion, it "did not work" and he resumed at half-back.

The Maryportians continued their season with a combination of Cumberland Senior League fixtures padded out by friendly matches. By the time mid-February arrived Maryport had won four and drawn three of ten league games so far, resulting in mid-table respectability. They had performed less well in the friendly matches, losing six out of seven including a 6–3 loss across the Scottish border at Langholm and a 7–0 reverse on the east coast against South Shields. James was not yet the scoring machine of later years and failed to increase his tally since the five points against Wath Brow during October. But, at the age of 19, he was still learning his trade. It was also an era of low-scoring matches, the Maryport team overall only managed four tries and no goals in that period. Nonetheless, there were encouraging comments about his "tricky" and "fine" running and kicking.

During February things began to change dramatically for the Maryport club. It was not so much because of what was happening on the field of play, but more through what was said behind closed doors. On Saturday 19 February Maryport were due to play at Aspatria in a league fixture, but the match was called off. Aspatria had eight players in the Cumberland side that faced Devonshire in a county game at Exeter that day and consequently had difficulty in raising a side to take on Maryport, who had no players involved in the county game. What seemed like a standard, legitimate postponement had ramifications later on.

Meanwhile, the following week saw the first round of the Cumberland Challenge Cup take place; Maryport eliminated visitors Whitehaven on home turf 11–0. On a cold afternoon and pelted by heavy showers and hailstone, Maryport achieved their success on the back of three tries after James came close to opening the scoring with a missed drop-goal, then worth four points. Seven days later – 5 March – another home draw favoured them for the second round tie against Workington. The match kicked off at 4.15pm, 40 minutes later than planned because Workington had missed their train. With Maryport leading 4–0 at the halfway stage following a drop-goal by centre D. Semple, it was James who proved to be the hero of the day. According to the *West Cumberland Times*, "a scrimmage was formed at the centre from which Lomas got possession and, dashing through the Workington backs, scored a magnificent try in a good position." Semple's conversion made it 9–0 and, although the visitors landed a penalty, Maryport prevailed 9–3. Unfortunately, tempers became frayed towards the end resulting in the dismissal of Hayton (Maryport) and Hatchin (Workington) after they "came to blows".

Maryport were through to the semi-final stage of the Cumberland Challenge Cup. The only problem was that the win over Workington would be their last match under the auspices of the RFU. Maryport's membership were incensed through the Cumberland Rugby

Football Union suspending Hayton, reportedly without anyone from the Maryport club – including Hayton – being present to defend the case of a player they felt was not the perpetrator. In addition, the team was ordered to fulfil the previously postponed fixture at Aspatria on a Wednesday, 16 March, rather than the usual Saturday, a decision they felt unacceptable given the difficulties of raising a team in midweek.

On Friday 11 March, Maryport's players and officials held a special meeting in the town's Coffee Tavern. Clearly unhappy at their "unjust" treatment from the county authorities they were on the verge of resigning from the Cumberland RFU. The *West Cumberland Times* said there was "a lot of ill-feeling amongst the Maryport players." A vote was taken; 25 favoured joining the Northern Union, three felt the club should disband and not one was for staying with the Cumberland RFU. The decision to join the NU was "enthusiastically received" by the great majority of those present and it was immediately resolved not to fulfil the next day's league fixture at Penrith or the rescheduled Aspatria match on the subsequent Wednesday.

The Cumberland RFU reacted by calling a special meeting at the start of the following week. Held at the Station Hotel, Workington, Maryport had four representatives present; club official Mr Bleasdale, and players Joseph Robley – the team captain – D. Semple and J. Hayton. Cumberland RFU president Mr R. Westroy clearly meant business because he had also invited the Reverend Frank Marshall, a school headmaster based in Huddersfield who was infamous for his zeal in routing out professionalism in rugby union. The Maryport men seemed unclear as to the precise reason for their presence. Hayton, for instance, had attended thinking it an opportunity to defend his dismissal against Workington. He was told in no uncertain terms that the Cumberland officials were not there to discuss his case and suggested he left the room. What was on the agenda was Maryport's defection, Mr Westroy said that he had heard the club intended to leave the Union and wanted 'proof'. Evidently he was acquainted with the details of the vote. He knew the exact count and attempted to build a counter-argument based on it not including all members of the Maryport club, claimed to number over 50. However, any implication of conspiracy was emphatically denied by the Maryport attendees.

The whole tone of the meeting – certainly in the manner in which it was reported by the *West Cumberland Times* – was akin to naughty schoolboys being paraded before the headmaster, which, of course, Marshall was. The committee seemed to have little interest in what the Maryport men had to say. Maryport carried through their decision to leave, causing the Cumberland RFU problems because they had reached the semi-final stage of the Cumberland Challenge Cup. Rather than asking Workington, Maryport's victim's in the last round, Whitehaven were invited to take their place, probably because there were rumours that the former was also about to abscond!

Indeed, on Saturday 19 March – the same day Maryport played at Barrow in their first Northern Union match – the news broke that Workington had also defected. Maryport's action had led to a 'domino' effect and, before the season closed, Wath Brow and Brookland Rovers had also jumped ship, quickly followed by Whitehaven and Whitehaven Recreation. Twelve months later only four clubs remained in the Cumberland RFU and, having been runners-up to Kent in the 1897 County Championship, they were forced to abandon their own county cup competitions due to a lack of participants.

Maryport's first taste of Northern Unionism was not very sweet and they were well beaten 31–0 in their friendly with Barrow. The team who played in that historic match at a sunny Cavendish Park was: Robley; Semple, Clark, Hayton, Mandall; Lomas, Lanningan; Barnes, Osmotherley, Milligan, Graham, Young, Hutton, Smith, Scolley. Maryport concluded the unexpected finale to their season with five more friendly fixtures in April; Workington, lost 13–8, Millom, won 3–0, Wath Brow, won 8–0, Brookland Rovers, won 2–0, and Wath Brow again – a 0–0 draw. Except for the latter, all the matches took place at the Cricket Field in Maryport.

The *West Cumberland Times* said that, for the first of those home matches, against Workington, "a large number of spectators gathered to witness the new game and it was universally admired." James appeared to have little difficulty in adapting to the new environment. In the win over Wath Brow he took possession of the ball and raced towards his opponent's try-line where he "jumped over one of the opposing backs and scored a magnificent try." Those three points were the first of many under Northern Union rules.

3. 1898 to 1900: A shiny medal and a prized cap

James Lomas's first full season in the Northern Union (NU) was mostly fought out in Cumberland and north Lancashire. At the time, the bulk of the Northern Union clubs played in separate Lancashire and Yorkshire Senior Competitions. Each had Second (Division) Competitions, the Lancashire version for 1898–99 included Millom and northerly Lancashire outfits Barrow, Lancaster and Ulverston. All four also competed in the North Western League which, as the name implies, was a contest for Cumberland and north Lancashire clubs. Maryport – along with Askam, Dalton and Workington – also had a place in what was effectively the rebirth of a similarly named competition that had existed under Rugby Union auspices a few years earlier. Additionally, Maryport arranged friendly fixtures with old West Cumberland adversaries Brookland Rovers, Seaton, Wath Brow, Whitehaven and Whitehaven Recreation.

An incredible eight and a half hour rail journey, that began at 4.30am, was followed by an opening 3–0 defeat at Birkenhead Wanderers of the Lancashire Second Competition in a friendly on 10 September. Maryport then began their North Western League quest with the shorter trip to Workington seven days later. Although they lost 12–0, the *West Cumberland Times* spoke well of James, pointing out that he "worked wonders" during the match and had "hard lines in nearly, but not quite, getting over [for a try]" at the start of the second period. The Maryport team in what was the club's – and James's – first competitive Northern Union match was: J. Robley; M. Clark, J. Steel, Moore, H. Graham; J. Lomas, J. Patterson; W. Orr (captain), W.T. Smith, Walker, J. Brown, R. Barnes, A. Scholey, J. Bell, T. Milligan.

By the end of October, Maryport had played four more league fixtures. They lost at home to a strong Millom side 6–0, but then won the remaining three; Ulverston, 7–4 at home, 7–6 at Askam and 3–0 at home to Lancaster. James played at outside-half in all of them; his influence, based on the newspaper reports, was clearly growing. His surging runs and ability to dribble the ball long distances was becoming a regular feature and he was also developing his awareness for an opportunity, such as a pass interception or an off-the-cuff drop-goal attempt. After the victory at Askam, the *West Cumberland Times* said: "Lomas and Patterson played well at half and now seem to understand each other thoroughly."

James, though, had yet to score any points in the new campaign, something he rectified on 12 November when Wath Brow visited Maryport's Cricket Field for a friendly fixture. Maryport won 22–2, James broke through the defence following a scrum to close the first half scoring at 7–0 and then added two second half conversions. He was again among the points in December. On the 10th, in a 21–0 North Western League win over visitors Askam, he scored three second half goals through a penalty and two conversions. The latter was a family affair after a try by his step-brother W.T. Smith. He also gave the final pass that sent centre J. Hayton over the try-line for a touchdown in each half.

At this point in his career James was not the regular goalkicking choice for Maryport. Against Askam he was given the ball for every conversion and penalty attempt; that duty usually fell to threequarters Hayton, A.H. Mandle or D. Semple. However, James was clearly the designated marksman on 31 December, when he scored six goals – all conversions – in a 39–0 friendly win over visiting Whitehaven. His personal contribution was increased to 15 points through notching one of his side's nine tries.

His next points came from a try against visiting Whitehaven Recreation in another friendly encounter on 11 February. Maryport won 14–2. He was also entrusted with two of his side's four conversion attempts, including the one following his own score, but was unable to find the target on this occasion. By the end of February, Maryport's 11 league fixtures had produced a respectable record of five wins and two draws. The arrival of March, however, brought with it a new silverware opportunity. The Northern Union (later Rugby League) Challenge Cup was in its third season and Maryport had a chance of competing in the first round proper provided they overcame nearest and dearest rivals, Brookland Rovers, in a qualifying tie.

Played on the Maryport Cricket Field on 4 March, the tightest of contests was settled by James's well struck first half penalty – for a scrum offence; his team won 2–0. The reward was a formidable looking visit to Hunslet in the first round two weeks later. Before that encounter, though, Maryport had a return friendly against Whitehaven to fulfil. Despite sending a weakened side, Maryport secured a morale-boosting 22–0 win with James scoring the last of six touchdowns.

It was inevitable Maryport would lose at Hunslet, but they performed remarkably well against the side that would eventually finish as beaten finalists that season. At half-time they only trailed 3–0 and, when James scored an early second half drop-goal to reduce the deficit to just one point, there was a possible upset. Maryport fought tooth-and-nail to contain the Parksiders during a second half onslaught. James played a significant role by clearing the constant danger with long, raking kicks downfield. But it was a matter of time and a try under the posts from the great Albert Goldthorpe – which he converted – set Hunslet on the path to an 11–2 win.

The following week Maryport completed their home league fixtures with the visit of Barrow; the Shipbuilders won 12–0. James tried his best on a soggy ground, particularly in the first half when he was off course with drop and penalty goal attempts and unlucky not to put centre W. Skelton in for a try, but the latter lost the ball. Maryport played a further six matches before the season closed, two in the league, the rest were friendlies. The latter category included their one remaining home fixture, against Brookland Rovers on 12 April, in which James contributed two conversions towards the Maroons' 16–6 win.

Their final North Western League fixtures were severe tests; a 13–6 defeat at Millom, whose 100 per cent record gave them the title, and 14–0 at runners-up Barrow. It left

Maryport in mid-table with five wins and two draws from 14 games. James scored 42 points from 15 goals and four tries in all matches, both competitive and friendly, in the campaign.

Maryport's second Northern Union season in 1899–1900 heralded a restructuring of the league competitions in their part of the world. The North Western League contracted to five clubs with Maryport taking on Barrow, Millom, Whitehaven Recreation and Workington. There was also a Cumberland Senior League that, like the North Western League, was the revival of a competition that previously existed during the rugby union period. In this Maryport would lock horns with Brookland Rovers, Seaton, Wath Brow, Whitehaven, Whitehaven Recreation and Workington for the right to be called county champions.

With James again at outside-half, Maryport began their campaign with an unlikely looking fixture at their Cricket Field enclosure against 'J. Elliott's Team' which, in effect, was the Maryport Wheelers Cycling Club! Played on a Wednesday evening, 13 September, one would have expected the cyclists to lose heavily, but Elliott's side won 6–3, such were the vagaries of sport in an era when sportsmen were often involved in more than one discipline.

Maryport had better luck when opening their Cumberland League account the following Saturday, and won 4–3 away to Whitehaven Recreation. James's second half penalty wiped out a 3–2 half-time deficit. Next up was a trip to Workington for another Cumberland League fixture, but this time they lost 5–0 in a match played in good weather over four quarters rather than the usual two halves. James was possibly not as downcast by the loss as he might normally have been due to the outcome of a meeting of the Cumberland Executive Committee the previous evening, Friday 22 September. At 20 years old James had been selected for his first representative match as a member of the Cumberland team for their forthcoming meeting with Cheshire.

Played at the Whitehaven Colliery Recreation Ground on Saturday 30 September, the Cumberland side on this most significant of dates in James Lomas's rugby career was: Bill Eagers (Millom); John Timoney (Maryport), T. Teasdale (Wath Brow), J. Leck (Millom), J. Young (Millom); Sammy Northmore (Millom), Lomas (Maryport); J. Atkinson (Workington), J.H. Buckett (Millom), S. Hoggarth (Millom), M. Linton (Millom), H. Nixon (Brookland Rovers), W.P. Robinson (Maryport), G. Steel (Workington), D. Wilson (Millom).

On a wet and windy day, the Cumbrian forwards dominated proceedings although there was only one score. That fell to James who, just before half-time, gained possession from a scrum and kicked the ball towards Cheshire winger H. Clayton. He then "robbed" his adversary of the ball before dribbling it over the try-line near the corner to claim a try, the difficult conversion proved to be too much for skipper Buckett. Cheshire played better after the interval, but Cumberland held on to win 3–0, the *Athletic News* commented: "(Cumberland) half-backs Lomas and Northmore combined fairly well, the first named putting in some splendid work."

The following week James was back with Maryport for the 19–0 home victory over Wath Brow in another Cumberland League fixture. He began the match in lively fashion despite being off-target with two penalties, a drop-goal, and the attempted conversion of a try from new half-back partner 'Buggy' Messenger. Ultimately, though, it was not his lucky day, and he injured a shoulder, which caused the match to be held up for a while to allow treatment. He continued but, to quote the *West Cumberland Times*, "one arm was practically useless" and he was forced to quit at half-time. Despite that setback, James was back in harness the following weekend, 14 October, and played his part in defeating Whitehaven Recreation 9–5 at home in the first of Maryport's North Western League fixtures.

Meanwhile, a few days before the game against the Recreation side, the Boer War began in the Transvaal and Orange Free State as the British sought to extend their influence over that part of southern Africa. The bulletins from the conflict dominated newspaper headlines throughout the remainder of the 1899–1900 season.

James was back in Cumberland's blue and white jersey on 21 October, this time against the might of Lancashire at Oldham. It must have been an exciting time for the young Cumbrian who entered new territory by appearing at the Watersheddings, a ground that would become very familiar to him in later years. Cumberland lost 17–7 in front of around 8,500 spectators, a figure the *Athletic News* felt was "moderate" compared to the club's league attendances. This time James was in partnership with Workington's R. O'Hara, described by the *Athletic News* as "the most indefatigable of the halves" in a Cumberland side whose players "fumbled and rarely did anything above mediocrity." James – who did not score – may still have been feeling the effect of his shoulder injury, although he was applauded for some "clever" runs during the match. One consolation was that, having made two Cumberland appearances, he qualified for a county cap.

The suspicion that he may still have been injured was supported by him not taking part in Maryport's next two games, both at home; a 0–0 draw with Workington in the North Western League, and a 29–0 win over Whitehaven in the Cumberland League. James did not return to action again until 25 November when he made his third Cumberland appearance, against Yorkshire at Millom, where he was reunited with Northmore at half-back. Cumberland – who then had a policy of only selecting players still attached to their clubs – did well to hold the Yorkshiremen until succumbing to a late drop-goal from Batley's Joe Oakland that gave Yorkshire the spoils, 7–5. Play got rough at times, the *Athletic News* said: "It was distinctly a novel, and not a pleasant experience to see the referee, Billy McCutcheon of Oldham, in a county match take two men out by the collar, and publicly admonish them for the way in which they had jointly tackled an opponent."

With the inter-county programme completed, James was free to devote the remainder of his season to Maryport's quest for league success. December began with a Cumberland League victory at Seaton's Lowca Lane ground, James's second half drop-goal logged the final points of a 5–2 score-line. A few weeks later Seaton forced a scoreless draw in the return at Maryport but, that apart, the Maroons won their remaining matches of 1899 including away successes in the Cumberland League at Whitehaven, 13–2, and Brookland

Rovers, 3–0, on Christmas Day, and 13–0 at home to Whitehaven Recreation in the same competition when James scored the second of Maryport's three tries.

As 1899 gave way to 1900, James was becoming a more dominant force in the Maryport side. His defence was solid and he was earning praise for his powerful attacking surges and uncanny ability to brush experienced predators aside. Having claimed just one touchdown for his club so far in the campaign, his try count slowly, but surely, began to increase. He was also being trusted with a bigger share of the goalkicking responsibilities.

Having almost scored a try during the narrow 4–0 victory over traditional rivals Brookland Rovers at the Cricket Field on New Year's Day, he was more successful for the visit of Workington five days later in a vital Cumberland League fixture. Maryport – whose only defeat in the competition was at Workington in September – were closing in on the title and their opponents posed the biggest threat to their aspirations. Workington took the lead through an unconverted O'Hara try, but James came to the rescue when his spectacular dribble ended in a "wonderful" try, tying the score at 3–3. Unfortunately, Hayton failed to add the goal that would have secured victory, but the result meant Maryport, with one match left, were virtually there.

James almost grabbed another try the following week on a visit to Aspatria Hornets in a friendly, but did make Hayton's try in their 3–0 win. Next up on 20 January was a visit from the strong Barrow combination in the North Western League. James excelled throughout and, having headed a rush towards the Barrow in-goal, was on hand to accept Messenger's pass from a scrum and, "after a fine dodgy run," scored the only points in another 3–0 win.

In February, Maryport completed a friendly 'double' over Seaton, overcoming their opponents 8–2 away and 8–0 at home. The first match was delayed by 30 minutes as the players waited in snowy conditions for the referee to arrive. Eventually, they used a substitute official; James subsequently converted a second half try and then warmed himself up on a cold afternoon by sprinting over the Seaton try-line for the concluding score. The weather was much more pleasant for the return game when James scored his first brace of tries. He broke away down the touchline and outran the chasing posse for an exciting score. Timoney's goal made it 5–0 at the break. James then got on the end of a passing move to register his second try near the corner flag.

Their clashes with Seaton had sandwiched a 5–3 defeat away to Whitehaven Recreation in the North Western League. They did, however, ratify their status as Cumberland Senior League champions with a 12–0 win at Wath Brow on 3 March. James climaxed what was described as an early "onslaught" by the Maroons to score in the corner, which gave his team a 3–0 lead at half-time. He continued to impress after the restart; he produced some wonderful breaks and kicked a great drop-goal. It had been a good campaign in the Cumberland League, Maryport drew two and lost one of 12 league matches.

The Challenge Cup broke the routine the following week. Maryport – who did not have to qualify this time around – received a first round away draw, although their journey was relatively short compared to some of their Cumbrian colleagues. While Wath Brow and Millom were both despatched on the long trek to Hull to oppose the fishing port's two senior clubs, the Maroons visited Westmoreland to play Kendal Hornets. With a heavier pack who won most of the possession, they had little problem in securing three tries for a 9–0 win.

The following week – 24 March – Maryport were away once more in the second round. This time it was in Cheshire where Runcorn awaited. It could hardly have been a tougher draw because the Linnets were well on target to win the Lancashire Senior Competition, and eventually did so with only two defeats in 26 matches. Under the circumstances, Maryport did well to only lose 12–0, having trailed by just four points at the break.

Maryport completed their competitive fixtures with three matches in the North Western League. They defeated Millom at home 7–0, but lost 3–2 at Workington and 8–0 at Millom to finish third in the table. The two latter defeats had dashed hopes of a championship double, Maryport finished just two points behind both their opponents in the league ladder. Millom subsequently defeated Workington 9–3 in a decider at Whitehaven.

There was just one other game for Maryport in this period. Arranged for the 'benefit' of the Cumberland Senior League – who presumably needed the funds – it was touted as the Champions – Maryport – versus runners-up – Workington. It took place at Workington on 7 April but, despite its grandiose billing, drew only a moderate attendance. Workington won 3–0, although James came close to equalising near the end but was bundled into touch.

All in all, it had been a satisfactory season for both Maryport and James. The 'Prominent Salford Sportsmen' series, published by the *Salford City Reporter* in 1926, said: "He was captain of the team when they won the Northern Union Cup (Cumberland District) for the first time, and the medal which was presented was the first he had ever gained." The cup referred to would certainly be for the Cumberland Senior League and it is interesting to see the claim that James was the captain. Unfortunately, contemporary reports do not say who the team captain was, although there is no reason to doubt it was James because, in all probability, he would have been interviewed for the feature. James, himself, reiterated the point in his memoirs[1], saying that "While playing for Maryport we won the Cumberland League championship the first year it was at Rugby League. I was captain."

James ended his campaign with eight tries and four goals in all games, including representative and friendly games; his 32 point haul was down on the previous campaign. However, he was not yet 21, and, as captain of Maryport with a shiny championship winners' medal to show off as well as a prized county cap, he had the world of rugby in the palm of his hand. The only problem for Maryportians and Cumbrians in general was that that world lay elsewhere.

---

[1] James Lomas's memoirs were written in note form in the 1930s and never published. They were transcribed for this book by the author with permission from his family.

4. 1900–01: The man from Stanningley

It was to the Maryport club's misfortune that at least one of its concluding matches of the 1899–1900 campaign happened to be witnessed by an iron worker from Yorkshire. The man in question hailed from Stanningley in Leeds and was spending time in Cumberland working on the erection of a new bridge. He was clearly impressed by the performance of James Lomas and, on returning to West Yorkshire, reported his discovery to Bramley officials – the Barley Mow club was located not far from his Stanningley home.

His intervention almost certainly altered the course of the 20-year-old half-back's career. At that time James was hidden away in the backwaters of Cumberland, playing most of his rugby in that region. It is perfectly reasonable to assume, however, that, having already represented his county at a young age, he would ultimately attract attention from the financially stronger Lancashire and Yorkshire clubs. That premise was all the more likely because he was in the 'shop window' whenever Cumberland visited those counties. Had that scenario run its course it is doubtful whether Bramley would have been in a position to compete for his signature.

Two of Bramley's star threequarters, Albert Hambrecht and J. E. Parker, played for Yorkshire against Cumberland at Millom in November 1899 when James was at half-back for the latter. Whether the two Yorkshiremen returned home with glowing reports of the Maryport youngster is unknown. As it happened, James does not appear to have stood out in that match and it was some nine months before Bramley made a move.

A story appeared in the *Yorkshire Evening Press* in 1913 which claimed that James joined Bramley "after being rejected by the Leeds club". It may have been that the Stanningley worker had approached Leeds before Bramley, although, at that time, both were competing in the Yorkshire Senior Competition, with little between them in terms of on-field achievement. Headingley was certainly a more impressive venue than Barley Mow, but Leeds were not the power of later years and their average crowds not much greater than Bramley's.

Either way, once alerted to James's blossoming talent, Bramley moved in August 1900 to secure him for the forthcoming season. Among the entries in the Bramley treasurer's book are two for 2 August and 23 August, both listed as 'Delegates expenses Maryport', the amounts reading £2 and 2 shillings (£2.10p) and £1 and 5 shillings (£1.25p). The first of those long trips to the seaport must have borne fruit for the Bramley representative because, on 10 August, there is another entry stating 'Registration fee Lomas and Holden, 5 shillings (25p)', the latter being a forward who appeared in around 20 games for them over the next couple of seasons.

The Yorkshire Senior Competition committee meeting at the Green Dragon Hotel, Leeds, on Thursday 16 August confirmed James's transfer from Maryport to Bramley. It was one of around 20 ratified that evening including winger George West from Beverley to Hull

Kingston Rovers who, like James, would establish records that stood the test of time. As a footnote, a feature on James in the *Salford City Reporter* in 1926 claimed he "threw in his lot" with Bramley the day after his 21st birthday which would have been 27 August.

How much James actually received for transferring his affections is unclear, but it was at least £30. Entries for 1 and 8 September, on the occasion of his first two matches for Bramley – both at home, to Halifax and Brighouse Rangers respectively – show 'Bonus Lomas, £20' and 'Bonus Lomas, £10'. Whether he had already been enticed with some 'cash on the table', as was the usual practice of Northern Union officials, during those meetings in Maryport is not recorded.

Bramley – founded in 1879 and based in west Leeds – left their rugby union roots behind in 1896 to join the Northern Union and, for most of the 100 years or so that followed, they played third fiddle to the city's two other senior outfits, Hunslet and Leeds, except for their singular success when they won the 1973–74 BBC2 Floodlit Trophy. Possibly because they existed in the shadows somewhat they took on the aura of a 'Cinderella' club and for many Yorkshire fans, unless they actually supported Bramley, they became a 'second favourite' team. The club folded after the 1999 summer season, but was thankfully resurrected as Bramley Buffaloes in 2004 and, at the time of writing, are members of the Rugby League Conference.

When James arrived at the Barley Mow, Bramley were, as previously stated, members of the Yorkshire Senior Competition and, by implication, played most of their matches within the confines of the White Rose county. It was a time of optimism for the club. Apart from the arrival of James, other new recruits included threequarter W. Young from Hunslet and forwards T. Barnett from Bingley and P. Connolly from Otley St Joseph's. Bramley already boasted established Yorkshire county players in threequarters Hambrecht and Parker, and forward Harry Topham, plus reliable, popular full-back Charlie Dixon. When James wrote his memoirs years later, he listed Dixon, Hambrecht and Parker among his list of "old time giants". Although not about to win any trophies Bramley were building a side that commanded respect. More so after James was added to their playing register.

It was not the best of starts for James or the club, the first four matches ending in defeat. As at Maryport he took his place in the side at outside-half. His debut, a home match against Halifax, which drew a "fairly good" crowd, was lost 14–5. The *Yorkshire Post*, though, claimed Hambrecht's first half try for Bramley was the day's best effort, he had retrieved the ball after kicking over centre Reggie Mallinson's head. James was one of several players making Bramley debuts, including the aforementioned Young and Barnett, and, according to the *Leeds Mercury* reporter, all of them "created a favourable impression"; the writer went on to say that "Lomas played a fine game at half back, though hampered by the timidity of his partner [Hewitt]". Bramley's full line-up was: C. Dixon; A Hambrecht, W. Lee, H. Brayshaw, W. Young; J. Lomas, J. Hewitt; T. Barnett, H. Bradshaw, G. Clarke, G. Fielding, C. Hambrecht, D. Horn, G. Smith, H. Topham.

The next match, against Brighouse Rangers and another home fixture, drew mild criticism of James from the *Yorkshire Post* correspondent. Apparently, following a scoreless opening half, he "should have dropped an easy goal for Bramley soon after the restart, when he had a fine opening, but the ball went wide". As it was, Brighouse, in an exciting finish, scored a converted try in the corner five minutes from time to seal the match 5–0.

James scored his first points for the Villagers – as Bramley were known – in his fifth outing, against Liversedge at Barley Mow on 29 September. Neither team had won thus far, so something had to give and it was to be the Liversedge XV that did so. Bramley's forwards took command from the start, controlled the ball and allowed James and half-back partner Bentley to enjoy plenty of possession. The *Yorkshire Post* noted that they "worked the ball out to the next [threequarter] line in capital style" and provided them with plenty of running and passing opportunities. Things looked bleak for Bramley, though, when new forward signing Connolly, on his debut, injured his ribs just before the interval and had to come off, which left his colleagues a man short for the remainder of the match. Shortly after the break James opened his account through converting a penalty-try, Liversedge's T. Midgley had obstructed Bedford as he attempted to place a hand on the ball. Just before the finish James doubled the score to 10–0 by "outwitting the defence" to race beneath the posts, and added the goal for good measure.

A second consecutive victory eluded them when they went down 12–2 at Huddersfield the following weekend. There was some encouragement for James though as he adjusted to the pace of life with his new team-mates. As the rain began to lash down at Fartown towards the end of the match he scored Bramley's only points with a penalty. He also caught the eye with two telling breaks; his first, just before half time, almost produced a try for Parker who was "grassed" just in time, the second effort after the interval, came when he intercepted a pass and "galloped down the field" before Huddersfield centre Walter Dewhirst intervened. In the report for this match the *Yorkshire Post* writer labelled him the "Bramley crack". After just six matches he was clearly making an impression.

James was again the only points contributor in the following week's home game against another Leeds-based club, Holbeck, but this time it brought his team success. His moment of glory came just before the break when "playing magnificently" he took a pass from Hewitt to dash over. Unfortunately, and amidst much disappointment on the terraces, Parker failed to add the extra points. However, Bramley retained their 3–0 advantage until the final whistle because James demonstrated another facet of his capabilities by starring in defence as Holbeck pressed hard in the closing stages.

The next Saturday, 20 October, Bramley's standing in the code was fully illustrated through the selection of three of their players – Hambrecht, Parker and Topham – for the Yorkshire side that took on Cheshire at Wakefield. Indeed, according to a feature by 'Pakeha' in the Wellington-based *New Zealand Truth* in March 1909 (reproduced in the *Salford Reporter* in February 1911) James, having joined Bramley, was also selected for

Yorkshire "but some objection was made as regards qualification, and he was deprived of honours for two counties". In fact, as James was later to add Lancashire caps to those for his native Cumberland, he achieved that dual-distinction anyway.

Meanwhile, while his three colleagues busied themselves in claiming six of the tries and three of the goals in Yorkshire's resounding 40–0 victory, James and his remaining team-mates faced Leeds at Headingley. Leeds, who had no players in the Yorkshire side and would finish the season two places below Bramley in the league table, had, nonetheless, anticipated an easy victory. But it was not the case and, watched by 7,000 the match remained scoreless, the spotting tactics of Bramley paid off while James and half-back partner Bentley earned plaudits for "opening out the play" behind a dominant pack.

That match began a run of six league games without a win, a sequence that included three defeats and two further low-scoring draws, both at Barley Mow; 0–0 versus Batley and 2–2 against Castleford. The latter, incidentally, was a different outfit to the one that plays today and disbanded in 1907. The only time James bothered the scoreboard during that spell was in converting a try in the 13–8 reverse away to Hull KR on 24 November, having done likewise in an 8–2 friendly win at Keighley seven days earlier.

Bramley's third league win of the campaign was their most unexpected and celebrated of the season and the highpoint of James's time at the club. Indeed, he was the hero of the hour with a late contribution that would have produced banner headlines had it happened today. It occurred on 8 December when they entertained Bradford, the current Yorkshire Senior Competition champions and league leaders having won 12 and drawn one of their 13 matches to date. In contrast, Bramley entered the fray with just two wins and three draws from the same number of fixtures and lay third from bottom in the 14-team table. The attendance was 8,000, many of whom had travelled over expectantly from Bradford. Their heroes began with a strong wind in their favour, but the points avalanche did not materialise, their only first half reward was a try in the corner by Frank Murgatroyd shortly before the interval. Finding themselves only three points in arrears, Bramley played with commitment and confidence during the second half, but Bradford defended well. Then, with only five minutes left, James made a name for himself. It all unfolded from a scrum just inside Bradford's half. Parker took possession before delivering the ball to Hambrecht who then shrugged off several opponents in his charge towards the try line. When finally apprehended, he managed to squeeze the ball out to the supporting James who completed what the *Leeds Mercury* described as "a superb movement" by placing the ball for the touchdown. Victory was assured when James tagged on the conversion, which sent the home fans into raptures.

Bramley fell to earth with a thump in their next two matches, losing 18–0 at Halifax, who would finish as league runners-up to Bradford, and 20–6 away to Brighouse Rangers, their two biggest defeats of the season. The Villagers could claim mitigating circumstances in the former. James lost fellow half-back Hogg with a bad ear injury before half-time, which necessitated some hasty reshuffling among their 14 remaining men. The young Maryportian did not trouble the score-sheet during those two defeats. He missed a goal attempt from a mark at Halifax, the ball just fell short, and failed to convert the first of his side's two tries against the Rangers.[2] James was in better form with the boot in the next three games, all of them played at Barley Mow over the Christmas period and won by Bramley. The first took place on Christmas Eve against Leeds Parish Church, one of five Leeds-based clubs in that season's competition. The match had been brought forward from New Year's Day and club officials were rewarded with an 8,000 crowd. Bramley were quickly out of the blocks with James looking particularly potent. He almost scored an early try and then created a chance for Parker, who failed to take his pass. The duo combined more successfully when James picked up the ball from a scrum in midfield and set off towards the opponent's '25' area where he kicked across field for Parker to pick up and go in under the posts. James added the extra points and then landed a penalty shortly afterwards from the 25-yard line, for an 'informality' at a scrum. Bramley led 7–0 at half time. There was no further scoring, the *Yorkshire Post* said that the "Churchmen" were "a well beaten team at the close".

Two days later, on Boxing Day, they hosted Wakefield Trinity. Over 4,000 saw James give the Villagers an early boost through a 5th minute drop-goal. A try by Hambrecht – James missed the conversion – gave Bramley a 5–0 lead at the interval, a just reward after dominating the opening half territorially. They had a scare when Wakefield winger Horace Price, a future team-mate of James's, almost scored after a 75-yard run. Wakefield had more of the game in the second half, but the gap remained the same, finishing 7–2 after a drop-goal by Hambrecht was replied to in kind by Trinity centre Jack Goodyear.

The winning treble was completed three days later. Hunslet succumbed to the rejuvenated Villagers 11–3. Again the match attracted a good attendance, estimated at around 5,500. James was still wide awake to opportunities, almost getting over for a try from the kick-off before being held at bay. It was a temporary reprieve for the Parksiders who conceded three tries before half-time; James converted the second with a magnificent touchline effort, although he failed with the other two. Hunslet came back with a consolation try in the second half through Billy Hannah, but the victory was well-merited against one of the competition's strongest teams.

James missed the next match, at Liversedge on 5 January 1901, although no explanation is given in either the *Yorkshire Post* or *Leeds Mercury*. Despite his absence, that afternoon's events are still worth recounting. The Liversedge club, who were struggling financially, had started to use the ground of neighbouring Cleckheaton although, unfortunately, the main stand had recently been destroyed by fire. On a bitterly cold day, the press and spectators

---

[2] A 'mark' occurred when a player caught the ball cleanly from an opponent's kick and marked the spot with his heel. It allowed his team a free kick, attempts at a goal from a mark being abolished after 1921–22.

had had to await the late arrival of Bramley, the match eventually started at 3.30pm. It was so cold that the press box emptied before kick-off as the journalists tried to get their circulation moving after the thermometer "had gone below freezing". The *Leeds Mercury* writer found wry humour in the depressing set of circumstances saying "the delay meant spectators had ample time to look at the charred remains of the grandstand – all that was rescued from the recent fire." With daylight fading the match was played in two halves of 30 minutes each, Bramley unexpectedly lost 3–2 to provide the basement club with its first win of the season.

Undeterred, the Bramley players quickly rediscovered their improved form, winning five and drawing three of their next eight games. Huddersfield were the first to fall, losing 5–3 at the Barley Mow on 12 January, James opened the scoring with a second-half try. Seven days on they travelled the short distance to Elland Road, the future home of Leeds United AFC, to meet Holbeck. In terrible weather and on a ground referred to as a "swamp", Bramley snatched a thrilling last minute win when, losing 2–0, Parker scored the winner, James added the extra goal points. It was Bramley's first away success of the season. A scoreless home draw with Leeds followed, a repeat of their earlier encounter at Headingley, before rugby matters were placed on hold.

The scheduled trip to Mount Pleasant to meet hosts Batley on Saturday 2 February was postponed, along with every other Northern Union fixture and sporting activity. It was done as a mark of respect for the late Queen Victoria whose funeral was taking place that day in Windsor. She had passed away on 12 January following a reign of over 63 years, the longest ever for a British monarch. The history books say that Queen Victoria presided over a period of change and prosperity. What they do not generally impart is that her reign also witnessed massive change in the sporting lives of its people, particularly the working classes. It was a time of sporting development on a grand scale. New sports appeared and all manner of football clubs were founded with the formation of the Football Association in 1863, the Rugby Football Union in 1871 and, of course, the Northern Union in 1895.

Back into action, an in-form Bramley steadily continued their climb up the league ladder towards mid-table respectability with two further away wins; 6–0 at Manningham and 7–5 at Castleford. The latter match was significant for James as he was picked in the centre for the first time in his senior career and reportedly played a "prominent" part. The Villagers leapt into a 7–0 half-time lead; James opened the scoring with a difficult penalty kick and found the target again after a long-distance try from Hambrecht.

He was restored to his accustomed outside-half position the following Tuesday afternoon, 19 February, when Bramley visited Crown Point to take on Leeds Parish Church. A reasonable 4,000 crowd saw another scoreless game. It apparently had "too little science and too much force," the *Yorkshire Post* writer claimed the encounter was "not calculated to increase the popularity of Northern Union football." Indeed, at the end of the season Leeds Parish Church did fold, although the primary reason was notification to vacate their ground, eight players subsequently moved to Headingley to join Leeds.

Without a fixture for the following weekend, Bramley entertained York, then topping the East section of the Yorkshire Second Competition, which they eventually won, in a friendly. James made his second and last appearance at left centre for the Villagers. The result was another 0–0 draw, Bramley's fifth of the season. Next up was a trip to Rochdale Hornets for the opening round of the Challenge Cup. In what was their only match of the season outside Yorkshire, Bramley led a tight encounter 5–3 at half time, a try by Parker – converted by James – was responded to by a touchdown from Berrill. James stretched the lead to 7–3, through a goal from a mark made by Parker. Roared on by the home support the Hornets bombarded the Bramley defence but they held firm, the scoreboard operator was not troubled again.

That result deprived Rochdale of a lucrative home tie with their great derby rivals Oldham in the following round. In those early years the ties were pre-drawn through to the final, similar to today's major tennis championships. Thus it was to the Barley Mow that Oldham travelled, where an attendance reported as around 12,000 packed into the tiny ground; nearby housetops and trees were precariously used as vantage points. It was suggested that so deep was the crowd around the playing area perimeter that many saw nothing. Oldham presented a tougher challenge than had their Lancashire Senior Competition rivals Rochdale, even though Bramley had the advantage of a home draw.

James raised the hopes of Bramley's excited supporters early on with a well taken penalty, awarded because of an 'informality' at a scrum. The goal encouraged his team and Hambrecht, following up a punt by centre Walton, lifted expectations further, but his touchdown claim went unheeded. The home team, though, was undeterred and James was instrumental in the next score. His ambitious, mammoth drop-goal attempt just went to the right of the posts, but an alert Wilkinson followed up to score a try. Surprisingly, James missed the goal, but made amends just before half-time with a more difficult, touchline effort after Hambrecht had made a mark. The opening half had seen the powerful Oldham forwards control most of the possession, but the Villagers had defended well and, inspired by James, entered the break with heads high and a 7–0 lead.

But the second half quickly turned Oldham's way on the back of incessant attacking. After just 10 minutes, from a scrum near Bramley's line, Arthur Lees picked up the ball and kicked towards the posts, colleague Tom Fletcher followed up for the score. Joe Ferguson converted and suddenly Bramley's lead of two points looked fragile. Somehow they held on for most of the half but their hearts were broken when, from another scrum on Bramley's line, Lees initiated a passing move that brought Viv Huzzey a try in the corner. Ferguson failed to add the extras, but Huzzey kicked a late goal from a mark for a 10–7 win to shatter Bramley's cup dreams – and James's – for another year.

Having failed in their bid to reach the last 16 of the Challenge Cup, Bramley returned to the bread and butter world of the Yorkshire Senior Competition. There were just four matches remaining, the first of those was the rearranged match at Mount Pleasant against Batley, the team destined to win that season's Challenge Cup. Played on the following Tuesday afternoon, it ended in another defeat, this time 4–0, having been level at the interval. Bramley rediscovered the winning formula for the next two matches, both at home against the two Hull clubs. Hull KR were the first, arriving with a weakened side due to their forthcoming Challenge Cup match at Brighouse despite the latter being seven days hence. Unsurprisingly, Bramley were by far the stronger combination and logged their highest score of the season, 23–0. Having failed to convert Bramley's two first half tries, James contributed four goals after the interval; the first from his own mark, the remainder through converting his side's three further touchdowns.

The reported 3,000 crowd was matched three weeks later for the visit of Hull. Bramley narrowly led 3–2 at half-time thanks to a late try from Hambrecht. It was left to Parker to attempt, and miss, the conversion, James was possibly overlooked through missing with two earlier shots at goal. He was given the chance to redeem himself during a second half described by the *Yorkshire Post* as "very fast", tagging the points onto Parker's try as the Villagers triumphed 8–2.

The concluding match of the season looked, on paper, to be the toughest of the campaign. It involved a visit to Park Avenue on Easter Monday, 8 April, to take on Bradford who had already secured the Yorkshire Senior Competition championship. In the event, Bramley did reasonably well in losing 10–3, the home team scored two tries to one in a vigorous encounter in which injuries were frequent. James did not get on the score-sheet, having missed the goal attempt following Parker's touchdown. The Villagers finished 11th in the 16-team league, winning 12 and drawing five of their 30 matches, while James had the satisfaction of ending the season as Bramley's top scorer with 54 points. His team mate Albert Hambrecht scored 56 points during the season, but 20 of those were for Yorkshire.

With Bramley's campaign concluded it is probable that James returned to Maryport for the duration of the close season, something he was apt to do during his future years as a player. Certainly he was there in the remaining days of April because he was invited to play for Maryport, something he did with Bramley's blessing. Maryport played several matches towards the end of that month and, although there is no mention in the *West Cumberland Times* of which specific match or matches James took part in, the implication is he must have appeared in at least one of them. The *Yorkshire Post* subsequently described it as "appearing in a holiday match last season in Cumberland".

Unfortunately, the brief reunion with his old club had severe repercussions for all parties. The Northern Union authorities fined Maryport two guineas (£2.10p) and Bramley one guinea (£1.05p) on the basis that their arrangement was made with the knowledge that James was out of work, a situation presumably created as a consequence of his temporary return to Cumberland. It had been a stipulation of the Northern Union since 1898 that a player could not turn out for a team unless involved in *bona fide* employment during the

26

preceding week. Referred to at the time as the 'work clause', the only exceptions were for extenuating circumstances, in which case a playing 'permit' had to be obtained from the Northern Union. This was usually applied for by the appropriate club secretary on the eve of the match, something that had evidently not occurred on this occasion. James also suffered through his misdemeanour by being suspended until 15 September, thereby missing the start of the next season.

April was an ill-fated month altogether for the Bramley club. On Wednesday 17 April, a dozen of the leading clubs from the Lancashire and Yorkshire Senior Competition's met to debate the formation a new Northern Rugby League, a previous unwieldy attempt having been shelved after 1895–96. The idea was eventually approved by a Northern Union committee meeting on 6 June, 14 clubs took their place among the elite. It was, in effect, the Super League of its day, comprising as it did some of the best supported clubs in the Northern Union. Bramley, though, were not one of them. The plan incorporated promotion and relegation between that competition and the remnants of the Lancashire and Yorkshire setups. At a subsequent meeting on 10 July, the Lancashire Senior Competition clubs accepted that olive branch, but their Yorkshire counterparts – Bramley included – did not.

It was a messy situation that alienated the Yorkshire Senior Competition, and created a divide that allowed the new Northern Rugby League outfits to entice their players without the approval of their clubs. Bramley, in particular, suffered through this unfortunate turn of events, and ultimately lost four high profile players; Hambrecht joined Hull, Dixon and Topham headed for Oldham, and James signed on for Salford.

For James's brother, Tom Smith, however, April 1901 was the pinnacle of his football career. On 20 April at the Crystal Palace in south London, he lined up for Tottenham Hotspur against Sheffield United in the Football Association Cup Final watched by 114,815 spectators. The result was a 2–2 draw and seven days later the two teams met again in the replay at Burnden Park, the then home of Bolton Wanderers. Having trailed 1–0 at half-time, Smith became one of the London sides heroes, his "low shot" 14 minutes from the end put his team 2–1 ahead, the final score was 3–1.

Whether James travelled to Bolton to cheer for his sibling is not recorded. What is known, however, is that fate would decree he never played another match at the Barley Mow, not even in opposition colours.

James Lomas's brother, Tom Smith (third down on left), featured on a 1930 John Player & Sons cigarette card celebrating Tottenham Hotspur's 1901 FA Cup Final victory.

5. 1901–02: A half-back from Cumberland

On 17 August 1901 the *Salford Chronicle*, previewing the Salford club's prospects for the forthcoming 1901–02 season, confirmed the "principle candidates" for the half-back roles would again be the established Welsh pairing of Ben Griffiths and Dai Davies with W. Phillips as "understudy". That was followed by an insignificant-looking snippet: "There is a prospect of a half-back from Cumberland who had, in addition, gained a lot of experience in the broad-acre county [of Yorkshire]." No one, including the club officials, could have foreseen that they were about to witness the arrival of one of the Reds' most legendary players.

James Lomas's impact during his Salford debut season was immense. Almost from the start he reigned supreme in a team that had been on the fringe of success for several years but, thus far, failed to make that final step towards silverware. Since belatedly joining the Northern Union in 1896, the Reds had hovered around mid-table in the Lancashire Senior Competition. Their best efforts were finishing fourth in 1897–98, third in 1898–99 and fifth in 1900–01. They had, though, stirred things up more significantly in their quest for ownership of the Challenge Cup, failing in two successive semi-finals; 5–0 to eventual winners Batley in 1898, 15–8 against Hunslet the next season and then, in 1900, finishing runners-up to local rivals Swinton 16–8 in the Final at Fallowfield Stadium, Manchester.

Salford were well equipped for the rigours of the Challenge Cup, possessing a vigorous no-nonsense set of forwards that intimidated most packs they came across. Some commentators, particularly those that followed the fortunes of the Yorkshire clubs, had claimed on more than one occasion that they were a 'dirty' combination, an assertion Salford officials were quick to refute. However, there was no escaping the fact that five of their forwards – Jack Rhapps, Billy Brown, Harry Woodhead, Miles Gledhill and E. Jones – were given 'marching orders' in that 1899 semi-final against Hunslet, with Brown, in 1900, becoming the first player dismissed in the final itself. Salford, though, were not bereft of talent among the backs, especially with the Welsh duo of full-back Dan Smith and skipper and centre Tom Williams.

The Salford supporters had had great players to cheer in the past – forwards Tom Kent and Harry Eagles had both been selected for England duty in the club's rugby union era – but James was to be extra special. He was not simply an eye-catching star performer that put the icing on the cake; he was a major ingredient in the cake itself.

The precise date that James signed with Salford is unclear because the official Northern Union club registration books for that particular period have long since disappeared. The *Salford Reporter* first mentioned him by name on 31 August 1901, implying his imminent arrival with the news that neither he nor centre John Varty, another Cumbrian who had joined Salford from Aspatria the previous November, could appear for the club until after 14 September due to an "infringement of a rule last season". In James's case it was his punishment after playing for Maryport without having a 'proper' job and, presumably, Varty's 'crime' was similar.

Despite the impending ban, Salford supporters were given a foretaste of his talent on Saturday 31 August, when he appeared in the club's final trial match, held at New Barnes. In what was once a regular pre-season ritual whereby each club held a series of up to three trial matches for aspiring professionals – mostly local talent and rugby union men from Wales and other outlying areas – who would be put through their paces. The most prominent would be included in the final trial, usually the weekend before the season opener, when they would be matched against the main contenders for first and 'A' (reserve) team duty. It was in the latter that James was at half-back for the 'Reds' against the 'Stripes', partnering Ezekiel Harter in the opening half and J. Daniels after the break.

The following edition of the *Salford Reporter*, on 7 September, confirmed James – "a first class half-back who will make his first appearance in the Leigh match" – had by then been added to the club register as had Wakefield Trinity wingman Horace Price. As was the case with James, Salford took advantage of the Yorkshire Senior Competition's estrangement to entice the Trinity man. James's contract rewarded him with £2 and 10 shillings (£2.50p) if the team won, £2 and 5 shillings (£2.25p) for a draw, and £2 if defeated, good money at a time when skilled shipbuilders commanded slightly less than £2 a week and labourers around £1 and 8 shillings (£1.40p).

Having been forced to miss the opening two matches, both at home, a 16–0 victory over Brighouse Rangers on 7 September followed a week later by a friendly against South Shields when the Durham outfit lost 25–0, James, as predicted, made his debut at Leigh's Mather Lane enclosure, taking Griffiths's place. The Reds' line-up was: Smith; Herbert Dyson, Tom Williams (captain), Radcliffe Thomas, Herbert Hadwen; Davies, Lomas; Brown, Herbert Buckler, Rhapps, Robert Shaw, Hugh Shore, Pat Tunney, Jack Williams, J. Worthington. Watched by 5,000 spectators, James kicked off the match and also opened the scoring with a penalty. His day was sullied somewhat through the Reds' inability to protect that early lead; they fell away badly in the last 20 minutes and conceded three tries in an 11–2 defeat. James had the consolation of being hailed in the *Salford Reporter* as "the best man on the field", the opinion was that had he and Davies received the same support as the opposing duo, the result would have turned out differently. The same writer was clearly impressed by James, and commented: "He is the strongest man that has come to Salford for many a day, and is likely to be one of the most reliable of the backs."

James's strength for a short man would earn admiration throughout his career, combining his elusive "tantalizing swerve" with an ability to literally shove bigger opponents out of the way with his "long arm poking out like an iron bar". His physicality was something the Salford selectors quickly latched onto and, for his second outing – a trip to Fartown to take on Huddersfield – he was switched to right centre. In what was viewed as "sweeping changes" to the threequarters, Price, as James's outside partner, and Ernie Bone were also brought in on the wings, skipper Tom Williams was the only man to retain his place in the line. Griffiths also benefitted through reclaiming the half-back slot vacated by James. Before 5,000 spectators, and on a perfect day for rugby, the reconstruction of the backs paid off in the first half, James proved to be not only a dangerous attacking option, but a steadfast defender as well. When Bone received the ball from a scrum he shot down the touchline before passing inside to James who pushed his way over the try-line with two opponents vainly clinging on. He missed the conversion attempt, but his first Salford try was enough to give his team a 3–0 half-time lead.

Although Huddersfield levelled the scores after the break, the Reds regained the upper hand with a touchdown from Price, James grabbed his second off a Griffiths pass, to which he added the goal for an 11–3 verdict. The *Salford Reporter* journalist was again impressed with Salford's rising star, and said that James "promised to be a giant in the Salford ranks". He added, almost poetically, "where Price and Williams are weak, he is strong, where they are strong he is stronger, and in the match was the best man on the field with the exception, perhaps, of [Salford full-back] Smith. As a centre threequarter he proved a tower of strength, not least useful of his efforts being his contribution to the score." Unfortunately, the defeat did not go down too well with the home supporters who apparently "lost their heads and threw stones at their Lancashire visitors." After Tom Williams protested to the match officials, a Huddersfield committee man was despatched to the spot in the crowd where the missiles were coming from and "eventually soothed their angry passions".

It was in James's third match for Salford that he finally appeared in a home fixture. The visitors were Bradford on 5 October, the reigning Yorkshire champions who he and his former Bramley colleagues had unexpectedly defeated at Barley Mow the previous season. There was no such luck, though, with his new club who went down 14–10 on a wet afternoon before around 6,000 spectators. Salford were considered lucky to be only 6–2 down at the interval, Bradford's two tries had come as the result of a dominating pack. James, who had missed an earlier penalty due to a strong wind, opened the scoring with a goal from a mark by Buckler after the forward had defused a clearance punt from Bradford half-back George Marsden. Worse came for Salford after the interval as Bradford extended their lead to 14–2 before James inspired a comeback. He excited the home crowd with a tremendous break before transferring to Bone. Although the wing man was tackled by Bradford's full-back, the resulting quickly taken scrum saw the ball move smartly through the hands of Tom Williams and Griffiths for James to score under the posts and add the goal. The revival continued through a Tom Williams try, James this time missed the conversion. Although losing in his home debut, the Maryport man earned plaudits, the *Salford Reporter* said "Lomas was the pick of the lot from all points, whether aggressive or defensive, and his great strength must have been an eye opener for his opponents."

Salford were at New Barnes again the following week, Halifax provided the opposition in the first-ever competitive fixture between the two clubs. James returned to the halves, replacing an out-of-favour Davies. It was a role he retained through all his remaining appearances that season, all but one as outside partner to Griffiths. The prospect of again seeing their new hero in action boosted crowd numbers to 9,000 and the home contingent were not disappointed. He roused them midway through the opening half with a break deep into opposition territory, setting up Griffiths with a chance that just failed to mature due to a strong defensive effort. Then, after Billy Little had given Halifax the lead with a drop-goal, he replied in kind before edging his team 4–2 ahead via a penalty just before half-time. In the second half Salford increased their lead following a scrum in the corner near Halifax's line. James received the ball from Griffiths and slung out a long pass for Tom Williams to score. James obliged with the extra points and, although a further drop-goal followed from Little, the result was a 9–4 victory for the Reds.

Salford lost their two remaining October fixtures, both away from home; the short journey to Wheater's Field for the big local derby against Broughton Rangers 3–2 and the longer trip to the east coast to take on Hull at The Boulevard, 14–5. In the former, which drew over 15,000 spectators, James scored Salford's only points, his long-distance second-half penalty the only response to a first half try by Rangers winger Arthur Widdeson. It was a match James only just made after working earlier in the day and arriving late at Rangers' headquarters, the Grosvenor Hotel. Following an "impromptu wash", presumably to remove the sweat of his half-day toil, he quickly changed and travelled by cab to the ground, his last minute arrival causing "a buzz of excitement" inside the enclosure. The match at Hull was the first time that James failed to score for Salford. He did have a hand in Bones's try, but missed the conversion; the remaining points resulted from an earlier Griffiths drop-goal.

The defeat at Hull – albeit minus Smith and Tunney who were representing Lancashire against Cheshire that day – caused consternation for Salford officials as well as supporters. Three wins and four defeats in the opening seven outings fell way below pre-season expectations, when it was believed they had created a side capable of challenging for the Northern Rugby League title.

A turning point was reached with the following week's match against the Challenge Cup holders Batley at New Barnes. Salford won 14–6 and James was again a pivotal figure in providing the go-ahead points. With his side trailing 6–3 he pushed his way over the Batley line early in the second half following a dribbling run from his forwards, and added the goal points. This match has its place in history through being recorded for posterity by the Mitchell & Kenyon Film Company, based in Blackburn. Rediscovered and restored it was, as mentioned in the introduction to this book, featured in a BBC2 television series in 2005. In addition to James's try and goal, it shows the two sides emerging from their changing rooms at the London & North Western Hotel on Cross Lane, Salford's headquarters at that time, and then being conveyed by horse-drawn wagonette to the ground.

It was followed by three further victories. The first was 24–8 away to Brighouse Rangers

– James contributed a try direct from a scrum and another after charging down a clearance kick, plus two conversion and another goal from a mark; 11–3 at home to Leigh, where he forced his way over for a touchdown off a Buckler pass and landed a conversion in a match that saw Gledhill dismissed for kicking an opponent; and 11–5 against Hull, when his penalty goal opened the score. In all three matches James continued to make his presence felt as the outstanding performer. The latter game, played on 30 November, was also a significant day in Salford's history because it was the last first team match at New Barnes. The club had to move to accommodate the expansion of the Manchester Ship Canal. The final curtain came down at New Barnes on 14 December with an 'A' team fixture with Rochdale Hornets.

In the annals of the Salford club December 1901 was an important month. It was also a low scoring one, the Reds registered an aggregate 11 points to nine in the six matches played. The first two, away to Halifax and Rochdale Hornets – the latter was a fixture in the six-club South East Lancashire League – both ended scoreless, although, in hindsight, they could so easily have lost both. Jack Williams did not help the Reds' cause at Halifax – played in stormy weather – when he was sent off for "rough play" in the opening half, but the handicap they faced in the Rochdale meeting was far worse. It escalated into a mini-farce after a series of events that seem incredible now. When playing permits for five players – James, Griffiths, Buckler, Price and Davies – were routinely applied for by club secretary Victor Wright under the work clause rule, a response had not been received by the morning of the match. As the team – including the five players – travelled to Rochdale, Mr Wright travelled to the Oldham home of Northern Union secretary Joseph Platt, hoping to resolve the situation. But Mr Platt said the requests had not arrived and Salford had to take to the field in a snow-storm with the remaining 10 players, plus travelling reserve forward W. Howarth, against the Hornets' 15. There was more misfortune after Tunney returned alone to the dressing room during the interval and was accidentally locked in by an attendant. It was 10 minutes into the second half before his banging on the door was heard.

The following week, 21 December, was a landmark fixture when Salford played their first match at The Willows. It could not have fallen better because near-neighbours Swinton provided the opposition. The *Salford Chronicle* had no doubts about the sense of occasion saying: "The rivalry of the Reds and the Blues is almost historical and so far as this part of the world is concerned the contests have become classical and are locally of more importance than the Oxford and Cambridge boat race." The pitch had been covered by straw the day before to protect from a possible frost and was in good condition as the near 17,000 crowd built up while being entertained by the South Salford Silver Band.

The match itself was well contested with little to choose between the two teams. As usual James caused problems, the *Chronicle* noted that "his immense strength must have been a vexation to his opponents, amongst whom there seemed somewhat of a disposition to play on him." And it was the Cumbrian who settled the match, although it took him two

33

bites of the cherry to do so. From a scrum in front of the Swinton goalposts Griffiths got the ball out to him but, as he attempted a drop-goal, he was brought to ground, being slightly injured in the process. Undaunted, they repeated the move moments later and this time James sent the ball neatly over the crossbar, loudly cheered by the home fans. The narrow victory was something James recalled with fondness in his memoirs: "Salford had not beaten Swinton for some time and it was my first match against them. We won by a dropped goal to nil and I dropped it towards the end of the game. The points you score that decide a match makes them look the best!"

The Yuletide programme soon followed with visits from Broughton Rangers on Christmas Day, Stockport on Boxing Day, another South East Lancashire League match, and a trip to Runcorn on 28 December. The performance against Rangers was poor in comparison to that of four days earlier against the Lions. Salford deservedly lost 3–0 in front of around 6,000 fans. The 7–0 win over Stockport was less of a formality than anticipated and James registered a first half conversion and penalty towards the end. The visit to Runcorn saw the hosts overcome a tired-looking Salford 6–2. James claimed a goal from a mark made by Varty. The latter match – played on a heavy, treacherous pitch in "pitiless rain" – was highlighted by James's territorial kicking duel with Linnets' half-back Jim Jolley. It was something that the Cumbrian became noted for over the years, his prowess at propelling the ball deep into opposition territory was one of his major strengths.

Less complimentary was the reference to his Christmas Day performance against the Rangers. The *Salford Chronicle* observed that "here is a suspicion that Lomas's fine work has at times an element of selfishness in it and has a tendency to run his men off their feet." The writer was, of course, suggesting that sometimes James chose to run when he would be better advised to pass to a better placed colleague who, consequently, runs out of space by the time the pass is finally made. It was a criticism that resurfaced in match reports throughout his career, particularly if his team lost. When he moved to centre, where he spent much of his career, he was often accused of ignoring his winger. The fact was that James had great belief in his ability to beat a man, something he did time without number. On the occasions where he failed to break through the defence he would, like many of the top rugby league players since, risk the accusation that he was trying to win the match on his own. It is something that all great players in team sports endure. James was, by all accounts, a modest man but he was without doubt a match winner and he knew it.

James was absent for the New Year's Day match, a 7–0 home defeat to Hunslet, due to the work clause rule, but travelled to Oldham three days later for yet another 0–0 draw, played out in muddy conditions. This time both of Salford's half-backs, who had earned praise earlier in the campaign, came under the *Salford Chronicle* microscope: "Griffiths has a holiday look yet about his play and does not give the support to Lomas that is necessary for the latter to make much headway. So far as Lomas is concerned it is worth his while to pay a little more attention to his centres, and not attempt everything. Good man as he is he can hardly hope to win matches without the assistance of the other fourteen."

On 11 January the Reds travelled to Durham to face South Shields in the return friendly on what, for a change, was a fine day. James, following up a kick by Bone, scored a try under the posts and dropped a goal in a 13–7 win. It was at this stage of the season that Salford discovered the form most thought they were capable of and, of the next 16 matches, only one was lost, a run that took them to runners-up spot in the league and a place in the Challenge Cup Final.

First up, the Reds avenged their recent home defeat to Hunslet by winning 11–3 at Parkside on 18 January. James claimed all Salford's points with a try under the posts following a scrum near Hunslet's line, and added the conversion, a penalty and two drop-goals. The *Salford Chronicle* writer was full of praise, saying: "There is no getting away from the fact that he is the most versatile man in the team. It has been alleged that Lomas plays a selfish game. Perhaps he does but nothing succeeds like success and the question is just now not worth debating. Nobody in Salford cares who wins matches so long as they are won and when they find that of the 130 points standing in the clubs credit in the League competition Lomas has contributed 64 the supporters of the borough club will pray that the next capture may be as good a man."

The fine line between praise and damnation in sport was proved when James got into the 'bad book' again through missing the next fixture, a 6–0 home win over Oldham. Although selected, it was generally known by Saturday morning that he would not take to the field. The *Salford Chronicle* commented: "Jimmy had not complied with the working clause, and there are some very inquisitive people who would like to know why this has happened a second time, and how often it is likely to happen again." The previous occasion referred to was for the New Year's Day match against Hunslet, although, as already outlined, the mechanics associated with the rule also cost him an appearance at Rochdale in mid-December through no fault of his own. In all probability, James was struggling to find reliable employment. As previously mentioned, he had trained to be a ship's riveter when living in Maryport, a trade that was subsequently entered on his marriage certificate in 1903. However, it was a skill he was unlikely to be able to pursue in Salford. There was, of course, the new inland docks area, but no shipbuilding industry.

James was back in harness for the wins at Bradford, 2–0 on Shrove Tuesday thanks to his 10th minute drop-goal; at Batley, 11–9, when James converted George Heath's last minute try; and at home to Warrington 16–6, with two tries and two conversions from James. His two second half tries in the latter, watched by 10,000 at The Willows, showed him at his spectacular best. Each time he accepted Griffiths's pass before racing around full-back Jack Hallam to score. While acknowledging the forcefulness of Salford's forwards in the club's recent upsurge, it was at half-back where the cutting edge was applied, the *Salford Chronicle* pointed out: "Griffiths works the pack and Lomas does the rest, and the latter cannot be accused of selfishness on Saturday's display. Both his tries were the fruit of level-headed observation and acceptance of opportunity."

The Shrove Tuesday triumph at Bradford had been followed by the singular loss, 13–5 at Swinton, James's drop-goal had opened the scoring. The only other blemish on their league run-in was another 0–0 draw, this time against Runcorn the week after beating Warrington. It provided dreary viewing for an 8,000 Willows crowd. Salford's biggest league win of the season was 57–0 against Huddersfield on 31 March; the Fartowners had deliberately sent an understrength side to The Willows just five days before they faced each other again in the Challenge Cup. In a farcical and one-sided match James claimed two of the 13 tries, one in each half. He had had to leave the field shortly after the first of them with a leg injury, "the result of his opponents' unnecessary attention", but resumed in the second half, although on the left wing. He also landed five conversions, but the real star of the afternoon was Price who notched five touchdowns.

The final league match on 14 April produced a tightly fought 8–7 win at Warrington, enough to secure second place in the table, just one point ahead of Runcorn. It was a heroic performance by the Reds given that, but for one change, it was the same line-up that had played two days earlier in a Challenge Cup semi-final, whereas Warrington had been inactive for nine days. Small wonder there was a hint of "leg weariness" about Salford. Kicking off at 6pm on a Monday evening, the teams agreed to play 35 minutes each way.[3] A Price try in the corner gave Salford a 3–0 lead at the break, James missed the goal attempt. After Jack Fish had narrowed the gap with a goal, Davies made a sensational break for the Reds for a second try. James added a difficult goal to open up a vital six-point gap, enough to ward off a Warrington rally when they added a converted try five minutes from the end.

During this period, Salford also won two further matches in the South East Lancashire League. They defeated Rochdale Hornets 19–3 at The Willows on Monday 3 March, a fixture originally fogged off in November, and Stockport 8–3 at Edgeley Park on Good Friday, 28 March, when most of Salford's first choice men, including James, were rested due to them appearing in the Challenge Cup tie the next day. Against the Hornets, it was James's break that created the opening try for Price before he scored two himself. Both were from passes from half-back partner Griffiths. It was also Griffiths who made the mark from which James kicked his only goal, the pair, apparently, doing almost as they liked with James "as usual, head and shoulders above the rest."

But it was in the Challenge Cup where most excitement was generated. Could Salford's good form land them the prestigious trophy, and erode the disappointing defeat in the 1900 final? The first round was on 15 March, Salford had a home draw against Pontefract, who operated several rungs below them in the Yorkshire Second Competition. The visitors did remarkably well in the first half and were only 5–0 down at the interval. James's long distance break put Bone in under the posts. James converted and, after the break, again

---

[3] This option was withdrawn in 1911 when it was decreed that all games must last for 80 minutes.

gave the final pass for another Bone try. James placed the ball for his touchline conversion attempt back near the 25-yard flag to take account of a strong wind, and succeeded with what was described as "the finest goal so far kicked" at The Willows. Salford added four more tries, including one by James who, having taken a pass from Griffiths, "made one of his characteristic dashes for the line" to score under the posts. He also added three more conversions. Pontefract avoided a 'nil' score with a late penalty as Salford won 28–2.

The next round took the Reds to Dewsbury of the Yorkshire Senior Competition for a match that ended in mayhem. James got an early goal from a mark made by Gledhill, establishing a two point lead that remained unchanged throughout a contest that became vigorous and heated on the field and just as hostile off it. It escalated during the second half when half-back L. Ross appeared to land an equalising drop-goal for Dewsbury but referee, Mr Ashton from Oldham, had already blown for offside by Salford. Ironically, the resultant penalty attempt from Dewsbury's full-back Rhodes was off target. Then, when Salford were awarded a free kick, the agitated home crowd started to hoot loudly. Mr Ashton halted the game and stood in the centre of the field with his arms folded until peace was restored. After the final whistle blew, according to the *Salford Chronicle*, "three Dewsbury men were engaged in a cowardly attack on Lomas by attempting to ram his head into the ground." The police had to draw truncheons and form a cordon around the referee as the crowd surged onto the pitch pelting him with mud and cinders. The Salford players fared little better. James recalled in his memoirs: "They kicked us off the field and stoned the [wagonette] horses. One was bad. They took it to a veterinary surgeon. The referee drove to Batley in a cab. Horace Price ran to [his home in] Wakefield." In fact, despite police protection, several of the Salford party were, reportedly, injured by stones and bricks while being conveyed away on the wagonette. The following Monday the Northern Union committee suspended use of the Dewsbury ground until 27 April.

Salford drew another club from the Yorkshire Senior Competition in the third round, and played Goole at The Willows the day after meeting Stockport in the South East Lancashire League, although, as already pointed out, the Reds fielded mostly 'A' team players in the latter. Goole unwittingly provided Salford with their biggest ever win, 67–0, up to that point in their history. Two of the Reds' players also made an imprint on Northern Union's individual records; James's 31 points set a new high, overtaken in 1905 by Hull KR's George 'Tich' West with 53, while Bone equalled the try-scoring best of six, set by another Salford player, Frank Miles, in 1898. Despite a wet pitch where boots sank into the ground, James kicked 11 goals – all conversions – the first time he reached double figures. Another personal milestone was that in scoring three of Salford's 15 tries, he recorded his first try 'hat trick,' and a 'true' one at that. He scored the last try before half-time and the first two of the second half, all off Griffiths passes. Two days later came the 57–0 demolition of Huddersfield; the Reds scored an aggregate 124 points to nil in the two matches. James claimed 47 of them.

Huddersfield also provided Salford's fourth round opponents on 5 April, a place in the semi-final was the prize. Although Huddersfield deserved respect and were, like Salford, competing in the 'elite' Northern Rugby League, they were not then the powerhouse combination that would later become 'The Team of all the Talents'. Nonetheless, a trip to Fartown was not to be taken lightly. The attendance was 9,000 on a cold and wet day with pools of water covering the playing area. The Yorkshire side twice took the lead with unconverted tries and both times James had a part in levelling the scores. For the first he kicked across field for Davies to touch down and the second came when he took possession from a miskick by Walter Dewhirst and ran over at the corner. With the score tied at 6–6 Salford's task was made harder after the interval through the loss of full-back Smith. Brown took over his duties, leaving the Reds a man short in the pack. As tension mounted and with only five minutes left to play, Price broke away and, having kicked the ball towards the in-goal area, beat Llew Deere to the touchdown in the corner. Although James missed the goal, the visitors held on to their 9–6 lead to reach the last four.

On 12 April Salford had a semi-final date with holders Batley, the fifth consecutive time the Reds faced Yorkshire opponents in the 1902 competition. A keenly fought first half failed to produce any points and it was James who broke the deadlock in the second half. Again, it began with the reliable Griffiths, who took possession from the scrum before quickly passing to James. Although he was pulled down several times during a magnificent run, "the Batley backs could not withstand the determination of Lomas" and he regained his feet on each occasion to eventually score. James himself recalled this critical try in his memoirs: "It was one of the biggest individual efforts I ever made from halfway. I was up and down half a dozen times before I scored under the posts." James added the goal and the Reds now had the whiff of victory in their nostrils. Buckler had a try ruled out and James and Bone both got held up on the Batley try-line. The verdict was sealed towards the end when Davies – playing at centre – took the ball from the scrum and pushed his way through for a second try. The 8–0 win put the Salford fans in good heart as they left the ground with James once more hailed as their hero. The *Salford Chronicle* declared: "The followers of the scarlet runners were not only glorious but happy on Saturday as they left the splendid Watersheddings and wended their way to the (railway) station, stopping occasionally to buy a red flower or a card issued in pious memory of the Batley team."

Two days later, as previously mentioned, Salford secured the league runners-up spot through winning at Warrington. There was no play-off system then in place and top-placed Broughton Rangers took the title. It was the Rangers who lay in wait for the Reds at Rochdale's Athletic Grounds on 26 April to contest the ultimate destination of the Challenge Cup. The stand on the railway side of the ground had been closed after a late inspection had ruled it unsafe. Extra caution was taken in the wake of a terrible disaster at Ibrox Stadium, Glasgow, on the same afternoon that Salford and Huddersfield had met in the Challenge Cup. A total of 25 spectators were killed and around 500 injured when a wooden stand collapsed at the Scotland versus England association football international.

It seemed Salford had the majority of the support at Rochdale, red being the "prevailing colour" on the morning of the match. Salford's team was: Smith; Bone, Tom Williams (captain), Davies, Price; Lomas, Griffiths; Brown, Buckler, Gledhill, Heath, Rhapps, Shaw, Tunney, Jack Williams. The match started 25 minutes late due to Salford's train being delayed despite the comparatively short journey from Salford Station. When they did eventually arrive Salford gave their worst performance of the season for what was their most important match and were well beaten 25–0. The star of the afternoon was Rangers' captain Bob Wilson with three tries, while for Salford only their forwards received any credit, the backs were considered to have had an "off day".

The *Salford Reporter's* Broughton Rangers correspondent gave a disparaging and maybe biased view of James. He suggested that "While [Lomas] has been a most successful performer this season, it can hardly be said he is a 'class' man, and not being quite on the top of his form to which must be added that he was well watched by his opponents, he for once found his match." The *Bradford Daily Telegraph* was kinder, and said that, for Salford, "Only Lomas played anything approaching a descent game amongst the backs, and it was in single-handed efforts he was most noticeable. He would have done better in the first half for his side had he tried oftener on his own." Years later, James acknowledged that Broughton Rangers team as one of the three best he came across, the others were Huddersfield in the years before the First World War and Swinton in the late 1920s.

James concluded his season the following Tuesday by appearing in a combined Salford and Swinton team against a Broughton Rangers-Oldham combination at Rangers' Wheater's Field in a benefit match for their former centre Harry Chapman. James partnered Swinton's Dai Davies at half-back (not to be confused with the Salford player of the same name), winning 20–6. James's innocent looking contribution would have unfortunate repercussions for him at the start of the following campaign.

It had been a disappointing end to the season but, for James and his colleague, they at least had the consolation of being runners-up in both major competitions and who knows what the next season could bring? On a more personal note he had the satisfaction of establishing new Salford club records of 52 goals and 164 points, the latter figure also put him at the top of the Northern Union's point scoring list for the season.

On a statistical note, it was previously believed that James had set a new Northern Union point scoring record for a season of 172 during 1901–02, surpassing the 169 by Hull's Billy Jaques in 1898–99. Research for this publication now shows that he actually scored 164, although he would, on two occasions, set new records for this category in the future.

James in his Lancashire jersey.
He represented his adopted county nine times from 1903 to 1906.

6. 1902–03: A world record

When James Lomas became the subject of a world record transfer fee in 1902, it was a tribunal committee rather than the two clubs involved who determined what that figure should be. It was a situation that arose as a direct result of the rift between the Yorkshire Senior Competition and Northern Rugby League being healed, a process that began in April 1902. Suddenly clubs such as James's former employer Bramley were again part of the establishment in an expanded Northern Rugby League, one that would contain two divisions in the upcoming 1902–03 campaign. But the entente-cordiale also meant that players spirited away from the Yorkshire Senior Competition some 12 months earlier now had a value placed on them and there was a price to be paid if their new owner wished to retain their services. That price was decided by a three-man arbitration panel because then, as now, the seller's valuation usually exceeded that of the buyer.

The three officials chosen to form that panel were D.F. Burnley (Batley), J.E. Warren (Warrington) and W.J. Rich (Millom). Bramley had demanded £250 for James, but the price tag placed on him was £100. The Reds were instructed that should they not wish to retain him he should be returned to Barley Mow along with £30, presumably a payment for playing him in 1901–02. While it still equated to the first-ever three-figure transfer, £100 was a sum Salford were more than happy to pay and small wonder after the impact he made at The Willows the previous season. It was also reported that Bramley would have been willing to pay £100 for his return. Hull, on the other hand, decided not to retain James's former colleague Albert Hambrecht and he went back to Bramley. Interestingly, Salford refused to pay the £75 required to hold onto Horace Price, despite him having scored 20 tries in 31 appearances in 1901–02, and he rejoined Wakefield Trinity.

All in all, it was a scenario that again proved the old adage that there is never anything new under the sun. In 1987, another three-member tribunal panel was set up by the Rugby Football League to settle transfer fee disputes arising between clubs following the scrapping of the antiquated 'retain and transfer' system. The new system of contracts allowed players to join another club when their agreement period ended, although still subject to a transfer fee. It was a situation that lasted until 1998 when – influenced by football's 'Bosman' ruling – it was decided transfer fees no longer applied for out-of-contract players.

James spent the 1902 close season back in Maryport. Whether he was there primarily to share time with his family or, more likely, his future wife, Annie, is not known. What is known, however, is that during those summer months he was once more employed in the shipyards alongside the River Ellen. This may have had some appeal because it seemed that throughout his life, after originally leaving Maryport in 1900, he found it difficult to obtain guaranteed regular employment in what were difficult times for a working man. That difficulty was very likely the reason why he sometimes fell foul of the work clause rule in that he found so-called *bona fide* work elusive.

Whatever his motivation for working in the Maryport shipyards during the 1902 break, at least three people had good cause to be eternally grateful, including former Wigan winger John Timoney who had returned to Maryport as captain of James's former club. All three were rescued from drowning in the River Ellen by James that summer, something he had twice done before. The *Salford Reporter* commended him, saying "these rescues are conclusive proof of natural smartness and resource under trying circumstances."

Salford did not bring in many new recruits for 1902–03, although they did obtain another Maryport player in threequarter Thomas Bell. A less publicised signing was that of Dave Preston, a half-back from the Salford Trinity junior club. First seen in action by supporters during the club's pre-season trials, he went on to have a long career with the Reds. Meanwhile, James took no part in the three public trial matches and, although back in Salford at the beginning of September, it was reported at that time that "it will be another fortnight before Lomas can take his place in the team."

The reason was that – just like 12 months earlier – he had been suspended for the opening two matches. Again it was due to the 'work clause' although, surprisingly, it related to his appearance in Harry Chapman's benefit game at the end of the previous season. At their meeting on 13 May, the NU committee decided he should have applied for a permit to play, having been unemployed on the day of the match, a Tuesday, and the day before. The *Salford Reporter* correspondent was cynical about the committee's decision, and said that "Having regard to the nature of the occasion and the manner in which similar breaches of the employment clause were dealt with at the same meeting one is not surprised to learn that the sentence passed on Lomas is strongly resented in Salford football circles as an act of tyranny."

He also claimed: "There is a strong suspicion that nothing would have been heard of the affair if Lomas had turned out for the match on the following day; Broughton Rangers v The Rest of the League." James had pulled out of the latter, at Wheater's Field and organised to celebrate Broughton Rangers' championship success, after being selected at outside half. But, whereas he may have considered he did not require permission for a benefit fixture, did he withdraw from 'The Rest' because he had not fulfilled the requirements of the work clause? Whatever the underlying reason, he did not reappear until Salford's third match, at home to Widnes. By that time he had become club captain with forward Jack Williams as vice-captain, decisions that had been announced on the eve of the season.

There were approximately 6,000 people at The Willows to witness the visit of Widnes, the previous season's Lancashire Senior Competition runners-up and one of four clubs admitted to the expanded top division of the Northern Rugby League. Just before half-time, James opened the scoring with a try after taking a return pass from his former captain, Tom Williams. James was wide with the goalkick, but the Reds led 3–0 at the break. It was not until almost the end that James concluded the scoring in the Reds' 5–0 victory with a magnificent long-range penalty, given for offside. There were some interesting comments about the game in the *Salford Reporter*. One person "who had come for the purpose" counted that there were 122 scrums, or 'scrimmages' as they referred to them at the time, which roughly equates to three every two minutes. It added up to what was described as an "unentertaining" match that "passed through a series of cycles, something after this fashion:- heel out – pass – tackle – scrimmage – heel out – punt – reply to touch – scrimmage again, and so on for the 80 minutes." James, at least, was absolved of criticism: "If Lomas had not played the result would have been drawn. The Salford man is about the only man in the contingent capable of bringing off Saturday's points under the conditions prevailing."

It was Salford's third successive win, but their 100 per cent record was dented the following weekend against Bradford, with a 2–2 draw at Park Avenue after James had put his team ahead with an early penalty for 'feet up'. Another narrow home victory came on 4 October when Huddersfield were the visitors, James's 40-yard penalty for offside was followed by a drop-goal from Billy Brown for a 4–0 win, all the points came in the opening half. An interesting piece of play began the second half after James – usually so accurate in this situation – kicked off and the ball, aided by a strong wind, went directly into touch near the corner. The rules then said it had to be retaken until the ball arrived in the field of play and, after a second attempt had followed the same route, his third was caught by a Huddersfield defender two inches from touch in almost the same spot so the game was underway again. There was concern about the dearth of tries so far and, in particular Salford's lack of "a really first class wingman" with Price and Ernie Bone no longer on the team sheet.

Two days later, on Monday 6 October, James swept club issues out of his mind when he played at Widnes's Lowerhouse Lane ground in the Lancashire trial, having earned 'residential qualification' through his association with Salford. He lined up at half-back with the Possibles, partnering Leigh's Jimmy Molyneux. Opposing them in the Probables were brothers Willie and Sam James of Broughton Rangers. James did not let himself down, and scored all his side's points with a first half try, after 'fast passing' with Molyneux, and the conversion to tie the score 5–5 at the interval. He added a penalty for a 7–5 lead. The Probables, however, took control and eventually won 21–7. After the trial, the James brothers – who were in the driving seat having been utilised for the previous campaign – retained their places, although James was named as one of the reserves for the opening match against Cheshire later that month.

Salford's next fixture was at home to Warrington. James had a hand in the opening try, scored by Tom Williams in the corner, but missed the conversion and a subsequent penalty "by inches" before Warrington tied the score at 3–3 before the interval. James claimed the next try, taking a pass off Bell before "shouldering off all opponents and scoring in a favourable position for augmentation." Unfortunately, James's 'augmentation' was not forthcoming and Salford clung to a 6–3 lead that was finally extended when Bone – making a rare appearance – raced over near the corner flag. This time Brown failed to gather the extra points, but Warrington were held at bay until Taylor added a goal from a mark in the last minute to close the scoring at 9–5. Overall, the match had been open and well contested. James – who hit his best form again – was lauded in the *Salford Reporter*: "The style of Lomas is well known and in his own particular tactics he has no compeer. Keeping steadily before him the necessity of making a score and endeavouring to win a match he does not follow the orthodox methods, and this was apparent on Saturday. Nothing succeeds like success and he succeeded."

Having remained unbeaten during their opening six matches, Salford suddenly hit a wobbly patch losing all three of their remaining October fixtures; 4–0 away to Brighouse Rangers, 5–0 at home to Broughton Rangers and 9–5 at St Helens. The visit to Brighouse took place on a Monday to coincide with the annual pig festival held in the town, the return fixture at The Willows – as the *Salford Reporter* pointed out – "being set down for the feast of the indigestible pancake in February." The paper welcomed full-back Dan Smith back from his honeymoon, but added that "while wishing him every success in life, there is a faint suspicion that the loss of the match was in some measure the outcome of celebrating the event." Played in pouring rain, it was a surprise defeat against Brighouse, who were destined for the league's wooden spoon. The nearest to a Salford score was when James's first half penalty hit a post.

With Salford and Broughton Rangers among the league leaders, their meeting at The Willows attracted 14,710; the £367 gate was reported as a record for the Reds. There was plenty of incident around the terraces when, on two occasions during the first half, the perimeter fencing was brought down as the crowd surged, the latter instance resulting in "a couple of hundred" fans running across to the Pavilion end, the referee, momentarily, halting play. It was the away supporters who left the match smiling, a second half try from Bob Wilson, converted by Willie James gave their team the win. James, who attempted a penalty from just inside his own half which just dipped below the crossbar, came in for some criticism in the local paper. The *Salford Reporter* was quite candid in its review: "The Salford captain only sparingly gave to his threequarters, Tom Williams being the most favoured recipient ... his individual efforts were fruitless in spite of unflagging industry all the afternoon. The amount of work he got through was marvellous and betakes his possession of an immense amount of physical strength. The Rangers of course watched him so closely that he was no sooner seen with the ball than he was surrounded by half-a-dozen of them and pulled down. Seeing this he might have saved himself several maulings by passing out – but he didn't."

The last of their trio of defeats, at St Helens, was another upset given that the Saints had won only once so far and ended the season one place above Brighouse. James kicked a 40-yard penalty after just 10 minutes, one impressed St Helens spectator exclaimed "Yon man means business", a comment that the *Reporter* correspondent said "speaks well for the sportsmanship of the town." With Tom Williams and Bell both injured from the previous weeks match, James played at left centre and gave his usual industrious performance but was again well marked. Williams, who had damaged a knee cartilage never played for Salford again, although he attempted a brief, unsuccessful comeback with Swinton in 1908. Sadly, he died of a fever in 1915 during the Gallipoli campaign in Egypt.

An unusual situation prevented James from participating in Salford's next match, at home to Runcorn on 1 November. Cumberland – whom he had last represented in 1899 while with Maryport – had surprisingly selected him for their meeting with Yorkshire at Headingley on the same day. This was despite him having already appeared in Lancashire's trial and being reserve for the Red Rose's 25 October match versus Cheshire. The Cumberland county committee claimed he had refused "for insufficient reasons" to play for them and cited his birth qualification and the fact he had won a Cumberland county cap. For his part, James had already written to the Cumberland committee and, while thanking them for the "proffered honour", said he "desired to be released". The Cumbrian response was to send him a telegram declining his request and warned him against representing Salford on that date. There was a feeling that Cumberland had deliberately picked him in retaliation for his decision to play for Lancashire. Possibly because of these events, the July 1903 Northern Union Annual General Meeting agreed that, in future, a player, having already represented his birth county could not, without that the consent of that county, represent another.

In 1960 'Elbra', writing about James's career, gave a Cumbrian perspective, saying: "His decision to leave Cumberland's side for the Red Rose caused great bitterness and controversy in Cumberland because he was a potential match-winner in his own rights any time. In those days the home county championship match of Cumberland was the big game of the season." Either way, it put James in a difficult position and he stood down from the Salford team against Runcorn. He missed out on a match that had an exciting finish, with Bell – who had been disappointing since joining Salford – cast as the hero. In an important match between two of the leading sides, Runcorn had led 6–5 at the interval. It remained that way until two minutes from time, when Bell took a pass from Ben Griffiths and beat several defenders before rounding full-back Sammy Houghton, aided by a neat dummy pass, to score. Brown's goal made the final score 10–6, and created "scenes of enthusiasm and cordiality" among the 7,000 crowd.

Meanwhile, Salford contacted both the Northern Union and Lancashire county officials in a bid to clear up the dispute over James's county credentials. It was evidently resolved because a few days later he was again selected as reserve for Lancashire in their forthcoming match with Yorkshire, scheduled for The Willows on 15 November. Interestingly, while James was forced to sit out Salford's match against Runcorn, Bradford centre Bill Eagers scored two tries for Yorkshire against Cumberland despite having already represented the latter on six occasions.

It was back to action with Salford for James at Batley on 8 November where, despite him producing another excellent display, it was not sufficient to avoid a 5–2 defeat during an afternoon of pouring rain. Smith grabbed Salford's points with a drop-goal. Following a weekend off while Salford staged the Lancashire versus Yorkshire fixture in front of a reported 14,000 crowd, the Reds entertained Halifax on 22 November. It was a significant game in James's career. Having returned to half-back for the Batley trip, he was again picked in the centre, a role that would endure – with a few exceptions – for the rest of his playing career. The change came about for two reasons. One was the Reds' weakness at centre due to the loss of Tom Williams and the poor form of Bell. It was a problem alleviated by the recent acquisition of Swinton's Bob Messer for £50, although it was still considered a vulnerable area. The second reason was that James, as a half-back, was often perceived as holding onto the ball instead of releasing his threequarter line. As already stated, James believed, with some justification, that he could beat any man that barred his path but, of course, that could not happen every time and, when it did not, he invited criticism. Moving James to a wider position would provide opportunities for him to create even more mayhem.

On his wing against Halifax was the improving Bell who looked more comfortable patrolling the touchline than he did in the centre, the pair formed an all-Maryport left flank, while Messer slotted in at right centre. With the formidable Salford pack virtually picking itself and experienced threequarter Ezekiel Harter gaining a new lease of life in covering James's former outside-half berth, the team settled into a line-up that served them well for the rest of the season. James, whose penalty gave Salford a 2–0 interval lead over Halifax, put Bell in for a try in the corner following good approach work by Harter and Griffiths. He then landed another penalty after "shady work" by Halifax's pack for a 7–0 lead and completed the scoring in the final minutes by converting the goal to forward George Heath's try, crowning a 12–0 success. Although involved in many aspects of play, James's performance was rated as "hardworking without being brilliant" with Messer and Harter being feted as the two outstanding individuals. The latter, along with Griffiths, was credited with keeping play open.

James's star shone very brightly again during the next match, at Leigh. It was a low scoring affair and only a Griffiths drop-goal separated the two sides at the break, although James, ably supported by Messer, constantly punched holes in the defence as he "got through an immense amount of hard labour." In the match's closing stages he claimed a try that had the crowd buzzing with excitement. It began after a charge down the field by the Reds' pack was followed up by Harter giving possession to James, who "carefully running well within himself [then] threaded his way through the whole of the Leigh backs and scored." He could just about be forgiven for missing the resultant kick in a 5–0 win.

Salford drew 3–3 with visitors Hull seven days later, but James was not on the field because once more he failed the 'work clause' rule. The problem this time, apparently, was that he had not worked three full days. An injury sustained at Leigh stopped his attendance at the start of the week and then he was laid off by his employer on Thursday. The *Salford Reporter* seized on the injustice and anomalies associated with the rule: "It seems that just at present the firm by whom he is employed are in 'short time' and of course Lomas is unable to work any longer than any other man. The Northern Union sub-committee absurdly note 'short time' is not 'full time', unjust under the circumstances. Lomas could not help being injured at Mather Lane, nor be responsible for slackness of work."

Although James did occasionally suffer through not fulfilling the conditions associated with the work clause rule, he was nonetheless a supporter of its principles. The rule was dispensed with prior to the 1905–06 season, from which point so-called 'open-professionalism' was allowed. James, though, said in his memoirs that "It was a bad blow to the players when they finished the working clause." His reasoning was that rugby players should be encouraged to work because it contributed to their well-being, manual work in particular being a good way to keep in condition for the rigours of the sport. In a 1930s interview he said: "When I came into the Northern Union game it was a condition that you had had to work before you could play. Now it doesn't matter. But I have always believed that a professional footballer is all the better for having a regular job providing it is a healthy one."

It seemed that every week there was as much news off the field as on it. The match at Watersheddings on 13 December resulted in a 2–0 win over Oldham thanks to a Smith drop-goal in the first half, but the talking point was the 'low' attendance of 5,000 with fans staying away due to a smallpox scare.

James and his colleagues were then inactive until Christmas Day when they faced Broughton Rangers at Wheater's Field, a match that attracted almost 20,000. Before the start there were queues a quarter-mile long outside the ground and many climbed in. If they expected a points-fest, they would have been disappointed because the only time a score looked likely was when James intercepted a Frank Harry pass intended for Wilson and ran over half the length of the field before he was despatched over the touchline at the critical moment. Two days later Hull KR arrived in Weaste for the first time, although it was a fruitless journey. Salford won comfortably 17–0. James chipped in with three second half goals; from a mark made by Heath, a conversion and a penalty.

New Year's Day 1903 required a short journey to Chorley Road to meet Swinton. A 14,000 crowd saw Salford take a 6–0 interval lead thanks to tries by Herbert Buckler and Bell, the latter after a passing move involving James. The Salford skipper was less productive with the boot, and missed both difficult touchline conversions although he had been close earlier on with a long-range penalty and a drop-goal attempt. Swinton, who enjoyed the slope advantage after the turnaround, replied with two touchdowns of their own to tie the match at 6–6. In the opening phase of the second half Salford had brought Brown out of the pack to assist his backs stem the Swinton attack. This was not an unusual tactic at this time, but the *Salford Reporter* writer was quick to point out that, in his opinion, the pressure had been self-inflicted and "for this Lomas has had to bear a lot of adverse criticism". The reasoning behind the comment was that, as captain, James had erred in choosing to play downhill in the first half having been "warned" to choose differently. Presumably, James believed his side could build a winning lead before changing ends.

Just two days later, in a game described as "fast and exciting", James's performance during the 16–2 triumph at Hunslet was beyond reproach; he helped to set up Bell for the second of his side's four tries and scored the final two himself. He was, though, off the pace with his goalkicking, his one success was an early second half penalty, Brown notched the Reds' only conversion. One feature of James's kicking armoury that was still potent, however, was his towering kick-offs. Despite playing in the centre he continued to take the responsibility, invariable finding touch near the opposition corner flag to immediately place his team on the offensive.

Having already succeeded at Central Park, Salford confidently expected to dispose of Wigan in the return fixture on 10 January, but were beaten 13–0, although there were mitigating circumstances. As in the first encounter, James was absent. In this instance it was to make his debut for Lancashire in a team that also included four Salford colleagues; Smith, Heath, Jack Rhapps and Pat Tunney. Ironically from James's point of view, it was against Cumberland in Millom; he was paired at half-back with Sam James of Broughton Rangers. On a bitterly cold day, continuous rain for the past two days, that only ceased just prior to kick off, had made the playing area very heavy. It was Lancashire's fourth and final match of the campaign, their 21–3 victory gave them a 100 per cent record and the county championship, something they were assured of before the match. Lancashire's half-back duo earned praise for their contribution, although James did not get on the scoreboard, having attempted and missed the goal following the opening try by Broughton Rangers' winger Andy Hogg. Incidentally, Cumberland's try was scored by Timoney, the Maryport player that James had rescued in the summer.

Following the postponement of the match at Widnes on 17 January, due to frost, Salford returned to winning ways for the remaining two matches of the month, 14–0 at home to Bradford and at Huddersfield, 12–6. They were welcome results for the Reds who were in contention for the championship along with Broughton Rangers, Halifax, Oldham and Swinton. Bradford were a well-beaten side by the finish. James scored the first try from Preston's pass and returned the favour by taking part in the move that put Preston under the posts for the second. He added the goal for the latter as Salford led 8–0 at the interval. After finding time to race across the field to prevent a certain touchdown from Bradford centre Frank Murgatroyd, James had a significant part in Salford's final try of the afternoon, escaping the clutches of winger Bill Sinton, Murgatroyd and full-back Ward to put Bell in. Surprisingly, James and his co-centre Messer were chastised for their "tendency to run [wingers A.] Norris and Bell too close to touch before passing" adding that "if this was remedied there would be chance of a return pass and Lomas and Messer could benefit."

The victory at Fartown saw James add yet another try to his tally, scoring the last one before the interval after beating three men, following a scrum, to go over at the corner. It gave Salford a 9–3 lead but, in a goal-less game, Huddersfield pulled back to 9–6. James tried his best. He intercepted a pass and ran halfway down the field only for his pass to Bell to be ruled forward. He then had a try disallowed for an infringement. Relief came on the stroke of time when he helped send Bell racing over the try-line for the clinching score. In fact James had a hand in all four Salford tries, having helped set Norris up for the first two. Unfortunately, there was trouble at the match, some home fans tried to reach Widnes referee Jack Smith shortly before Bell's try, clearly unhappy at his decisions. Visiting Salford fans were also hustled at the end, and mud and cinders were thrown at the team. Brown was struck in the eye. Later, the crowd gathered around the hotel that Salford had gone to, the Reds contingent required police intervention to make their exit.

The next Thursday, Salford fulfilled the previously postponed fixture at Widnes, but came unstuck 7–3. They did better two days later at Warrington; James made a now rare appearance at half-back as replacement for Preston who had injured a leg at Lowerhouse Lane. Salford won 11–2, having led 3–0 at the break. James converted the Reds' second try, scored by Bell after the interval, before he set up the third and final try for Messer. The supporters' fickle nature was shown in the second half when James received "derisive shouts" from Salford fans "for finding touch too often" rather than keeping the ball in hand.

The following Saturday, 14 February, saw the start of the 1903 Challenge Cup campaign. Salford were one of several clubs to receive a bye into the second round seven days later. Their opponents were Leigh who brought around 2,000 supporters to The Willows, although the attendance was a 'disappointing' 7,000, attributed to a miserable, wet day. The tie was scoreless at half-time, James – back at centre – had done his best to alter that situation. He hit the post with a penalty, missed a drop-goal and was held up on the Leigh line in the final moments before the interval. Harter was the first to score, racing over following a scrum, Bell got a second off Messer's pass. With Brown adding on the goal points for the latter, Salford led 8–0. It was left to James to seal it 11–0 with a try described by the *Salford Reporter* as "perhaps the best thing in his football career." It began when Bell dribbled the ball from his own '25' area. James – who had been struggling to show his usual running style in the difficult underfoot conditions – took over and propelled it by boot all the way to Leigh's in-goal for the score. He missed his second conversion attempt of the afternoon, but it was good enough to put the Reds through to the last 16. There was a feeling of optimism in the local paper that, with great rivals Broughton Rangers and Swinton eliminated in the opening round, it was their best chance for some time to win the Cup.

However, before the next round was due, Salford had league business to take care of against Brighouse Rangers and Runcorn. Brighouse visited Weaste on the Tuesday following the cup tie. James converted Hugh Shores' opening touchdown as Salford built an 8–0 interval lead, and scored the final try in the corner following a dribbling move by his forwards. James and co-centre Messer earned respect for an excellent display in the 14–0 win, just as they had in the Leigh game. With Salford in the title hunt, the following weekend's 4–0 defeat at Runcorn was considered a disaster. The Reds gave a poor display against an improving Linnets side that eventually finished fourth in the table.

Salford picked themselves up from this disappointment, and went through their next 10 games unbeaten. The run began with the third round Challenge Cup match at Second Division Rochdale Hornets on 7 March. Excitement was high; 2,000 supporters on three special trains followed the Reds to the Athletic Grounds. They were rewarded by seeing five unconverted tries in a comfortable 15–0 victory. James scored three of them. His first was the only score of the opening half; he ran from distance to touch down as rain began falling heavily. He also claimed the final two, first through recovering a loose ball following an excellent touchline run by Bell and later dribbling into the Hornets in-goal area before scoring. The result put Salford in the last eight for the fifth time in six seasons.

Two more home league victories followed – Swinton, 10–0, and Batley, 28–8 – as Salford continued their title quest. The match with the Lions drew 13,312 through the turnstiles, the £430 takings were a record, exceeding that of the early season Broughton Rangers fixture. A drop-goal by Griffiths got the Reds off the mark, James then deprived Swinton full-back Alf Chorley of the ball when he attempted to retrieve a kick towards the left flank. Shrugging off Bob Valentine, he placed the ball under the posts, and added the extras for a 7–0 half-time lead. Swinton had defended well, but Salford's forwards, encouraged by James's wonderful touch kicking – at which he was considered a master – gave the Reds the edge. Harter sealed their success with a late try.

Two days later, on a wet Monday against Batley, James notched two of his side's eight tries. Both came during the second half and were scored under the posts; first off Bell's pass, and then after controlling a bouncing ball before grounding. He also converted the Reds' first try, scored by Bell, who went on to claim a hat-trick. Despite having a part in most of Salford's touchdowns – "if Lomas failed himself he was the cause of others scoring" – the old chestnut about his holding the ball too long again emerged through comments such as "Lomas was selfish at times and this kept the score down." This came after Salford's biggest win of the season so far.

Salford travelled to York on 21 March for their fourth round cup tie. Again, Second Division opposition lay in wait; the Reds had few problems in delivering a 25–2 victory. The signs were ominous when James kicked off and produced his usual party piece of finding touch near the opponents' corner flag. York managed to resist this early threat, but succumbed in the 10th minute when slick passing concluded with James sending out a long pass for Messer's simple run in. Bell got a second and then James, with a supreme effort, "fairly bluffing all opponents," ran in at the corner after accepting a pass from Griffiths. Salford held a 9–2 lead at the break; further tries followed from Norris with two, Bell and

Robert Shaw. Harter also added his name to the score-sheet with a drop-goal. As on most occasions, James was singled out for praise by the *Salford Reporter*, although given with an unusual tinge of regret in saying his performance "was a grand example and rather astonished the York spectators by his clever running and dribbling and it certainly was galling that we could not claim him as a genuine Lancastrian."

There were, however, other more pertinent comments about his goalkicking prowess. During the York match he had managed just one conversion while missing several reasonable opportunities. It triggered the remark that "for some reason Lomas is not successful this season in his attempts at goal." Certainly, his strike rate was down on his Salford debut season. In 26 matches so far, he had succeeded with just 17 place kicks whereas in the previous campaign he hit the target 45 times, including five drop-goals, after the same number of appearances. Despite his count falling, he was still considered to be the club's number one marksman, although there were times when the ball was handed to others to try their luck, most notably Brown.

However, to put things in perspective, it is worth pointing out that, compared to today, goal attempts during this era were far less fruitful. Goalkicking had not developed into the art form seen today and its exponents were still to achieve the level of skill and consistency of later years. This was partly due to the more rounded, cumbersome shape of the ball, its propensity to become heavy in wet conditions and the kicking style used. Usually, the ball was put on the ground pointing towards goal, the kicker took a short run before booting it towards the posts. All very different to what developed later; the ball carefully placed in an upright position, the measured run up, and a variety of kicking styles. James would end the 1902–03 campaign with just 22 goals, including two in the Lancashire trial, whereas the season's leading goal-scorer, Hunslet's Albert Goldthorpe, although way ahead of the Salford captain, still only managed 48.

Salford's next date was with Leigh at The Willows on a wet afternoon that saw a heavy fall of hailstone midway through the opening half. A dribbling move from the home forwards towards the end of the first 40 minutes created the position for James to open the scoring. Gathering up the ball, he raced over in the corner, evading winger Frank Ganley and full-back Edgar Pearson in the process. As if to prove his detractors wrong, and despite the awful conditions, he added a magnificent touchline conversion. In the second half, James made a tremendous break that covered over half of the field, almost getting Rhapps over, but the forward was tackled just in time. James continued to feature strongly as his team added three further tries, although he missed all three goal attempts. Salford finished the match 14–0 to the good.

It was back to Challenge Cup business the next weekend, 4 April. Oldham were the obstacle to a second successive appearance in the final. The match took place at Broughton's Wheater's Field ground. There were 19,000 fans present. It was a fine afternoon, although the pitch was in a poor state. Salford were considered fortunate to hold the Roughyeds at bay for a 0–0 draw. James received credit as "one of the best men on the field." The replay took place four days later, on Wednesday afternoon, at the same venue. The ground was in a better state and play was much faster than the previous encounter. James proved himself to be the man for the big occasion and, having already been hauled down a yard from the try-line following an incisive break, he broke away again, and burst through a crowd of opponents to score under the posts accompanied by "a hurricane of cheers". There was no icing on the cake though; James struck the underside of the crossbar with his goalkick, so Salford led 3–0 at the break. Joe Ferguson missed an Oldham penalty and James almost claimed a second try in a keenly fought start to the second half. Griffiths extended Salford's lead with a drop-goal, Roughyeds' full-back Dickie Thomas failed to reply in kind. Again, James nearly got over for a try, this time in the corner. Norris cemented an 8–0 win near the end after forcing his way across the whitewash. This time Brown took the kick, but hit the post. Salford had played well in the second half, with James rated "head and shoulders above his confreres in the Salford threequarter line."

The Reds had reached the Challenge Cup Final for a third time, but supporters' joy turned to despair when James was injured in the following match. As luck would have it, Salford met Oldham a third time in eight days through their league encounter at The Willows the following Saturday, fielding the same XV as in the replay. The first half was scoreless, its highlight being a tremendous run from James, who weaved in-and-out of a host of opponents before he was brought down by winger Tommy Cash. The incident resulted in him damaging a thigh muscle and he left the field until half-time, Brown took his place at centre. The Salford skipper returned for the second half, but had to withdraw later. His colleagues, meantime, secured a 3–0 victory through a try from Griffiths; Brown hit the crossbar with his goal attempt. The *Salford Reporter*, showing concern for James, bemoaned "if he is missing for any length of time it will prejudice their championship chances." Sure enough, James was absent for the next game two days later on Monday, although Salford kept their aspirations alive with an 11–3 win over visitors St Helens.

The next match was of paramount importance in the championship race; Salford travelled to Halifax just three days later on the Thursday. The two teams were locked at the top of the table, both having 44 points with three matches each remaining, including their clash at Thrum Hall, which drew 14,000. There was relief in Salford's camp that James was able to reappear for such a vital game. Halifax – Salford's opponents for the forthcoming Challenge Cup Final – took first blood to lead 5–0 at half-time, their try and conversion came from former Salford player Herbert Hadwen. Any doubts about James's fitness were dispelled during the second half after he received a quick pass from Griffiths. The latter had been supplied by Harter direct from a scrum. Running at full pace through a melee of defenders, James handed off assailants in typical barnstorming fashion before scoring between the uprights, tagging on the extras to level the match at 5–5. It was the game's final score. It left them all-square on 45 points and meant the pair could not be overtaken.

James awaits the result of the coin toss by opposing skipper George Frater of Oldham. This is probably prior to the 1903 Salford versus Oldham Challenge Cup semi-final at Wheater's Field.

Halifax's Archie Rigg tosses the coin as James makes the call for Salford prior to the 1903 Challenge Cup Final at Headingley. This photograph appeared in *The Book of Football 1905*.

The *Yorkshire Post* was quick to praise James, saying "Halifax need a strong scorer and individualist in their back division such as Salford have in Lomas. The old Bramley player enabled Salford to draw the match, just as he succeeded in winning the replayed tie with Oldham last week. With such a man, capable of pushing an attack home, there would be no difficulty in making Halifax favourites for the Cup."

Salford appeared to have glory within their grasp. With two matches remaining in the championship against clubs in the lower half of the table, together with a cup final against a team they had taken three points off in the league, surely the double was a realistic ambition? But, with the finishing line in view, Salford's bubble suddenly burst and, instead of silverware, what resulted was disappointment and thoughts of what might have been.

The first outstanding league match was at The Boulevard against Hull on Monday 20 April, five days before the cup final. Salford – despite sending their proposed line-up for the final – finished well beaten, 12–5. They were 12–0 down at the interval, Norris's second half try and James's touchline conversion closed the scoring. James had quite a time of it in more ways than one, his discomfort was a consequence of the non-appearance of appointed referee Frank Renton of Hunslet. After a 25 minute delay, touch judge Mr Mellor of Goole took charge, an official from each club took up the flag-waving duties, Harry Eagles fulfilled the role on Salford's behalf. The *Salford Reporter* accused Mr Mellor of "biased" judgement and "poor errors", claiming that, but for Eagles's intervention, James would have been dismissed during the first half, adding "readers who would like to know the reason of this action had better ask Mr Mellor." Reportedly, James had retaliated having been "the recipient of marked attention" of the kind "usually bestowed on clever players", which had prevented him opening out play.

It was another anti-climax for James when he led his team against Halifax in the Challenge Cup Final at Headingley. Watched by 32,507 – a new attendance record for the code – Salford lost 7–0; all the points came after the interval. The *Yorkshire Post* said: "Lomas has seldom been seen less conspicuously. That was not his fault. It was the want of opportunities. At half-back Harter and Griffiths in the first half made for touch as they considered it a haven of refuge." In part, this was due to a keen defensive display by the Halifax forwards and half-backs. James hardly handled the ball at all during the second half, except to take free kicks. The Reds XV was: Smith; Norris, Messer, Lomas (captain), Bell; Harter, Griffiths; Brown, Buckler, Heath, Rhapps, Shaw, Shore, Tunney, Jack Williams.

At Hull KR's Craven Park on the Monday afterwards, the Reds lost 16–0 in wet conditions. Halifax completed the double by winning their last two league fixtures. It was another disappointment, although James was exempt from criticism. For the second consecutive season, Salford had finished runners-up in both the league and Challenge Cup. James finished third in the NU's points list with 104 from 20 tries and 22 goals.

7. 1903–04: A fine day

James Lomas had far more than rugby on his mind when the 1903–04 season started. On the second Saturday of the new term, when Salford were due to meet Keighley for the first time ever, he exchanged wedding vows with Annie Mary Blackburn. Her mother was Mrs Sarah Bell, who was the innkeeper of the Cross Keys Inn in Maryport, a hostelry on King Street, one of many situated in the vicinity of the harbour and its shipyards. Whether James first met Annie there as he quenched his thirst after a day's work is unclear, but what is known is that their marriage on 12 September 1903 lasted for almost 56 years, during which time they produced four daughters who were all born in Salford.

Annie Mary Lomas (Photo: Courtesy Rob Dellar)

They were married on a fine day by the Reverend Arthur Botterill at the Stowell Memorial Church in Salford, the steeple of which survives today as a landmark at the corner of Trafford Road and Eccles New Road. Annie's father was the late Joseph Blackburn, a chief engineer in the shipping industry and she was born in Liverpool, as were her two elder brothers and younger brother. She was educated at Bedford Old Board School. Her mother subsequently married William Bell, and they settled at his home town of Maryport, where he was employed as a brewer's cellarman.

Typical of James, not wishing to let anybody down, he made his way to The Willows following his wedding and turned out against Keighley. Considering the circumstances, it was unsurprising that the *Salford Reporter* should say about his performance that he "worked very hard but he has played much better, and his kicking at times was poor." Nonetheless, he did score the first try. He deceived the Keighley backs as he sped under the posts to finish off good approach work from half-backs Ezekiel Harter and Dave Preston. James missed the simplest of goal attempts, but subsequently converted both of A. Norris' first half tries, Salford eventually won 24–2.

Talk in pre-season had included a debate within the game on whether to decrease team numbers from 15 to 12, shedding two forwards and one centre. The *Salford Reporter* correspondent was moved to reminisce about the old days when clubs had nine forwards and only three threequarters – a centre and two wingers – arguing that Salford's late–1880s trio of Jack Anderton, Alf Barrett and Herbert Cook was as effective as any of "today's four [threequarters]". The idea was rejected for club competitions, but an agreement was reached to test its effectiveness in county championship fixtures. As far as the Reds were concerned there was optimism that "Salford's chances of recovering the lost championship are very bright."

Meanwhile, the club had made a significant signing following their public pre-season trial match on 22 August. He was a 22-year-old Welshman from the Aberavon rugby union club. William Strother Thomas, otherwise known as 'Willie' was a right-centre whose legacy with Salford during those pre-First World War years would stand second only to James Lomas. Including wartime fixtures, he played over 500 matches for the club, the last in 1921. He and James appeared as co-centres on 122 occasions and were paired at half-back on another five. James recalled in his memoirs that Thomas "was a clever player and got his Welsh [Northern Union] cap [in 1911]". New Zealander Lance Todd, who, as a Wigan centre, opposed Thomas many times, said in an early 1930s feature that "Willie Thomas was a real good centre, not of the flashily brilliant type, but sound and solid, and made a perfect partner to Lomas."

Thomas had a promising debut in the season's opening fixture at Batley on 5 September, and grabbed a try in each half. With the interval score tied at 3–3, James put the Reds 5–3 ahead with a penalty and subsequently enhanced Thomas's second touchdown. There was a scare for James – and no doubt Annie Mary considering their impending marriage – when, near the end, he was tackled by T. Turton as "a great cheer went up" from the home fans, and was seen to be limping badly afterwards. His performance in that opening match was summed up in the *Salford Reporter* thus: "We hope to see Lomas play a still better game than he did, but that aspiration does not detract from his splendid defensive tactics when needed." He had played well but, such was the expectation, given his outstanding talent, that his performances were forever monitored through critical eyes. He could be the best player on the field – and usually was – but anything less than a five-star showing, as judged against his own high standards, was viewed as below par. There was an additional burden for James because in most matches he was far more closely marked than most players.

He recovered from his injury and declared fit and well for both his wedding and the game against Keighley the next weekend. There was some relief, though, among supporters, to see James in the team for the local clash away to Broughton Rangers on 19 September. The reason for their anxiety was because the inflexible work clause did not seem to take account of Northern Union players wanting to celebrate getting married. It seemed to be a question on everybody's lips, the *Salford Reporter* explained "wonder was expressed as to whether the indispensible Jimmy would spare sufficient time from his honeymoon to fulfil the conditions of the working clause." Happily for the Salford fans – if not for domestic harmony – James did work enough days to qualify for a match played in front of an 18,000 crowd, with "a large contingent [of Salford followers] making the journey across the [River] Irwell," no doubt encouraged by the sunny weather.

The Reds made it three wins out of three with an emphatic 20–6 result. James claimed all the early points as Salford took a 7–3 lead; his penalty was followed by a try when he raced through the defence from a scrum to go beneath the posts, and added the goal. It was 10–3 at the halfway stage. James scored first in the second half with a touchdown after he recovered a dropped pass by Rangers' captain Bob Wilson. He almost had a hat-trick of tries; a first half effort was disallowed and he went close on several other occasions. Overall, James received praise for his high work rate and was, as usual, the most influential threequarter. But again, he was judged to be "not seen at his best" and "apparently forgot that there was such a person on the field as Willie Thomas." It could have been, of course, that James was simply protecting the young Welshman who, despite the fact that he was "coming on splendidly" was, after all, only making his third appearance. Where James was suspect, though, was with his goalkicking and several failures saw Billy Brown given the responsibility of successfully converting the Reds' two second half tries.

Salford's splendid start to the campaign continued and they raced to the top of the League with three further victories; 18–2 against Hunslet at home, 13–0 at Widnes and 8–0 at home to local rivals Swinton. Hunslet had also won their opening three fixtures, but were well beaten at The Willows in front of a 10,000 crowd on a baking hot, sunny day. After Dan Smith had dropped a goal, James scored the first try, recovering a ball kicked by colleague Harter before shrugging off full-back Herbert Place. At 5–0, the referee signalled half-time, but then realised there had been only 30 minutes played, a mistake possibly induced through the match starting 10 minutes late after Hunslet's delayed arrival. Salford made full use of that remaining 10 minutes and James converted a George Heath try. James – who toiled hard "never failing to make some headway" during the afternoon – also converted one of his side's two second half tries.

The journey to Widnes again reaped its reward for James. He scored a try in the opening half, accepting the ball from Thomas following a scrum and kidded the opposition to score behind the posts, adding the extras. Down by eight points at half-time, winger Dick Wailing almost brought Widnes back into contention, but James shoved him into touch at the corner flag. Shortly afterwards, the Salford skipper incurred the referee's wrath and was penalised for "rough play" although it was claimed he "was the main subject of attack during the afternoon and only a man of almost iron constitution could have come through the ordeal safely." In fact, play on both sides became a bit heated and "iron constitution" or not, James was injured during a rush by Widnes's forwards, although he recovered sufficient to add the goal following Salford's final try by Norris.

Several of the Reds players finished up "the worse for wear", the *Salford Reporter,* like most local papers over the years, projected a one-sided view, saying "Widnes were unnecessarily robust". The paper's exoneration of Salford also embraced Broughton Rangers and Swinton in saying "We always like to think that our three local teams are gifted with the harmlessness of the dove when they are performing the operation known as tackling and any Salford supporter will tell you that if his favourites show the slightest signs of diverting themselves of their dove-like methods it is only when suffering from the effects of severe provocation by the opposing teams."

It was against one of the other local clubs – Swinton – that Salford concluded their sextet of wins, all the points being scored in the second half. James who was "like a magnet in the way the visitors were drawn to him" set up the first try for Heath. He missed the goal, but added the extra points after Herbert Buckler's try; the forward had dropped onto the ball in the in-goal area as it rolled out of a scrum. Salford's 8–0 win gave them an aggregate 96 points to 13 in their six-match winning streak.

James's next match was two days later, on Monday 12 October in the Lancashire county trial at Warrington. Having played in the Possibles side the previous year, he found himself promoted to the Probables line-up this time. Selected at half-back, rather than his more recent club position of centre, he was paired with Rochdale Hornets' Johnnie Baxter, who was a late replacement for unavailable Sam James of Broughton Rangers. James scored a try and two conversions as his team built a 28–0 half-time lead and, for the second half, it was decided to swap all the backs over. As a consequence, James assisted the Possibles in 'winning' the second half 8–3, the final result was a 31–8 win for the Probables. James was hailed as "the best man on the field", his partnership with Baxter clearly impressed the officials because the duo were subsequently selected for all four Lancashire's fixtures, although James withdrew from the first through injury. In keeping with the format decreed for the county competition, the trial had two teams of 12 players. The *Manchester Guardian* commented "On the whole the 12-a-side game created a favourable impression, the players having more freedom of movement, while dribbling was of a more pronounced character."

Salford's excellent start was dented in their next two league fixtures by Hull KR and Oldham. James had an unfortunate role at Craven Street on 17 October when Hull KR scored the first try. Watched by a 12,000 crowd, Rovers attacked Salford's line when E. Sleep, on being confronted by James, passed to winger George West. The ball ricocheted off the Reds skipper's shoulder and bounced over the try-line, West followed up to touch down. James subsequently landed a penalty and was inches away from a second, but the

Reds trailed 5–2 at the break. Salford made a perfect start to the second period, Preston took the ball from a scrum and outwitted half-backs Jim Barry and W. Guy to score near the posts, James's goal put Salford 7–5 ahead. Unfortunately, James suffered a leg injury and had to leave the game although, surprisingly, he was allowed back on to attempt a penalty kick, which he missed – presumably with his 'good' leg – and then went off again. When Smith was hurt Salford were down to 13 men, forwards Brown moved to full-back and Heath to the threequarters. Their depleted six-man pack held firm until Smith eventually returned. Fate, though, was against the Reds and in the closing minutes, full-back Alf Carmichael, "amidst loud cheers", kicked a penalty goal to draw the match 7–7.

The following Saturday, Oldham visited Weaste and inflicted Salford's first defeat of the season in front of another 12,000 attendance. Despite his previous injury, James was back in the centre but, right from the beginning, he was clearly not fully fit. The *Yorkshire Post* reported that, when he arrived at the ground, he had reported ill. Whether it was injury or illness, his discomfort was touted as the reason Salford failed to capitalise on an early 15 minute onslaught. He moved to the right wing at the start of the second half, by which time the Reds trailed 5–0. Smith subsequently dropped a goal for the Reds, but a further Oldham try saw Salford defeated 8–2. It was argued in the *Salford Reporter* that James, along with full-back Smith and winger Alf Bedford "should certainly have had a rest," adding "but the committee and presumably the players decided otherwise." It seems that throughout the contest James was "only a looker on [with] what few things he did being of no practical use." It was also noted that the referee, Jack Smith, rigidly enforced the new scrum law that allowed only three players to pack in the front row. Introduced to make the scrums tidier and safer, it was the forerunner of scrums as they are today.

James's incapacity meant he missed playing for Lancashire against Cheshire at Wheater's Field on Wednesday 28 October. He was still missing when Salford lost 6–3 at Halifax the following Saturday. Their captain's absence was given by the local paper as the main reason for the defeat: "the muscular strength of the Cumbrian would have enabled him to get through his opponents where [Bob] Messer and Preston failed and Salford would have retained their unbeaten certificate in inter-league matches with Halifax."

James returned for the 16–3 win over Huddersfield at The Willows on 7 November. He began the scoring with a first half penalty and closed it with a try and conversion as darkness descended, evading several defenders to race over in the corner before turning inside to touch down behind the posts. Salford did not have a fixture the following week, which was just as well because they had five players appearing at Headingley for Lancashire against Yorkshire, including James. There was no score in the first 40 minutes. Bob Wilson made the breakthrough for Lancashire in the second half. He drew Halifax's Billy Little before passing to Broughton Rangers colleague Andy Hogg for the try. James converted and played a part in the move that led to Hogg's second; Lancashire won 8–0.

Two uninspiring games – against Wigan and Leeds – concluded Salford's November fixtures. James was "well watched" in both and had few opportunities to open out play. Wet and windy weather kept the crowd down to around 4,000 for Wigan's visit. James missed a penalty when it was "blown completely off course". He then failed with a drop-goal and another place kick following a mark. Brown took his chance and landed a magnificent penalty from halfway to give Salford a 2–0 interval lead. Winger George Baker added a try, although Brown missed the conversion, to complete a 5–0 victory. The match at Leeds saw even worse weather; Salford's forwards were out-muscled in a 6–0 defeat.

The weather played a significant role in the home match with Runcorn on 5 December, although this time it was fog, rather than rain, that provided the disruptive influence. Preston scored a try, converted by James, in the first half and, with fog descending, the interval was kept short. But with 20 minutes left the match was abandoned with Salford 5–0 ahead. What spectators managed to see was reasonably entertaining, James and his colleagues, apparently, had "plenty to do".

Midweek provided another inter-county fixture, this time against the combined Durham & Northumberland side at South Shields. James and six club-mates – Smith, Pat Tunney, Heath and Buckler for Lancashire, J. Bell and Robert Shaw for the host county – made the long trek to the north east on the Wednesday. The match resulted in a cake-walk for the Red Rose, who won 42–0. James scored two of 10 tries – one in each half – and also converted two during the second period. The real star, though, was Warrington's legendary winger Jack Fish, who claimed three tries, one after running the full length of the field, and four goals – three conversions and a spectacular drop-goal from midfield. James had tremendous respect for Fish and, in his memoirs, wrote that "Jack Fish (was) the human ferret. I have never seen his like before or since. He could get through the eye of a needle."

It was another foggy Salford day on Saturday 12 December when Hull came to town, although not as dense as for the Runcorn game. Nonetheless, it kept the attendance down to about 4,000; James's three penalties created a 6–0 half-time lead. Play became rough in the second half and James and the Hull winger Laurie Parry were cautioned by the referee "for hugging each other too earnestly". James was, however, sufficiently composed to be able to tag on an excellent touchline goal to a late Norris try, the final score was 11–0. With Thomas temporarily missing, Tom White earned credit for his stint at right-centre, the *Salford Reporter* said "The Llanelli half-back seems to share the same fate as Lomas in the way of earning a reputation as a threequarter." Both were well watched by Hull, the writer noted: "It is needless to say that Lomas had a particular fascination for the visitors. He usually has. Very rarely was he allowed to travel far."

On the following Wednesday, 16 December, James was selected by the Northern Rugby League committee for his first international match, due to take place on New Year's Day at Oldham's Watersheddings ground. They picked both teams for what would be the first ever Northern Union international: England versus Other Nationalities. The idea for such a fixture was originally raised by the Yorkshire committee; players in the infant code could at that time only aspire to county level because no other nation was involved in the sport. Using the 12-a-side format adopted for the county matches, James was chosen at half-back, along with Lancashire colleague Baxter.

The next Saturday, 19 December, Salford were considered lucky to come away from Leigh with two league points. James provided the vital difference in a 5–0 win by intercepting a pass and then, after an excellent run, he passed to Heath for the try. He also added the goal. On Christmas Day, Salford were at Bradford for a match that turned out to be crucial in deciding the outcome of the championship. Suffice to say Salford lost 9–0, conceding three tries in front of a crowd that, understandably, projected "a holiday atmosphere", most of the damage was inflicted by the home forwards. The next day's Boxing Day fixture with visitors Warrington was also fruitless and another defeat resulted, this time 11–3. There was no first half score, James wowed the estimated 8,000 Willows crowd after the interval by striking a post with an ambitious penalty attempt from halfway. Having had no Christmas Day fixture, Warrington were the fresher outfit and that advantage told as the match wore on, with James – who had protested strongly against the Wire's opening try by former Salford player Dai Davies – the only Reds player who "seemed to have much energy left".

A third match in four days, and the last for 1903, was again at home, on Monday 28 December, the replayed Runcorn fixture having been shoe-horned into the holiday schedule. Salford won convincingly enough, 19–0, 16 points came after the interval, when James scored from the first scrum of the half. He received the ball from Preston and dissected the opposition like a hot knife through butter, covering over half the field. He added the goal and was instrumental in setting up the final try for Norris.

The 1904 New Year opened in splendid style for James although the international match, scheduled for 1 January, fell victim to a severe frost. He more than made up for that the following day with a personal 24-point haul, four tries, six goals, in Salford's emphatic 39–0 home victory over Batley. The first to score, with a penalty, he claimed the opening try and another just before half-time, under the posts after White fed him from the scrum, as the Reds built a 13–0 interval lead. The first of his two second half touchdowns was planted in the corner, the second after he picked up the ball "from the toes of his opponents" and raced over the line. He also added a second penalty and four conversions.

James's first try against Batley drew an interesting reaction from the *Salford Reporter* journalist who suggested that he "at last succeeded in his apparent desire to score himself." This followed earlier observations in the match report that "he held too long before passing" and "only selfishness on the part of Lomas in not opening out the game prevented a score." Those thoughts – which reflected play prior to Salford's nine tries – may have been borne out of frustration. It was certainly a very different mood from the same writer when he summarised the match: "Lomas played a great game of the true old-fashioned Lomas type and if his performance was any guide to the future, the Maryport man seems to have come back to his form of two seasons ago." These comments are interesting on two counts. First, they recycle the observation made many times over about James's desire to take on opponents himself, an issue previously considered. Second, they imply that, after his opening season with Salford, his form dipped. Again, this is something discussed already, but the fact remains that James Lomas stood out, to a greater or lesser degree, in virtually every match he appeared in and one can only assume that his "come back" to form related to him reaching the higher expectations he faced.

Keighley was the Reds' next destination, a tight struggle finished 2–2 after James's first half penalty, for foul play, was matched by half-back Harry Myers's drop-goal in the second, the same player hitting the crossbar with another attempt in the final minutes. James claimed a touchdown early on in the match, but the pass from Thomas was ruled forward.

Four days later, James was again in midweek action for Lancashire, this time against Cumberland at Wigan. The 15–0 win assured the Lancastrians, with four wins from four matches, of the county title outright, having begun the match level on points with Yorkshire, who had completed their fixtures. On a ground that was considered sloppy and unfit for purpose, the *Manchester Guardian* writer seemed to find humour in the event suggesting the "holiday crowd" – it was Wednesday half-day closure in Wigan – found it to be an "occasion for laughter" saying: "You saw a man in white playing costume measuring his length in the mud and when he got up his clothing was white no longer and his face was something like that of a miner fresh from the coal pit." James, who kicked a penalty goal in the first half and converted both second half tries, was exempt from negative criticism: "There was, of course, some football skill shown and a man who can handle the ball and dodge his opponents and keep his feet under such circumstances must be credited with the gift of adaptability. Such a man is Lomas, the Salford half-back. He is not one of your midget half-backs, but a man of fully average inches and more than the average weight, and he can show a clean pair of heels to a good many men who class themselves sprinters. Today the Cumberland players seemed to be hopelessly in difficulties whenever Lomas got into his stride. He somehow managed to keep his feet while they clutched at the swift-moving, bulky figure, lost their foothold and were virtually left sprawling." The 12-a-side match was reduced to 11-a-side before the interval; opposing wingers Fish (Lancashire) and W. Crane (Cumberland) were injured in a collision and took no further part.

James was the hero of Salford's next match, a local affair with Broughton Rangers that was seen by 12,000 at The Willows. In a dramatic finish, the Reds, after trailing 3–0 at half-time, produced the winning score as the final whistle beckoned. James recalled in his memoirs: "Time was up first time the ball was dead. We got a free kick. I kicked it up and followed along with the rest. I managed to secure the ball and score a try and kicked the goal from the touchline and win 5–3." It was a thrilling moment for the home fans, and generated scenes of wild excitement in the ground. The *Salford Reporter* said that "all the ancient rivalry was in evidence as marked as in days when both the Reds and Mrs Boardman's Boys were next door neighbours," a reference to the 1880s when Rangers played at Walness and used Isabella Boardman's Bridge Inn as their headquarters.

Salford had their colours lowered the following week at Hunslet when well beaten 12–2, James landed a second half penalty that was mere consolation to a side already 12 points adrift. It was a vital match because Hunslet – like previous foes Broughton Rangers – were among the championship's leading contenders. There was some excuse for the Reds' poor showing in that James was unwell with a sore throat. Harter had travelled with the team as standby in case he stood down. In fact, having started the game back at outside-half, James spent the second period playing wide of the threequarter line. The chief architect of their downfall was the evergreen Albert Goldthorpe, who operated from outside-half and had a hand in most things that emanated from Hunslet.

James was back in the centre when Salford welcomed Widnes, and remained there for the rest of the season. The visitors were continually pegged back throughout the afternoon by his long downfield kicks and he forced his way over for the first try, which he also converted. James had another touchdown disallowed, but provided the scoring pass for the winger Hugh Allen, a recent signing from Barrow St George's, as they built up a 14–2 half-time lead. Proving that habits today were no different all those years ago, it was noted that, during the interval, the bulk of the Salford support made their way to the end that Widnes would defend in the second half. They were rewarded in seeing Allen score his second try after excellent passing from Thomas and James, the Reds won 17–2. There were unpleasant scenes towards the end when the exchanges became a bit more physical than normal, Preston was sent off after an altercation with Widnes forward M. McDonald. An irate Salford crowd on the Popular Side, who clearly felt the dismissal unjustified, became even more incensed moments later when James followed his colleague to the dressing room. In fact, the Salford captain had not been sent off by the referee as fans had thought, but retired through a twisted leg. Nonetheless, Salford officials had to ask police officers, situated along the touchline, to escort the referee off the pitch after the final whistle.

Success over Widnes was the start of six consecutive league victories as Salford reaffirmed their credentials as potential champions. Their other wins – during which no points were conceded – were 11–0 at Swinton, 16–0 against Hull KR at home, 2–0 at Oldham, 5–0 at The Willows against Halifax, and 21–0 at Huddersfield. The match at rain-swept Swinton drew in 10,000 hardy souls. James scored first after dribbling the ball across the muddy pitch and, as the *Salford Reporter* put it: "cleverly outwitting [Swinton half-back Jimmy] Molyneux, and the home backs generally, with a bit of work worthy of [Manchester City players Billy] Meredith or [Billy] Gillespie." He added a second half penalty, but was off-target in his attempts at converting the Reds' three tries. More miserable, wet weather lay in store for Hull KR's visit and only 4,000 came to watch. On a boggy pitch, with players sliding in all directions and dribbling generally considered the best method for territorial gain, the Salford skipper once more began the scoring. He touched down after taking a pass off Thomas, and then converted a second try, scored by the latter, to give his team an 8–0 interval lead. Having exchanged their mud-caked garments for a fresh set of jerseys and shorts, Salford scored two further touchdowns; James tagged the extra points to Rhapps's score and then set up the final one by Heath, Brown missed the conversion.

The thawing of an overnight frost, followed by heavy rain, produced another precarious surface for the match at Oldham, although plenty of sand was applied to the pitch. The only score to occupy the attention of a 10,000 crowd was James's penalty midway through the opening half after Oldham's pack were judged to have not packed down correctly. The ever-improving Thomas was given the accolade as Salford's best threequarter, but the *Salford Reporter* was keen to explain that verdict: "This remark is not intended to diminish the value of Lomas' services, which were invaluable to the side, and whose example was contagious. But the Salford captain is such a compound of every position in the field that his play hardly comes within the scope of criticism when you want to say 'who was the best man' in a given department of the game. Lomas played at Oldham as he alone can play, and Salfordians know what that means."

In the following fixture, against Halifax at Weaste, James was again influential. He landed a first half penalty and created a Jack Williams try in the second half, having dodged his way through several defenders. One early incident, involving James, was described as follows: "[Bob] Winskill tackled Lomas, and would not leave him when the whistle sounded so, after a stiff wrestle, the Salford man picked the burly forward up and laid him on his back to the delight of the home supporters." It was over to Fartown for the next encounter, James crossed the whitewash twice as his contribution to the Reds' five tries as the visitors had too much pace for Huddersfield. His first was after receiving the ball from Thomas, who had intercepted a pass, and outran the chasing defenders to go under the posts, his goal made it 10–0 at the interval. He then converted another try and hit the post with a further effort, before he scored his second touchdown from a pass by Rhapps.

The winning streak continued when Salford turned their attention to the Challenge Cup, first round opponents Brookland Rovers were a very familiar name for James. Rovers gave up home advantage in lieu of a £50 payment from Salford, having eliminated James's former Maryport club 2–0 in the preceding intermediate round.

It was reported that at 1pm on the day of the match, 12 March, some "40 of 50 strangers" were seen in Manchester's Market Street "most of them carrying handbags." They were players and friends of the Brookland Rovers and Parton clubs who had travelled together by train from Cumberland. The latter had also waived home advantage to play Broughton Rangers. Apparently they had all been travelling since 5am. The *Salford Reporter* was rather patronising about the Cumbrians, and said they were "no doubt duly impressed by what they saw in that ancient thoroughfare [Market Street] and two hours later the party would probably be still more dazzled by the scenery of the royal borough [Salford] and the

Salford 1903-04. Back: V. Wright (secretary), P. Tunney, G. Heath, J. Williams, J. Rhapps, R. Shaw; middle: B. Mesley, D. Preston, E. Harter, J. Lomas (captain), H. Shore, unidentified, W. Brown; front: H. Buckler, A. Bedford, D. Smith.

Rovers' section of it by the palatial pavilion of the Salford Club with hot and cold [water] always on tap, and flourishing laurel bushes on the extensive lawn. When to these luxuries are added a ground of good condition, and opponents in the pink of condition, what more could the visitors desire?"

The match itself ran a very predictable course, Salford won comfortably 57–0; their 15 tries included three from James who also slotted over five conversions. Hopefully this did not spoil their fans' day out too much.

The following week, Salford were on the east coast for the second round tie against Hull. It produced an unexpectedly easy victory for the Reds who won 23–5 in front of a 12,000 crowd after leading 8–3 at half-time. Having failed to open the score with two early drop-goal attempts, James managed three conversions plus a goal from his own mark after catching a ball kicked by Hull full-back Harry Taylor. That score put Salford 13–3 ahead and, apparently, had a "depressing effect" on the Hull team. James – who scored the final try after running through "the whole of the Hull backs" – was again the shining star: "The game was an object lesson at showing the influence of Lomas on the Salford team as he certainly infused a lot of dash into his men."

Before resuming their Challenge Cup quest, Salford had two home league fixtures to deal with; Leeds, 12–3, and Bradford, 4–2, were both defeated to extend their winning run to 10 games. Leeds attracted 10,000 and helped produce one of the season's best matches at The Willows. Buckler scored Salford's first try after five minutes. Leading 6–0 at half-time, James twice came close to a touchdown after the interval, but it was his side's third try – scored by Bedford after "leaving his jersey in the hands of [Leeds centre G.W.] Andrews" – that proved crucial when the visitors had pulled back to 6–3. James – who stamped his usual authority on the match – failed to score for the first time since Boxing Day; he missed all four conversion attempts.

The meeting with Bradford came two days later on the Monday and had a vital bearing on the championship race which now virtually rested between the pair of them. The tightness of the score created a tense, exciting contest. James gave Salford a 2–0 lead just before the break from an audacious penalty kick from just inside Bradford's half. Having tried to open out in the first half, Salford decided on a tighter approach after the interval, and relied on their forwards to play a rushing game. During one piece of foraging, as the two packs booted the ball around inside Bradford's 25 yard area, Heath took a flying kick at it as it lay on the ground, sending the ball over the crossbar for a remarkable and rare field goal. This mode of scoring has long since disappeared from the rule book, but it was sufficient, at the time, to put Salford 4–0 up. Bradford rallied, encouraged by an Erving Mosby goal following a mark, but Salford held on.

The result left the Reds in a healthy position, sharing top spot with Bradford on 44 points and, with five matches left, Salford had the advantage of a game in hand on their Yorkshire rivals. The only others still in contention were Hunslet on 41 points and Broughton Rangers with 40, although Leeds on 38 and Oldham on 35 still had a mathematical chance.

Third-placed Hunslet awaited Salford on 2 April in the third round of the Challenge Cup at Parkside. Again James provided early inspiration, kicking a penalty goal, for obstruction, from distance for a 2–0 lead. By half-time, though, Hunslet gained the initiative through a try from Place, converted by Walter Goldthorpe. Hunslet controlled most of the second half play although no further points accrued and Salford were eliminated 5–2.

Somehow, the Reds managed to swallow their disappointment to win 5–2 in the league at Wigan two days later. Played on a Monday, it was the rearrangement of a fixture postponed from 19 March when both sides were involved in the Challenge Cup. On a fine day, the ground conditions at Central Park were good, which was just as well because the venue had hosted a Wigan League versus Manchester League clash in the morning. A 15,000 crowd saw Wigan take the lead after half-time through a penalty by full-back Jack Mason, but Salford were not about to allow their championship hopes to drift into the same gutter as their Challenge Cup aspirations. Preston scored under the posts after a weaving run and, although James frustratingly missed the conversion, the captain redeemed himself with a tremendous drop-goal. The result took the Reds two points clear of second-placed Bradford in the championship table, both having played 30 matches.

Possibly James should have packed an overnight case because he was back in action at Central Park the next day and was late for the kick-off. The occasion was the staging of the historic first international, switched to Central Park after a second postponement at Watersheddings on 8 February when heavy rain made the ground treacherous. The two line-ups suffered through Broughton Rangers and Bradford having to replay a drawn Challenge Cup match on the same day, forcing the withdrawal of several players. It was still 12-a-side but, unlike the original selection, the teams had a full complement of threequarters, the forwards reduced to just five, possibly to vary the experiment following the conclusion of the county games. As a result, James was relocated from half-back to centre. The England team was: Billy Little (Halifax); Frank Spottiswoode (Oldham), George Dickenson (Warrington), Lomas (Salford), Jack Fish (Warrington); Johnnie Baxter (Rochdale Hornets), Johnny Morley (Halifax); Anthony Starks (Hull KR), Pat Tunney (Salford), Jack Riley (Halifax), Billy Bulmer (Halifax), Joe Ferguson (Oldham). The Other Nationalities line up was: Dan Smith (Salford); Tom Llewellyn (Leeds), Dai Harris (Wigan), David Lewis (Oldham), Willie Thomas (Salford); Eli Davies (Wigan), Phil Brady (Huddersfield); Jack Rhapps (Salford), Jim Moffatt (Leeds), George Frater (Oldham), Dai Thomas (Oldham), Herbert Buckler (Salford). The latter selection included nine Welshman, two Scots, Moffatt and Frater, and Brady – an English-born player of Irish descent.

James's delayed arrival – he was a few minutes late – meant England started with only 11 players, although he was on hand to attempt the conversion after Fish scored the opening try, his touchline shot hit a post. He was later cheered for "a brilliant piece of work" that almost got Spottiswoode in for a second try, before Dai Thomas equalised with a touchdown for Other Nationalities. It was the 'combination' team that eventually won 9–3, through second half tries by Harris and Willie Thomas.

Back in the bread and butter world of league action, James was in Salford's team that returned to The Boulevard on Saturday 9 April, three weeks after their convincing Challenge Cup success there. This time Hull showed sterner stuff and the Reds lost 7–0. It was certainly a blow to the Reds' title prospects. The *Salford Reporter* opened up old wounds: "The great question [that is] troubling the followers of Salford is whether the team are going to cut up badly as at the fag end of last season. Then through a variety of causes the final for the [Challenge] Cup was lost and the championship of the league was thrown away. Just now there is the prospect of a repetition of these performances." Again, a lot of expectation was placed on James's broad shoulders. True, he had missed a handful of penalty goal attempts at a windswept, rainy Boulevard, although several were quite difficult, and failed to score any tries, although he almost forced his way over the line in the first half. A suggestion that "Just now Jimmy is not the terrier he once was" perhaps did not take account of it being his fourth match in eight days.

His endeavour was stretched to five matches in 10 days when he led his troops out at Canal Street on the Monday. Perhaps James 'passed the test' on this occasion – he laid on Salford's first try, by White, and roared over for a second himself after an intelligent round of passing, to lead Runcorn 6–3 at the interval. He was at the fore in widening that gap after Runcorn full-back Sammy Houghton spilled the ball, James gained possession to race in behind the posts. The only blemish on his performance was that he missed the three conversions, Brown concluded the scoring at 11–3 with a drop-goal.

Salford went into their last two league fixtures with 48 points from 32 matches, the same as Bradford, with Hunslet, 45 from 31, and Broughton Rangers, 42 from 31, as the only other challengers. Of the foursome, Salford were the only side in league action the following Saturday, 16 April; Bradford and Hunslet had Challenge Cup semi-finals to settle and Broughton Rangers had no fixture. It allowed the Reds to steal a march on Bradford with a convincing 28–6 verdict over Leigh at The Willows, a result that eliminated Broughton Rangers from contention. It was a first class performance by the Reds on a warm, sunny spring afternoon. A well-struck drop-goal by Smith and a try by Thomas, shortly before half-time, gave Salford a five point cushion at the interval. After the resumption Thomas claimed his second, James's excellent touchline kick built a 10–0 lead. The next try was Preston's, he raced over the line after gathering the ball from James's cross-field kick. James added the goal and also obliged – off the crossbar – after Harter scored under the posts. At 20–0 it was virtually over, although both teams added a couple of tries each to the score, the last of them from James, who picked up and placed the ball beneath the posts after a dribbling move by his forwards, and added the goal.

Seven days later Salford were at Wilderspool to meet Warrington – destined to win the Challenge Cup a week later – and easily won 19–3, all the points were scored in the opening half. It was another glorious day, forward George Thomas got the home side off to a perfect start with a try after only three minutes. The Reds, though, came back with three of their own, James converted the first two to go 13–3 up. It was the Salford leader that added a fourth after he "dodged through about half-a-dozen players" although he missed the goalkick and again failed when Bedford's touchdown closed the scoring.

Bradford won 13–2 at Hunslet on the same day, and trailed Salford by two points in the table and, if they lost their remaining fixture, the championship was heading for The Willows. Salford fans hoped that neighbours Broughton Rangers would do them a favour by beating Bradford at Park Avenue two days later, but it was not to be, the Yorkshiremen claimed a 5–0 victory. It left the teams tied on 52 points and, although Salford had a superior scoring record, it was ruled that a play-off was necessary to separate them.

Salford therefore met Bradford on Thursday 28 April at Halifax, in what was effectively the first ever championship final. The Reds put the following team on the field: Smith; Ike Lewis, Thomas, Lomas (captain), Bedford; Harter, Preston; S. Bebbington, Brown, Buckler,

Heath, Rhapps, Shaw, Tunney, Williams. In front of a reported 12,000 crowd on a wet day, lady luck was not smiling on the Reds who, yet again, finished runners-up in a major competition. It was scoreless at half-time; James came closest for the Reds in attempting an ambitious penalty from near the middle of the field. Despite Bradford having met Broughton Rangers only three days earlier, it was the more rested Salford side that tired during the second half. Bradford centre Mosby succeeded with a penalty goal and their forward J. Hutt scored the only try with under 10 minutes remaining to seal the Championship on the back of a 5–0 win. The Reds and their supporters could hardly conceal their disappointment as their opponents received the trophy at the final whistle.

James ended his season with several personal scoring achievements attached to his name; he was the NU's leading goal scorer with 65, 21 ahead of Bradford's Mosby who finished second, and set a new points record with 214, Fish of Warrington trailed him on 158. He also made an impact in the try charts, his 28 for the season placed him joint-second with Fish.

James and his Salford colleagues in Lancashire jerseys. They had all represented the county in 1903–04. Back: G. Heath, P. Tunney, G. Cook (trainer). Front: J. Rhapps, D. Smith, J. Lomas, H. Buckler.

8. 1904–05: In good trim again!

The *Salford Reporter* gave James Lomas a glowing testimony in its preview for the 1904–05 campaign, saying "It is not necessary to write much about the popular Jimmy, he is too well known. Suffice to say he is in the best health, and looks in every way fit to lead the team on to victory and the championship." No doubt the writer anticipated that Salford could go one step further this time. After all, they had been runners-up in the league for three consecutive years and Challenge Cup finalists twice during James's tenure at The Willows. Things, though, begun to slide a little as the season unfolded. The club's popular, reliable full-back Dan Smith had departed for a new life in Canada, although several new players were unearthed during the three pre-season public trial matches during August. James took part in the latter two when it was observed that "Lomas, the idol of the Salford crowd, is evidently in good trim again."

The Reds certainly got off to a promising start by winning at Halifax and defeating visitors Hull in the opening two fixtures. Not for the first time James was the saviour of Salford after they fell three points behind to Halifax on 3 September through Joe Riley's try in the corner. When Halifax wingman Haley Backhouse dropped a ball kicked downfield by Salford's Dave Preston, the alert Cumbrian rushed up "much to that young man's amazement" and dribbled the ball through the defence to score. He also added the goal, which gave Salford a 5–3 interval lead that they maintained until the final whistle. The following week, a beautiful sunny afternoon welcomed Hull to The Willows, A. Norris, off a pass by James, touched down near the corner. James was only a fraction wide with the goal attempt, but was successful in tagging on the points to his side's two remaining tries as they secured a 13–7 win. It was noted in the match report that the Hull pack "tightened their belts and inflated their lungs with Arnold's Automatic Antiseptic, the invigorating properties of which are too well known... to need any encomium on our part." Whether the writer was on commission is not recorded.

Meanwhile, as was so often the case since moving from New Barnes, the South Salford Silver Band provided pre-match and interval entertainment for the crowd. While appreciating the 'sweet music' the *Salford Reporter* journalist felt that they played too close to the main stand, where the press were, and that it would be better if they moved to the middle of the field or the 'popular side' opposite, suggesting "it would greatly facilitate the arrangements of the press for distance lends enchantment to the sound and telephones are very sensitive. We like the bands, but the editor wants 'copy' and when he can't get it he says things that are calculated to terrify his subordinates and interfere with the discharges of their very different duties on the day that comes in between Saturday and Monday."

Having made a positive start to the season's journey, Salford's train became temporarily derailed over the following weeks; they lost three consecutive league fixtures, their worst run since April 1902. Their defeats were at Bradford, 11–3; 9–3 at home to Leeds and 10–3 at Runcorn. The match at Bradford was attended by 12,000 people who were possibly enticed from their home through the bright, sunny weather. Led by a dominant pack, the Park Avenue side led 8–0 at the break, an in-form Jimmy Dechan claimed his third try after the interval. Meanwhile, Salford's 'Jimmy' – whose progress thus far had stalled on several occasions through the combined attention of three or four opponents at a time – finally found himself on the end of a passing move, and scored a try. As with every match James appeared in, he was well policed with, in this instance Erving Mosby – whose "surveillance of Lomas was the feature of the afternoon" – acting as his prime marker.

Leeds drew a crowd of 7,000 for their visit to Weaste who were again entertained by the South Salford Silver Band. Presumably, club officials must have read the *Salford Reporter* because the band was positioned further away from the main stand. Salford led 3–0 at half-time after Preston, "the smart little half-back, in Lomasian style, worked his way through his opponents and scored." Salford suffered a blow when winger Alf Bedford twisted his knee during the opening period which resulted in his withdrawal from the match. The numerical disadvantage did not help the Reds' cause and they conceded three tries in the second half. As usual, James toiled away. He scattered opponents with his charges to their line and proved solid in defence, although he still picked up the barbed comment that he "was alright on his own, but he will try to do too much."

The headline after the Runcorn defeat read "Poor Salford! What next?" On another sunlit day, James came close to giving Salford an early lead, but the ball rebounded back off the crossbar when he attempted a goal from his own mark. Instead it was the Cheshire side that gained the initiative, and took a favourable 2–1 try count into the interval, to which they later added two drop-goals. The *Salford Reporter* lamented afterwards that "the Linnet flaps his wings in the face of the dyspeptic Red", adding that James, who had returned to outside-half for this match, had "a bad time" due to the close attention he again received. This time it was the Runcorn halves J. Richardson and Jim Butterworth that "laid themselves out to spoil Lomas". It was a recurring theme as far as the Cumbrian was concerned. The message that all the Reds' opponents appeared to take into a match was 'stop Lomas and you stop Salford'.

The *Salford Reporter* tried to make some sense of it all, saying "Seldom is he allowed to get away from his opponents and most of the afternoon [against Runcorn] was spent at bay with half-a-dozen Linnets clinging on to him. The amount of work he gets through is enormous but it is of a desperate character and when operating at half-back and behind erratic forwards, he is more easily bottled up than when in the threequarter line." It was certainly a frustrating dilemma for James. In an era when the senior, more experienced players dictated a team's tactics, such as they were, there was no such thing as a coach on hand to offer advice and direction. Of course, the obvious remedy had to be with the forwards. If they could overpower the other pack, the life of the half-backs and thence the threequarters was infinitely easier. Sadly, and although they still looked a solid line-up on paper, Salford's forwards seemed no longer to be the fearsome force they once were.

The pressure eased somewhat through the defeat of Oldham in the next match. The Roughyeds had started the campaign well, and before visiting The Willows had lost only once in what would turn out to be a championship winning season. On their previous visit, almost a year earlier, James had played despite being unfit and Salford had been beaten. This time he appeared keen to erase the memory. According to the press, "from the moment he stepped on to the field it was quite evident that the Salford captain meant business... and in the end accomplished his desire." As so often happened, he opened the scoring, this time with a penalty, an effort that, while creating "intense joy" for the majority of the 8,000 fans, also pleased club officials and dignitaries situated in the main stand: "The gentlemen on the scarlet cloth-covered benches smiled and the ladies, no doubt thinking it was the correct thing, smiled also." Oldham were quick to respond with an unconverted try by Tommy Cash, then Preston reclaimed Salford's lead with a try at the corner. James missed the goal, but succeeded with a spectacular effort from halfway after debutant forward J. Graham made a mark, putting the Reds 7–3 ahead at the break. A further try by Heath cemented an acclaimed 10–3 victory.

On the following Wednesday, 12 October, James played in the Lancashire trial match at Wigan, having been selected at centre for the Probables in a 15-man-team. The previous season's experiment of reducing the number of players had been shelved. The form book was slightly upset as the Possibles claimed a 17–15 victory. James, though, did himself proud, first with an early penalty from near the halfway line to place his team 2–0 up, and then with a try that he also converted to bring about a 10–2 half-time score. He added a further conversion in the second half. After what was deemed a "remarkable game" the team for the opening fixture with Cheshire was chosen. Several Possibles had earned selection ahead of the favoured Probables, but James had done more than enough to guarantee his inclusion.

He returned to Wigan on Saturday with Salford, which resulted in another 10–3 score-line in the Reds' favour, watched by 15,000 people. Salford led 3–0 at half-time, winger Hugh Allen beat three men to score in the corner from James's pass after only five minutes. Wigan's famed wingman James Leytham levelled the scores before James, with a goal from a mark made by Jack Williams, restored the Reds' lead at 5–3. The goal inspired Salford and a further try, by winger Robert Parry which James converted, concluded the scoring. That latter goal did not receive the 'usual signal' by the officials and the press initially reported the final score as 8–3.

James had had a fine match, but again came under scrutiny, this time for his lack of proficiency with the boot. The *Salford Reporter* commented that "Somehow or other Lomas does not seem to be as effective in his goalkicking as he used to be. His shots are marvellously well directed and usually fail by inches only – but they do fail – a fate which befell the attempt to augment the value of Allen's success." It is difficult – impossible even

– to take issue with an observation made over a century ago by someone who clearly watched James week-in, week-out. His kicking accuracy was certainly an enigma; on the one hand he missed easy chances close to goal, but then found the target from near the touchline or on the halfway line as he had in his previous two games. It was true, as already stated, that the consistency and accuracy of his goalkicking at that time was way below later levels achieved in the sport. James's inability to cash in on some of the simpler chances was not, however, unique as match reports of that period will testify. Nonetheless, he had so far managed only 10 goals in his opening eight games and three of those were in the Lancashire trial.

The next challenge was from Swinton, who – along with 12,000 fans – made their way to The Willows on 22 October. James was playing his fourth consecutive match for Salford in the halves, although it was the last time he would do so at club level for almost three years. The Reds received an early blow when Bedford suffered a recurrence of his knee injury and took on passenger status for the remainder of the match. Meanwhile, the Lions built up a 5–0 interval lead that they extended to 8–0; Billy Brown scored a late consolation try for Salford with James again off-target with the goal.

Four days later, James represented Lancashire at Runcorn in their opening county match. Despite excellent weather it was a low-scoring game, Cheshire won 3–0 through a first half try by Runcorn's J. Richardson. The *Manchester Guardian* confirmed that, even at county level, "Lomas was too well watched to shine".

October's commitments were brought to a close with a visit to Knowsley Road to take on St Helens. Their hosts, promoted from the previous season's Second Division, had won two matches so far and, in a close contest, increased that tally to three. James was on better form with his marksmanship; he converted Salford's only try and was successful with three penalties, the latter one reduced the margin to 13–11 to St Helens with 10 minutes to go. It caused great excitement for Salford's supporters, but the score remained unchanged at the end. The result left Salford ninth in the 18-team table with four wins and five defeats.

Hull KR provided Salford's next opposition at The Willows on 5 November. Salford won easily enough, 15–4, James threaded through another long-distance penalty from just inside the Rovers' half as Salford built up a 5–2 half-time lead. He also made the vital passes for Willie Thomas and Bob Richards to each touch down after the interval. With James failing to convert the Reds' first two tries, Brown kicked the latter. James redeemed himself through having the final say when, after making a mark, his resultant goal concluded the scoring. The match had begun 10 minutes late, the Rovers players waiting patiently on the pitch for a Salford side delayed by the late arrival of their captain. It was James's seventh consecutive Salford appearance without scoring a try, the *Salford Reporter* again made the point that "owing to the shadowing to which he is subjected... this great player is thereby terribly handicapped."

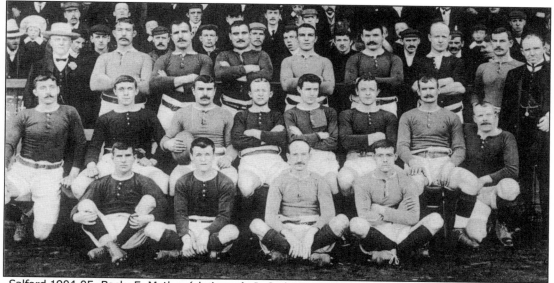

Salford 1904-05. Back: E. Mather (chairman), J. Graham, J. Williams, J. Rhapps, D. Rees, P. Tunney, R. Shaw, S. Bebbington, G. Cook (trainer); middle: G. Heath (kneeling), W. Thomas, J. Lomas (captain), A. Bedford, R. Parry, W. Brown, A. Norris, I. Lewis (kneeling); front: R. Richards, D. Preston, E. Harter, W. Lambert.

Salford won their next match at Batley 7–3, but James, along with Herbert Buckler, was on duty for Lancashire at Oldham, where Yorkshire triumphed 14–5, ending any hope the Red Rose county had of retaining their title. James was at half-back, partnering Warrington's Tom Hockenhall, who retired from the game after 25 minutes with a bad cut to the head when Lancashire led 5–0. The *Athletic News* writer 'Philistine' said "Lomas at half-back was a clever worker, as he always is, and the amount of defensive work which fell to his lot was neatly and effectively accomplished."

James opened his account with two penalty goals the following weekend when Hunslet visited, and then put Allen over for a try in the left corner. He scored and converted the next himself, after he raced through the defence off a neat pass from half-back J. Maddocks. Salford were handily placed at the break with a 12–4 advantage. James almost returned the compliment to Maddocks in the second half; he intercepted a pass and sped downfield only to see the latter spill the ball. The final score came from Albert Goldthorpe's penalty for Hunslet.

Salford's next match, at Widnes on Saturday 26 November, was postponed due to a cocktail of fog and frost. They next played at Broughton Rangers' ground on 3 December in front of a healthy 14,000 attendance. The Reds were totally outplayed by the Rangers. They scored a first half try by Pat Tunney after the ball rebounded off a goalpost. James's conversion tied matters at 5–5, but the hosts led 14–5 at half-time. Three of Broughton's opening four tries had been on Salford's left flank, defended by S. Pemberton, a reserve half-back from the Heyside club, drafted in on the wing due to a dearth of wingers. During the interval, James decided to swap Pemberton, who was making his debut, with half-back Maddocks, who was himself a reserve having made his first team bow two months earlier. Although it tightened things up out wide, Salford lost 20–5 after leaking six tries.

Back on home soil, Salford did better in the next fixture. They won 5–0 against Warrington through a late try from James. Receiving the ball from Thomas, he avoided several opponents in a magnificent run to the try-line, and subsequently added the goal. James played on the right wing, based on the need to subdue the threat of the Wirepullers' winger Jack Fish. It was an idea that worked well, the *Salford Reporter* claimed that James's try "was about the finest thing he has done at The Willows and has rehabilitated him as a player to be reckoned with," adding "it is just possible that the experiment will be continued in view of the fact there are now three capable centres available and Lomas can be trusted in any position." The other two centres were Thomas and Richards, the latter having made his debut in the senior side two months earlier after initially signing from Llanelli as a full-back. The wing positions, meanwhile, were becoming a nightmare for the selectors, particularly since Bedford's injury. The *Salford Reporter* had said at the start of the season that the club urgently needed to recruit a top wingman and that was borne out by the fact that the club would eventually use 17 different players on the flanks, including James, during the course of the campaign.

James continued to patrol the right wing for December's remaining three fixtures; away to Wakefield Trinity and at home to Leigh and Halifax. His performance at Wakefield was a memorable one. Trinity were the better side in a scoreless first half, but were handicapped by the loss through injury of forward Cox during the second. Richards was the first to score through a drop-goal, James later picked up a loose ball near the touchline on halfway and worked his way through the opposition in spectacular fashion towards the centre of the field with Thomas supporting on his outside. When James reached the 25-yard line, he passed to the Welshman who beat off two more defenders before touching down in the corner, which put the Reds 5–0 ahead. James, clearly relishing the extra space out wide, beat virtually the whole Trinity team in another breathtaking run, full-back Jimmy Metcalfe just managed to grab him around the ankles when a try looked certain. In the final minutes, the Cumbrian retrieved another wayward ball and broke away, again with an amazing burst of power and pace as he "completely took his opponents by surprise" and bypassed every defender that barred his way before scoring under the posts. He added the goal to complete a 10–0 victory. His effort was described as "sensational" by the *Salford Reporter* which added "it says much for the sportsmanship of the Wakefield spectators that they applauded the effort and cheered the [Salford] team as they left the field."

Playing James on the wing was hailed a success, his partnership with Thomas at centre created "a powerful combination". Reportedly, "he was, long before the finish, the sole topic of conversation on the stand, and almost the sole objective of the Wakefield players."

Having won at Wakefield in such convincing fashion, albeit against 14 men for much of the match, the Leigh fixture, played on Christmas Eve, looked a certain home win, but the Reds had a shock awaiting them. James scored all Salford's points with two tries, but it was not enough to avoid an 11–6 setback. His first came after he raced over at the corner off a Thomas pass, which reduced the deficit to 5–3 just before the break. The tide looked as though it would turn after the restart; Leigh forward Paddy O'Neill was dismissed for rough play and then James grabbed his second try – again after running into the corner – to put Salford in front for the first time. Leigh, though, proved worthy winners in the end, although, reportedly, James "might have done more had he been better supported." It looked as though the Reds might lose again when Halifax arrived at The Willows seven days later when Joe Riley put the Yorkshire side ahead with a try. Richards narrowed the gap with a drop-goal before James, off yet another Thomas pass, went over for a try by the corner flag. He then added a wonderful touchline goal to give his side a 7–3 lead at half-time. With no further scoring, Salford held on for the win, helped by James's relieving kicks. One item of note in the second half was a penalty given against Salford for "four men in the front rank" of a scrum, instead of the now mandatory three.

The first match of 1905, played on Monday 2 January, was the rearranged game at Widnes. The Chemics won 2–0 through a second half penalty, although Salford were without James, who represented England that day in the second of the now annual New Year international fixtures. The opposition was again Other Nationalities, who included Salford's Welsh forwards Herbert Buckler and Dai Rees. Played at Bradford, it was, as the saying goes, 'a game of two halves.' Other Nationalities scored all their points in the first half and England, who won 26–11, registered all of theirs after the interval. The change of fortune was attributed to England's forwards taking control of the second half scrums which allowed their backs more freedom. James – paired with Bradford's George Marsden at half-back – scored one of his side's six tries, but the real star was Wigan's Leytham who managed four. The *Manchester Courier* commented: "It is rare nowadays to see in one match so many brilliant movements."

Whether or not it was due to Thomas being unavailable through injury, James was back in the centre for Salford's next match, at The Boulevard on 7 January. It was the first of three successive defeats – 18–0 at Hull, 14–3 at home to Bradford, and 15–10 at Leeds – as their indifferent form continued. The Hull forwards dominated the first match and won two-thirds of the scrums. It was suggested that "If [trainer] George Cook could put another 10 yards [pace] on the forwards it would be an improvement." Under such circumstances it was hardly surprising that James "was not seen to great advantage and was only twice or thrice notable for his characteristic runs."

It had been anticipated that Salford would put on a better show against Bradford, partly because Thomas and Bedford were available again, and J.E. Davies, just signed from Hunslet, was making his debut on the left wing. With James selected in the centre, the threequarter line, on paper at least, looked more potent. But then James and Thomas had to stand down. In Thomas's case it was because his injury had not properly healed but, for James, it was due to a very sad bereavement. The 24-year-old wife of James's brother, Tom Smith, the former Tottenham Hotspur player, had passed away, having been in 'delicate health' since undergoing an operation. Tom – then landlord of the Sun Hotel on Maryport's Wood Street – had only been married a few months. James travelled to Maryport to attend the funeral, which was on the day before the Bradford match. He also withdrew from the Lancashire team that met Cumberland in Whitehaven on the following Monday.

James and Thomas were both back in the centre for the game at Headingley, the Salford skipper missed with two early penalty shots before instigating a move that led to Salford's first try. Having passed the ball to Davies, the latter kicked ahead. Thomas followed up to take possession and put James in for a score that he also converted to put Salford 5–3 ahead. It seems the Leeds fans got hot under the collar over something because they began 'hooting' James during the time he was placing the ball and taking the kick. Later they were "almost hysterical with delight" when he was tackled. Salford retained their two point advantage until half-time although, reportedly, if James "had not played in his best style it would have gone hard with the Reds." After the break Salford went behind 6–5 before, according to the *Salford Reporter*, "[Leeds forward E.] Watts and Lomas got at logger heads and there were loud cries for the Salford captain to be sent off, although the Leeds man was the aggressor." Leeds increased their lead before Salford forward Ike Lewis's try and James's goal tied the score at 10–10, but a last minute converted try won it for the home side. James, meanwhile, must have won over the hearts of the home spectators by the finish: "Lomas was seen at his best, his powerful kicking and his rescue work being such as to earn him much praise from the spectators – after the match. How Salford would have gone on without him it is hard to say." Again, the blame for defeat was put on a pack that lacked the necessary 'dash' to win matches.

One positive point from the match at Headingley was the debut of Welshman William David 'Dai' John, a lightweight five feet, two inches half-back who became a great crowd-pleaser at Salford. Signed from Penygraig rugby union club, he played for the Reds until 1922. In a newspaper article published in the early 1930s he said one of the happiest recollections of his career with Salford was his association with James: "We understood one another very well. I think my cut-through made a good many tries for him, but everybody knew, of course, that half an opening was enough for Jimmy. He was a great player to have in one's side."

Salford returned to winning form against Runcorn on 28 January, a match that brought 6,000 customers through The Willows turnstiles. The Reds won 8–0 in a game of contrasting fortunes as far as Salford's wingers were concerned. On the right flank, Bedford again broke down and had to retire before half-time, while on the left wing R.M.H. Bell – a speed merchant just signed from Bridgewater Albion rugby union club and, reportedly, a

Somerset county player – made his debut amidst high expectations. The match got off to an unusual start: after just three minutes play, the ball burst and had to be replaced. James scored the first try after he recovered a ball dropped by Hesketh as the Runcorn centre was tackled by John. Running at full pace, James dribbled the ball, keeping it "at his toes" for half the length of the field before he dropped on it over the try-line and added the goal. In the second half, Bell showed his quality after James despatched him down the left touchline. As he was about to be tackled he returned the ball to his skipper who beat the remaining defenders to claim his second try, although he missed the goal. It was later said that the combination of James with Bell was one of game's best features. During the match there were several displays of petulance, and Runcorn forward W. Wood was sent off in the second half.

February was the best month of the season so far for Salford, who went through all four matches unbeaten. The first, at Oldham, was a draw without a point scored. In spite of that deficiency the *Salford Reporter* reckoned that "taken altogether the play was interesting and fairly open for a modern Northern Union struggle", implying that some matches were not quite so entertaining. There was also a shift of attitude about James playing as a winger, a position he took again at Oldham. Whereas a month earlier, the *Salford Reporter* correspondent believed it to be a successful idea, the feeling now was that "Lomas got few chances and very little of the ball, and as a wingman this player is simply wasted under the present conditions. Either give him a daring centre or put one of the other men on the wing." In fact, Thomas played as his centre just as he had on the previous occasions, but clearly the combination did not work quite so well at Oldham.

The remaining February fixtures produced victories, the first time they had strung three together all season; 14–2 at home to Wigan, 8–3 at Swinton and 19–2 at home to St Helens. In the match against Wigan, James again played on the right flank, his last ditch tackle prevented his opposing winger, the ever-dangerous Leytham, from scoring an early try. Instead, it was James himself who opened the score. He collected a ball kicked by Wigan full-back Jack Mason and raced through to touch down. Although he missed the goal, he converted a second try, scored by John, and the Reds led 8–2 at half-time. Salford added a brace of tries after the break. James missed both goal attempts and the verdict again was that he was "neglected and wasted" on the wing.

A strong wind awaited both sides at Chorley Road for the Swinton versus Salford clash. The Reds officials endorsed the opinion of the *Salford Reporter* by switching James back to the centre; he replaced Richards who was moved out to the wing. James did not make the best of starts, with a knock on after receiving a good opportunity to score off a Thomas pass. Then the elements foiled him when, having made a mark, a howling wind blew back the ball in his attempt at kicking a goal, colleague Herbert Buckler – who was standing behind him – caught it. Eventually, after Salford full-back Billy Lambert had a drop-kick effort charged down, Thomas recovered the ball to send in Arthur Buckler, Herbert Buckler's recently signed brother, for a try. James added the extra points and Salford led 5–0 after 25 minutes. Swinton pulled three points back with a try from winger Jack Flynn, before James, who had missed another glorious opportunity by untypically dropping the ball a second time, redeemed himself 10 minutes from the end with the final try, pushing his way over from a John pass.

St Helens' visit produced an easy win for the Reds. James thought he had scored an early penalty, but it was disallowed through offside by a team-mate. He remedied that disappointment through scoring the second of Salford's three first half tries. He received the ball from Preston and kidded the defence with a dummy pass to Thomas before scoring at the corner. Salford extended their 9–2 interval lead with further tries, by Preston and Lewis, James converted both. He also shook off the gremlins that had infiltrated his play over the past few games. The *Salford Reporter* said: "The shocking exhibition of fielding given in the Swinton match by the Salford captain again threatened to be on view, but it was only of a temporary character and though faulty at first an improvement was shown later on."

Although Salford were well out of championship contention, their improved results had seen them climb into the top half of the league table and, with a first round Challenge Cup match awaiting at Second Division Keighley on 4 March, thoughts turned towards another successful cup run. It was anything but. One post-match headline said "Defeated and Disgraced", a reference to Salford's woeful performance at Lawkholme Lane in losing 8–0. In a match where they were beaten in all departments, the Reds' threequarter line was not alone in being labelled "a poor quartet" although James, at least, was deemed "the pick of the lot and kicked well".

Whether it was a hangover from the cup defeat or not, another poor show followed in the league with a scoreless home draw with Batley. Perhaps the supporters sensed this would happen because only 3,000 bothered to turn out. A blank weekend followed due to their Challenge Cup dismissal, the Salford players had a fortnight off before meeting Widnes at The Willows on 25 March. They duly rediscovered some semblance of form with a 23 points to 2 triumph. James – who was back on the wing – scored 17 of them. He claimed the opening try by pouncing on a ball dribbled into the Widnes in-goal by Jack Williams and added the extra two points. He then had a hand in the next two, scored by Bell and Richards, and successfully tagged a touchline conversion to the former for a 13–0 interval lead. Widnes were unlucky in that they lost forward Sam Aspey due to a sprained ankle and he did not reappear in the second half. George Aspey, meanwhile, got two points back for them with a penalty before James completed the scoring with a couple of tries under the posts, the first after recovering a ball dropped by Widnes wingman Jim Hughes, the second after receiving forward Silas Warwick's pass. He also added both goals. The *Salford Reporter* thought that the two-week break had benefitted the Salford players: "In no case was this more notable than in that of Lomas, the popular captain giving us a sample of his old-time form."

The cup exit gave Salford another Saturday off before the journey to Warrington on 8 April. Salford lost 5–0, but played with a man short for all but the first five minutes. Lambert tried to catch a ball with the sun in his eyes but, failing to collect it, he slumped to the ground, his right kneecap having been very badly damaged. It was a bizarre incident and, transported to Warrington Infirmary, he was hospitalised for several weeks. Having proved an ideal replacement for Dan Smith, it was thought he would never play again although he did courageously reappear, but not until December 1910. The incident left Salford on the back foot throughout the match and James, who was back in the centre, endured the usual ordeal of being "well watched" by the defence.

The Reds recovered from that setback to win their next four games, a run that earned them sixth place in the league, a position that looked unlikely a few months earlier. The first two victories were at home against Wakefield Trinity, 21–0, and Broughton Rangers, 7–0. Salford led Wakefield 8–0 at half-time, James added the goal to the second of two tries. Three further touchdowns followed, the second of which was claimed by James; he intercepted a pass on his own try-line and raced "quick as lightening" the full length of the field with two or three defenders in vain pursuit. He also landed the extras to Salford's final try of the afternoon. The match drew only 3,000, but the following fixture against the Rangers, on Good Friday 21 April, attracted 14,000. James played, despite struggling with an instep injury after colleague Jack Rhapps accidentally trod on it during the Wakefield game. Despite the discomfort, James kicked a penalty after 20 minutes, the only points of the opening half. Midway through the second period, his injury got the better of him and play was stopped while he received attention before continuing. Broughton had the best of the second half exchanges, but were undone when Thomas stole the ball from their skipper Bob Wilson and ran 60 yards for a try near the corner flag. With James struggling, Brown added a superb touchline goal to complete the score.

James's injury sidelined him for the next day's game at Leigh, which Salford won 16–2, but he was declared fit for the trip to Parkside on Tuesday 25 April, when Hunslet were overcome 16–11. Salford recovered from a 3–0 deficit through a Preston try, goaled by James, to lead 5–3 at the change of ends. The Reds just about retained their grip after the interval by outscoring their hosts three tries to two. James claimed two of them; latching on to a Thomas pass for the first shortly after the restart to climax a sweeping passing move, the second one came after a pass from winger Colin Walton after Preston's spectacular break. The latter score, which James converted, was crucial because Hunslet had drawn level at 8–8.

Salford concluded a hectic finale of four matches in six days by travelling to play Hull KR the next day. Rovers had the forthcoming Challenge Cup Final on their minds three days later and put out a weakened team. Only one of the players that faced the Reds, D. Read, appeared in the final, which they lost 6–0 to Warrington. Who was the most disadvantaged

– a fatigued Salford or understrength Rovers – is arguable, but the Reds, 5–3 down at half-time following a try by Thomas – James missed the conversion – eventually lost 14–3.

It had been another barren season for Salford, although James, despite comments about his goalkicking in the early stages of the campaign, again finished the season as the Northern Union's top point scorer with 144 from 22 tries and 39 goals in all matches.

9. 1905–06: No need to show his paces

During the 1905–06 season Salford gave a hint that their finances were not all that could be desired when they announced what must have been one of the earliest ground-share agreements. The rent earned from their tenants, the fledgling Salford United Association Football Club, was clearly an incentive as, from a monetary viewpoint, was scrapping the club's 'A' (reserve) team after 25 years, to accommodate them. In fact there had been discussions two years earlier on the desirability of disbanding the 'A' team to reduce costs. The forerunner of Salford United were Weaste Amateurs, who had played four matches at The Willows towards the end of the 1904–05 season with a view to sharing the ground.

Although the income was clearly welcome, the move could have backfired on the rugby club as there were several instances of Northern Union clubs disbanding in favour of association football, which was growing in popularity at this time. Salford United, who had joined the Manchester League, later applied for Football League membership in May 1907, although they failed to be elected. Subsequently, and due to falling behind on their rent, they left The Willows for a new ground close to the junction of Eccles New Road and Stott Lane, but disbanded in 1911. Their demise may have been hastened through Manchester United relocating from the Clayton district of Manchester to nearby Old Trafford in 1910. Certainly the vast following commanded by that great club over the years since then has provided a stern challenge for Salford's rugby team in its battle for support.

The impact of scrapping the 'A' team was first felt by the supporters in the club's pre-season trial matches, held at The Willows on 19 and 26 August. With a reduced squad, the usual Reds versus Whites games – composed of Salford players and would-be Salford players – were replaced both times by a run-out against the local Egerton junior club. The latter were members of the Manchester and District Rugby League, a competition that Salford had intimated as a probable base for its fringe players. Whether James Lomas had spent another summer in Maryport is not known, but he took no part in either game, the second of which attracted some 4,000 spectators. Possibly he was the one player at the club who did not need to show his paces, so assured was his place in the team.

The two division league format had been scrapped due to the precarious finances of the old Second Division clubs, and a new all-embracing Northern Rugby League competition took over. With 31 clubs it was clear not everyone could meet, so each club was allowed to organise their own fixtures. A minimum of 10 home and 10 away matches was decreed, most arranged over 30 overall. With clubs playing an unequal number of games, it was decided to determine places on a percentage system, based on the number of points gained from those available; thus, for example, if a team won 15 and lost 15, their figure would be 50.00 per cent.

In Salford's case, 34 fixtures were agreed, the first a visit from Hull on 2 September. Under 'threatening skies' and watched by 6,000 supporters, James showed he was just as adept at preventing tries as he was at scoring them. He raced across field to make an early vital tackle on Hull's Irish left winger Albert Freear as he was about to touch down. Later, when Willie Thomas found himself surrounded by defenders, he succeeded in off-loading the ball to James, who sidestepped his way through for Salford's first points of the season as the cheers rang in his ears. That score lifted Salford, who eventually won 12–3 in a match where all the points accrued from tries. Two days later, James had cause for even greater celebration through the birth of his first daughter, Annie Alexandra.

The next game was at Swinton, where rainy weather kept a disappointing derby-day crowd down to around 6,000. James dominated events during the first half. Playing "a hard game", he opened the score with a penalty and then broke through the Lions' defence, after taking a pass from a colleague, for a try in the corner. He was fractionally wide with the conversion attempt. He later made a sensational run from inside Salford's half to within a few yards of Swinton's line before passing to Jack Williams, who was tackled just short. With Salford ahead 5–0 at half-time, James continued to make a nuisance of himself after the restart, full-back Jack Flynn just prevented him from scoring another touchdown. It was Reds' new winger Vernon Hampson that eventually clinched it three minutes from the end; he claimed a try after some excellent passing by Dave Preston and James. Hampson – a former Swinton player signed from York – was praised in later years by James as a man that "could get tries when given a chance". Although James missed the goal, Salford were safe at 8–0. The *Salford Reporter* said "Seldom has the Salford captain played better, and the master hand was evident throughout the scoring."

The excellent start to the season continued with a third straight win, this time against Batley, whose late train delayed the scheduled 3.30pm start by 17 minutes as some 6,000 souls patiently waited on a sunny, though windy afternoon. Forward Jack Spencer scored the opening try for Salford, James added a super touchline goal to place the Reds 5–0 up at half-time. Salford added four more tries during the second half, James converted two for a 21–6 triumph; Batley's response was from two penalties and a drop-goal from the boot of Wattie Davies.

Salford's first defeat of the campaign was at Mather Lane on 23 September, 8–5 to Leigh. This time it was Salford's turn to be held up by the train, the match kicked off 22 minutes late. All the points were scored in the second half, Salford were already eight points down when Willie Thomas scored a try two minutes from the end, converted by James. The Salford skipper's next appointment was at Wheater's Field the following Wednesday for the Lancashire trial. Representing the Probables, and playing in the centre, he scored two goals in a 31–15 win over the Possibles. The *Manchester Guardian* was not enamoured with James's attitude, and commented: "Lomas was good and bad in turn and did not appear to take the game seriously". Either way, James was selected for Lancashire's opening match 10 days later.

Prior to the inter-county game, James had a league fixture to fulfil against St Helens at Weaste. The Saints took an unexpected 5–0 lead. This prompted a few stunned Salford supporters to shout 'buck up,' which James certainly did. He broke through the defence and, when tackled by full-back Tom Foulkes, despatched R.M.H. Bell over at the corner. James missed the goal and, shortly afterwards, fisticuffs broke out between Jack Rhapps and Foulkes; both were dismissed. James then "electrified the crowd [with] one of his brilliant dashes." He timed his pass to Arthur Buckler to perfection, the young forward's try – allied to James's goal – put Salford 8–5 in front. After the interval Willie Thomas kicked the ball downfield and James, following up, gathered it from the feet of St Helens' centre Tom Barton to score near the posts and added the goal. Play became rough and, after a mass brawl, Salford forward Ike Lewis also received a 'one way ticket' from the referee. Despite the numerical disadvantage, Salford claimed the next try through Hampson; James's goal made the score 18–5. It became 13 players-a-side when Barton was sent off on the intervention of a touch judge. Salford then rounded off the scoring with drop-goals from half-back Joe Morgan and Willie Thomas, and a try in the corner by James, from Morgan's pass, to win 25–5.

His performance against St Helens had been outstanding, but Salford had to release their skipper for the next match – a 4–3 defeat at Runcorn on 7 October – due to his commitment to Lancashire. The opposition was James's native Cumberland and the match, at Wigan, drew a very healthy 12,000 crowd, despite drizzling rain that made the playing surface difficult. One of the interesting things from a rugby history point of view was the Lancashire three-quarter line of James Leytham (Wigan), James Lomas (Salford), Bob Wilson (Broughton Rangers) and Jack Fish (Warrington) – all legendary names in the annals of their clubs. Possibly due to the conditions, it was not a great game, particularly in the second half which the *Athletic News* described as "poor and uninteresting" and, for the majority of the aforementioned quartet, it was an afternoon of varying fortunes. The *Athletic News* painted a dark picture of the two centres, and declared that "Wilson and Lomas were erratic, and both men repeatedly knocked on with chances staring them in the face." Worse was Fish's experience. He scored in the 10th minute off a pass from James but, in doing so, fell heavily and fractured his collarbone. It left Lancashire a man short although from that point there was no further score. M. Jenkinson of Wath Brow had scored an earlier try; Billy Little (for Cumberland) and James missed the respective conversions – both failures attributed to the state of the pitch – so the match ended 3–3.

The following Saturday, 14 October, saw Salford's first appearance in a new competition, the Lancashire Challenge Cup. A Yorkshire Challenge Cup was simultaneously launched across the Pennines. Both survived until 1992. The first round draw favoured Salford with a home tie against Swinton, 8,000 fans entered the ground to witness the event. Just one score settled the match, Willie Thomas passed over James's head to an unmarked Hampson for a try in the corner. James missed the goal and also a penalty attempt in an exciting second half when the result could have gone either way. Both James and his co-centre Willie Thomas made threatening runs, but they were foiled by the slippery conditions.

The Reds returned to league duty the following week, and took on Rochdale Hornets at the Athletic Grounds. Scottish winger Tom D'Arcy made his Salford debut and scored two tries, including the first of the afternoon. It was 11–0 at half-time, James had scored – and converted – Salford's third try of the half. He raced 60 yards before touching down beneath the posts. Salford added two more tries after the break, James claimed the last of them after another long-distance sprint, covering 75 yards before again going under the posts. He added the goal to make the final score 19–0. Salford deserved the spoils, but Rochdale were unlucky in having two players carried off injured; half-back Bobby Schofield in the first half and centre Charles in the second.

The Lancashire Cup second round followed on Saturday 28 October, with another home draw, this time against Oldham, for a place in the semi-finals. On a fine day, the *Salford Reporter* claimed the excellent 11,300 paying crowd – the total was estimated at 13,000 to 14,000 when club members and the press were taken into account – was "Proof at least that the handling game has not lost all its attraction for the working man." Early on, James had raised the home spectators to "a pitch of excitement" when, having caught the ball, he sprinted through the opposition before being tackled as he attempted to sidestep full-back Dicky Thomas. Salford, though, eventually lost 10–0; their forwards had performed below expectations and James's own contribution was given a poor rating as a result.

Salford went down at home again the following weekend, 8–5 to Hull KR. James, though, was absent, having travelled in the opposite direction to fight for Lancashire's cause at The Boulevard against Yorkshire. There were more than 8,000 people at the county match, despite a damp day that brought a mist to the ground that affected visibility. Lancashire won 8–0 and, in contrast to its previous review of the match against Cumberland, the *Athletic News* said "Lomas and Wilson in the centre made an admiral pair". There was also an additional, interesting comment related to James: "Lomas was not personally so prominent as he has been seen in representative matches. He certainly fitted in well with his colleagues, but he did not give one of those extraordinary displays of individual ability which made his name famous two years ago." It is an observation that fitted with other previous suggestions – particularly in the *Salford Reporter* – that, although James was still a potent force and worth his place in any representative side, he was perhaps not as effective as when he first burst onto the scene at Salford. Then again, had the opposition got wise to the dangers he threatened? Many of Salford's match reports at that time, as has already been outlined, refer to the fact that he was always marked by several players.

Before leaving the Roses match, there was one other fascinating view in the *Manchester Guardian*. Their correspondent acknowledged that Lancashire's success was "due to a clever back division and a better conception of the possibilities of Rugby football" and went on to say that "without approaching the standard to which the New Zealanders have attained in passing and running, the Lancastrians gave a really good exhibition in these arts." This, of course, refers to the historic 1905 New Zealand rugby union tour of the British Isles that was then taking place. On Saturday 4 November, the day that Lancashire met Yorkshire in Hull, the New Zealanders were hammering Blackheath 32–0 in London. It was the 15th match of their tour and they had won them all and, in the process, scored 493 points against just 15. They were certainly a revelation to the rugby union code, but was it really superior fair to that offered by the Northern Union? Incidentally, several of those New Zealanders subsequently enhanced their reputations in the NU code including Charlie Seeling and William 'Massa' Johnston, who both played for Wigan, and George Smith who joined Oldham.

James was back with Salford at The Willows on 11 November. He landed a first-half drop-goal against Oldham to win the match 2–0 and avenge their recent Lancashire Cup exit. He was out of luck in the second half; he hit an upright with a penalty and, in the last minute, almost scored a try, but the Roughyeds' full-back Sam Irvine managed to grab his legs. With the next Saturday reserved for the county cup semi-finals, Salford arranged a friendly with Leeds at Headingley. The current league leaders were also without a fixture after being eliminated from the Yorkshire Cup. In the event, the match was abandoned through fog after 30 minutes during which time "the phantom Lomas hovered about the field in a half material state." Salford trailed 5–0 when it was stopped, but gained some value by trialling Richard Waugh at full-back and Johnny Cochrane on the right wing. Both were from Maryport. It seems probable that James recommended them but, either way, they retained their places for the next league match, at Barrow on 25 November.

The long trek to north Lancashire was a profitable one, Salford easily triumphed 26–5. The Reds trailed 2–0 from a penalty, but responded with three tries, all converted by James, to lead 15–2 at half-time. The Salford captain had scored the second himself, his mesmerising run enabled him to bypass Barrow full-back Harry Gifford and score under the posts. James was to the fore as his side added three further tries after the interval, and converted one of them. He was looking more like his old self and playing with a gear to spare, the *Salford Reporter* said that he "did well and kicked splendidly and no doubt if necessity had arisen would have done better."

His performance received another 'thumbs up' the following week when he "played a magnificent game," albeit in defeat away to Hull KR on 2 December. Early on, he made a good opening for Cochrane, although the winger failed to collect the ball properly and an opportunity was lost. James received better value when supplying Hampson, the wingman beat several defenders before touching down in the corner. The Reds' skipper was wide with the goal attempt, but continued to keep the Rovers busy. He picked up a loose ball and just failed to get around full-back Herbert Sinclair for a second try. He landed a penalty, however, which increased the lead to 5–0. There was no holding James at this stage and he completely bamboozled the defence in another magnificent spurt for a try that he also converted. Salford – and James – were in sparkling form and, following a Rovers penalty from George West, led 10–2 at the interval. Unfortunately, from a Salford point of view, the momentum shifted in the second half, helped in part through the dismissal of Reds forward Silas Warwick, after Rovers had reduced the difference to 10–7. Thereafter, three penalties from the trusty boot of Rovers forward Anthony Starks were enough to sink Salford 13–10.

The six remaining matches in December proved more rewarding. Salford won five with only the Christmas Day defeat at Broughton Rangers to spoil the festive celebrations. Their first victims were Widnes, who were well beaten 25–3 at Weaste on 9 December. James scored the opening try near the posts, his exciting run came after receiving an inside pass from Hampson, who made the initial break from Salford's 25-yard line. Hampson claimed the second and third touchdowns for himself; James scored a fourth near the posts from Willie Thomas's pass. The strong wind blew the ball away as James was about to attempt the goal but, because he had been on target following the first two scores, the Reds held a comfortable 16–0 lead at half-time. Anticipating more tries from Salford, most of their fans changed ends to stand by the area they were attacking in the second half. It was Widnes, though, that got the first one of the half through winger Dick Wailing before Salford rewarded their supporters with three further tries, none of which James enhanced.

Salford travelled to Mount Pleasant the following week, a disappointing Batley crowd of around 1,000 witnessed the Reds' 13–2 victory as James continued to impress. Batley actually had the better of the first half, and entered the second period with a 2–0 lead through a Wattie Davies drop-goal. Salford, though, had more fire in their bellies during the remaining 40 minutes, a try from Hampson was followed up with two from James; the first from a Preston pass following a scrum and, in the final minutes, he raced through the entire Batley back division for another. James converted both his own efforts, the *Salford Reporter*, while highlighting his "splendid form", commented that "Salford may congratulate themselves on possessing a strong threequarter line [Cochrane, Thomas, Lomas, Hampson]." It appeared that the Reds had turned a corner following the previous season's quest for a settled foursome.

The third consecutive win, 10–0, came against visitors Swinton on 23 December. Salford were 2–0 up at half-time after James, "amidst loud applause," landed an excellently taken drop-goal. With confidence oozing, he opened the second half by attempting a penalty from the centre of the field. He missed the kick and then came close to touching down for a try after an exciting run towards the corner flag. Eventually a forward rush led to Dai Rees picking up the ball to send Warwick over. James tagged on the goal and then hit the post after Bell had scored in the dying minutes. James could do no wrong: "The best man on the field was Lomas. His kicking was judicious and his tackling safe, whilst his attempts to score were unsuccessful simply because the marking was numerous and true."

The Reds loss at Wheater's Field on Christmas Day was seen by an 'overflowing' 12,000 holiday crowd, most of them happy to see their arch-rivals put to the sword. Broughton Rangers led 8–0 at the interval, Salford were handicapped through the loss of winger Bell after 20 minutes following a head-on collision when the score stood at 5–0. In the second half, James again thrilled the crowd and the *Salford Reporter* described his next move as "a sensational performance by Lomas who, profiting by a mull [dropped ball] on the part of Wilson, picked up in his own quarter and, after a splendid run in which he was pursued by Wilson and accompanied by Hampson, beat all opposition and scored a try and kicked a goal." Only 8–5 down, the score lifted Salford's hopes, but the Rangers withstood the resultant pressure, Andrew Hogg's try in the corner sealed the Reds' fate, 11–5.

The Boxing Day match at Warrington produced the narrowest of victories, Rees scored a vital first half try for Salford under the posts. Taking a pass off Preston, it was the culmination of a fine dribbling move by the pack. James's goal provided the Reds with a 5–0 cushion at the break. Fish – restored to the Wirepullers' team after his injury with Lancashire – pulled the score back with two second half penalties, which gave the Salford fans an anxious time before their side won 5–4. Another victory followed on 30 December when Bradford were soundly beaten 13–0 in Weaste. A drop-goal from James was followed up by three tries. He scored the second himself after grounding the ball in the corner to tail end a move by half-backs Preston and Dai John. The Reds' captain also converted the third try in a match that was played at a fast pace and Salford's forwards – well led by Warwick, Evan Thomas and Spencer – dominated their opposition.

New Year's Day 1906 was described as "bitterly cold" and was made even more miserable for the Salford fans through their side being well beaten 9–0 at home by a well organised, quick-passing Leigh. James did not play against the team that would ultimately top the Northern Rugby League table and claim the title of Champions and, even if he had, it was thought "doubtful he could have averted the disaster". Instead, he was involved once more in the annual international fixture, played this time at Central Park, Wigan. With Broughton Rangers' Wilson unavailable through injury, the captaincy transferred to James. Points did not accrue on the scoreboard until James – playing in the centre – scored a second half try for England after combining well with Leytham. The Other Nationalities subsequently equalised through a Willie James touchdown, the final result was 3–3. James was considered the best of the Englishmen on view, his wing partner Fish had a less memorable time for, having recently returned from injury, he damaged his leg in the first half and retired from the match.

Central Park was again the setting for James's next match five days later, on the Saturday. On a muddy pitch and in pouring rain, Wigan and Salford fought out a 0–0 draw. James tried his best; was a yard short with a penalty from halfway and had a drop-kick charged down in the final minutes. It was considered a credible performance from the Reds. Willie Thomas – who had spent the preceding three days ill in bed – started the match, but badly injured his ankle before the interval after colliding with the perimeter railings and took no further part. Seven days later, 13 January, Salford had another scoreless result when Broughton Rangers travelled to The Willows. Again, the playing area was a mud-bath, with "the going heavy and the ball as solid as lead." Three different players attempted goals, but the ball refused to rise each time, small wonder that James "did not shine in any of those brilliant individual efforts that are looked upon as his peculiar prerogatives." On a political note, Sir Lees Knowles, Member of Parliament for West Salford – who arrived "to great cheering" while the first half was in progress – kicked off the second on behalf of the Rangers. The reason for his presence was because a General Election was due the following month but, following 20 years as a Conservative MP, he lost his seat.

The two remaining January fixtures were both lost by Salford; 9–5 at Hunslet, and 8–6 at home to Warrington. At the time of Salford's visit to Hunslet – a miserable day of rain and bitter cold winds – the Parksiders were the league leaders; they eventually finished second. The Reds got off to a promising start when a passing movement which involved Preston and John ended with James scoring a try and adding the goal. He later attempted a drop-goal and was just wide. There was another chance to extend the lead when James broke away but, after he drew the full-back, Hampson dropped his pass with the line open. As so often happens, the home side recovered and centre Billy Eagers scored in the corner to reduce Salford's lead to 5–3 at half-time. The Reds slipped four points behind thanks to two goals from Walter Goldthorpe and another from Eagers. James thought he had turned things round after another brilliant run; he beat "all opposition" before he placed the ball down over the line. The touch judge, however, ruled he had put his feet into touch first, something with which the Reds disagreed.

Despite Salford missing several players for Warrington's visit, James claimed the afternoon's first scalp with a try near the posts, although off course for the goal attempt. The Wirepullers drew level 3–3 by half-time thanks to Tom Hockenhall's response and the Reds were undone in the second half through a converted try by their former forward George Heath. As usual, James did his upmost to avert defeat, and scored his second try after charging through a host of defenders to cross in the corner off Preston's pass. Unfortunately, his goal shot again failed and Warrington survived.

In both those recent defeats James was described by the *Salford Reporter* as "head and shoulders" above the other Reds players and virtually carried the team. It was a dilemma for the club. Against Warrington they were missing, for various reasons, Hampson, Willie Thomas, Bell and Jack Williams. In addition, they had been unable to replace Lambert at full-back and Cochrane had filled in, the latter's vacated wing slot left another void. Winger Harry McWhirter had recently re-signed for the club, but he was not a regular try-scorer. The team was sliding down the league table and their officials had tried desperately to recruit new blood, including "well known ones" although, according to the local paper, they were "well paid where they are" and reluctant to move to The Willows.

It was a cause for consternation among supporters and a flurry of letters were published in the *Salford Reporter*. After the scoreless match with Broughton Rangers in mid-January, 'A Disgusted Supporter' wrote about the non-appearance of an 'A.N. Other' on the wing, his absence necessitating a reshuffle of the threequarter line and the introduction of inexperienced half-back Frank Drake in the centre. The letter writer complained: "There is not a capable threequarter [at the club] in case of accident." On 3 February, a letter appeared from 'Tin Hat' criticising Salford's officials for "not parting with money for good players" saying that, of the "dozen" signed that season, "only two are worthy of a place". A Salford director responded in the next edition, the unnamed official rebuked the "scandalous and vile accusations" made against the board, both during the previous season and at the present time. A week later, 17 February, another letter, from 'Disgusted No.3' – who claimed to be a shareholder – appeared, expressing disappointment at what he perceived as the shortcomings of club officials in building a decent side saying, with an obvious reference to James, "My opinion of the team is that it is a one man team and has been so for a year or two now. We cannot expect a team, where one man has to do nearly all the scoring every week, to get at the top of the League, or win the cup."

It was a tricky situation for the directors because then, as now, supporters always expect more without comprehending, or even caring about the financial implications. The move to The Willows in 1901 had come at a price, and club officials, having formed a limited company in February that year, had been hit by the high cost of bringing their new home up to scratch. In March 1903, they had organised a 4-day 'Bazaar' at the Groves Lads' Club on Regent Road as a focus for raising £2,000 "to place the Club in a sound financial position". Based on its annual reports and reading between the lines, the scrapping of the 'A' team for example, it had continued to struggle with its bank balance ever since, a situation not helped by falling attendances. Club officials clearly wanted to strengthen their team, but appeared to lack the "financial muscle" to fulfil their ambition, something that obviously, although understandably, frustrated the supporters.

The team returned to winning ways on 3 February, a poor 3,000 Willows crowd witnessed the 8–0 victory over Rochdale Hornets. Willie Thomas returned to action in the centre, but James, although fit and able, was rested "with a view to the Oldham match". That fixture took place on 10 February, a significant day in naval history and something James would have appreciated given his background. The 'super' battleship, H.M.S. Dreadnought, then the most powerful warship in the world, was launched at Portsmouth by the Royal Navy. It was an event that caught the imagination and even the powerful Wakefield Trinity pack that led them to Challenge Cup glory in 1909 became known as the "Dreadnoughts".

Oldham were one of the leading contenders in the league and Salford's trip to Watersheddings was viewed as a greater challenge than that posed by Rochdale, who were languishing near the bottom. On a quagmire of a pitch, Salford held their hosts to a 0–0 draw. According to the *Salford Reporter*, Oldham's supporters took to booing their visitors "in a most unsportsmanlike manner and especially manifested their fear of Lomas" adding "it must have been something of that kind when the Salford captain took a shot at goal." James and Oldham's great forward Joe Ferguson both tried in vain to break the stalemate with several worthy goal attempts. In the second half, James managed to dribble over half the length of the field but stumbled on the ball when he reached the in-goal area.

Salford filled in a blank Saturday, on 17 February, with a friendly against Swinton to inaugurate the ground of the recently formed Liverpool City club that intended applying for a place in the Northern Rugby League for 1906–07. There were approximately 3,000 spectators at the Edge Lane venue, which was previously the home of Liverpool Old Boys rugby union club, former opponents of both Salford and Swinton in their pre-Northern Union days. Salford were losing 8–3 at half-time, Hampson then scored a second half try after a length of the field run when the winger and his centre partner James passed and repassed the ball in exciting fashion. It brought the Reds to within two points, but James just missed with the goal kick and Salford lost 8–6.

There was an additional date in James's diary on Wednesday 21 February, when he represented Lancashire against Cumberland in a county championship play-off, the pair having finished level at the top of the table. It was not a great game to watch, the *Manchester Courier* summed it up as being "as flat as can be [with] not a sprightly feature about it," and added "scrummage after scrummage followed in wearying succession." In between the scrums, Huddersfield winger Billy Kitchin gave the Cumbrians an interval lead with an unconverted try, Lancashire equalised when a smart piece of play from James got Broughton Rangers' Frank Harry over. The final 3–3 score meant there was no outright winner and the title was shared. It was James's fourth appearance at Central Park that season, each ended in a draw; 0–0 with Salford, 3–3 with England and Lancashire twice.

Salford's next three games were all away from home. The first was at The Boulevard on 24 February when on a greasy, slippery pitch, Salford lost 13–2. The Reds could have scored early on when James made one of his spectacular bursts, only for Hampson to drop what would have been the scoring pass. Instead, it was the hosts who led 5–0 at the interval. Preston injured his leg midway through that opening period and left the field. He returned for the start of the second half, but lasted only a few minutes, leaving the Reds a man short. James moved to half-back and Billy Brown joined the threequarter line. Worse came when James was also injured and retired from the match some 20 minutes from the end, Salford's only points came from a drop-goal by Brown. James had had problems of a different kind before the half-time break, having a set-to with Hull half-back G. Hall. Apparently, James was the victim but "wasn't having any", both players received "severe" cautions from the referee.

Despite his earlier injury, the Salford captain was available for the next game away to Rochdale Hornets, a first round Challenge Cup match. James had been on the left wing –

with Hampson as his centre – for the recent clashes at Oldham and Hull, but those positions were reversed for the cup tie which Salford won 6–0. Hampson scored a first half try and James, who had just been held up on the try-line before the interval, added another in the second half. He outran his opponents to score near the posts after good approach work by the pack was continued by John and Willie Thomas. James's place-kicking, though, was not spot-on; he missed the goal from a good position, and had also failed with an easy looking penalty earlier in the half.

A week later it was back to league action at Halifax. James was again on the left flank, a move that seemed to work. Having been "not quite up to his usual standard" at Rochdale, at Thrum Hall he was "assuredly never in better condition, and worked hard for victory, but spoiling did its deadly work and the Salford captain did not score." The latter comment presumably referred to touchdowns, because James did land a magnificent touchline goal following an Arthur Buckler try to level the half-time score at 5–5. Halifax, though, through a try and goal from winger Bill Wedgewood near the end, won 10–5.

Four days later Salford had their first home game in over five weeks with a Wednesday fixture against Wigan. In front of a poor crowd, estimated at 2,000, the Salford contingent among them gained early optimism through a try by Hampson. James just missed the goal and was unlucky when he attempted another from a mark shortly before half-time. The Reds increased their lead to 6–0 after some excellent passing put Willie Thomas in, but James again was wide with his kick. Maybe the Reds could have done with those extra points because Wigan fought back to win 8–6, their winning try was a personal disaster for the usually reliable Salford captain. His poor clearance kick from under the posts was fielded by forward Tom Whittaker who went in for a simple score.

It was back to Challenge Cup action with an intriguing home tie against Egerton in the second round. The junior club were making their fourth visit to The Willows that season, having provided the opposition for Salford's two pre-season games and had used it as a home ground in defeating Leigh Shamrocks 9–0 in the previous round. The club had its roots in the area of Salford close to what is now the Mancunian Way and used Swinton's Chorley Road ground as a base after previously playing in Trafford Park. On a fine afternoon, 2,355 people paid to see the game, which reached approximately 3,000 with members, the so-called 'Young Blues' showed endeavour in their 38–5 defeat. Salford scored 19 points in each half, their visitors had the last word with a popular late converted try. As anticipated, James "had a day out". He scored the first two of Salford's 10 tries; under the posts after Rees was pulled down short and in the corner after a dummy pass to Hampson. He notched up a third during the second half, again beneath the posts after indulging in some quick passing moves with Hampson that "mystified" the junior side, and converted four tries.

The cup victory was costly, Salford's three star backs – Willie Thomas, Dai John and James – were all left out of the next league match at Bradford "having sustained some hard knocks in the Egerton match, the anxiety of the blues to tackle the great artistes leading up to some foolish work on their part." Certainly James, during the course of the Egerton tie, "was frequently tackled by his nimble opponents" but were the illustrious trio truly indisposed, or did club officials have an eye on the following week's big Challenge Cup match against Broughton Rangers? Whatever the truth was, Salford were hammered 33–0 at Park Avenue, the *Salford Reporter* suggested that, based on the their performance, "the destination of the Northern Union Cup will not be at Weaste."

The third round Challenge Cup clash between Salford and Broughton Rangers on 31 March brought 15,241 paying customers through The Willows turnstiles which, according to the *Salford Reporter*, "with the addition of ticket holders [members] and deadheads make it 16,000". The tie developed into a mini-epic and covered three matches. James, restored to the centre after playing his last three games on the left wing, created the early excitement through a third minute drop-goal after receiving possession from Preston following a scrum. Just before half-time, though, Wilson replied in kind and the scores were level at 2–2, a situation that was unchanged when the final whistle sounded. It seemed the rival captains suffered the same fate: "Lomas and Wilson were, as usual, the most ubiquitous men on the field, but somehow there were always two or three men waiting for them."

The following Wednesday afternoon at Wheater's Field, battle recommenced with approximately 12,000 spectators being present on a fine, although very windy afternoon. Twenty minutes of early Salford pressure was repelled and Wilson's try for Rangers provided the first score. Undeterred, the Reds continued to press. A clearance kick by Rangers' winger Billy Harris resulted in the ball landing into James's welcoming arms and he combined with Hampson and the latter got over the try-line. The 'try' was, however, disallowed but, moments later, John took possession and dodged his way through the opposition forwards to score just before half-time. James's attempted conversion just missed and the match was tied at 3–3. The second half was a stalemate with both defences too eager for the respective attacking plays and another draw ensued. Unfortunately for Salford, the vigorous second half challenges resulted in injuries to James, who had been in sparkling form for much of the game, and their full-back, Cochrane.

Two days later, Friday 6 April, the trilogy concluded with a second replay at Central Park, Wigan. Cochrane was declared fit to play but James, who had injured a heel, was not. Thanks to a dominant display from the pack, the Reds squeezed through to the semi-final 5–3, a try by scrum-half Drake – who had replaced James in a reshuffled back division – and goal from Brown gave Salford a 5–0 lead at the break. There were some complaints that the tie had not been played at Swinton, which kept the crowd down to 4,378.

Having met their old enemy three times in just seven days, the Salford players probably felt they needed a rest. Instead – on the day after the Central Park encounter – they made the long trip to Barrow for a league match. James was still unfit but, apart from the introduction of three other players, it was the same side that had won the cup tie. Barrow were among the lower group of clubs in the league but, after their exertions, it was hardly surprising the Reds lost 24–0.

The following Saturday, 14 April, Salford met Keighley in the Challenge Cup semi-final at Wilderspool. The Lawkholme Lane side were no pushovers; they had eliminated the Reds in the previous year's competition and, apart from reaching the last four this time, were going well in the championship race, and eventually finished fifth. Salford were at full strength, and included James who resumed his position in the centre. It was the Yorkshire side that almost opened the scoring when their full-back Bob Walker struck the upright with a penalty. Instead it was John, after kidding the opposing halves, who claimed the first points with a try in the corner, Brown just missed the difficult goal effort. The Reds retained their 3–0 lead until the interval, following a keenly fought, fast paced opening half. After the restart, James attempted a drop-goal, but slipped in the effort and missed. Shortly afterwards he almost got John in for his second try. It was Preston – running in at the corner flag following a scrum – who finally enhanced Salford's score, although James was wide with the kick. Keighley were not finished and Harry Myers – who, sadly, was fatally injured during a match seven months later – scored with a try that Walker was unable to convert. At just 6–3 to Salford, Keighley piled the pressure on, but could not break through. James – already struggling through his heel problem – injured his shoulder when he fell awkwardly on it, but carried on and was just wide with another drop-goal attempt. Then Willie Thomas hurt his foot but he, too, remained on the field, which left both of the Reds' centres in a "crippled state". Somehow, Salford resisted Keighley's onslaught to book their place in the final once more.

The final was set for 28 April but, before then, Salford had four league fixtures to cram in, including two that had been postponed due to their cup run. With no hope of championship honours, the Reds prioritised the cup final, their line-ups in the league games were almost unrecognisable compared to the usual team. James did not play in any of them, the reason given was his shoulder injury from the semi-final, and neither did Willie Thomas. There were many other changes – officially through injuries – and 29 different players took part in the four games, several had not played all season. They managed to beat Halifax 21–3 at home, but lost the others heavily; 33–0 at home to Runcorn, 11–0 at Widnes, and 26–12 at home to Hunslet.

The Challenge Cup Final was against Bradford, their third meeting of the season, each had won the home league fixture. With the exception of forward Arthur Buckler, who had a knee injury, Salford fielded their strongest team as follows: Cochrane; McWhirter, Willie Thomas, Lomas (captain), Hampson; John, Preston; Brown, Alf Foster, Lewis, Rees, Rhapps, Spencer, Evan Thomas, Warwick.

On an overcast, wet and windy afternoon, James led his team onto the Headingley pitch, followed by Bradford and, having won the coin toss, decided to start with the strong wind at their backs. There was no scoring during the first half, the *Yorkshire Daily Observer* claimed

Bradford "had done exceptionally well in keeping out their opponents". Try chances were few during that opening period. James missed two penalties – one from long distance that was well short, another from 25 yards – and Willie Thomas hit the woodwork with a drop-goal attempt. The second half got heated and Warwick, along with Bradford forward Harry Feather, was sent off after exchanging punches. Fifteen minutes remained when half-back Sammy Brear struck the first blow in Bradford's favour with a superb individual try. Alex Laidlaw added a penalty two minutes from the end and Salford were beaten 5–0.

It was the fourth time in four attempts that the Reds had lost in a Challenge Cup Final. Interviewed by the press after the match, James gave credit to the Bradford forwards and conceded that "Bradford were just slightly the better team" although he made the point that "a few of our men were not fit to start with." The *Leeds Mercury*, summing up, said: "One cannot help feeling sincere sympathy with Salford in their many last-minute failures, and particularly with Lomas, who had done more than any other member of the team to give Salford their high standing during the past few years. The Reds' captain played a lion-hearted game on Saturday, and one could not help admire his pluck in the later stages of the game when Bradford had scored and apparently made their victory secure. To the end Lomas showed all his old grit, and he deserved all the sympathy that was bestowed upon him in one more disappointment." Amazingly, Bradford left the NU a year later and took up association football as Bradford Park Avenue; Bradford Northern arose from the ashes.

One game remained, but it was not without incident. On the Monday after the cup final, the Reds took on St Helens at Knowsley Road, and suffered another disappointment. They lost 11–0, all the points were scored in the first half. A patched up Salford, who made three changes from the cup final, lost the services of stand-in full-back E. Lancaster with an injured knee in the second half and this was followed by the dismissal of half-backs T. Hall of St Helens and Salford's Preston. The *Salford Reporter's* journalist said that referee Billy McCutcheon paid scant attention to the hosts' "shady tricks" in the second half, had lost control, and claimed "these matches are harming NU Football and gates are likely to fall."

The match ended in turmoil with bricks and stones thrown at the Salford players and several were struck. One unnamed Reds player said he had not seen anything like it in 13 years as a player. The journey by omnibus from the ground to the Talbot Hotel changing rooms was also hostile because players of both sides shared the transport and several blows were exchanged. James recalled the match in his memoirs: "There was some rough work during the journey. After getting dressed we had to have an escort to the railway station at night as the crowd would not go away." It was an unfortunate end to the season.

Salford finished 18th of the 31 clubs, with 14 wins and three draws in 34 matches, a significant drop from 6th in the former First Division. But the team deserved credit for reaching another Challenge Cup Final in what had been a difficult season. James had continued to log up the points, his 22 tries and 36 goals made up the 138 that put him into a clear second place, behind Wigan's Leytham, as the NU's leading points scorer.

Salford 1905-06. Back: J. White (trainer), W. Brown, J. Williams, J. Rhapps, E. Thomas, S. Warwick, J. Spencer, D. John, D. Rees; middle: J. Cochrane (kneeling), R.M.H. Bell, W. Thomas, J. Lomas (captain), V. Hampson, I. Lewis, D. Preston (kneeling); front: S. Holbrook, H. Buckler, A. Buckler.

Salford 1906-07: Back: T. White (trainer), W. Brady, A. Foster, I. Lewis, E. Thomas, S. Warwick, D. Rees, W. Lambert (asst. trainer), J. Cochrane; middle: A. Buckler, C. Garner, W. Thomas, J. Lomas (captain), V. Hampson, A. Mason, W. Brown; front: D. John, D. Preston.

James with his England jersey and 1908-09 cap, a season when he represented his country three times against the visiting Australians. (Courtesy Rob Dellar)

A 1900s 'Baines' card featuring James. The cards, which first appeared in the 1880s, were popular collectors' items at the time.

10. 1906–07: A season like no other

The 1906–07 campaign was a significant and historic one for James Lomas and the Northern Union game in general. He shattered the NU point scoring record for a single season, set a new high for goals, and, in addition to those categories, broke the Salford club record for tries. On top of that he set a championship fixture record that stood until 1992. It was a season like no other as far as James and his point scoring prowess was concerned. A major reason for the upsurge in points was the most defining change made by the Northern Union since breaking away from the Rugby Football Union in 1895. Alterations such as the abolition of the line-out from touch in 1897 and the recent introduction of the play-the-ball rule after a tackle were certainly distinctive and influential in the development of the code, but it was the reduction in the number of players from 15 to 13 that divides the rugby codes in many people's minds.

It was achieved by shedding two forwards, estimated at saving around £100 a season on each club's wage bill, a decision that opened up more space for talented backs such as James to exploit, and thereby increased the entertainment value for the paying customers. It certainly worked because, as demonstrated by James's increased haul, point scoring increased significantly. Salford scored 462 points in 34 League matches compared to 272 in 1905–06 from the same number of matches. This growth was reflected throughout the competition; Wigan, who had the best points per match average in both seasons, registered 12.97 a game in 1905–06 and 19.29 in 1906–07.

Salford's final pre-season practice match at The Willows on 26 August 1906 was watched by around 3,000 spectators. The Reds, who included James who scored two tries and three goals, beat the Whites 40–3. The *Salford Reporter* commented: "Needless to say, [Vernon] Hampson, Lomas and [Dai] John were seen to advantage and [Willie] Thomas was in far better condition than at the close of last season." The same paper also commented: "Already in the practice games there has been some difference of opinion amongst the whistle blowers, notably as to the interpretation of the play-the-ball rule."

Salford opened their season on 1 September with a home match against Batley, the club's first ever 13-man line-up read: Willie Thomas; Harry McWhirter, Walter Clessold, Lomas (captain), Hampson; John, Frank Drake; Billy Brown, Alf Foster, Ike Lewis, Jack Rhapps, Jack Spencer, Charlie Swindells. It was a baking hot, sunny day, reaching almost 100 degrees Farenheight. Apparently the spectators struggled in the heat through having to wait an extra hour for kick-off due to Batley's late arrival. James got his own season off to a good start with a goal from almost halfway after Swindells called for a mark. Clessold, a new signing from Penygraig injured his knee and eventually quit the match; Thomas returned to his usual centre berth as a consequence and Brown moved to full-back. The highlight of the afternoon followed when, from a scrum on Salford's 25-yard line, a pass intended for Batley centre A. Senior was seized upon by an ever alert James who "electrified the crowd" as he roared downfield, "leaving all in his wake" to score under the posts. Minutes later, Hampson also placed the ball behind the posts following an exciting move that also included John, Thomas and, of course, James, who made the try a certain bet before passing to the scorer. With Salford's captain succeeding with both goals, the Reds led 12–0 at half-time. With Salford a man short in the pack due to Clissold's absence, Batley had far more of the game after the break and pulled back seven of the points, but the Reds prevailed 12–7.

The *Salford Reporter* match summary made interesting reading: "Whatever else has been revealed by the opening match the Reds may congratulate themselves that Lomas is in the pink of condition and that the new rules suit him." Further comments in the same paper extolled the impact of the new rules, saying "this new style of play is a great improvement on the old and the spectators were delighted with what they saw. Nobody had seen a faster game for many seasons. There was not an uninteresting moment [and] the sister code will have to look to its laurels. The smaller number of players gives more scope for open work among the backs; the play-the ball rule lessens the number of scrummages to a big extent while the touch rule, of course, is bound to produce play of more open order ... the Northern Union have reason to be proud of these changes and throughout the whole series of League games on Saturday the verdict is the same – a great improvement."

Salford travelled to Edge Lane to take on newcomers Liverpool City on the second weekend of the season. The Liverpool team was referred to as a "comparatively scratch side" with "a distinct flavour for rugby union tactics" and included former Salford forward Harry Woodhead in their selection. James grazed the wrong side of an upright with a penalty before he opened the score after 15 minutes. He ran and weaved his way through defenders from some 20 yards out to score in the corner. He missed the goal, and a long distance drop-goal effort, but was on target after Willie Thomas and Drake scored the next two tries. A further try, by Jack Williams, followed by one from City forward Cook put the Reds 16–3 ahead at the interval. With the wind and sun at their backs in the second half, Salford may have anticipated building up a big score, but Liverpool defended much better and just 12 points were added, a drop-goal by John was followed by touchdowns from Hampson and debutant former Pendlebury forward Tom Rickers in the final minute; James converted both to complete a 28–3 win. It may have been a new club but, as is so often the case with a star player, James, who was twice unlucky when his powerful running just failed to produce further tries, was singled out by home fans for the usual derisory remarks.

Several players had been rested in anticipation of the home fixture with Leeds; half-back Dave Preston and forwards Dai Rees and Evan Thomas appeared in their first match of the season against the Headingley men. In front of 6,000 spectators, Leeds threatened early on, and took a 2–0 lead through a penalty from A. Brayshaw, a former Bramley colleague of James's. The *Salford Reporter* reassured its readers there was no reason for early panic: "In view of the rapid changes that nowadays come over the game there was no need for the home spectators to be unduly alarmed." Sure enough, James twice came close to scoring; he nudged the outside of a goalpost with a penalty and then lost the ball "after carrying it over [the try-line] in his best style". Eventually, it was Preston who made the breakthrough from John's pass, a second try followed for Rees. James tagged both goals and the Reds led 10–2 at half-time. It was noted that an eight point deficit was a lot to make up by Leeds in the second-half "yet under the new rules the game is of such a character that it is not quite as formidable a total as last season." As it happened, Leeds could only add a second Brayshaw penalty, James's goal from a mark and his conversion of further tries from Hampson and Spencer completed a convincing 22–4 score line.

The *Yorkshire Post* wrote perceptively that Leeds "lacked the lead of a man with the commanding genius of Lomas. What Lomas has done for Salford will never be fully realised until his football days are over. That day is not yet, and, great individualist that he is, he looks likely under the new conditions, to win more games off his own foot, so to speak, than he had done in the past. Certainly Saturday's victory was Lomas's victory [and] he made at least three of the tries [while] playing with a dashing fearlessness that brooked no denial he was at once the leader and inspiration of the side."

Just three weeks into the season the new rules had revolutionised the NU code. Having ended the previous season as a sport that often produced a boring stalemate dominated by the forwards, it was now seen as a quick and exciting spectacle. The *Salford Reporter* scribe was running out of words when trying to describe it: "So rapid now are the transitions that they are not only difficult to follow but equally difficult to describe. The [passing] movements, in fact, so much resemble one another that language fails to repeat them without becoming tautological and saying the same thing time after time in the same way."

The sparkling run of three opening wins was soon dulled through three successive away defeats; 17–5 at Hunslet, 35–5 at Bradford, and 33–3 at Warrington. James was closely marked at Hunslet, and had less freedom to manoeuvre than in the earlier fixtures. His penalty had put the Reds 2–0 ahead, but by the interval they trailed 9–2. The Salford captain put Willie Thomas over in the corner for a late consolation try, but his tricky goal attempt bounced back off a post. As at Hunslet, the Salford forwards were blamed for a below-par performance at Bradford that allowed their backs to be overrun. James scored a touchline penalty in the first half but, after he had put Preston in for a try in the corner after the break, was unable to convert it. It was said that, despite the freedom afforded the Bradford backs, James had played "a great game" although he was booked, along with Bradford winger J. Dunbavin, during the second half following an altercation between the pair. In defence of Salford's heavy defeat, it was observed that "under the present conditions games are apt to be one-sided after one team has got a lead."

Salford's loss at Warrington provided further cause for concern, particularly the number of points they again conceded. They did, though, have five players, including James, absent due to their involvement in a county fixture that day. It was a match that was a bit special for James because it marked his return to the Cumberland side and, furthermore, it was played in his home town of Maryport at the Athletic Ground. The opposition was Lancashire who had earlier selected him for the usual Probables versus Possibles trial match, held at Wheater's Field on Wednesday 26 September. However, he declined the invitation, and said that his intention was to revert to Cumberland. James explained his point of view in his memoirs: "Cumberland had neglected me since I left there, therefore Lancashire had first claim under the existing rules at the time. After a while a few of us decided to go back and play for the County of our birth. We [Cumberland] won the championship twice [outright] before the [First World] War and I got medals for Lancashire."

James had followed the example of two other Cumbrian greats, Halifax's Billy Little and Oldham's Joe Ferguson, who had turned out for their birth county the previous season having represented Yorkshire and Lancashire, respectively. The *Athletic News* welcomed the change in the qualification rules, and commented: "the lack of excitement in the county championship series was notorious, and only one match, namely Lancashire v Yorkshire, was thought worthy to be played on the usual half-holiday [Saturday]." The writer also said: "An alteration in the rules which gave a player the right to play for the county of his birth, rather than that of his adoption, inspired those footballers who have wandered from the sylvan shades of Cumberland to the wilds of Lancashire and Yorkshire to find the contingent that would defeat the other counties and send the championship to Cumberland." However, the title was not yet destined for that county and Cumberland lost to Lancashire 15–4, the second of James's two penalty goals, following half-time, tied the score at 4–4 before the Red Rose pulled away.

Salford had a break from the league with a first round Lancashire Cup game against Wigan at home on 13 October. It was 3–0 to the Reds at half-time thanks to a 10th minute try by John, James increased the margin to 9–0 with three goals, two penalties and a mark, before Foster's effort in the corner made it 12–0. Wigan's obstruction try made the final score 12–3. Yet again, James was the best player on view: "His kicking, running and tackling proves that he has lost none of his old skills. But he lacked support. Twice in particular he made splendid openings (but there was) no one at hand."

It was back to the league on 20 October and another torturous away defeat, this time 26–3 against local rivals Broughton Rangers. It was a score home fans in the 17,000 crowd would have enjoyed. Salford trailed 17–3 at the interval with only a try from Brown to their credit. Salford entertained Runcorn in the next round of the Lancashire Cup the following Saturday. James's penalty from almost halfway gave his side the lead, but their progress in the competition was eventually halted through a 3–2 defeat. The Salford skipper stood out as usual and, with his side pressing strongly near the end, he was just short with a goal attempt, again from midfield.

The cup tie caused the postponement of the return fixture with Warrington, which was delayed until the following Wednesday. This time the tables were turned and the Reds won

8–5 after a dramatic try from James. With the match tied at 5–5, he intercepted a Warrington pass intended for centre Ike Taylor and, having got through several opponents with the ball in hand, he dribbled it towards the opposition line, and covered some threequarters of the field. As the ball crossed the try-line he just got the touch ahead of a pursuing Taylor to win the match. The Reds had led 5–0 at the interval after another long-range penalty by James, which he followed up with a try after combining with Lewis.

Salford were at Runcorn the following Saturday, 3 November. The Willows, meanwhile, hosted the Lancashire versus Yorkshire fixture. Lancashire won 19–0 watched by around 5,000 fans. Rees was missing from the Salford line-up at Canal Street due to Lancashire commitments and James was also unavailable through injuries received against Warrington. The Reds lost 17–2, a result that put the Cheshire side on the league summit with Leeds.

Over the next four weekends Salford won three home games, and it could have been a sequence of four consecutive victories, but for an abandoned match at Oldham. The three home triumphs came against St Helens, 26–13, Leigh, 17–8 and Wigan 7–2. The Reds were trailing 8–7 to St Helens. James had converted a Hampson try and kicked a penalty, before Hampson turned the game around with his second touchdown. James's goal made it 12–8 and home spirits lifted. Salford ran in four further tries, James – who also crossed the try-line in the second half, but was ruled to have stepped in touch before grounding – converted one of them. Hampson took the eye with his four touchdowns, but the star show came from James, who had a hand in every try as well as kicking brilliantly in general play.

He took that excellent form into the next match against Leigh, despite a storm that enveloped the players, which made conditions very difficult in the pouring rain. Salford trailed to the reigning champions 8–4 at the break. James had landed two penalties. Salford were a different side after the interval, though, and scored three tries with James adding two goals through a penalty and conversion. Wigan's visit on 1 December was a tighter affair. James, as he often did, opened the scoring with a penalty. By half-time it was 5–0; Preston gained possession and scored after James had booted the ball across the field. James Leytham's excellent penalty from halfway for Wigan made it uncomfortable for Salford at 5–2 before the Reds' leader added a further goal from a penalty for obstruction.

The Wigan fixture dissected two visits to Oldham, the first of which was the aforementioned abandoned game. In a bizarre sequence of events that would probably grab headlines today, the match was halted through bad light in the second half with Salford leading 7–0. James – who again had an outstanding match – had added the goal to a first half try by Charlie Garner, and kicked a long-range penalty after the interval. The *Salford Reporter* journalist – possibly disappointed to see a good lead against one of the championship contenders sacrificed – believed there was sufficient light to continue, and said "another 11 minutes would have made all the difference". In other words, in his opinion, the game could have reached 70 minutes play, at which point the result would have stood. However, it was a certain railway porter that was the real culprit rather than referee Jack Smith. The reason the game ran out of light was because it began 45 minutes late after Salford's kit had disappeared during their journey. When the train carrying the Salford party from Weaste Station arrived at Manchester's Exchange Station, they changed trains for the onward journey to Oldham. Unfortunately, the porter forgot to transfer the kit and it returned from whence it came, and finished up at Patricroft Station, near Eccles. Fortunately, when the train next arrived in Manchester the kit was still on it and the journey continued.

An interesting observation was that an 8,000 crowd at Watersheddings showed that, despite disappointing attendances at The Willows, Salford were still an attraction elsewhere. This may, of course, have been due to James's presence in their team. The replayed match was on the Monday afternoon following the Wigan fixture and, consequently, the crowd was much lower, around 3,000. Although Salford battled well during the second half, during which they scored two tries – which included one by Warwick after excellent dribbling by James – they were beaten 10–6.

Bradford came to Weaste on 8 December. Salford inflicted revenge for their cup final defeat and the annihilation at Valley Parade earlier in the season with a 16–0 win. James excelled yet again – "as fine a game as we have seen him do this season" – and scored the third of the Reds' four tries. It came after winning a race with winger Jimmy Dechan in pursuit of John's deft kick before he touched down, his follow-up goal provided the second of his two conversions. The December weather was starting to bite, a slight frost was in evidence for the following weekend's game at Barrow. James missed with his almost customary early penalty strike, accompanied by loud cheers of derision from the home fans. Instead, Barrow took command and led 8–0 at the halfway point. After changing ends, half-backs John and Preston broke away before passing to Arthur Buckler. He passed to James "who beat all opposition in characteristic style" to score a try that he also converted. With only three points in it, Salford raised their game. James missed with a penalty attempt, but Barrow produced the knock-out blow with their third touchdown for an 11–5 victory. The *Salford Reporter* reiterated its view that James was back to his best, although it was clear the north Lancashire side must have done their homework on him: "He is so well watched that he rarely scores. He was within an ace of adding four more tries."

Seven days later, worse conditions awaited the Reds, only 4,000 bothered to turn out on a dark, fog-filled, cold and damp afternoon at Chorley Road where Swinton awaited. Yet again, Salford came away a beaten side, this time 15–6. All the points came from James's boot in the first half with a long distance effort from a mark, plus two penalties. Behind 8–6 at the break, Salford tried to recover in the second half; James was held on the line and missed a goal attempt following another mark, and Warwick had a try disallowed.

Salford entertained their other local rivals, Broughton Rangers, three days later on Christmas Day. This time the weather was sunny and conditions dry, which enticed 11,000 spectators away from their Yuletide festivities. The first score was placed against James's account; he touched down for a try following a loose scramble for possession on the Rangers' line. He added the goal, but was off the pace with a succeeding drop-goal attempt. The Rangers, though, drew level at 5–5 by the interval following some "exceedingly keen" first half play. The Salford skipper again demonstrated his importance to the cause by landing an impressive drop-goal after he received the ball from John, which restored their lead at 7–5. There was no further scoring but, in a hard fought conclusion and with points at a premium, James tried to register further goals, but failed with two drop attempts, another effort from a mark, and a penalty from halfway.

Boosted by their success over Broughton, Salford travelled to Headingley on Boxing Day in search of a double over Leeds. Unlike the previous day's conditions at The Willows, there had been a heavy fall of snow and a precautionary covering of straw had been removed and piled up around the sides of the pitch. For the fourth successive game, James scored all his side's points with two second half tries, but it was insufficient to avert a 14–6 defeat. He also claimed a try in the first half following a powerful run, but referee Ted Smirk ruled it out. Instead, it was Leeds who opened the scoring, and stretched a 3–0 half time lead to 14–0 before James's double strike. With their 1906 commitments over, Salford found themselves drifting in mid-table, having won half of their 20 league fixtures.

James should have been back at Headingley on New Year's Day to represent England in the annual fixture with Other Nationalities. The match – which would have been the first 13-a-side international – was called off the previous evening "owing to the state of the ground" because the pitch was heavy following a thaw. Although announced as a postponement, it was not subsequently played and no further New Year's Day internationals were planned again. The Other Nationalities side went into storage until 1921, probably due to the emergence of international opposition from the other side of the planet.

This cartoon, from *Athletic News*, of the Swinton versus Salford match played at Chorley Road on 22 December 1906, captures the awesome power of James's hand-off.

England's loss was Salford's gain, and James was able to turn out at The Willows against Hunslet on the same day. The match ended controversially when, in the final minute and with Salford staring defeat in the face at 11–10 down, James took a penalty shot at goal. The home fans cheered as the touch judge waved his flag to signal a goal, but the referee, Bradford's J.H. Crompton, decided that the ball had travelled beneath the crossbar and overruled him, which gave Hunslet the win. Salford's stand-in wingman Albert Mason had been the first to trouble the scoreboard operator with an eighth minute try. When John scored a second for a 6–0 lead it looked hopeful for the Reds, but it evaporated into a 9–6 reverse by half-time. After the break, however, drop-goals by John and James restored the Reds' lead, 10–9. Seven minutes from the end Albert Goldthorpe spoilt Salford's day with a penalty that ultimately sunk them, an appropriate metaphor for a match played throughout on a saturated pitch due to continuous heavy rain.

Salford put their disappointment to one side enough to win the next two matches, both at The Willows; 27–0 against Swinton and a closer 17–15 over Oldham. James enjoyed one of his best days against Swinton, and scored 18 points including four tries. Having converted John Cochrane's opening score, the ball landed on the crossbar and rolled over, he scored the next two touchdowns himself. The first came after Willie Thomas fumbled a John pass, but somehow managed to get a foot to the ball, James followed up to go in under the posts. The second came via a return pass from Hampson following a move when all the backs had handled the ball. Having, surprisingly, failed to add the goal to his first try, he succeeded with the second, which put Salford 13–0 ahead at the break. After the restart, James claimed his third try. He picked the ball up after a Swinton move broke down to go over in the corner. He made it four on the run after Warwick, who had galloped towards the Swinton 25-yard line after gathering up the ball in midfield, gave him possession. The skipper then handed off forward Billy Lloyd to go beneath the posts. His goal raised the margin to 21–0, Willie Thomas added two further tries. Despite his four tries, it was felt James could have had "another try or two," the *Salford Reporter* credited Swinton centre Albert Valentine's defence, who "watched him like a cat".

James missed out on the narrow victory over Oldham on 12 January, a match that was hailed as a thriller, Salford overcame a 15–9 deficit against their illustrious visitors. The *Salford Reporter* exclaimed that after the final whistle "The crowd cheered again and again [and] seldom has so much enthusiasm been seen at The Willows." Contrary to opinions that claimed that Salford were a one man team, it proved they could rise to a challenge without James's presence. His absence was due to Cumberland's match against Yorkshire at Huddersfield, in which he scored and converted both of his county's tries, which helped them to an impressive 12–5 interval lead. It took just five minutes for him to get the first, near the posts, after a sustained period of pressure. His second effort came off a return pass from his wingman, Huddersfield's Bill Kitchin. Unfortunately, Cumberland showed less exuberance in the second half, and eventually went down 15–12.

Four days later, James was at Mather Lane with his Salford colleagues for a Wednesday afternoon fixture against Leigh. It produced a comfortable 22–4 victory for the Reds. The visitors were off to a flying start when Willie Thomas scored a try after just three minutes, James added a second, from Hampson's pass, and converted two further tries for a 16–2 interval lead. The following Saturday, the Reds took a trip over the Pennines to take on eventual champions Halifax. The home side led 9–0 at the break and it could have been worse for the Reds, had not James pushed winger Percy Eccles into touch after he outwitted several defenders. Having been outclassed, Salford revived in the second half and James was on target three times. He landed two penalties, including a spectacular effort from halfway that the home fans sportingly cheered, plus the extras after a late try from John. Unfortunately for James and his men, a Bill Wedgewood penalty was just enough to sink Salford 11–9.

Having completed a hectic eight day schedule, Salford's players had a fortnight's rest because the following week's home fixture against Barrow was a victim of frost. Action was resumed on 2 February in a record-making home game with Liverpool City. Salford's 78–0 win was their biggest ever, unchallenged until March 2003 when they twice defeated an unfortunate Gateshead Thunder in the National League Cup 90–8 away and 100–12 at home. James's contribution was exactly half – 39 points – a record for a league fixture that was not surpassed until 1992 when Dean Marwood scored 42 playing for Workington Town. As well as his 39 points being the most scored in a single match for Salford, so too were his 12 goals. James also got five tries, four of them in the first half as Salford amassed a 44–0 interval lead. The *Salford Reporter* said: "If the 18 (tries) were earned without too much trouble, the same can hardly be said of the goals. Whatever the quality of the other players, goalkicking is a science apart and, as such, good goals may be kicked in a poor game as in an important one. Lomas, therefore, performed a feat worth recording by taking the 18 places, and from 12 of them adding the extra points." The result was another nail in the coffin of the Merseyside club who lost all 30 of its League matches and folded at the end of the season.[4]

Liverpool City's annihilation began a sequence of five victories that ran through February, their best run for almost three years, further victims being Batley, 11–7, away, Barrow, 49–0 at home, Wakefield Trinity, 26–2 at home and Halifax, 9–5 at home. At Batley, the Reds found themselves trailing 7–0 after 20 minutes before Hampson's high kick was followed up by James who kicked the ball over the line and touched it down. A brilliant run by John led to a try for Hampson and, as James added the goal, Salford had an 8–7

---

[4] Hull KR's George West scored 53 points (11 tries, 10 goals) in 1905, against Brookland Rovers, but that was a Challenge Cup match, rather than a league fixture. Marwood's points were scored against Highfield, the successor to the second Liverpool City club. In his time a try was worth 4 points; under that scoring system, James's efforts would have been worth 44 points.

lead by half-time. James completed the scoring in the second half; he took a wide pass from Preston and dodged between two defenders to go over in the corner. The Barrow game was on the following Wednesday, 13 February, following its January postponement, the inconvenient timing kept the attendance to a meagre 2,000. Again, James was among the points with four of Salford's 13 tries, two in each half, and tagged on five conversions.

A tremendous penalty from near the halfway line by full-back Ward gave Wakefield Trinity a 2–0 start at The Willows, but James once more came to the rescue. He took a perfectly aimed long pass off Preston to touch down near the posts, and added the extra points. A few moments later, while Salford were defending, he gained possession and broke away, started a passing move that concluded with a Cochrane try under the posts, which put Salford 8–2 ahead after 20 minutes. There was no further scoring until the second half, when James evaded defenders on another of his powerful runs to put Warwick in at the corner. Having missed the previous conversion from in front of goal, James confounded the odds by landing this one from the touchline. Following another try by Cochrane, this time near the corner flag, James charged down the ball following a clearance kick from Ward. He retrieved the ball on the rebound, and raced from the centre of the field to place it over the try-line. He added the goal, and did likewise after the final try by Warwick.

There were around 12,000 spectators at The Willows on 23 February, many drawn in to see champions-elect Halifax, who had earned many admirers during the campaign. Only two points separated the teams at half-time; James had slotted over a goal for Salford following Hampson's mark. The Reds' captain doubled that tally after a Halifax player was penalised for not playing the ball correctly, and excited Salford fans further when he made a break and, as he was tackled by Billy Little, passed to Arthur Buckler for a try. James missed the goal. The 7–0 lead was eroded when forward Ike Bartle was awarded an obstruction try and Wedgewood converted. With two points in it, the match continued "amidst much excitement" before, in the final seconds, John caught the ball from a clearance by centre Ernest Ward and called for the mark. In dramatic fashion and possibly to eat up the clock, James took his time placing the ball which ultimately sailed over the crossbar as the final whistle sounded, which left Salford fans to celebrate a famous win.

James had performed well throughout his side's winning run, one report suggested that when he had possession "he put life into the play" and he "rarely makes a slip with every movement having method in it." However, Salford, and James in particular, suffered a slight hiccup in the next fixture, at Wigan on 2 March, losing 10–5 in a match watched by 14,000. For James, though, it was not mere defeat that was on his mind after the match ended, but the fact that he had been sent off for the first time in his career. He was dismissed early in the second half by referee W. Robinson of Bradford, along with Wigan's Welsh centre Tommy Thomas, for fighting, following the intervention of a touch judge. The *Salford Reporter* was quick to defend James, and said "Thomas had not played previously against Lomas and like many another man, was anxious to show off against Jimmy, who was beating his man time after time," and added "he was subjected to great provocation [throughout the game], and it is to be hoped that the full facts will be narrated when the matter comes before the committee of the Northern Union."

At the time James marched off Salford were losing 7–0. Although they pulled it back to 7–5 with a Willie Thomas try, converted by Brown, who had taken James's position in the centre, a further Wigan touchdown from centre Sam Johnson sealed Salford's defeat. Despite the mitigating circumstances proposed by the local paper, James was suspended for one match. Unfortunately for Salford they had already agreed to a St Helens request to postpone their next league fixture – scheduled at Knowsley Road on 9 March – until April. It was a decision that backfired on the Reds because it meant James would, instead, be unavailable for the opening round of the Challenge Cup on 16 March. Salford, though, just managed to survive the temporary loss of their captain, and beat Leigh 10–5 at home to progress to the second round the following week, and another meeting with Wigan, this time at The Willows.

On this occasion James and Tommy Thomas managed to stay on the field, with no repeat of the exchanges three weeks earlier. Instead James extracted retribution in a way that only he could – by almost single-handedly destroying the opposition. He set Salford on the road to success by bursting through the Wigan defence and despatched Willie Thomas towards the corner flag for a try. When the Colliers' Johnny Thomas fumbled a pass from his half-back partner Billy Anderson, Willie Thomas grabbed the ball and returned the earlier compliment by sending James in under the posts. James missed the simple conversion, but more than made up for it with a penalty from near halfway after Cochrane was fouled, which put Salford into an 8–0 lead. Next up, Arthur Buckler sent out a wide pass to James who transferred to his wingman Hampson, the latter then dashed to Wigan's 25-yard line before he returned the ball to his skipper who took a diagonal route to score under the posts. His goal gave Salford a very healthy interval advantage of 13 points. After the break, a try by centre Bert Jenkins, converted by his wing partner Leytham gave Wigan some crumb of hope, but James was having none of it. When Willie Thomas crossed the visitors' try-line but lost possession, he rushed up to gather the wayward ball and score, and added the goal to complete an 18–5 win.

Circumstances surrounding the tie with Wigan implied that Salford were continuing to struggle with their finances. Two weeks earlier, on 9 March, Salford 'A' team, which had been resurrected this season after being shelved the previous term, were due to entertain Wigan 'A', but the match was switched to Central Park for purely commercial reasons, the entire gate receipts from an attendance of around 2,000 were handed over to the Reds. When the two clubs were drawn together in the Challenge Cup, Wigan offered Salford £250 to switch the tie. Clearly they felt Salford were susceptible to the possibility although, in the event, they declined the offer and were rewarded with a bumper attendance estimated at around 15,000.

The success against Wigan meant Salford faced an incredibly hectic Easter weekend; Runcorn at home on Good Friday, a third round Challenge Cup match with Leeds at The Willows the next day, and the aforementioned rescheduled game at St Helens on Easter Monday. For James it was even more hectic because Annie presented him with their second daughter, Evelyn, just two days ahead of the Runcorn match.

Salford spurned the temptation to bring in reserves against Runcorn with only Cochrane, with a slight injury, and Willie Thomas, who was rested, omitted from the line-up that would face Leeds. There was a reasonably good attendance of 7,000 for Runcorn's visit. James was again in the thick of it in the opening half. He had a penalty kick charged down and a try disallowed before he kicked a goal from a mark made by Mason on the stroke of half-time. Injuries reduced Runcorn to 11 players although, with the Leeds match in mind, the Reds did not exert themselves, a try by John concluded the scoring at 5–0 to Salford.

There was an estimated 12,000 (10,933 paid) at the ground the following day for the eagerly anticipated cup match with Leeds. Like Salford, the Headingley outfit were in the middle of a similarly busy three-match-in-four-days schedule, and had lost 28–3 away to Broughton Rangers the previous day, and stayed overnight in Didsbury. James started the scoreboard ticking with a penalty after Leeds half-back Brayshaw had been given offside, forward John Stead responded with a touchdown in the corner to give his team a one point lead. James tried to restore the Reds' advantage, and missed a drop-goal before the referee – Mr A. Smith of Halifax – blew his whistle for half-time. The crowd quickly made it known that only 25 minutes had been played and the players were subsequently called back. James then had another go at recovering the lead; he made a mark and was just wide with the resultant goal attempt.

Half-time was finally reached and there was concern in the Salford camp that they had not taken control of the tie nor scored a try. The *Salford Reporter* said "There were many anxious faces on the stands and that of the Salford captain was a study. What was going to happen next?" What happened next was that the home side – inspired by James – went up a few gears, John slipped through the visitors' defence close to their try line, to put Hampson over at the corner. James then landed a mighty penalty goal from 10 yards inside the halfway line to give his team a 7–3 lead and suddenly the relieved home fans were cheering. Moments later, having taken a pass from Preston – who had made the initial break – James raced away, and handed off several Leeds men before he scored in the corner. A successful penalty from Brown towards the end confirmed a 12–3 win and a place in the semi-finals once again.

Possibly because of their recent exertions, Salford lost heavily at St Helens on Easter Monday, 30–5, and thereby ended a four-match winning run. James scored the Reds' points; a fine first half goal from a mark made by Garner near the touchline – having earlier been just wide with a penalty from halfway – and a try near the end of the match after an excellent run and pass from Lewis. Salford finished with only 10 players; forwards

Evan Thomas and Arthur Buckler retired injured during the course of the second half, Hampson joined them towards the end after taking a knock. To be fair to St Helens, they were 17–2 up at half-time and heading for victory before Salford's misfortunes accrued.

Salford were falling off badly as the season began to wrap up and lost 29–5 away to Wakefield Trinity the following Saturday. James scored first with a penalty and, later in the opening half, Cochrane got over for a try at the corner, but they lagged behind Wakefield 11–5 at the interval and were overwhelmed after the resumption. James was accused of being "indifferent" and Willie Thomas was, reportedly, "unwilling to take any risks," the whole team, apparently, were similarly-minded. The probability is that their thoughts were occupied by the Challenge Cup semi-final seven days later. They were well off the pace for the inaugural top-four championship play-off. The defeat at Wakefield left them in 10th place, having won 18 and lost 14 of their 32 fixtures, whereas victory would have enabled them to leap-frog Broughton Rangers into ninth.

The Challenge Cup semi-finals were an all-Lancashire affair, Salford met Oldham at Rochdale Hornets' Athletic Grounds and Swinton took on Warrington at Central Park, both on 13 April. The Rochdale ground was saturated from earlier heavy rain and slippery underfoot. On a miserably cold and dark day, most of the colour was among the spectators who wore their club favours and waved flags. The unpleasant weather meant that "the man with the good overcoat or mackintosh came off best" because the venue offered very little shelter from the elements, although it was a good day for those selling pies and cough toffees. It was not, however, a good day for Salford. Lewis was sent off in the first half for some indiscretion in a tackle, and Preston also retired with an injury, which left a re-jigged Salford with a four-man pack. James tried his best, and failed with a penalty when the ball did not rise above the sodden turf, just missed with a goal attempt from a mark, and was held up "by half-a-dozen opponents" on the Oldham try-line just before half-time. Although Preston had returned, Salford's 12-man team was slowly worn down by the Roughyeds who scored two tries to earn their place in the final with a 6–0 win.

The defeat was another disappointment for the Reds' players and supporters and meant their campaign was over. The season had fallen below the expectations put on their shoulders eight months earlier. Their three defeats at the end of the term seemed to take away the kudos that had come their way in winning nine of the preceding 10 matches, a run that had taken them up the league and to a Challenge Cup semi-final. James also finished on a "damp squib", the verdict on his semi-final performance was that "seldom has Lomas figured less in a match." His overall contribution to Salford's 1906–07 season, though, was extraordinary. Time and again he was the outstanding player and a match-winner without equal, not least in the Challenge Cup victories over Wigan and Leeds and, in cold statistics, NU history clearly reflects this. His phenomenal scoring this season set new records for the NU of 275 points, beating his 214 in 1903–04, and 85 goals in all matches, and for Salford, with 261 points, 81 goals and 33 tries. Truly, the King of brilliance.

A 1907 photograph of James and Annie with their two
eldest daughters, Annie Alexandra, right, and Evelyn.
(Photo: Courtesy Salford Local History Library)

11. 1907–08: The mainstay of the side

The major, almost sensational news at the start of the 1907–08 season was the announcement of a New Zealand tour to England and Wales, commencing in October. As NU rugby was not yet played in that country, their party would be made up of leading disaffected rugby union players who felt they should receive more of the finances generated by the sport, particularly from tours. James Lomas, it was noted in the press, would be eligible to meet them in four guises; Salford, whose club officials were among the first to guarantee the required £100 to stage a match, Cumberland, England, and a combined NU team for the test series, although he was subsequently not selected for the latter.

As was often his habit, James had spent the summer months in Maryport and had arrived back in Salford "looking remarkably fit and well". Along with Vernon Hampson, he was given permission to miss the club's pre-season trial match on 24 August in order to take part in a six-a-side competition at Swinton. The pair were included in Swinton forward Dan Davies' Swinton & Salford team. Eleven sides participated, Dan Davies' team winning the tournament by defeating Joe Kewin's Barrow Marsh Hornets 15–3 in the first round, then Tom Davies' Swinton Hornets 26–0, Billy Simister's Swinton team 18–8 in the semi-final and Ike Bartle's Halifax 10–0 in the final. The composition of Dan Davies' winning side, who were all from Swinton except for James and Hampson, was: Richard Townson (full-back), Lomas and Hampson (threequarters), Billy Griffin (half-back), Davies and Tom Promfret (forwards).

James's reappearance at The Willows was for the final pre-season trial seven days later, playing in the Reds (first team) side that defeated the Whites (reserves) 22–0 and contributing three tries and two conversions. Reportedly he "electrified" the 3,000 supporters with a run that covered the length of the field, almost putting Willie Thomas over at the corner flag. Salford faced the campaign minus several notable forwards who had all retired, including Billy Brown, Ike Lewis, Jack Rhapps and Jack Williams. Fortunately, they still had plenty of experienced packmen on their register, a list supplemented by rugby union signing Tom Harris from Llwynpia, who had represented Somerset.

The opening fixture on 7 September, against Rochdale Hornets in Weaste, proved to be a much tougher challenge than expected and, by half-time and in front of 5,000 fans, Salford trailed 8–2. James – who started his season with a penalty that rebounded in off the upright – temporarily exchanged places with a struggling Dai John at half-back, the latter moved to centre in an effort to change things. The *Salford Reporter* said: "That the Reds captain was getting anxious could be seen by the determined look which his face bore." James began the second half filled with fire, and within 15 minutes had altered the course of the match. He played a prominent role in a stirring passing display that led to Hampson going over in the corner and then, with a typical burst, he charged like a marauding bull towards the Hornets line as he "refused to be brought down by half-a-dozen". James was

113

resisted, but a second Hampson try soon followed which he converted to put Salford ahead, 10–8. There were still plenty of tense minutes remaining and only towards the end, when James closed the scoring at 12–8 with a penalty following a foul on John was the match safe. According to the match summary, James had begun another season at his sparkling best: "Lomas was the shining light of the three-quarter backs, his kicking, tackling and running speaking well for the way in which he kept himself fit during the summer season."

Two days later, Salford took on Halifax at Thrum Hall, grateful for an evening 5.45pm kick-off following a baking hot Monday afternoon. The Reds were 5–0 up after only five minutes and 5–2 at the interval but, in the second half, their hosts got on top to win 12–7, James added a penalty to his earlier conversion. In defeat, it was comforting for Salford officials to see that John and Dave Preston had performed brilliantly at half-back after a worryingly inept display against Rochdale. The *Halifax Courier*, meanwhile, praised the Salford captain: "Jimmy of the Napoleonic stature seemed particularly anxious to see the match go in favour of the Reds, and he worked might and main to secure this end."

Apart from the upcoming New Zealand tour, the other international breakthrough in 1907–08 was the appearance of two Welsh clubs in the Northern Rugby League: Ebbw Vale and Merthyr Tydfil. As a direct result of this expansion, Salford found themselves on a Friday train out of Manchester heading for an overnight stay in Hereford, and resumed their journey to Ebbw Vale on Saturday morning. The accompanying *Salford Reporter* journalist did not seem to appreciate the excursion and said: "The worst part of the inclusion of Welsh clubs in the Union is the long journey". Nor was he too impressed with the Ebbw Vale ground and its facilities: "An altogether different piece of turf to the billiard table at The Willows whilst the arrangements for the spectators are correspondingly primitive." Salford won easily enough, 29–0, with "a most exhilarating display"; their handling of the ball was described as a "real treat" for the spectators – presumably by comparison to the rugby union they were used to watching.

The Reds held a 13–0 lead at the interval but, of greater significance to James, having scored two tries and two conversions during the opening period, was an 'awareness' around the ground during the break that he was six points short off his 1,000th for Salford. Five minutes after the resumption, Hampson's try allowed him to notch another goal, before the great man himself gained possession and beat off several backs before scoring under the posts. He added the extra two points to surpass the magical 1,000, as "the crowd signified their appreciation of this fine performance by loudly applauding the captain of the Reds for his star turn".

Salford welcomed St Helens to The Willows on 21 September, where there was a healthy attendance despite the counter-attraction of horse racing at the Salford-based Castle Irwell Racecourse. James, having received "cheers of recognition" for his feat of scoring 1,000 points, celebrated by being instrumental in the opening try by Hampson after seven minutes. A further three-pointer from Arthur Buckler and a third, from James – who outran

114

the opposition to score under the posts – brought up a 13–2 interval score. Midway through the second half, James burst through the Saints' defence, his perfectly-timed pass put Charlie Garner in. Reportedly, it was a try that "was well worked and once more demonstrated the fact that Lomas is a great player and leader." He was again involved when Hampson scored the fifth try and, through converting three of the goals, ensured a 21–2 victory for his side.

The threequarter line at Salford was remodelled over the course of the season. James and Willie Thomas were still untouchable as the first choice centre pairing, James having inherited a new left-wing partner in Jimmy Hutchinson from the Victoria Rangers club in Warrington. For the next match, at Leeds on Saturday 28 September, another 'Jimmy' was added to the group, newly signed James Henry Cook from Devonport rugby union club appeared on the right wing. In his memoirs, James rated the new arrival highly: "The best scoring wing man I had at Salford was Jimmy Cook. He held the record for try scoring in one season. It proves I wasn't selfish when my wingman would do that." Although Cook was indeed a prolific try scorer, James seems modestly unaware that his own 1906–07 Salford total of 33 tries beat Cook's best return of 26 in 1909–10 and 1910–11.

It was not a great start for Cook – the Reds were beaten 23–2. James was on target with an excellent first half penalty after "customary howling" as he placed the ball. Salford's forwards were outplayed for the first time that season while James was not above criticism, and "gave the impression that the Cumberland match may have been on his mind".

The Cumberland fixture was actually seven days later at Wheater's Field against Lancashire and James once more fired on all cylinders. The *Manchester Guardian* said that "Lomas, who was playing at half, instead of centre threequarter as originally chosen, backed up his forwards in splendid style and showed that even in his old position he is still very capable. He made two beautiful openings in the first ten minutes for [Workington's A.] Brown and [Huddersfield's Bill] Kitchin to score but both of them failed to take his passes." It was Lancashire's Jack Fish who scored first with a try after 15 minutes, Kitchin responded and James converted to give Cumberland a 5–3 interval lead. The Cumbrians, with their forwards dominating, had the better of the second half, although the only additional score was a drop-goal from their full-back Billy Little.

While James was busy in nearby Broughton, Salford took on and beat Leigh 16–8 at The Willows. He was back in Salford colours for the match at Hunslet on 12 October, the day after history was made through the arrival in New Jersey of R.M.S. Lusitania after the fastest ever Atlantic crossing. Unexpectedly, James played at outside-half again, the incumbent Preston was out with a damaged shoulder and replacement, Billy Brady, failed to turn up. With the Reds' other centre, Willie Thomas, unavailable due to an injured instep, the Salford threequarter line consisted of four wingers; Cook, John Cochrane, Hampson and Hutchinson. Under the circumstances Salford did well to earn a 12–12 draw and actually led 9–5 at the interval. James's portion of the scoring was three first-half goals from two penalties and a tremendous effort from the centre of the field after a mark was called by John. There was also an amusing incident in the first half when, with the score 5–5, the match was "considerably delayed through the antics of a dog [Hunslet full-back Herbert Place] eventually capturing the delinquent" before he took it to the touchline.

Hunslet skipper Albert Goldthorpe was his side's saviour, and rescued them with a last minute penalty. Like James, he was a prolific point scorer, although his haul mostly came from his goalkicking ability, and he finished the campaign with 101, the first player to top a century over a season. The *Salford Reporter* scribe was clearly a fan of the legendary player: "Goldthorpe is always so cool and collected on his own ground that he commands the greatest admiration, but in Lomas he usually meets his match as a kicker, and it came not as a surprise when Jimmy opened the scoring with a fine effort." There was, however, a slight criticism of the two men: "Lomas and John were a great pair of half-backs though the captain was rather neglectful of his colleagues, a fault that can also be laid to Goldthorpe's account." In his memoirs, James rated his old rival as one of the finest players and the most accurate goalkicker he played against.

James was again absent for Salford's next match, at Barrow on 19 October, due to another appearance in Cumberland colours. It was a worthwhile journey up to Whitehaven, though, as the 7–3 victory over Yorkshire secured Cumberland's first county championship. In a tight match with defences generally on top, James – again playing in the halves – was twice tackled on the Yorkshire try-line, but was unable to get his name on the score sheet. His Salford colleagues, meanwhile, lost 6–2 at Barrow, a result that cost them their early leadership of the Lancashire League, a new competition that, along with the Yorkshire League, was incorporated into the Northern Rugby League fixtures from that season.

The Lancashire Cup occupied the weekend agenda for 26 October. Salford received a visit from Wigan in the second round, the Reds had a bye in the first. Salford's 3–0 interval lead was increased to 8–0 after James – restored to the centre – converted Jack Spencer's try. Mist started to descend as half-back Johnny Thomas pulled three points back for the Colliers. James re-established Salford's two score advantage with a penalty following a foul on Reds' full-back Albert Mason. The situation looked precarious for Salford after Wigan grabbed a converted try, but they held on to win 10–8. It was a match in which new wingman Cook caught the eye beating James Leytham "3 or 4 times" for speed.

November's fixtures began with a visit from Warrington on the 2nd of the month, the result being an 8–8 draw. James was unable to play through an injured knee, but was back for the following week's fixture – also at home – against Broughton Rangers. Hutchinson delighted the majority of the 11,000 crowd with a try after just three minutes, although it was to be the only first half score. James – who almost got over for a score before the interval, but for a forward pass – came close after the restart but "succumbed to numbers". When Hutchinson grabbed his second, James's conversion opened up an 8-point gap and the Reds eventually succeeded 8–5.

The Cumberland team that defeated Lancashire 7-3 at Wheater's Field on 5 October 1907. Back: H. Hillen (St Helens), W. Winskill (Broughton R), J. Trotter (Broughton R), J. Ferguson (Oldham), W. Dixon (Oldham); front: J. Clampitt (Broughton R), A. Brown (Workington), J. Flynn (Broughton R), J. Owens (Oldham), J. Lomas (Salford), W. Kitchin (Huddersfield), W. Little (Halifax), C. Brown (Barrow). (Photo: Courtesy Mick Harrop)

Salford's 1909 international players with club officials. Back: J. White (trainer), J. Stoddard (director), J. Spencer (England), E. Thomas (Wales), S. Warwick (England), F. Crowshaw (director), V. Wright (secretary); front: A. Buckler (Wales), J. Lomas (England), D. Rees (Wales).

117

Salford received a home draw in the Lancashire Cup semi-final and Oldham travelled to Weaste on 16 November. The match attracted a 10,000 crowd, James provided all the Salford points but it was insufficient, the Roughyeds won 8–7. Oldham led by eight points before James, following a free kick by John, rushed up the field to recover the ball for a touchdown and added the extra points. Losing 8–5, Salford went into the second half full of gusto, James landed a penalty for offside. The Reds tried desperately to find the winning points, but it was not to be. Oldham's display justified their triumph, although James must have regretted hitting a post with a first half penalty.

However, it was another of his goal attempts that caused consternation in the Salford camp. Club officials were dissatisfied with the outcome of the match and protested to that effect at the following Tuesday's Lancashire County Committee meeting at the Grosvenor Hotel in Manchester. James had taken a penalty, the touch judge raised his flag to indicate a goal, but then lowered it to signal 'no goal'. James protested to referee Frank Renton, convinced a goal had been scored. Renton apparently told the Salford captain that he could not overrule his touch judge. The committee, though, dismissed Salford's protest. There were several irate letters in the *Salford Reporter*, 'J.B.', who claimed to be behind the goal, wrote "a perfectly fair goal was registered" while 'Fair Play' was of the opinion that the touch judge "must have had his eyes shut". Both letters suggested the touch judge changed his mind when Oldham full-back Dicky Thomas shook his head.

Salford endured further disappointment when Wigan returned to The Willows the following Saturday, 23 November. In what was Salford's fifth consecutive home game, Wigan gained revenge for their Lancashire Cup exit and won 13–10. On a day of hail, snow and rain that kept the crowd down to around 3,000, Wigan led 10–5 at half-time. A rush by the Salford forwards towards the Colliers' in-goal enabled James to plunge over for a touchdown to which he added his second conversion of the day to level the scores. Winger Joe Miller restored Wigan's lead with a try before the referee killed any thoughts of a late Salford rally by abandoning the game 10 minutes short due to bad light. As the minimum time had elapsed the score stood. Although defeated, James had played well following some indifferent performances – by his standards – over the preceding weeks, probably due to his knee injury, which had happened in the earlier meeting with Wigan.

Salford's run of home fixtures was set to continue on 30 November, but fog caused the postponement of the game with Widnes. Instead, Salford next played at St Helens, and started a run of three convincing victories. The Knowsley Road pitch was very slippery following heavy rain, a situation not helped by a pre-match schoolboys' game. James started the scoreboard ticking with a penalty, the only score in an opening half that ended with Preston badly injuring his knee and being assisted off by Willie Thomas and James. Salford's captain was to the fore yet again after the interval with two tries; he touched down following a dribbling move and then took a wide pass off Cook for the second. Having kicked the goal for the latter, the score stood at 10–0. Cook then claimed his first try for the club and John pitched in with a late try as the gloom descended. James's resultant goal finalised the outcome at 18–0.

The rearranged match with Widnes took place the following Wednesday. The home supporters in The Willows crowd were treated to a comprehensive 26–0 win by their favourites. The Salford forwards were the architects of the one-sided eight-try mauling, Hutchinson grabbed half of them. Unusually, James missed out on the try-fest and converted just one try.

Swinton were the next guests at The Willows three days later for a match that only attracted 5,000. The low derby match attendance was blamed on a lack of interest compared to past meetings; the Lions had slipped alarmingly in the league race over the past few seasons. Salford won 11–0; James failed to enhance any of his side's three tries but, conversely, kicked an awesome first half penalty from just 10 yards inside the Swinton half. Having been described as "brilliant" seven days earlier against St Helens, James's performance was an unusually below-par effort, the *Salford Reporter* said that "Lomas was only moderate and obviously did not relish the attentions of the opposing forwards."

As the Christmas holidays approached, Salford had a date at Oldham on Saturday 21 December. Shortly before the match – which they lost 6–5 – supporters realised that James would not be taking part. He had suddenly returned to Maryport due to the death of his wife's step-father, William Bell, the preceding Thursday. Mr Bell, whose funeral took place the following Monday, had passed away at the Cross Keys Inn where he had lived with James's mother-in-law, Sarah.

James was back for the Christmas Day fixture at Wheater's Field against Broughton Rangers. Losing 8–0 at half-time, he helped engineer a try for Preston, and added a goal that rebounded in off the upright. He again hit the post, but with less fortune, when he attempted a goal from a mark. After the Rangers had stretched their lead to six points, James's conversion of Silas Warwick's try left the Reds only 11–10 behind and "more excitement than ever was manifested by the crowd". But a try by Rangers' winger Billy Harris was the only other score in a tight finish, and the Reds missed out 14–10. Boxing Day saw the appearance of Leeds at The Willows, Salford gained ample revenge for their earlier Headingley defeat with a convincing 20–2 win. Leeds scored first with a penalty from forward H. Brown, but Cook's try, converted by James, put the Reds on the path to victory. Five more tries followed, including one in each half from Salford's leader, although none were converted.

Salford concluded their 1907 schedule just two days later, on Saturday 28 December, with a high profile fixture against the New Zealand tourists. Arriving as the 'All Blacks' – the name attached to their illustrious rugby union touring sides – they are remembered in rugby league folklore as the 'All Golds' due to them forsaking their 'amateur' status. There were approximately 12,000 people present at The Willows for what was the 23rd match of the tour. The Salford team was: Mason; Cook, Willie Thomas, Lomas, Bill Hyam; Preston, John;

119

Arthur Buckler, Harris, Dai Rees, Spencer, Evan Thomas, Warwick. Legendary Australian centre threequarter Dally Messenger – invited to join the New Zealand party – scored two first half tries to put his team 6–0 ahead at the break. James reduced the arrears with an impressive penalty from just inside New Zealand's half, but a further try from Edgar Wrigley gave their guests a 9–2 win. Afterwards, Salford officials put on a post-match dinner at Manchester's Corn Exchange Hotel for the two teams and members of the press. During a round of speeches, James, in his capacity as Salford captain, admitted that it was the first time he had seen the New Zealanders play, and added "they proved themselves the better team" although he pointed out that his own side was suffering from "severe exhaustion" after their Christmas fixtures against Broughton Rangers and Leeds. He also believed that Salford could learn from their style of rugby – a reference to their short, sharp passing and support play, as opposed to the wider passing moves employed by teams like the Reds – and wished them well for the remainder of their visit.

The New Zealand team included Lance Todd at five-eighths (stand-off) who would later make his imprint at The Willows through his management of Salford's 'Red Devils' team in the 1930s. Todd recalled that first experience of The Willows in a newspaper feature published in the early 1930s: "We had a very special interest in Lomas when we were touring, for, after our match with Broughton Rangers [on 19 October], a Manchester sportsman made a fairly substantial bet with one of our chaps that Jimmy would score a try against us if he was playing when we met at Salford. This was shared amongst a few of us, and you can wager we had a scout or two to watch him more than once to get a line on his style of play. When we met Salford, we definitely arranged our team with the one object of tying Jimmy down, and for this purpose Edgar Wrigley and myself were played together at five-eighths, and my set instructions were to work inside (Lomas) on all occasions and drive him out at all costs to Wrigley, where we trusted the great weight and strength of the latter to hold him.

We managed it alright, but that game lives in my memory, because never in my life have I seen a man come tearing and battling his way so desperately and so often, and the punishment he took without the slightest murmur was amazing. He may not have known of the wager, but I wonder what he would have been like had he known!"

Salford celebrated New Year's Day with an 18–12 victory over visitors Wakefield Trinity. Both teams registered four tries, but James's goalkicking was credited as the dividing line between success and failure through his ability to convert three of the Reds' efforts. Salford should have travelled to Warrington on the following Saturday, 4 January, but the match was called off through a frozen pitch. Four days later James was due to play for Cumberland against the New Zealanders at Workington, but was a late withdrawal along with Broughton Rangers' Jack Flynn.

Their absence was not explained in the press although, three days later, both faced New Zealand at Central Park as members of the England team. It was the host nation's first

120

international apart from playing against Other Nationalities. New Zealand had met Wales in the latter's debut on New Year's Day at Aberdare. The England team was: Harry Taylor (Hull); James Leytham (Wigan), Andy Hogg (Broughton Rangers), Lomas (Salford), Percy Eccles (Halifax); Harry Wallace (Hull), Jack Flynn (Broughton Rangers); Jack Beetham (Broughton Rangers), Joe Ferguson (Oldham), Dick Padbury (Runcorn), Asa Robinson (Halifax), Arthur Smith (Oldham), Harry Wilson (Hunslet). The Englishmen won a fast, entertaining match 18–16, although the general opinion of the press was that the visitors looked the slicker, better organised combination and, consequently, were unlucky to lose.

England led 8–5 at half-time. James was instrumental in their second try, scored by Padbury. He recovered a ball fumbled by Wrigley before passing to the Runcorn man who had a clear opening to the try-line. With the score 13–11 to England, Salford's skipper conjured up what proved the winning score; he dribbled the ball into the in-goal area and beat Wrigley and Jim Turtill to the touchdown. His extra points put England 18–11 ahead, and provided just enough breathing space after New Zealand came back with a converted try. England's half-backs, Wallace and Flynn, were, according to 'M.L.S.' of the *Athletic News*, "disappointing" and "did not help their centres by setting up play". The consequence was that both the centres, Hogg in particular, and James were "a trifle old-fashioned and cumbersome in their methods".

James's international call up meant he missed out when the Reds entertained Ebbw Vale on the same day, the first Welsh club to visit Salford since Newport in March 1894 in the club's rugby union era. Unlike their first meeting the previous September, Ebbw Vale performed far better, although Salford, even without James's services, won 15–2.

The following Wednesday, Salford travelled to Runcorn for a fixture previously postponed through Lancashire Cup commitments. There were only about 1,000 spectators at Canal Street, Hyam's try for Salford – James missed the kick – tied up the half-time score at 3–3. A Cook try put Salford ahead although James was again off the mark with his place-kick. He atoned with a touchdown when, according to the *Salford Reporter* he "dribbled splendidly to the Runcorn line where he picked up in marvellous fashion and scored a sensational try under the posts." This time James, described as "the best man on the field" added the goal, although he missed again after Willie Thomas scored. A late unembellished try for Runcorn gave the Reds victory by 14–6.

Three days later, Salford were back in that vicinity to meet Runcorn's neighbours from across the River Mersey, Widnes. It was another successful day for the Reds. A kick by Cook into the Widnes in-goal almost produced the first score, the ball just bounced dead before James, following up, could get a hand on it. Eventually, it was Cook himself that claimed the first try and James's goal gave the Reds a 5–0 advantage at half-time. Salford eventually secured the win 8–5.

The next Saturday, 25 January, Salford won yet again, edging out Hunslet – who were challenging for top place in the league – 7–6 at The Willows. James, having been wide with a penalty moments earlier, notched the first two points with a goal from a mark by John after the latter fielded a clearance kick by Walter Goldthorpe. James later missed the touchline conversion to a Willie Thomas try but, building on a 5–0 interval lead, he landed a penalty following a foul on Mason, which opened up a seven point gap. There was almost a try for James, but he lost possession as he got over the line. Salford then had their fans sweating by conceding two tries, and were fortunate that neither was converted. Hunslet's pack – known as the 'terrible six' – were considered to be their main strength and "although not fast they were persistent and would not be shaken off." It was also said that James – normally so calm and assured – "was apt to lose his temper" during the match. It was a notable success for the Reds because Hunslet created history at the end of the season as the first 'All Four Cups' winners; Northern Rugby League Championship, Challenge Cup, Yorkshire League and Yorkshire Cup.

Salford extended their winning streak on Saturday 1 February by completing the 'double' over Runcorn, 12–0, all the points came from tries. Cook scored the first near the corner flag, James's turn came next when, following a passing move, he received the ball, broke away and beat the defence to score at the corner. Following the interval, the Salford skipper completed his hat trick. He received the ball from Willie Thomas, handed on to Hyam, who returned the compliment with perfect timing to put his leader in near the corner. His final touchdown came after he picked up a stray ball to send Hyam on his way. The wingman beat a defender, slipped two yards short of the try-line, but somehow managed to return the ball for the try. It was Salford's seventh successive league victory, and lifted them to fourth place in the 27-team table behind Oldham, Hunslet and Wigan. James, who had been seen as playing below his usual high standard in recent weeks, produced excellent form in the match which "argued well for the [Challenge] cup ties which are fast approaching."

There was another previously postponed fixture to squeeze in on the following Monday, Salford's good run was slightly blemished through a scoreless draw at Warrington. Heavy rain made conditions difficult underfoot and the two packs dominated proceedings. The Reds managed to rediscover the victory trail the following Saturday with a 2–0 win at Swinton. Watched by 7,000 fans, James hit the upright with a first half penalty, a later attempt, for a foul on Preston, proved more successful, the "keenly contested" match produced no further score after the interval. The *Salford Reporter* repeated the oft-quoted comment that James was "well watched", saying "Lomas was not too pleased at [Albert] Valentine's attentions" clearly indicating that the Swinton centre had been tasked with policing Salford's danger man. The Swinton correspondent claimed in the same newspaper that James "was not nearly as prominent, either in running or kicking, as he usually is, and it was evident to everybody in the ground that he had no relish for the way in which he was frequently brought down."

The key to James's problems may be in a remark that "the strain in his knee spoiled his shooting for goal", which implied that James was carrying an injury against Swinton. If so, it could explain why his goalkicking success rate had fallen off since the turn of the year and his general performances were not as consistently high as usual. It may also have been a factor in him not taking part in any of the three Northern Union versus New Zealand test matches in January and February; the centre slots were shared by Welsh trio Tom Llewellyn (Oldham), Bert Jenkins (Wigan) and Phil Thomas (Leeds).

On the following Saturday, 15 February, while the final test was taking place at Cheltenham, James was in Leigh to help Salford to another win. He stamped his authority on proceedings in the 5th minute, scored a try and added the goal after a rush by Salford towards the Leigh line. It was 8–0 at the half-time break; Leigh reduced the arrears to three points before Cook sealed the match with a brilliant run from Salford's 25-yard line to finish under the posts. James – who was just prevented from scoring earlier off a Preston pass – added the goal for a 13–5 win that moved the Reds up to third place in the league.

Next up was a vital home match with top of the table Oldham, but earlier heavy rain that had flooded sections of the playing surface created a dilemma for Salford's officials. They decided to keep the doors locked to spectators until Oldham arrived, in case they objected to playing and the referee subsequently supported them. Unfortunately, Oldham arrived late and it was not until 3pm that the two captains and referee agreed the game should take place. Consequently, some 13,000 spectators were then admitted to the ground. In the first half they saw James somehow dribble the ball the whole length of the field before Oldham winger George Tyson managed to kick it dead. There was no score in the first half, during which John was taken off injured. He returned later, James had taken his place at half-back in the interim. Salford made the breakthrough when Evan Thomas scored near the posts following the collapse of a move between Ferguson and Birdie Dixon. James added the goal. It was the only score of the match; Salford's 5–0 win was Oldham's first defeat of the season, and ended an unbeaten run covering 30 matches. Having played the match in "wretched conditions" some felt that, although Salford deserved their win, there had been some luck involved. Either way, the *Salford Reporter* had no doubt about James's contribution: "one of the most welcome revelations of the day's play was the form of Lomas who, for once in a way, did himself justice and proved that he is still a great player. He led his men well, and both in footwork and tackling, was a menace to the other side."

Such a noteworthy scalp put Salford into a confident mood for the following week's Challenge Cup first round match with Widnes, who were struggling near the lower reaches of the league table. Further heavy rain, combined with snow showers, had turned The Willows pitch – already badly cut up after the Oldham game – into a parlous state, partly white with snow and partly covered with large helpings of sand. James announced his presence to the Chemicals players when he almost dribbled the ball over for a try, but for winger J. Ditchfield, who just managed to get the ball into touch and nullify the danger. It was Cook who got the first try, the touchline goal from James set up a 5–0 half-time score. Salford scored two further tries in the second half, both goaled by James, before Widnes managed a late penalty. The Reds went through to the next round 15–2. James's rejuvenation was again confirmed by the *Salford Reporter*: "Lomas is rapidly approaching his best form and on a ground that did not lend itself to pace he was exceptionally fast."

Salford had now gone 11 games without defeat since losing to the tourists and, apart from the prospects of another good Challenge Cup run, were handily positioned for a league play-off place. As in previous seasons, though, the Reds mysteriously floundered at the crucial run in. The following Saturday, 7 March, was originally a free weekend but, with their next Challenge Cup match in a fortnight's time clashing with the home game against Halifax, that fixture was brought forward seven days. In spite of good weather, there were only 6,000 present at The Willows for a match that involved two sides pushing for a top-four finish. It was a tight, competitive first half, James's two penalties kept his side in the picture although they were 8–7 down after the first 40 minutes were played. The second half was much the same, Hyam's go-ahead try for Salford was responded to by a Billy Williams touchdown and, with no further scoring, the Reds unbeaten record evaporated by just one point, 11–10. The reverse also pushed them into fourth place behind Oldham, Hunslet and Broughton Rangers.

More disappointment waited at The Boulevard for the second round cup tie with Hull. It started well enough when James landed a goal from the centre of the field amidst "a storm of cheers and yells" from the Salford fans. The Salford skipper – who was cautioned by the referee during a heated first half – tried another ambitious shot from just inside Salford's half that just went under the bar. As half-time approached, he found the target again following a foul on Mason, but Hull went into the second period with an 8–4 lead. Salford were unable to get close to the Hull try-line. James tried and failed with another long-range goal attempt. Disaster then befell James and his colleagues after his clearance kick was charged down by Hull centre Frank Cook who went on to score under the posts, Harry Wallace's goal left the Reds behind 15–4. Towards the end of the game, James's pass put Willie Thomas in under the posts for a try; he added the goal. But Salford were out of the cup 15–9, frustrated at losing to a mid-table team, although Hull – who went all the way to the final – were unquestionably the better team on the day. It was another bitter pill for James, although the *Salford Reporter* exempted him from any blame: "Lomas was head and shoulders the best and from his vigorous play throughout one could see how much he had the matter at heart and how seriously he was affected by the impending result knowing, of course, that he, single-handed, could do little to avert the sequel."

Of course, Salford still had the league play-offs within their sights but that dream, too, came to nothing as they lost three of their four remaining fixtures to slide to ninth place in the final table. The first of those games was at Wigan, another crucial fixture that attracted 15,000, with the Central Park side also aiming for a play-off slot. If the resultant 2–0 defeat was a disaster for Salford's fading ambitions, it was doubly so for James. For the second time in his career he was dismissed, the previous occasion having also been against Wigan at Central Park 12 months earlier. The incident occurred with around 20 minutes left. A melee broke out with Wigan forward Reuben Collier and James both on the ground, kicking at each other. The referee had no hesitation in marching them off.

The *Salford Reporter*, predictably, was on James's side and said: "It should be explained that the Salford captain had been put in possession of the ball and had beaten a couple of men when he was roughly pulled down by Collier and deliberately punched. It has been whispered, but we do not certify for the accuracy of the statement, that this player had been detailed for the special purpose of harassing Lomas, who is greatly feared at Central Park." James, himself, claimed he retaliated, and that after "Collier rushed at him and kicked him [James] handed him off, but the Wigan forward came again and kicked [him] twice". The local paper was of the opinion that the incident "led to [Salford's] downfall". It was after the dismissals that Wigan full-back Jim Sharrock, following several earlier attempts, landed a magnificent drop-goal after catching a punt by Salford's John. Perhaps unusually for Edwardian times, and carried away in the euphoria of the moment, recent signing Lance Todd "as a mark of appreciation of this fine effort kissed the goalkicker".

James was suspended for two matches; a 6–5 defeat at Rochdale and a 15–2 home win over Barrow two days later on Easter Monday. The last match of the season was at Wakefield Trinity. James resumed his place in the centre and his try produced Salford's only points in an 11–3 loss. He broke through the defence from a pass by half-back Brady. The *Salford Reporter* said: "Had it not been for the fine form of the Salford captain the score would have been a larger one. But one man does not make a team and when that man is 'spotted' there is not much chance for him." Salford had faded abysmally in the league race, although the same paper believed it had some of the answers: "There is not the slightest doubt that the absence of Lomas led up to the disasters at Wigan and Rochdale but the real weakness is amongst the forwards."

With James considered the mainstay of the side, it must have been with nervous trepidation that supporters read the speculation that filtered through towards the season's end. It appeared to suggest that his future was in the balance with the possibility of a move away from The Willows. On 28 March the *Salford Reporter* said: "For some three seasons it has been freely rumoured that Lomas wanted to go to Wigan and that the Colliers were prepared to pay well for his transfer and at present there is a belief in some quarters that at the end of the season an attempt will be made to bring matters to an issue. Of course the truth or otherwise of all this is buried in the bosoms of the directors of the respective clubs, but the reception that the Salford captain receives at Central Park does not point to its accuracy, though football crowds are as fickle as they are prejudiced."

The story implied that Wigan had been on James's trail since the 1905–06 season. Although not reported at the time, there could be an element of truth in that. It was certainly a move that could have, arguably, benefitted all three parties; Salford, Wigan, and James himself. Salford had clearly been strapped for cash for some time, the 'A' team was temporarily disbanded for 1905–06 and there had been letters published during that season by supporters disgruntled at the lack of quality recruits. Their predicament was something that Wigan officials were clearly aware of and, in 1906–07, they offered to stage the Salford versus Wigan Challenge Cup tie after the Reds had received a home draw. Although, as previously stated, an 'A' team match had been switched from The Willows to Central Park a few weeks earlier the idea was rejected and James played an outstanding part in Salford's subsequent victory.

Wigan had the financial clout; their crowds had steadily increased since their move to Central Park in 1902, which allowed them to recruit from near and far. There could also be no question that James's stunning display against Wigan in the 1907 Challenge Cup match would have reminded them in no uncertain way of his spell-binding talent. The mid-season signing of New Zealand tourist Todd had been the final piece in putting together one of the Northern Union's most famed threequarter lines; Leytham, Jenkins, Todd and Miller. The earlier signing of James could possibly have led to his name becoming part of that famous foursome instead of Todd. Who can say? James's carrot would have been that, apart from probably receiving a higher wage at Wigan, he may have reasoned that, having won nothing to date with Salford, he had a more realistic chance of honours with Wigan who were building a team that had future success written all over it. The question was: were the rumours true in the first place?

12. 1908–09: A shock in store

James Lomas had a shock in store for the Salford directors and the club's supporters in the summer of 1908. It was not, as had originally been feared, a desire to pursue his career at Central Park, but it was his written notice that he was quitting Salford and, in all probability, the NU code in general. It was at Salford's Annual General Meeting in June that the club secretary, Victor Wright, addressed the shareholders with the bad news: "It was through no fault of the directors or officers. He left entirely from a business point of view... to be the landlord of a hotel in Maryport. He had been satisfied during the seven seasons he had played with Salford. If ever it lay in his power to assist the Salford club he would do so." The chairman, Fred Hampson, added "Many people thought the directors had been unkind to Lomas, but that was not so. It was not in their nature to be unkind to anyone. And if he ever came back to Salford we will give him a hearty welcome." A shareholder asked if there was any prospect of him returning, the chairman replied "They had their eyes open".

The intention of the Lomas family was to leave their home in Lindsay Street, Salford, where their two eldest daughters had been born, and take over at the Cross Keys Inn where Annie's mother, Sarah Bell, had been the innkeeper, but had been widowed the previous December. There was, however, to be a twist in the tale as the 1908–09 season got closer. The *Salford Reporter* announced: "Considerable interest has been aroused as to the intention of Lomas for the coming season, and our readers will be glad to know that on Wednesday [19 August] he finally decided to sign on [with Salford for the new season]. For the present he will travel from Maryport on the Friday or Saturday and his inclusion in the team will be heartily welcomed."

It was a major boost for everyone associated with the club, but what had made James change his mind? Did the lure of playing rugby prove too irresistible? Was the hotel trade not quite what he expected? On the latter point he did not remain as a hotelier for long. He did, indeed, commute from Maryport for matches once the season began and was still doing so until the end of November, at least. But James and his family were certainly back in the bosom of Salford by 21 January 1909 when his third daughter, Olive, was born at their new home address on Broadway. James had just had his 29th birthday at the start of the 1908–09 season, so there were still several years' rugby left in him. Of course, it is very likely that Salford enticed him back with an offer he could not refuse, although there were still concerns about the club's finances after they announced an adverse balance of £114 on the previous season.

It was to be a landmark season in other respects. Hot on the heels of New Zealand, there was to be a tour by Australia. Both countries had set up their own domestic competitions. Expansion continued as well in South Wales with the addition of four more clubs although, unlike the Antipodes, the Welsh adventure died out by the start of the First World War. Salford held two pre-season public trials. Collections at both were donated to

127

Salford Royal Hospital. James was selected for the second of the trials on Saturday 29 August, but was one of five players who did not appear. However, there seems to have been nothing sinister reported about that, and a full strength line-up was announced for the opening match.

It had been reported that "Lomas is sanguine that, with the assistance of the strong team he will have in charge, the position of Salford will be considerably raised in the league results." There were the usual new signings with two of them destined to make an impact; Bernard Mesley, a centre from Twickenham rugby union club who had represented Middlesex, and Ephraim Curzon, "a big local forward" who hailed from the Manchester area, but had recently been playing rugby union for Kirkcaldy in Scotland. It was not the best of baptisms. Salford's previous end-of-season form continued and produced three defeats.

The first was against visitors Runcorn, "always an attractive fixture", on Saturday 5 September. James gave the scoreboard operator his first piece of exercise with a penalty after he had been tripped. He then scored the first try. He touched down in the corner after taking a pass from Dave Preston as the latter was about to be tackled. James's excellent conversion had given Salford a 7–2 lead, but by half-time it was 7–7 and when the final whistle sounded, 18–7 to Runcorn. The *Salford Reporter* summed it up: "To say home supporters were surprised is to put it mildly, but the much fancied Reds failed in what was regarded as their strongest point, that of lasting the full 80 minutes." Although Salford were already 13–7 down at the time, it is worth noting that Dai John was carried off with an injury, which reduced the Reds to 12 men. At least James received some praise: "Lomas was in fine form and the home supporters look forward to a fine season from the popular captain provided he steers clear of accidents. His dash was a marked feature of his display and the idea that he had lost his speed was quickly dispelled."

The following week, at the Watersheddings, a crowd in excess of 20,000 turned up to see Oldham comfortably see off Salford's challenge. James worked hard in the first half and, in one instance, dribbled the ball through "all opposition" only to see it kicked dead when he reached the Oldham in-goal area. The Reds were 12–0 down at the break and it was 20–0 when James got the ball over the try-line, only for the 'score' to be disallowed. Eventually, Arthur Buckler succeeded, but James hit the crossbar with his failed goal attempt. Willie Thomas rounded off the score at 20–5 with a drop-goal, a token effort that made little difference to the final result.

The third defeat came when Wigan, embarking on what would be a tremendous season for them, well and truly trounced Salford at The Willows 36–7. James scored all Salford's points. He closed the first half scoring, when his team was already 11 points down; he recovered the ball following Reds' winger Jimmy Cook's kick and then, after rounding James Leytham, scored beneath the posts and added the goal. His other two points came from a penalty. Well before the end, many of the disappointed home supporters among the 6,000 crowd began to leave the ground. It was a black day for Salford and was no better for

James. Wigan's Lance Todd – playing at centre – was lauded as the outstanding performer; the *Salford Reporter* said: "All the afternoon he gave Lomas a big handful and it was no doubt an eye opener to the Salford captain when the New Zealander got up after being tackled, and sprinted to the home line [and] scored at the corner." It added that James had given "a moderate display and lost his temper because Todd got the better of him."

They are interesting comments. James was rarely outplayed, but maybe he was fighting a losing battle given Wigan's superiority on the day. As for his temper, it was an observation that had been made more than once in recent seasons, although he was generally acknowledged as being a composed character, albeit with a very competitive nature. Todd, meanwhile, praised James when writing about him in the 1930s, and gave a unique insight into the Cumbrian's qualities. Writing about former Salford players he said: "The greatest of course, was Jimmy Lomas, probably the dourest and gamest player the game has known. Short of inches, but wonderfully endowed by nature with great strength he was the hardest and straightest runner I have met. He may, perhaps, have lacked just a yard or two of pace, but was fast enough for most purposes. Jimmy had no use for going round his opponents, and anybody who went for him above the knees surely got to know all about it. A great goal kicker and a real demon near the line, his one fault, if fault he had, was that he sometimes went just that yard too far before passing, thus allowing his partner in the movement being covered, but Jim had such unlimited confidence in his ability to get through that one can overlook this."

Salford broke their duck the following week with a win at Broughton. James played at outside-half, John was the 'scapegoat' after his poor display against Wigan. The match also marked the debut of Mesley, while the 'old warhorse' Billy Brown returned to the pack, having previously retired. It was a better performance by Salford who, viewed by 12,000 spectators, led 7–3 at half-time, James converted an opening try by Cook and Mesley demonstrated his prowess as a kicker with a penalty from halfway. The Rangers were handicapped through full-back Billy Barlow, who had been carried off injured in the first half and – although he returned – did not participate in the second. James scored another goal following a mark from Preston and then, with the match finely balanced at 9–5 to Salford, he scored the try that won it. He gathered up a weak clearance kick by Billy Harris, and handed off two of the Rangers players before touching down. His goal made the final score 14–5. James was a hero once more, the *Salford Reporter* confirmed: "Lomas had a grand game at half, and his presence there is for the benefit of the team."

James had Cumberland commitments seven days later, Saturday 3 October, as did forward Silas Warwick. The trip to Workington was a fairly short one for James, whose 'new' Maryport home was in close proximity. Their bid to retain the county championship did not get off to a good start, as they lost 15–8 to Lancashire. As usual their forwards were the mainstay of the team and "rushed the scrummages in the approved Cumberland style". At first it paid off, an early try to Lancashire by George Tyson was responded to by his Oldham club-mate Billy Dixon. James converted the latter and then, having supported a break by Hunslet's Billy Eagers, burst through for a try. It gave Cumberland an 8–3 half-time lead, but the second 40-minute spell belonged to Lancashire.

Salford, meanwhile, enjoyed a second success, and beat visitors Warrington 14–7. Although the Australians were opening their tour that day against Welsh newcomers Mid-Rhondda at Tonypandy, 14 members of their squad – which had been training at The Willows – were at the match. There were about 3,000 present when James made his return to the Salford team at Widnes. Despite the praise foisted on him following his display at Wheater's Field, James was picked in the centre, as he had been the previous week with Cumberland. John joined Preston at half-back. Mesley – who kicked a penalty from halfway and was praised for his tackling – struck up a good centre partnership with James. Salford led 3–2 at the break, James then augmented the first of two tries he set up for Cook on the way to a 15–2 verdict. The Salford captain was singled out for his fine kicking throughout an untidy match that was strewn with penalties and was "likely to become a record!"

The Reds had a welcome rest from league action on 17 October when they entertained the Australians in the fifth match of their tour. It was a prestigious fixture for the club but one that – not for the first time – brought it into conflict with Cumberland. The Cumbrians were to meet Yorkshire at Huddersfield on the same day and indicated to Salford that James, John Cochrane and Silas Warwick would "be called upon". The Salford directors, having met on the preceding Tuesday, made representations to "the proper quarters". They stressed the importance of the match to Salford and the value of the presence of their players, James in particular. Selection of the team was postponed pending a response, but in the end, Cumberland exercised their right and Salford took on the Kangaroos without them, and produced an exciting draw 9–9. As a postscript, and while Cochrane and Warwick represented Cumberland in a 30–0 defeat, James did not take part, although there is no explanation as to why. Maybe the Cumberland authorities felt it was prudent to omit him considering the controversy or maybe they were trying to prove a point. Whatever the reason, politics beyond his control had left him to idle away an afternoon when both his club and county were involved in high profile fixtures.

James resumed with Salford on 24 October for a match at Rochdale. He again played at outside-half in place of John, the Reds retained the same threequarter line that did so well against Australia. There were 5,000 present at the Athletic Grounds "who at times were anything but sportsmanlike in their treatment of Lomas" so one could imagine the scene when he thwarted Rochdale winger Kirk, who had looked a certain scorer until James shoved him into touch. Willie Thomas scored the opening try under the posts, but Mesley – who appeared to now be sharing the goalkicking duties with James – just missed the goal. James got his chance and kicked the ball between the uprights from a mark, so Salford led 5–0 at half-time. In the second half, with the score 5–2 following a Hornets penalty and the home team showing signs of taking control, James rallied his troops. He almost registered a try, just losing the ball as he went over, but it lifted the Reds. Cook scored in the corner and Curzon did likewise beneath the posts. James converted the latter and Salford won 13–2. The *Salford Reporter* said: "Only the generalship of Lomas saved the match, and to him in great measure belong the honours of success. Cool and level headed under severe provocation the Salford captain led his men by personal example to victory and two-thirds of the points were his by right. Seldom has the popular Cumbrian kicked and tackled better or been more in the thick of the fray and it is an open question what would have happened in his absence."

Saturday 31 October marked the closing of the London Olympic Games, held primarily at the White City Stadium – a future rugby league venue – which had been specifically built for the event. On the same day, the Reds were on the road again and travelled to St Helens to record their fifth consecutive league win, four of them away from home. On a bright sunny day, there was another 5,000 crowd to again witness Willie Thomas grab the first touchdown of the afternoon. When the second half commenced, the Saints had moved ahead 8–3, but a try by Cook and goal from James levelled up the scoring. It regenerated Salford's spirits, Evan Thomas went over from a scrum. James – who was back in the centre, but closely marked throughout the match – obliged with the extra two points to complete a 13–8 victory.

The Lancashire Cup provided a distraction on the following Saturday, Salford faced a tough first round tie at Oldham. Having originally been selected at centre, James found himself back in the halves as a last minute replacement for John. The resultant 20–5 defeat replicated the score for their league visit to Watersheddings earlier in the season. As in their previous meeting, there was another 20,000 crowd. They saw the home side dominate the opening half to build up a 20–0 interval lead. There was some consolation for the Reds' fans when Arthur Buckler picked up a stray ball and booted it towards the Oldham line, James got hold of it and charged forward. When he was tackled, the ball fell behind him, but he recovered it and forced his way over near the goal, then added the extra points. On the lighter side, the match incorporated Mayoral involvement. A recent cotton strike that had hit the Oldham area had been resolved partly though the intervention of Alderman Isidor Frankenburg, Salford's Mayor, and he was invited to kick-off as a token of appreciation. Oldham's Mayor, Dr Robert Gourley, did likewise in the second half.

It was back to the league and a visit from Leeds on Saturday 14 November. Only 4,000 turned up, partly blamed on the counter-attraction of Broughton Rangers playing Oldham at Wheater's Field. James was again at outside-half, a position he kept until the turn of the year. John, meanwhile, was played at full-back for the first time, and stayed there for virtually every game until the end of the following season. James kicked a penalty and then added a try after dribbling the ball right through the Leeds defence to go over near the posts; his conversion attempt failed. Following a passing move that also involved Willie Thomas and Cook, James raced over for his second, the conversion was successfully entrusted to Mesley. Before half-time, the latter failed with a penalty attempt following a foul on James. A drop-goal by Leeds forward Jim Birch was responded to by James's third try, again he dribbled the ball towards the line to score beneath the posts. He added the goal and was also successful after Bill Hyam touched down; the closing score was 20–2 to Salford. It was their sixth consecutive league win. The Salford captain must have enjoyed himself, the local paper described his match as "an afternoon out", and added that "as an attacking force Lomas is almost irresistible and although you cannot have too good a man as a custodian [full-back] he would obviously be wasted in the last line of defence."

The match with Leeds had taken place after the Headingley side had agreed to bring forward an end-of-season fixture to plug a gap in Salford's schedule caused through Halifax's involvement in the Yorkshire Cup semi-finals. Instead, the Halifax team visited The Willows on the following Wednesday afternoon and proved themselves the tougher of Salford's two West Yorkshire opponents. They swept into a 9–0 lead with three tries, James – as only he could – dragged Salford back into the reckoning when he burrowed his way through the sternest of defences for an excellent try, to which he added the goal. The momentum turned towards the Reds and, when James kicked the ball into the corner, Cook beat Halifax's Billy Little to the touchdown. Mesley missed the goal, but a rejuvenated Salford entered the second half only 9–8 down. Salford continued their positive attitude in the second half and again James was to the fore. He aimed another kick towards the opposition line which almost produced a score for Arthur Buckler, and then was just wide with a penalty goal attempt. He followed that up with one of his irresistible charges, took possession and dribbled at the opposition line, the ball was just kicked dead as he was about to place a hand on it. Salford were on top, but could not get that vital go-ahead score and, as so often happens, it was Halifax that had the last word through a late penalty by Little, the Reds lost 11–8.

Salford returned to Wheater's Field on the Saturday to take on Broughton Rangers in a benefit match for their half-back Sam James who was suffering from consumption. Salford lost 24–21. James – who had made his usual journey from Maryport to take part – landed three goals; a first half penalty plus a conversion in each half. Sam James was the third eldest of five brothers from South Wales who played for the Rangers. Sadly, his illness took his life the following March; it had also claimed elder brother Evan in 1901.

November's programme concluded with a match at Central Park against Wigan. Salford appeared to have a chance after taking a 2–0 lead just before half-time when James banged over a penalty after a foul on John. It was only towards the end of the match that Wigan roused the 8,000 crowd when New Zealander Massa Johnston scored a try after he charged down the ball from a clearance by John. Leytham's goal gave the Colliers a 5–2 victory. Although beaten, James, "making good use of the ball in every way", and his half-back partner Preston earned praise for their contribution to a great game.

132

James had a busy seven-match schedule during December, including six with Salford. There was another 8,000 at The Willows on the 5th for Swinton's visit and James, as he did so often, started the scoring. His two penalties gave the Reds a 4–0 lead. His next manoeuvre was to burst through the Lions' defence into open territory before he passed to Willie Thomas, who touched down after confusing the opposition with a dummy pass to the supporting Hyam. James obliged with the goal, the Reds turned round with a nine point advantage. Willie Thomas scored his second try, in the corner, James – in the closing stages – put his name on the score-sheet once more when he took the ball off the feet of his rivals and dribbled it under the posts for a try described as "a characteristic Lomas effort". He added the extras for a 17–0 triumph. James had again been the dominant force, the *Salford Reporter* commented that "whenever the home captain gained possession there was always trouble for the visitors defence."

Salford were less successful seven days later at Runcorn, where the general consensus was that the Reds were badly let down by their forwards. James was exempt from blame; he worked hard throughout, but his two first half penalties were the only response to two earlier unconverted tries by the Linnets. Their hosts added two more tries after the break and converted the latter, which took Runcorn to a comfortable 14–4 lead. James was injured at this point because he had been "badly kicked" and play was stopped for a few minutes. He was able to resume, but it was centre Jim Butterworth's drop-goal that gave Runcorn the final say in their 16–4 win.

The following Wednesday, 16 December, Salford began a run of three home games, all were won. There were only 2,000 in the ground for the afternoon clash with reigning champions Hunslet, and "the genius of Lomas" ensured success. The *Salford Reporter* said that "the play behind the scrimmage was entirely dominated by the versatile and dashing Lomas who, by means of his strong running, coupled with judgement in parting with the ball at the right moment, was the most aggressive individual on the field." Inspired by their leader, Salford took a 6–0 interval lead, courtesy of two Cook tries. James's renowned defence faltered when Fred Farrar got past him for a try in the corner, but it was a temporary blip. His pass sent Willie Thomas racing past three defenders for another touchdown. The Salford skipper converted and the Reds claimed two further tries – sandwiching a second effort from Farrar – and came out on top, 17–6.

There was another poor crowd when St Helens appeared three days later, the 2,500 attendance was blamed on the severe weather with rain falling heavily. Nonetheless, it was an entertaining game, James again played at his best or, at least, the best that was possible given the state of the pitch. St Helens crept into an 8–2 lead; a goal from James from a Willie Thomas mark provided the home points. The half-time score, though, was more respectable, James's penalty and a try by Mesley reduced the deficit to one point. However, it looked serious for the Reds when Hyam's obstruction-try was met with two touchdowns by Saints' winger Tom Barton, to give the visitors a 14–10 lead. James rescued his troops after Cook dribbled the ball into the Saints 25-yard area; he took over to score a try near the posts and his conversion just sneaked a 15–14 win.

The trio of successes was completed on Christmas Day with the derby against Broughton Rangers. In contrast to the Reds' previous game, the weather was pleasant and the ground good. An obstruction-try awarded to George Ruddick, converted by Claude James, gave the visitors a 5–0 advantage but, after James narrowly missed with two penalty attempts, the Reds were level at half-time when he kicked the goal from Mesley's try. The Salford captain finally landed a penalty, given for an incorrect play-the-ball, to put his team ahead, 7–5. Mesley and James were in great form, and they pushed Salford further in front, 12–5, through Mesley's second touchdown, converted by James. Rangers struck back. Andy Hogg's try coupled with Claude James's second conversion, created great excitement in the ground with Salford only 12–10 up. James again came up trumps. He got the ball from a scrum in midfield and raced towards the line – "the brushing aside of three men was the merest child's play to the famous half-back" – before he shrugged off Billy Barlow to score near the corner. Mesley added the goal with a brilliant touchline strike and he was on target again with an excellent shot from a mark made by Curzon. The final score was 19–10.

Salford's Boxing Day fixture was at Mather Lane, where they were just edged by Leigh, and lost 5–3, having taken the lead through a first half try from Hyam. James missed the goal and was unlucky in the second half when he got into the Leigh in-goal area with one of his trademark solo charges, but was stopped from grounding the ball by a posse of defenders. Towards the end of a scrappy game, Salford were awarded a penalty. James elected to kick the ball skywards towards the Leigh line in the hope of a winning try, rather than attempt an equalising goal. The local paper suggested that the latter option would "apparently have been more productive!" The result left Salford with a mid-term record of 10 wins and seven defeats in the league, which placed them 10th of the 27 teams.

James was required by England for his next two matches, and represented his country against Wales and Australia. Wheater's Field was the setting for the England versus Wales meeting on Monday 28 December. England won convincingly 31–7. James was the outstanding performer; he scored a try and five conversions. The *Salford Reporter* said "such was his form that nobody on the other side could adequately cope with him." Afterwards, the England selectors named their team to face Australia just five days later; James retained his place in the centre.

On Saturday 2 January James faced Australia for the first time. Ironically, the international was at Fartown, Huddersfield, the very ground where his presence had been required by Cumberland in mid-October, which caused him to withdraw from Salford's clash with the tourists. Picked as team captain, he certainly made the most of his opportunity in England's 14–9 win, 'Forward' in the *Athletic News* wrote that: "James Lomas of Salford was the leader of the [England threequarter] line. Rarely have I seen the old Maryport player more determined. Tasks that other players would have hesitated to take were cheerfully accepted by Lomas." The *Manchester Guardian* echoed those comments: "Lomas was the best player on the field and on his present form is probably the best centre in the Union." The only blot in his copybook was that on a slippery, heavy pitch, he failed with all four conversion attempts; he had scored his side's opening points from a penalty.

On the day that James played at Huddersfield, his Salford colleagues were at Barrow, and won 16–6. During the second half Arthur Buckler was sent off, alongside Barrow forward Chris Brown, following an altercation, the pair shook hands as they left the field. With James back in the side the Reds added two more victories with home wins over Rochdale Hornets, 18–3, and Leigh, 27–5. The game with Rochdale was plagued by foggy conditions, "a typical Scotch mist" according to one description. The players were difficult to spot by the 3,000 that turned up. Most expected it to be abandoned before the end, and so it was, but not until just five minutes remained, so the result stood. Cook had to cry off, so James was back in the centre in a reshuffled back division. Salford led 13–0 at half-time, the last of three tries was scored by James, who beat off numerous opponents before he touched down, following a pass from Curzon. James also found the target with two conversions, added a third during the second half following his second try, scored beneath the posts after he and Hyam had run the ball into Hornets' territory. Not surprisingly, the local writer had difficulty in covering events, but saw enough to confirm that James was "in rare form and scoring his tries in the old sweet way by thoroughly beating what, in the main, was a fine defence."

He was back at outside-half for the visit of Leigh, a position he kept – with a couple of exceptions – for the rest of the season. It was watched by a slightly better attendance of around 4,000, those that turned up were entertained by seven tries from Salford. James played a part in most of them. He claimed the fifth for himself after half-time after he received the ball from Preston just inside Leigh's 25-yard area. Handing off all the opponents who attempted to stop his progress, he finished under the posts after a move that was described as "probably an eye opener to the Leigh players". The resultant conversion was one of three he succeeded with in a match hailed as one of Salford's best performances of the season so far. The *Salford Reporter*, yet again, confirmed that "Lomas was, of course, the leading man of the Reds".

James achieved another personal first on the following Saturday, 23 January – two days after the birth of his third daughter Olive – when he was selected for the NU's second test against Australia. With home officials using the series to promote and, hopefully, expand the game, the first test had taken place at London's Park Royal, then the ground of Queens Park Rangers AFC. It produced an exciting 22–22 draw, but only attracted just over 2,000 spectators. This time it was another association football club venue, Newcastle United's at St James Park. The Northern Union was rewarded with a 22,000 crowd. The NU team was: Harry Gifford (Barrow), Billy Batten (Hull), Bert Jenkins (Wigan), Lomas (Salford), George Tyson (Oldham), Ernie Brooks (Warrington), Johnny Thomas (Wigan), Bill Jukes (Hunslet),

John Higson (Hunslet), Dick Silcock (Wigan), Billy Longworth (Oldham), Arthur Smith (Oldham), Asa Robinson (Halifax).

It was an excellent test debut for James. He first converted the opening try by Thomas and then, having had the ball passed to him by Brooks, the *Athletic News* said he "indulged in one of his characteristic dashes and [Australian full-back Mick] Bolewski had little chance of checking the impetuous Cumbrian". James touched down near the corner flag, his excellent shot at goal rebounded back off an upright, so the NU had an 8–0 interval advantage. In the second half, James slotted over a penalty before Dally Messenger, who was in his second tour following his 'guest' status with New Zealand, scored what was described as the "try of the match". Evading one defender after another, he placed the ball beneath the posts and added the goal, the score was then 10–5. The NU made the match safe with a try from Tyson and, in the final minutes, James landed a drop-goal to cement a 15–5 victory.

Athletic News correspondent 'Forward' was delighted by James: "His handling of the team was admirable, and his punting always judicious. He found touch in a manner which I can only describe as marvellous, and the numerous penalty kicks were invariably used to advantage. His strong rushes always needed Colonial attention and when Lomas had the ball the heavyweights of the opposition were generally requisitioned. And they were needed too." The *Manchester Guardian* said: "Lomas played a remarkably clever game, and although faced by Messenger he managed during the afternoon to score a try and kick three goals. In fact his brilliant all-round work was the chief feature on the Northern Union side and, on his present form, Lomas is undoubtedly the finest centre in the Union."

Although the trip to Northumberland would have been arduous and time consuming, he was probably quietly relieved that his test call-up exempted him from Salford's match at Ebbw Vale on the same day, particularly in the light of what transpired. The Salford party left Manchester's London Road (now Piccadilly) railway station on Friday afternoon bound for an overnight stay in Newport. On Saturday morning, they arrived in Ebbw Vale only to be told that the match was off; the frost-ridden pitch was too hard and rutted.

Salford's next venue was a bit easier to reach with a fixture against Widnes in Weaste. Lowly-placed Widnes shocked the Reds with an early try; James eventually put his side ahead 5–3 after a magnificent goal from touch, which followed Mesley's try. It gave the home side impetus and, after James had sent the ball back into Widnes territory with a beautifully judged kick, he took possession from the resultant scrum and beat off the opposition for a try that had fans roaring their approval. It took the Reds into half-time 8–3 ahead, and Salford eventually won 14–8. The Reds just about deserved the verdict but, once more, James was the inspiration. The *Salford Reporter* said: "As it was, it was only the resourcefulness of Lomas that kept the Reds attack together, and with his judicious kicking the Salford captain played a great part in the victory."

136

James and Annie, seen here in a Maryport photographic studio, contemplated a permanent return to the seaport town during the summer of 1908.
(Photo: Courtesy Rob Dellar)

His excellent form justified James's place in England's next match, played the following Wednesday, 3 February, and – as with the test series – the NU saw a development opportunity, and took the game to Glasgow's Celtic Park, the first played by the code in Scotland. The attendance, on a day of drizzling rain, was only about 3,000 and they looked lost in the vast stadium. The match contained an amazing turn around in fortune. England led 17–2 midway through the second half, James had embellished all his team's three tries and succeeded with a first half drop-goal after "steadying himself" at the halfway line. Australia, though, staged a great rally with three converted tries to tie the result, 17–17.

James was certainly seeing plenty of the countryside because the next day he was in Carlisle to face the Australians again. This time it was on behalf of Cumberland at Devonshire Park, the then home of Carlisle United Football Club. James was the only player in the Cumbrian team to have played the previous day, but 11 of the Australians took part in both matches, including their entire back division. Perhaps, under those circumstances, it was little wonder that the fresher Cumbrian side, led by their powerful pack in wet and muddy conditions, won 11–2. The *Manchester Guardian* recorded that: "Lomas played a good game for Cumberland and his try – which he converted – in the second half was a fine effort." Those five points came at a time when the Cumbrians were clinging to a narrow 3–2 half-time lead and, effectively, turned the match in their direction.

The Salford captain's unrelenting schedule rolled on with club matches quickly following at Wakefield Trinity, on Saturday 6 February, and Ebbw Vale two days after that. Salford won both as they continued to rise up the league ladder in pursuit of an appearance amongst 'the charmed quartet,' in other words, the top four play-off places. The *Salford Reporter* remarked that, at Wakefield, the home supporters were "chivalrous enough to give Lomas a great reception on entering the field and, generally speaking, behaved themselves much better than the average Yorkshire crowd!" A possible reason for James's warm welcome may have been that posters advertising the match read "Come and see England's greatest threequarter and the miniature full-back," the latter reference concerned the vertically challenged, but supremely talented John. The kick-off was delayed by seven minutes as the teams "were put through the ordeal of photography".

Trinity led by two points at the interval thanks to a Jimmy Metcalfe penalty. James looked slightly tired due to his "knocking about" during the previous week. However, he was on his mettle in the second half when he put the Reds 3–2 in front by racing into the Trinity in-goal on the end of some excellent passing from Salford's backs. The hosts regained their lead, though, a converted try put them 7–3 up. But James and his half-back colleague Preston showed great form, and initiated one attacking move after another, the former – evidently revived – brought his side level with two penalties. With 15 minutes remaining, Salford were knocking on the Wakefield door, but it remained bolted until five minutes from time when the speedy Cook evaded three Trinity defenders for a try. Although James was off target with the goal, Salford held on for a hard fought, narrow 10–7 win. Salford's match winners were credited as being James, who "as unfit as he was, was the mainspring", Preston, Cook and Mesley, who all "worked with a will".

An unchanged team took on the demanding excursion to Ebbw Vale after their wasted trip a couple of weeks earlier. Salford won 20–6 against "a disappointing and disorganised" Welsh side. James was singled out as "the shining light" of Salford's team. The *Salford Reporter* said "he made the home defence look small on several occasions [and] it was chiefly to his ingenuity that Salford owed their success, as he had a hand in practically every movement which brought about tangible results." He scored the third of Salford's four tries just before half-time; he burst through the defence in his usual manner to cross the try-line. His two first half conversions were followed by two second half penalties, the first a spectacular long range shot.

The following Saturday Salford entertained Barrow, the Reds' 29–2 victory was their seventh on the run. James scored the Reds' second try just before the interval and added the goal for an 8–0 turnaround lead. Five more tries followed for the home side in the second half, James improved three of them. The *Barrow News* correspondent 'Cosmo' commented that "Lomas at half-back was a great power. He had something to do with every bit of scoring on his side. He has done well this season had Lomas, whether for his club or in the inter-colonial matches."

Two days further on – Monday 15 February – James was at Villa Park, Birmingham, representing the NU in the final test against Australia, his 11th match of 1909. He missed a simple looking goal attempt following Johnny Thomas's try under the posts that had opened the score, although he subsequently had a significant role in the passing move that led to Tyson's winning touchdown. This time his kick, from the touchline, was better struck, but went just wide. The NU won 6–5 to clinch the first Anglo-Australian series.

The next port of call for James was Headingley on Saturday 20 February, where Salford's push towards a top-four finish received a hefty jolt. The Reds' forwards held their own against the Leeds pack and James's kicking throughout was exemplary but, as happened in so many games, he was, rightly, singled out by the Leeds defence as the danger man. Closely monitored throughout the game, Leeds strangled his supply of possession to the threequarter line at source. True, he began the scoring with a penalty but, by half-time, his side had conceded two tries and trailed 8–2. The deficit extended to 13–2 before James landed a second penalty and Silas Warwick grabbed a touchdown. The Reds lost 13–7, their first league defeat since Boxing Day.

The following weekend Salford had a break from their league campaign when they entertained Dewsbury in the Challenge Cup first round, watched by approximately 6,000 supporters, 5,500 paid at the turnstiles. Unlike their infamous 2–0 victory at Crown Flatt in the 1902 competition – the only two survivors of which were Dewsbury forward Kilburn and James – Salford won far more comfortably although there were still a few controversial incidents. Just before half-time Salford forward Tom Coates was sent off for fouling Dewsbury full-back Jack Garrity, and then, in the second half, the visitors' half-back Everson was dismissed for punching Preston. It left Dewsbury short of both their half-backs as A. Brayshaw did not return to the fray after the interval due to a broken finger. It was described in the *Salford Reporter* as a "typical cup-tie full of exciting incidents and robust tackling." James hit an upright with a goal attempt from a mark before succeeding with two penalties as the Reds built a 7–0 first half lead. After the interval, there was a third penalty from the Cumbrian, followed by a try when he accepted a return pass from Cook. As the second half wore on, the one man disadvantage made the task more hopeless for Dewsbury and, when Cook completed a hat-trick, converted by James, Salford led 20–0. James then made a break, shook off defenders like the proverbial rag-doll, to score under the posts and add the goal, Preston's try finished the scoring at 28–0.

On the Wednesday James took part in England's third meeting with Australia, this time in Liverpool, at Everton FC's Goodison Park. Although not a 'test' series – some press members seemed to struggle with the notion of both the Northern Union and England meeting the Australians three times each – England, courtesy of a 14–7 win, could claim to be unbeaten, with two victories and a draw. The miserable, wintry conditions – there was snow on the pitch – kept the crowd down to around 4,500. James had a fine game, the *Yorkshire Post* correspondent said "despite the unnecessary severity with which he was handled [he] played good football." He was involved in both his side's tries and kicked three goals; from a penalty, a conversion and a mark. Unfortunately, he wrenched his left hip, which cost him his place in Salford's side at Swinton three days later, although they won 11–6 in his absence.

With the Australians having completed their tour, James – who had faced them six times – could now concentrate on domestic obligations. He was declared "fully recovered" for

Salford's difficult looking second round Challenge Cup match at Broughton on 13 March, which drew 13,000. On a fine afternoon and in a tight match, there was a flurry of penalty and drop-goal attempts by both teams during the first half. James was the only one to succeed, kicking from distance after a Rangers player was penalised for not playing the ball correctly. Salford did not help their cause when Evan Thomas was dismissed after the interval for "rough play" although, in truth, it evened up the numbers as Rangers' winger Jimmy Barr was injured before the break and took no further part. In a half that had a similar pattern to the first, it was again Salford's captain who put the only points on the board with another powerful long range penalty after Barlow had tripped John.

While again saluted as the match winner, it was claimed James lacked "fire and speed" and twice attempted drop-goals when he should have opened out. Whether this was a fair criticism is difficult to say and it has to be acknowledged that the writer of those comments obviously witnessed the match. There was no escaping the fact, though, that James, despite being declared fit, had not played for 10 days due to an injury, one that had come on the back of a demanding two month playing schedule. As a footnote, it was revealed that the Rangers had spent a few days preparing for the match at a brine baths in Northwich whereas Salford, apparently, "had made no special preparations, the officials trusting more to the offer of a substantial bonus than to brine baths".

Four days later, James and company were in action once more. Ebbw Vale made the lengthy mid-week journey to Weaste; the original fixture had been postponed due to Salford's cup-tie at Wheater's Field. Willie Thomas was injured in the latter match, and was unavailable for the visit of the 'Valians'. James switched back to centre and Billy Brady covered him in the halves. James was the first to score. He obtained the ball following a scrum and split the defence to go under the posts and add the goal. Ebbw Vale gamely fought back and levelled the score at 5–5 before James was off on one of his 'trademark' unstoppable charges. He beat a path through one defender after another before supplying Cook, who returned the ball to his skipper for a great try. A further touchdown from Coates just before half-time gave the Reds an 11–5 cushion to take into the second period. Ebbw Vale gallantly fought back, the progressive score read 11–8, 14–8, 14–11 and 14–14, which set the scene for James to complete his hat-trick of tries and win the match in true *Boy's Own* style. He missed the conversion, but landed a late penalty to clinch a 19–14 victory. While James was praised for his great form, "the visitors being quite unable to hold him", it was suggested in the *Salford Reporter* that "Salford did not exert themselves unduly but seemed to score whenever they liked."

Salford had again placed themselves in contention for honours at the "business end" of the season, having climbed to fifth in the league and reached the quarter-final stage of the Challenge Cup. But they had a difficult task ahead of them because second-placed Halifax provided their next opposition in both competitions. Those two matches – which concluded their March schedule – could make or break the season for Salford. There was an excited

12,000 crowd at Halifax for the league fixture on Saturday 20th. It was "a fitting tribute to the attractive powers of Lomas and his troops" according to the *Salford Reporter*, although many would also have been there to cheer the home side closer to a possible championship triumph. With Willie Thomas still not recovered, James was again a late switch into the centre from his selected position at outside-half. The Halifax team began in an uncompromising mood and had swept to a 10–0 lead by half-time. The second half was even worse from a Salford point of view and the Reds eventually lost 22–2, a penalty by James – the "only man in the quartet [threequarters] to do himself absolute justice" – being the sole entry to their account. It was a disastrous result for the Reds who had been challenging Batley for the fourth spot. They were hoping the Gallant Youths would slip up, but while Salford were being blown out at Halifax, they disposed of Bradford Northern 39–0 and then won 5–0 at Bramley the following Wednesday. This put Salford four points behind Batley, with four games each to play.

Meanwhile, Halifax travelled to The Willows on the 27th of the month for their third round Challenge Cup tie. Despite heavy showers before kick-off, 13,976 passed through the turnstiles, but the Salford contingent would have been dismayed with their side's first half performance. Little slotted over a penalty for the visitors after only six minutes and by half-time, the Reds were 9–0 behind. They did slightly better after the interval, but eventually lost 12–7. For once, James did not score, his team's two goals came from the boot of Mesley. With Willie Thomas returning, James resumed his position in the halves, but it seems he did not have the best of games. The *Salford Reporter* concluded that "Salford's biggest weakness was at half-back where Lomas did far too much kicking and some of his lengthy punts lacked judgement, while he was never able to shake of the attentions of [half-back Tommy] Grey and [centre Joe] Riley."

Out of the Challenge Cup, Salford were eliminated from the championship race with the following weekend's defeat at Hunslet. Salford began well enough at Parkside, a Hunslet try by Farrar was responded to by Willie Thomas. James then rescued a loose ball, beat off three defenders and scored under the posts, his goal gave Salford an 8–3 lead. The Salford skipper tried to increase the advantage with an ambitious penalty from near halfway that just failed. Instead, it was Hunslet that claimed all the remaining points as the Reds went down 16–8. This time James was complimented on his hard work, having "made many attempts to retrieve the fortunes of the day" despite being heavily marked. While Salford had been losing to Halifax [in the cup] and Hunslet, Batley had gained two further league victories to confirm their fourth place in the table.

A disappointing end to the season was concluded with three Easter fixtures that produced mixed results. The first, at home to Wakefield Trinity on Good Friday, was a resounding 11-try 53–0 win. James ran in two second half touchdowns and logged six conversions. In fairness, Wakefield's half-hearted resistance owed much to the fact that they fielded a weakened side due to a Challenge Cup semi-final date with Wigan the next day, a tactic that paid dividends as they eventually won that competition. The following day the Reds, inspired by James, made one of their best ever comebacks in their match at Wilderspool. Despite warm weather, there was only a small attendance, possibly due to an early start, the action began before midday and ended at 12.50pm. Reportedly, the teams had agreed to play two 30-minute halves. James made a typical run early on and beat 'half a dozen' defenders, but was unable to get his pass away cleanly. Instead, it was Warrington who got on top, and increased a 12–0 half-time lead to 15–0. Mesley's try under the posts, followed by another from James – who raced through for an exciting try off John's pass – sparked a revival. James added both goals so there were only five points between the sides and Salford had their tails up. Then, when Mesley broke away, he cross-kicked to James as the tackle came in, and the skipper obliged by planting the ball down for a try which he also converted. Naturally, with the score, at 15–15, there was tremendous excitement, but time ran out and honours were even. The *Salford Reporter* reckoned that if the match had been played over "full 40s" the Reds would have won "on stamina".

The Reds' league programme concluded on Easter Monday with a home match against Oldham. Salford performed fairly well in a 19–13 defeat after again finding themselves in a situation of having to chase the game. Already losing 8–0 at the interval, they conceded two tries after the break to extend the arrears to 14 points. Then James put Mesley over in the corner, the latter added the goal and suddenly Salford had belief. Mesley again got over in the corner, but Oldham replied and Salford trailed 19–8. Evan Thomas's try, goaled by James brought the Reds to within six points, but there was no further scoring. The *Salford Reporter* said: "Lomas tried hard to stem the tide of disaster, and at one time it looked as if his efforts were to be crowned with success, but the rally came too late."

Salford ended their season by undertaking the time-consuming railway journey to South Wales for a friendly against Merthyr Tydfil the next day. It was their fourth match in five days and was probably the last thing the players wanted after such a depressing conclusion to their season. Watched by approximately 4,000, it resulted in an 8–8 draw after Salford had led 8–0; James contributed a try.

James was once again an NU chart-topper, heading the list for points with 274 and goals with 89, quite an achievement when taking account of the fact that he had a long commute from Maryport to undertake in the first half of the season.

On a statistical note, it has long been thought that James had set a Salford club record for a half-back during 1908–09 by scoring 23 of his 28 tries from that position, a figure matched by Emlyn Jenkins in 1932–33. However, research for this publication shows that, due to late team changes in two matches, James's total from half-back was actually 21. A new record was established in 2003 when New Zealand stand-off Cliff Beverley registered 32 from that position.

13. 1909–10: The road to Runcorn

James Lomas continued to impress his critics during the 1909–10 season. His form throughout was of such consistently high calibre that it would provide the springboard for his finest achievement in the sport. He returned to action at The Willows for the second of Salford's two public trial matches, played on Saturday 28 August. There was, however, no news of any major signings at the club although the Reds' officials had tried, unsuccessfully, to capture Jum Turtill the New Zealand full-back who had impressed on the 1907–08 tour. He joined St Helens instead.

The Reds kicked off the 1909–10 season with a trip to Runcorn on 4 September; the *Salford Reporter* blamed their 13–5 defeat on the energy expended by the players in getting there. As their correspondent explained: "The road to Runcorn is surely one of the most awkward to travel, and it seems an anomaly that in this present day of airships and motor cars one has to journey 45 miles to reach a town that is not more than 28 miles from the starting point. It is quite certain that when we arrived on the Cheshire side of the [River] Mersey our men were thoroughly jaded, and some of them actually walked from the [railway] station to the ground to loosen their joints." It was not the best of days weather-wise either, drizzling rain made the pitch slippery and the ball like a bar of soap. James scored the season's opening points for Salford; first with a penalty from halfway and then through a try near the posts after a great break by Dai John. James missed the conversion, but the Reds led 5–0, only to fall away. Runcorn turned the game round, were 8–5 ahead at the interval and never looked back.

The following week, 10,000 spectators gathered at The Willows for the season's first home match. The opposition was the powerful Oldham side. The crowd enjoyed an exciting contest. James's penalty gave Salford the lead, but staunch defending by the Roughyeds prevented any further home points and it was Oldham who led at half-time, 5–2. A thrilling second half began to unravel when Salford centre Sidney Adams – recently signed from Welsh rugby union club Newport – scored under the posts and James added the extras to put Salford ahead 7–5, only to see George Tyson reply with Oldham's second try and sneak back in front 8–7. James earned praise when "amidst tremendous cheering" he landed a penalty, given for offside, to put the Reds 9–8 up, a score-line they kept until the final whistle. The Salford captain, who "was ever in the thick of the fray", was showered with plaudits, his half-back partnership with Dave Preston in outplaying Oldham pair Billy Dixon and Tommy Brice was considered pivotal to his side's success. It would prove to be one of only three league defeats suffered by Oldham during the season, who were destined to top the table and capture the championship.

Buoyed by their success over Oldham, the Reds travelled to Central Park with a feeling of self-belief, despite Wigan emerging as a powerful force in the code. There were some 15,000 present, many of them apparently aware of the threat posed by the Salford leader as they "barracked Lomas to their hearts' content when he placed the ball for a shot at goal". On a sunny afternoon, though, James and his colleagues were "out of sorts" and they were down 17–0 at half-time. There was a significant improvement in the second half, although not enough to win the match. James scored an early try from Preston's excellently placed pass and Willie Thomas got a second after he took James's pass with one hand. James missed both goals and when Leytham scored his second touchdown of the match, converted by Johnny Thomas, the Reds lagged well behind, 22–6. Some respectability was given to the score-line when James shrugged off an opponent after gathering the ball from a cross-field kick by Bernard Mesley to go in under the Wigan posts. His goal made the final outcome 22–11.

Salford produced better form the following week when Broughton Rangers were entertained in front of some 10,000 souls at The Willows. The Rangers started the better of the two, but their early 4–0 lead was quickly overcome and the Reds established a 20–4 advantage. James who, reportedly, "was the victim of some nasty tackles" and closely marked throughout the game, engineered the Reds' crucial opening try for Ephraim Curzon and landed three conversions, two of which were excellent touchline efforts. A consolation try from visiting wingman Jimmy Barr closed the score at 20–7. Salford followed that up with another difficult fixture, this time at Warrington. It was a disappointing afternoon for the Reds who trailed 8–3 at half-time. James, who had missed the conversion of Silas Warwick's try and been off target after Mesley had called for a mark, succeeded with a fabulous second half penalty from halfway, but it was not enough to avoid an 8–5 defeat.

James's attention was temporarily diverted from club matters the following Monday, 4 October, when he represented Cumberland against Lancashire in Barrow[5]. He forsook his now regular outside-half slot with Salford to appear in the centre in a match that was a disappointing spectacle for the 3,000 gathered inside Cavendish Park. Cumberland won 8–3, although James did not get on the score-sheet and was repelled several times from entering Lancashire's in-goal area. The Lancashire pack included Curzon, who had made a big impact during his first season with Salford and would have a significant part to play in James's greatest honour at the end of the current campaign.

Hunslet arrived at Salford on the following Saturday for another closely fought game, this time won by the Reds, 17–12. James kicked four goals – two conversions, a penalty and a mammoth long range shot following a mark from forward Edgar Morton. The half-time score was 7–7. Salford had an advantage after the Parksiders lost their centre Jack Manchester for the second half due to a damaged collarbone. On the next weekend James and his pals were due for another long train journey to visit Treherbert, one of the Welsh clubs that had recently joined the league. Unlike the previous season, when they journeyed

---

[5] This was when the town was considered part of Lancashire and not Cumbria.

to Ebbw Vale only to find the match called off, this time they received an earlier warning. Having gathered at Manchester's London Road station on the Friday, they were about to board the 2.45pm train to Cardiff for an overnight stop at the Grand Hotel when a message reached them just in time. A telephone call had been received advising that the Treherbert pitch was flooded due to heavy rain in South Wales and the trip was hastily abandoned.

It was another wet day when Salford beat Widnes 11–5 at home on Saturday 23 October; the players were drenched as they skidded around the pitch. James, though, was otherwise engaged, playing for Cumberland against Yorkshire at Maryport's Athletic Ground. It was virtually a home game for James and he did not disappoint the local people. The *Athletic News* said that "The Salford captain was on native soil and encouraged by his fellow townsmen he made the opening which resulted in [Barrow's Sammy] Treloare scoring a try". That score gave Cumberland a 4th minute 3–0 lead, but an injury to Jack Flynn of Broughton Rangers depleted their side, and resulted in James moving from the centre to service the scrums. A try and goal from Hunslet's Billy Batten gave Yorkshire a 5–3 interval lead and that was still the score when heavy rain again played a significant role, and forced the referee to abandon the match seven minutes into the second half. James did well after switching to half-back. The *Athletic News* correspondent 'Forward' noted that "when the ball came out on the Cumberland side, Lomas went on his own. His bursts were not devoid of method and a further 10 minutes of the Salford captain in the second half would I feel confident have brought about the downfall of the Tykes." It was intended to replay the match, but it never happened because agreement could not be reached between the two counties on a venue. Cumberland wanted to play at Oldham or Wigan for financial reasons, whereas Yorkshire wanted to replay in Cumberland and asked for £25 towards their expenses. With both sides having defeated Lancashire, they were subsequently declared joint champions.

The next Saturday, Salford entered the Lancashire Cup at the second round stage, having received a bye in the first. The draw took them to Mather Lane to face Leigh on another slippery surface. It was certainly an eventful first half for James, whose 7th minute penalty for offside was followed by a drop-goal from John, which rolled over off the crossbar, and try by Leigh wingman Tom Johnson to give the Reds a 4–3 advantage. However, the game was halted shortly afterwards while one of the touch judges marched James over to referee Bill McCutcheon for allegedly kicking out at Leigh half-back Sam Whittaker. No further action was taken and, in the second half, after a drop-goal by full-back Ellis Clarkson had put Leigh in front, James regained the lead with a goal from a mark by Mesley. However, two further Leigh tries vanquished Salford from the competition, the Reds lost 13–6.

It was claimed in the Salford press that "Lomas was not too much in the thick of the fight, and perhaps a little more energy on his part would have been serviceable." However, a clue as to the reason behind his "poor" performance and his lashing out with a boot was provided after his late withdrawal from the next two matches. Salford beat Barrow 25–6 at home and Hull Kingston Rovers 3–2 away. His absence in both was reported as due "to the soreness of his rib, consequent upon kicks received early on in the Leigh match." James was back on the pitch with his colleagues on Thursday, 18 November, having travelled to Treherbert to play the previously postponed fixture. Significantly, James was restored to the centre, swapping with Willie Thomas who took over the outside-half position, an arrangement that remained for most of the season. The Reds won 19–2; James scored two tries and two goals – a conversion and a penalty.

A poor crowd of "not more than 2,000" greeted Salford two days later when they played York at The Willows. The reason for the poor attendance was that dense fog covered the ground and it was doubtful the match would even kick off. Salford had just played Treherbert for the first and, as it proved, only time; the game with York was also a first because the clubs had never met before in a league match. They had clashed just twice in the Challenge Cup, the last time in 1903 and James was the only Salford survivor. Salford beat their Yorkshire visitors 27–10. They led only 11–10 shortly before the interval. James converted three of Salford's seven tries; the match reached its completion despite the fog thickening in the latter stages; the referee had turned the teams around without a half-time respite. Apparently, James's play "was not up to standard, some of his passes to Jimmy Cook being too low down." He was, though, lauded for other aspects of his performance: "In defence the Salford captain did all that was required and was always there to take full advantage of any slip by the attackers."

November's fixture list concluded with a trip down Chorley Road, where Swinton awaited their guests. There were roughly 7,000 people at the game, a smaller figure than anticipated, blamed variously on "doubtful weather" and the counter-attractions of the Leigh versus Wigan Lancashire Cup Final at Wheater's Field and horse racing at Manchester Racecourse, which was actually in Salford at Castle Irwell. Swinton led 3–0 at the interval, James – playing well in all other respects – missed the target with three penalty attempts. Salford had a huge second half advantage when Swinton lost both their centres; Eric Young, with a knee injury, did not reappear after the break and then Jim Wharton had to be taken off. The latter returned, but by then three tries had put Salford 9–3 in front, James rounded off the scoring with a drop-goal and the Reds won 11–3.

James was selected for England to play Wales at Wakefield Trinity's Belle Vue ground on Saturday 4 December for the first of two international matches between them that season. The *Athletic News* correspondent 'Forward', referring to a second-half touchdown by James, wrote: "I always expect a thrill when Lomas is in form and I was on this occasion not to be disappointed. It was a try worthy of the man. The Salford captain received the ball from [Hunslet's Fred] Smith about the halfway line. He had half a dozen opponents to face, but the deed was done and a beautiful swerve took him safely past [Leeds's Frank] Young and [Hull KR's Phil] Thomas for the try of the match. He placed the goal and the effort was well worth five points." His endeavour put England 19–8 ahead after they had fallen 8–6 behind at the interval. The final score was 19–13; James also converted a Joe Ferguson try.

Although without James – and Evan Thomas who was Wales's reserve forward – Salford overcame Leigh 23–8 at home, their eighth successive league win. It was a result that put them among the league leaders with just three defeats in 13 matches. The run ended at St Helens the following week when they lost 7–3. It was decided to play James on the left wing so as not to disrupt the centre pairing of Mesley and Adams that had performed well against Leigh. A General Election was due in the new year, so local Conservative candidate Rigby Swift kicked off the first half, and current St Helens Labour MP Tom Glover the second. It was noted that "If their skill as 'kickists' is anything to go by, Labour had it." Salford led 3–2 at the interval. James was just wide in attempting to convert Preston's try and missed with an earlier penalty from halfway. With the pitch in a very poor state, St Helens exchanged their muddied jerseys for clean ones during the break. Salford, meanwhile, made an exchange of a different kind; Lomas swapped places with Mesley, the Salford leader's formidable talents had been wasted out wide. The effectiveness of the switch was soon demonstrated when James almost put Cook in, but the winger lost the ball. Instead, Salford went behind due to a Turtill penalty, James missed with three attempts of his own, including one that struck the post, before Saints' half-back Arthur Kelly's late try sealed Salford's fate. Although James played in two positions the verdict was that "in neither did he shine when judged by his own standards."

It was an unexpected and disappointing defeat for Salford, but they made reparation through winning December's three remaining matches; Runcorn, 20–0 at home, Broughton Rangers, 10–5, away, and Swinton, 10–3 at home. The match with Runcorn was deemed "a splendid exhibition" which, in keeping with the political climate, had each half kicked off by the grandly named Lieutenant Carlyon Bellairs, the Conservative and Liberal Unionist candidate for West Salford. Salford scored four tries, the last was claimed by James who was again playing on the wing. He put the ball beneath the posts after he received possession following an Evan Thomas break. He also converted three tries and was successful with a second half drop-goal after he picked up a loose ball. Salford led by only five points at the interval, the visitors were handicapped through the loss of half-back Watton and forward H. Rees when the score stood at 8–0. James again had a tough time on the wing, with Runcorn centre Jim Butterworth "paying particular attention" to him.

Salford were up against it almost from the start at Wheater's Field on Christmas Day when Preston was sent off after seven minutes play for punching Broughton Rangers half-back Claude James. Surprisingly, forward George Thom took his place among the halves rather than moving James from the centre. In spite of the setback, Salford held a 5–0 advantage at half-time after James got hold of the ball after a scrum and kicked across field for Evan Thomas to retrieve possession and push his way over the try-line. For the second half, James was moved to half-back to partner Willie Thomas, the threequarters were reshuffled and Thom transferred to the wing. When James kicked the ball into Rangers' territory, the defending Barr failed to get hold of it and Adams picked it up to put Mesley under the posts. James landed his second conversion to bring up a 10–0 score-line, Rangers managed a late try and goal after Salford went two players down when Willie Thomas retired with a bloodied nose. It appeared James had recaptured his zest in the second half. According to the *Salford Reporter* "The great strength of Salford lay at half-back where... the brothers [Claude and Willie] James were no match for Lomas and Willie Thomas. The Salford captain played one of his best games this season, his bustling dashes being a source of worry to the opposing pair."

Two days later, on Monday 27 December, Salford played their other local opponents, Swinton. With rain falling and the ground muddy and under water in places, it was difficult for the 8,500 crowd "to distinguish [Salford] red from [Swinton] blue" as the match progressed. The trainers were kept busy as there was "much mopping of the eyes" during the afternoon. Cook scored the first try – Mesley missed the conversion – and James registered the second; he received a wide pass from Adams after the latter scooped up a stray ball. James was just wide with the goal kick, but added a penalty for a foul on John. A try from Swinton winger Billy Wallwork left Salford 8–3 up at the interval. The only second half score was another penalty from James, again for a foul on John, the match concluded in further heavy rain and virtual darkness.

Salford's winning run continued into 1910. They sailed through January with victories at Barrow, 15–0 and at home to St Helens 24–5 and Warrington 8–0. With Preston indisposed, James played in the scrum-half position in the first two, Willie Thomas played at outside-half. The New Year's Day trip up to Cavendish Park saw James – the main architect of Salford's attack throughout – score a try and two conversions on a damp, gloomy day in Barrow. Against St Helens, it was the Salford forwards who dominated matters, laying the platform for a comfortable victory. Salford set off like an express train and were 21–0 in front by the interval; James converted three of his side's five first half tries.

James was the star turn against Warrington on 15 January and scored all the points in a match that was once again played in heavy rain on a quagmire of a pitch. Shortly before half-time, he took possession and somehow managed to dribble the ball beneath the Wirepullers' posts for a try which he also converted. With the players getting drenched, no break was taken and the second half restarted immediately. James scored his second try; he pounced on the ball after Cook and Curzon had combined to dribble it through the slurry. It was a hard-fought, determined struggle throughout, with little between the teams except for one man. As the *Salford Reporter* writer gleefully noted: "As for Lomas, well, he was here, there, and everywhere, the Salford captain showing his best form." It was a vital result because it cemented Salford's league position of second, one place ahead of Warrington with Wigan fourth, the Lancashire-dominated top four being completed by Oldham in pole position.

148

James is surrounded by his Salford team mates, officials and backroom staff for this 1909 photograph.
(Photo: Courtesy Steve Haslam)

Salford still had two Saturday fixtures left in January, but both games fell victim to frost; at Widnes on the 22nd and Wigan's visit to Weaste on the 29th. They played on a pitch described as "mud, sand and water" when they visited Rochdale Hornets for their next match on Saturday 5 February, a legacy of the treacherous weather over the past month or so. Nonetheless, it did not deter James from continuing his irresistible, energetic form to produce what proved to be the match-winning try. The *Salford Reporter* said "Under the circumstances it was one of the most brilliant efforts that the Salford captain had made this season and will not readily be forgotten by those who saw it." The Hornets had drawn first blood through forward Joe Bowers's touchdown, Cook's try squared the match, 3–3, before James struck shortly before the interval. From a scrum on Salford's 25-yard line, Preston retrieved the ball and passed it to half-back partner Willie Thomas, his darting run taking him to the halfway line where he handed on to James. Salford's captain raced away, with Hornets' wingman Tommy West in vain pursuit, and he crashed over the try-line underneath the posts. His subsequent goal made it 8–3. James was also conspicuous during a scoreless second half when he again got over the Hornets line, but his appeal for a try was turned down.

Another tough looking fixture came when Halifax visited The Willows a week later, and the Reds were considered slightly fortunate to beat their Yorkshire rivals. James was again their life-saver, and scored all the home points in a 12–8 win. Halifax were leading 3–0 when he took full advantage of a dropped ball from a rival, and dribbled it into the in-goal

149

area for a try. He missed the goal, but his subsequent penalty, for offside, gave Salford the lead. Before half-time arrived he struck again, and completed a passing movement by placing the ball between the posts; his goal increased the margin to 10–3. At the start of the second period, James proved his value in defence, his excellent tackle thwarted a certain try from winger John Medley. And, after Cook was fouled in following up his own kick, James notched a third goal. A converted try by Halifax narrowed the gap to just four points and ensured a hectic finish; the referee admonished several players before the final whistle. James had an excellent afternoon despite the usual close marking he received. The Salford captain appealed several times to referee Mr W.H. Woods of Huddersfield about the "offside play" of Halifax's backs, but "little notice was taken of his objections".

Salford received Wigan the following Wednesday, 16 February, following that fixture's postponement a few weeks earlier. The Reds were in confident vein, and had hit their best run of form for several seasons, with eight successive league wins and only one defeat in the last 17 matches. It was a vital match for both clubs – defeat for Salford meant they would slide out of the top four – and 10,000 arrived at The Willows in anticipation. It was not the best of starts for the Reds, two tries by Leytham left them 6–0 down after only 10 minutes. James tried manfully, and played his "usual strong and skilful game". A great solo run ended when he was pulled down by weight of numbers. His endeavour encouraged his team-mates and they began to get on top; James's touchline penalty reduced the arrears to four points by half-time. He missed a couple of second half penalty attempts and, following a mighty charge through the opposition, outwitting full-back Jim Sharrock on the way, he almost scored a try. Just as he was about to place the ball down New Zealand forward Charlie Seeling managed to tackle him from behind. Salford's challenge fell away after that and with James being "well looked after" as usual, three further goals to the away side left the Reds 12–2 behind at the finish.

Three days later, Salford were at Mather Lane, scene of their earlier Lancashire Cup exit at the hands of Leigh. There was a reported 7,000 attendance for a match again played on a heavy looking surface. Salford scored first when Cook touched down near the corner flag after latching on to James's pass. The Reds, though, were soon depleted after Preston withdrew from the match with a dislocated shoulder. Aided by a strong wind, Leigh forged their way in front to lead 8–3 by the interval. Ten minutes into the second half, Salford had Cook to thank after he twice dribbled passed Leigh winger Arthur Booth to score in the corner, and completed his hat-trick. James converted the former, and edged Salford 11–8 ahead before he put the icing on the cake with a final try after John's cross-kick had provided Adams with an opening that he fully exploited. Reaching the Leigh line, he passed the ball to his captain, who shoved an opponent out of the way to score at the corner. He missed the conversion but Salford won 14–8.

While Salford were basking in the glory of their success at Leigh, another event had taken place that Saturday afternoon, 19 February, just a few miles from The Willows.

Manchester United had played their first match at Old Trafford, against Liverpool, in front of around 45,000 people. They had relocated from the Clayton district of Manchester. In the years since, and particularly since the period of the Second World War, Manchester United have drawn tremendous support from the sports-loving public of the Salford area, probably to the detriment of its rugby team.

Salford turned their focus onto the Challenge Cup the following week, the first round draw had presented them with a tie against York Irish National League (members of the York and District League). The Reds had drawn the junior side away, but persuaded them to travel to The Willows where, despite more bad weather, 6,000 attended. As expected, it was mostly one-way traffic, Salford won 64–0 and scored 32 points in each half. The junior outfit lost their full-back Kelly due to a knee cartilage problem at 13–0. Of the 16 tries, James scored four; two before half time – "threading" his way into the corner off Willie Thomas's cross-kick, running in his second from 25 yards out – and a couple after the break – off a Willie Thomas pass, and the final try of the match after following up a punt from Bill Hyam. James also succeeded with three of his six conversion attempts; the remaining efforts were shared by eight different players as Salford relaxed.

Salford faced a huge league fixture when they arrived at the Watersheddings on 5 March. It drew a 25,000 crowd, table-toppers Oldham had lost only three league matches, which included the one at The Willows, and won every home game. With Preston out injured, James was reunited at half-back with Willie Thomas and the pair were instrumental in breaking down Oldham's stonewall defence as Salford took a 3–0 lead. It came about after Thomas passed the ball to James who kicked downfield. Mesley, following up, beat Oldham full-back Alf Wood to the ball for a great try in the corner. James's conversion attempt was within a whisker of succeeding. It was a miss he later regretted when Sid Deane scored just before half-time to tie the scores. James tried hard to lift his team after the break, he attempted a goal from inside Salford's half from Mesley's mark, and twice crossed the Oldham line, but was resisted by "at least half a dozen" on the second attempt. The match ended 3–3, thus denting Oldham's 100 per cent home record in the league. Willie Thomas was declared "equal to any man on the field... except Lomas himself, who tackled without mistake". The *Salford Reporter* added a mildly amusing footnote: "For the game a new ball was brought out and it was in such an inflated condition that it caused a lot of trouble to the would-be directors of movement. Owing to this 'friskiness' Lomas had the worst of luck in touch kicking as the leather would go farther than it was wanted."

There was another bumper 25,000 crowd the following week. This time it was at The Willows and was, in all probability, the largest audience James played in front of at Weaste. The huge turnout was to see the mouth-watering second round Challenge Cup tie against top-four rivals, Wigan. It was said in the *Salford Reporter* that the hosts "have been paying strict attention to training and are sure to turn out in the perfection of condition." Mesley's early try under the posts got Salford off to the best possible start. James – who continued at half-back – added the goal points and successfully aimed a penalty after Wigan's Ned Jones was pulled up for not feeding a scrum correctly. The lead was pegged back to 7–5 by half-time, when the elusive Leytham managed to squeeze between James and John, Thomas converted. With the score so close and Wigan having the advantage of a second half wind, there were fears on the terraces that the Reds could let the match slip out of their grasp. Those fears were allayed by Cook who, following an exciting bout of passing, sidestepped Leytham and Seeling before he kicked the ball over Sharrock's head and reclaimed it to score beneath the posts. James's goal made the final score 12–5. The *Daily News* said "Lomas and Willie Thomas were an exceptionally clever pair" and had maintained the excellent form they showed against Oldham, although against Wigan it was Thomas who fed the scrums.

Salford had just seven days to go before the next round but, in the meantime, James had two matches to shoe-horn into his schedule. The first was on Monday 14 March, when he was required at Headingley to take part in a trial match for the forthcoming Northern Union tour, which will be covered in more depth in the next chapter. Two days later, Salford had to go to Widnes to fulfil the league fixture called off in January. It was a match Salford would have expected to win but, in the event, they lost 8–0, and severely dented their top-four ambitions. A meagre crowd of around 1,500 saw Salford give an indifferent performance due, perhaps, to a preoccupation with the Challenge Cup. For James – back in the centre thanks to the return of Preston in the halves – it was a third match in five days.

Salford had been drawn away to Ebbw Vale – surprise winners at Huddersfield in the previous round – in the Challenge Cup, but convinced the Valians to switch to The Willows. They guaranteed them £150, and they subsequently received £200 from the receipts generated by a 9,000 crowd. Salford succeeded in winning through to the semi-final stage although, after eliminating Wigan with such panache, they expected an easier passage than the one they had. The *Salford Reporter* said "At times they could do nothing right and it was only the magnificent play of Lomas which saved the team from defeat, the Reds' leader being on the top of his form. Time after time he extricated his side from difficult situations and in the second half made one glorious save when he sent the ball from behind his own line into touch near the centre flag." The first points came from Cook who scored in the corner after a move initiated by James; Mesley missed the tricky goal attempt. The second of Salford's tries also involved their captain, his pass put Adams in under the posts, and he added the extra points. Starting the second half with an 8–0 lead, James was unlucky not to extend it when his penalty hit a post. Ebbw Vale later pulled two points back with a drop-goal from full-back Dai Davies, but Salford finished 8–2 winners.

The cup tie had meant that the home league match with another of the Welsh clubs, Treherbert, had been called off. It was not subsequently played and they folded at the end of the season. The Easter weekend followed, and the Reds did themselves a massive favour in their quest for a play-off spot by winning all three games; 21–17 at York, 19–11 at home to Hull KR and 23–12 at home to Rochdale Hornets. The Good Friday match at York was played on a sunny day, the good ground conditions conducive to a fast, exciting match. James converted one of Salford's three first half tries and was desperately unlucky with a penalty from halfway. The Reds led 11–3 at half-time. After the break, he reacted like greased lightning to race over the York try-line after recovering a ball dropped by their half-back George Daniel. He added the extra points and did likewise after a subsequent touchdown by Preston. York added a second try, and the 21–6 score put Salford in a strong position. But it was far from over. In a frantic finish – during which James and York forward Carroll received "words of caution from the referee as to their conduct" – the home side added 11 points and only just missed out.

Hull KR attracted almost 7,000 into The Willows the next day, and they witnessed an enjoyable match, particular the Salford contingent among them. With the Rovers sporting red jerseys, Salford wore white, "much to the confusion of the press". A pumped up home side got off to a flying start with three tries in the opening seven minutes. James got the first two; he crossed at the corner after a determined attack involving Curzon and Willie Thomas, and gathered up the ball after a loose scrimmage to dash over. The third, from forward Dai Rees, made it 9–0, Mesley failed with the goal attempt for the second score and James missed the other two. Although Rovers managed to get their breath back, the Reds were 9–3 ahead at the interval. It got better for Salford after the break, James's pass in midfield despatched Mesley on his way to a spectacular try. The skipper's goal put his team 14–3 to the good, and with 20 minutes left everything pointed solidly towards a home victory. But the Yorkshiremen stormed back with two tries, and made it an uncomfortable 14–11 before Cook clinched the spoils with a fifth Salford try, James converted.

With some important games on the horizon, it was decided to rest James for the Easter Monday visit of Rochdale Hornets. The Reds' subsequent victory put Salford in third position behind league leaders Oldham and second placed Wigan. Incidentally, the Rochdale fixture featured the first team debut of Joseph Lavery at half-back. Normally a threequarter, he had arrived in Britain with the 1907–08 New Zealand tourists and subsequently played for Leeds and Leigh before he joined Salford in January 1910 as the club's first overseas player.

Salford embarked on a crucial stage of their campaign with a match at Wakefield on Saturday 2 April when they met Hull in the Challenge Cup semi-final. It was the Reds' eighth semi-final in the competition in 13 seasons and the fifth during James's time with the club. His return to the side saw him once more at half-back, a decision applauded by the *Salford Reporter* journalist: "It is much desired that the committee will play Lomas and Willie Thomas behind the scrimmage, for there is little doubt that the pair are better than the latter and Preston." Watched by around 11,000, the miserable weather was matched by a dire result for Salford who lost 20–6. James had the Reds' supporters cheering at the top of their voices with an early goal, kicked from a mark made by Willie Thomas. But they were not producing their best form and there was "no support for Lomas". Hull took a 10–2 lead into the interval. Salford should have been encouraged by the unfortunate absence of Hull forward Stan Britton for the second half after he had broken a collar bone, but it made little difference. James attempted a penalty from halfway, but it hit the backs of the Hull forwards lined up just in front of him. Mesley had better fortune with a drop-goal. James tried his hardest, but Hull defended well and the Salford talisman was brought down "time after time". The numbers were evened up when Adams retired with a damaged shoulder. Hull added two converted tries, which sandwiched a second drop-goal by Mesley. When the final whistle blew, Hull captain Billy Anderson was deservedly carried off the field by his jubilant fans. Salford's pack was outplayed but, as per normal, the spotlight fell on James, the *Salford Reporter* concluded "The Reds captain evidently had not derived much benefit from his idleness [being rested against Rochdale] for he played far below his form and had not a ghost of a chance to beat the tackling."

The semi-final had brought about the postponement of the visit to Halifax and this took place two days later, on Monday evening. With Adams unfit, James returned to centre, John – who had spent most of the season at full-back – joined Willie Thomas in the halves. There were barely 2,000 souls present at Thrum Hall to witness a disappointing match, although Salford at least won, 6–0, to keep their championship aspirations alive. James, who was "very conspicuous" in defence throughout, had his kicking boots with him in the first half, and scored three goals, two from marks and another from an excellently struck touchline penalty. With no further scoring after the interval, the result put Salford joint second in the table with Wigan, who had completed their fixtures. If the Reds could win their last match, at Hunslet, they would secure second spot and a home play-off with a third-placed Wigan.

Incredibly, Salford had to play that vital match at Parkside, on Saturday 9 April, without their star player. James was selected for England's international against Wales at Ebbw Vale. His absence, though, was more than balanced by three Hunslet players being included in the England side; threequarter Billy Batten, half-back Fred Smith and forward Bill Jukes. England, who led 13–11 at the half-time break, were eventually trounced 39–18 by the Welsh, their second half collapse attributed to the retirement of Batten through injury. The *Athletic News* writer, 'Forward', waxed lyrical: "I can best describe the scene as a duel between Welsh hares and English hounds. Invariably the hares ran to cover and the tired and limp hounds were exhausted long before the finish." James scored a late try after collecting a punt by Jukes for a simple touchdown, and added his second conversion having converted Smith's first half score. The *Leeds Mercury* said: "Lomas, although not in such good form as he has been seen in Wales was, nonetheless, a tower of strength to his side. He seemed to be everywhere, and was always in the thick of the fray."

Meanwhile, Salford beat Hunslet by the narrowest of margins, 3–2, to guarantee a home game in what would be their first top-four play-off appearance. As anticipated that match was against Wigan at The Willows, and took place on 16 April. Club officials hoped for a repeat of the 25,000 crowd that witnessed their Challenge Cup tie two months earlier. The attendance of 9,000 was, therefore, something of a disappointment, although terrible weather conditions kept many away. The bigger disappointment for Salford, though, was their 17–6 defeat although James, at least, could hold his head up; he was the Reds' best performer yet again. Joe Miller gave Wigan the lead with a try but, close to half-time, the Salford captain broke through the visitors' ranks and dribbled the ball towards their in-goal area, the Colliers' full-back Harry Price, deputising for the injured Sharrock, failed to collect and then obstructed James as he chased the ball over the try-line. The referee awarded an obstruction try although Mesley missed the goal; the score stood at 3–3 at half-time. However, disaster struck for Salford in the second half. They were overwhelmed by four Wigan tries to trail 17–3. James conjured up a consolation try in the corner after he chased a ball propelled by Cook over the head of Price, although he missed a difficult goal attempt.

There was an unusual finale to the match after Salford forward Charlie Rees had carried the ball towards the Wigan in-goal area. When the ball came loose, James raced up and placed a hand on it to claim a try, but referee Jack Smith ruled it had already gone dead and disallowed the score. It was a controversial decision because most of the Salford players believed it was still in play. After the final whistle, James 'invited' Mr Smith to walk with him to the spot in the in-goal where he had grounded the ball. This he duly did "accompanied by a couple of thousand spectators!" According to the *Salford Reporter*, the official admitted a fair try had indeed been scored, the explanation was that straw piled up behind the dead-ball line had spilled into the in-goal and covered the chalk marking the line. The referee, of course, said he could not alter his decision. One wonders how many referees today would dare review a debateable decision on the playing area while surrounded by thousands of spectators. Although unable to get his team into its first championship final, James had put on a good show. On the other hand, Lavery – who played at full-back – was ostracised for his poor performance, the local press complained that "Times without number Lavery was tackled in possession when a pass... would have removed the danger". It turned out to be the last of just four first team appearances by the New Zealander for the Reds.

There had to be mixed feelings associated with the season ending in the way it had for Salford. With limited financial resources, they had managed to reach the semi-final stage of the two major competitions, partly due to fielding a consistent line-up with only 20 players called on for first team duty. The problem was that the trophy cabinet, if, indeed, there was one, lay empty yet again. James Lomas had continued to shine and a huge part of Salford's success – such as it was – lay firmly on his broad shoulders. He ended the campaign second in the NU charts for points with 205, and goals with 62, and also scored 27 tries. But he was not about to put his rugby boots into temporary storage and spend the summer in Maryport as he had so often done in the past. He had a bigger adventure with the trip of a lifetime ahead of him.

The 1910 Northern Union tour party.
Back: T. Helm (Oldham), G. Ruddick (Broughton R), F. Shugars (Warrington), R. Ramsdale (Wigan),
E. Curzon (Salford), J. Leytham (Wigan), W. Winstanley (Leigh); third row: F. Boylen (Hull),
J. Thomas (Wigan), H. Kershaw (Wakefield T), F. Smith (Hunslet), J. Lomas (Salford, captain),
T. Newbould (Wakefield T), W. Jukes (Hunslet), J. Bartholomew (Huddersfield), W. Ward (Leeds);
second row: W. Dell (visitor), F. Webster (Leeds), W. Batten (Hunslet), B. Jenkins (Wigan),
J.H. Houghton and J. Clifford (joint tour managers), A. Avery (Oldham), J. Riley (Halifax), J. Davies
(Huddersfield), D. Murray (trainer); front: J. Sharrock (Wigan), F. Young (Leeds),
T. Jenkins (Ebbw Vale), F. Farrar (Hunslet).

14. 1910: The first Lions captain

James Lomas once said "I never played better than I did when in Australia", referring to the 1910 inaugural Northern Union tour, which also included New Zealand in its itinerary. James arrived in Sydney with a reputation that had preceded him but, after his side was beaten in the opening two matches, both against New South Wales, the Australian press claimed the NU players were not quite what they had been cracked up to be. Comments about excess weight and lack of fitness were aimed at them. It was in the third match – again facing New South Wales – that James shook Sydney's Agricultural Ground to its very foundations. In a sizzling, unbelievable performance James had the Australian fans cheering for him as he turned all pre-match predictions on their head. In one magical hour he had cemented his reputation down under; the *Sydney Morning Herald* said that "Lomas showed that he was a marvel". It was a performance that lifted his colleagues and their supremacy was rarely challenged after that match.

One of the players he opposed in that momentous clash was forward Bill Cann, a Kangaroo tourist to Britain in 1908–09 and 1911–12 who returned in 1921–22 as their joint-tour manager. Writing in the *Sydney Morning Herald* in June 1946, Cann said: "James Lomas brought the first English side to Australia in 1910. England had some great personalities. Indeed, I don't think their standard could ever have been higher than during this period. They had so many men with glorious records. The 1910 team had three great centres, Lomas, [Billy] Batten and [Bert] Jenkins. Lomas, a Cumberland wrestler, stockily built, was as strong as a bullock and hard to pull down [and] he was fairly fast."

Having welcomed touring sides to Britain from Australia and New Zealand, the idea of a reciprocal visit by the NU was first raised in late 1908. However, following a lengthy period of negotiations, it was not until 15 February 1910 that terms were finally agreed and a tour confirmed. The clubs were asked to nominate players "who will do honour to the Northern Union on and off the field." One player clearly at the top of the NU's wish list was James Lomas. On 26 February 1910, the *Salford Reporter* revealed that "Lomas has been offered the captaincy of the English team to tour in Australia, New Zealand, and, possibly, America." This appears to contradict a popular belief that James was elected after the full party was chosen and that his role may even have been determined during the voyage to the southern hemisphere. One of the reasons for this speculation is that contemporary reports, which announced the players selected, omitted to mention who the captain was, which implied it had not been decided. It seems the Australians had an inkling, though, because *The Mercury*, published in Hobart, Tasmania, on 20 April, included a list of the final tour party, sent from London on 18 April, which said that James "will probably be captain".

Apart from the obvious choice of James, the Salford officials, following a meeting with their players on 26 February, the date of their Challenge Cup match with York Irish National League, nominated Jimmy Cook, Dai John and Ephraim Curzon for consideration. An NU

157

sub-committee, following its meeting on 3 March, announced the names of the first 13 players invited to tour, four of whom, including James, had already agreed the terms offered; 10 shillings (50 pence) per week on board ship, £1 per week on land, and £1 per week for a player's family at home, if he was married. The team would also share a third of any profits. Of the remaining nine who still had to formally accept the terms, just three – for varying reasons – did not eventually make the trip.

Meanwhile, the other players required to make up the total of 26 were to be determined on the basis of two tour trial matches. The 'First Selected' (those who had already signed up for the tour) opposed the 'Yorkshire Probables' at Headingley on Monday 14 March and the 'Lancashire Probables' seven days later at Central Park. James took part at Headingley, and played in the centre for 'First Selected', who wore white jerseys while their opponents played in individual club colours. He scored two tries and a conversion in a 27–16 win over the Yorkshire aspirants. The *Yorkshire Post* reporter showed foresight in saying "Lomas was as resourceful as ever, and will probably be one of the successes of the tour."

James was not required for the second trial, a match that included Cook, John and Curzon. The latter was subsequently asked to join James on tour, a meteoric rise for the 26-year-old forward after less than two seasons as an NU player. According to the NU's official tour guide, published by the *Athletic News*, Curzon was born in Crumpsall, although the *Salford Reporter* once gave nearby Cheetham Hill as his birthplace. He had played rugby union in Cape Town in South Africa before he moved to Scotland where he spent two seasons as a threequarter for Lismore in Edinburgh and one with Kirkcaldy in Fife, prior to joining Salford. His wanderings were due to his work in the legal profession. Having played both codes, he gave his thoughts on their merits to the *Salford Reporter* in October 1908, saying that he "admired the Northern Union game which he admits is faster than that of rugby union, but he is strongly of the opinion that there is a terrible want of combination in the front rank as compared with scrimmages under the parent code."

On Monday evening, 18 April, the Salford directors held a celebratory dinner at the Victoria Hotel, Manchester, to honour the departure of their two players. All the club officials and players were invited. Club chairman, Fred Hampson, paid tribute to the pair, and concluded that "all followers of the sport in Salford trusted that they would cover themselves with glory out there." Further speeches followed, director Mr Crossfield announced that he would present both players with a photo of the R.M.S. Osterley, the steam ship that would convey them to Australia. Another official, Herbert Dawson, gave James a mascot "in the shape of Policeman William, who could no doubt look after them in foreign climes." Their playing colleagues presented them with a "handsome pipe" each and a "stock of tobacco". The vice-captain, Willie Thomas, received a round of applause after he said he would "personally watch their career and trusted them to do honour to the club they represented". Loud cheering followed when James arose and, having said he "much regretted the unfortunate finish to the Salford season" he was "going out to Australia to represent Salford and Cumberland, and incidentally Cumberland was England." He intended "to be a credit to Salford [and could be] depended on to do his level best to keep up his reputation and that of the club." He signed off to showers of applause after he said "it was a great honour to be selected". Curzon also gave "a neat little speech". Finally, the directors presented each player with "a full and complete outfit" of clothes and provisions plus a cheque "to assist them in holding their own with other representatives going out."

The majority of the tourists departed from Tilbury Docks near London on Friday 15 April aboard the Osterley. The Lancashire section of the party, including James, had missed their train from Manchester, but arrived in time to meet up with those who had travelled down from Yorkshire. Several suffered with sea sickness early in the voyage and, by the Saturday evening, joint tour manager Joe Houghton reported "we looked like a deserted ship" due to so many having sought refuge. There was welcome respite with a one-hour stop at Gibraltar before the long six week journey continued. It was while at sea that news came through of the death, on 6 May, of King Edward VII due to pneumonia. His place on the throne was taken by King George V, who became patron of the Northern Rugby Football Union in April 1911, although there is no record of him ever actually witnessing a match.

They arrived in Sydney on Thursday 26 May where they were to stay at the Grand Hotel, situated in the Waverley district. The party was met by several representatives of the New South Wales Rugby League and a posse of pressmen eager to interview the players. One unnamed player said he would be glad to start training, something that had been difficult to properly do on board, which led to the players increasing their waistlines. They were joined one week later by the six remaining players, who arrived on the R.M.S. Malwa on 2 June. Their later journey — they left London on 27 April — was because five of them played in the Oldham versus Wigan Championship Final on 23 April, while a sixth, Hunslet's Batten, required extra time to prove a knee injury had healed satisfactorily.

The first match of the tour was played on Saturday 4 June, at The Royal Agricultural Society Showground, commonly referred to as the Agricultural Ground, in Sydney. The opposition was New South Wales. Any concerns as to whether the tour would be a financial flop were dispelled by a crowd reported as 33,000. It was claimed to be the largest so far for the NU game despite it being a miserable, overcast day. The playing area was 'sloppy' after earlier rain. There was a sense of theatre before the match; the Australians emerged with a kangaroo in tow while the NU team was followed by a man who wore a lion costume with laced trousers and boots. As both sides emerged a band played *Three cheers for the red, white and blue*. The blue represented the colours of New South Wales, the red and white that of the NU side whose tour livery was red and white hooped jerseys, which signified the red and white roses of Lancashire and Yorkshire, respectively, with the NU badge on the left breast, and dark shorts.

The NU side, which was referred to in Australia as 'England' despite the inclusion of seven Welsh players and one Scot in the party, for this historic opening match was: Frank

Young (Leeds); Jack Bartholomew (Huddersfield), Lomas (Salford), Chick Jenkins (Ebbw Vale), Fred Farrar (Hunslet); Johnny Thomas (Wigan), Fred Smith (Hunslet); Frank Boylen (Hull), Bill Jukes (Hunslet), Dick Ramsdale (Wigan), George Ruddick (Broughton Rangers), Fred Webster (Leeds), Billy Winstanley (Leigh). Understandably, it was not the best of starts. One of the tourists said "our form… was frightful and our forwards hopelessly beaten for possession five times out of six", and admitted part of the problem was they were out of condition having not trained properly nor played a game for some time. The signs were good when James won the toss before kick-off and began the match with a favourable wind. There was little in it at half-time, the New South Welshman led 8–6. All the tourists' points were scored by James with three penalties. His first, awarded for a scrum infringement. was a 40-yard effort that was scored "amidst great cheering", his second gave the NU an encouraging 4–0 lead after 10 minutes play. One Sydney newspaper, quoted in the *Oldham Evening Chronicle*, said: "After the kick-off England was awarded a free-kick and Lomas displayed great generalship. His deliberate attitude was most pleasing and he punted high towards the centre of the goal, when the forwards swooped on to it and rushing down like one man had New South Wales in trouble." It was an incident that illustrated the Maryport man's determination from the onset, his resolve continued throughout the tour.

The game was played at a terrific pace, the new code excited the Australian crowd to the point where they were described as being "in a ferment". The tourists, though, wavered after the interval as New South Wales gained the ascendancy. There were probably three reasons for this. First and foremost there was the lack of fitness by the NU men that took its toll as the match wore on. Second was the loss of Farrar with a shoulder injury shortly before half-time, which reduced them to 12 men throughout the second half. And, finally, there was the interpretation of the rules by referee Tom McMahon. The tourists did take a 9–8 lead after a try from Thomas – their first of the tour – after Lomas, who failed with the conversion, had made the initial break following "a loose rush". There was an unusual occurrence when Dally Messenger took a penalty for New South Wales, one touch judge raised his flag, the other – who the referee agreed with – signalled no goal. Undeterred, the Australians forged out an 18–9 lead, the NU then claimed a second try, by Ramsdale under the posts. It came after James had created mayhem by sending the ball skywards from a penalty awarded on halfway, Webster gathered the ball and made the scoring pass. Thomas landed the goal and with 10 minutes left they trailed 18–14. But the effort required was too much and a couple of further tries from the hosts gave them a 28–14 victory. The *Sydney Morning Herald* concluded: "[The NU] on reputation played much below their form. It was too bad to be true. At the beginnings there were some misgivings when Lomas, the English captain, had put on four points to nil. These, however, were the outcome in the first place of infringements of the law by New South Wales. Having been given the chance of a free [penalty] at goal, the visiting captain showed that he was a

160

The NU side that played New South Wales in the first ever tour match. Back: T. Jenkins (Ebbw Vale), W. Winstanley (Leigh), R. Ramsdale (Wigan), G. Ruddick (Broughton R), J. Thomas (Wigan). Middle: F. Young (Leeds), W. Jukes (Hunslet), J. Lomas (Salford, captain), F. Boylen (Hull), J. Bartholomew (Huddersfield). Front: F. Webster (Leeds), F. Farrar (Hunslet), F. Smith (Hunslet).

James strikes the ball during the goal-kicking competition held before the first test match at Sydney Agricultural Showground on 18 June 1910. He defeated Australia's Dally Messenger by 3 goals to 2.

pretty sure left-foot goal-kicker. Thereafter the New South Welshmen shook themselves into their stride and took command of the game." There was, however, acknowledgement that it had been a great game to watch, "wonderful in pace and in incident of individual and collective value."

There was post-match comment in the Australian press that the NU officials had not allowed the injured Farrar to be replaced. Australia, some 50-odd years ahead of Britain in its thinking, allowed a man to come on in such circumstances, but NU rules forbade it. There was a quick discussion at the time of the incident "but the English managers were determined to play to their own rules." It was also clear that the NU had an issue over the way the Australians fed the scrum, the ball frequently hit the leg of one of their forwards and bounced back to the scrum-half, who was allowed to play on. Even the Australian journalists sympathised with the Northern Union on that anomaly.

Two days later, on Monday, there was another bumper crowd of around 40,000 to witness a rematch at the same venue on a cold, but dry day. James missed with an early penalty opportunity, but soon found himself among the points. He followed up a rush by his forwards to dive on the ball in the New South Wales in-goal for a try that he converted with an excellent goal shot. After 25 minutes play his main adversary, Messenger, levelled the scores at 5–5. He had thrilled the Sydney crowd with a mesmerising run for a try which he also goaled. Another converted try put the state team ahead before James's penalty made the score 10–7 in the Australians' favour at half-time. In a match that was often played at a quick pace, the men in blue raced ahead in the second half to lead 27–10. The NU side staged a late revival which, while not turning defeat into victory, made the final score-line more respectable. First, Thomas found his way over the try-line, Leytham converted, before James, with a wonderful powerful run, broke through for his second touchdown, and added the goal. The tourists were again hampered by refereeing decisions; the continuing problem of the ball not entering the scrum from the Australians' feed allied to an adverse penalty count did not help their cause. There was also another aspect highlighted by an unnamed correspondent to the *Oldham Evening Chronicle*, who said: "The ball used here is somewhat different from the one used in the Old Country, which makes a material difference in the kicking of our Northern Union players, but it is one that will be quickly overcome."

New South Wales again supplied the opposition for the third tour game, the venue, once more, was the Agricultural Ground. Watched by 27,000 – which brought the three-match aggregate up to an amazing 100,000 – it was a landmark fixture for the tourists' credibility and probably the wellbeing of the venture overall. There had been many dissenting voices about the quality of the British side, based on the opening two fixtures, but all of that changed on Saturday 11 June. The *Sydney Morning Herald* said afterwards that an improvement in the visitors' form had been expected "but there was probably not one [person] at Saturday's great contest who anticipated that the visitors would run over New South Wales for five-sixth's of the game [the last 15 minutes favoured New South Wales]. It

162

is difficult to imagine that it was practically the same English side as that of the two preceding matches." The paper claimed the NU's performance "rivalled that of any combination ever seen in Sydney for brilliance, combination, pace and tackling."

The match was a triumph for James, the *Sydney Morning Herald* left its readers with no illusions whatsoever: "The hero of the match was undoubtedly Lomas, the English captain [and] he scored the whole 18 points first registered [it was actually 16, but who's counting?], doing it with play which will never be forgotten by those who had the good fortune to witness it. His goal kicking was remarkably accurate, and no distance seemed too long for him to span, one goal coming from more than halfway. The impression made by his success in profiting by the mistakes of the home team is shown by the fact that when an infringement occurred within 10 yards of his own goal some of the spectators cried, 'Have a kick for goal, Lomas!' But it was not only in goalkicking that Lomas proved himself a champion. The second try, which he secured, was brought about by a run from the home 25 to the corner, in the course of which he was tackled by half a dozen opponents, but so strongly did he go through them that they quite failed."

James's one-man point scoring crusade began early when New South Wales were penalised for scrum offences, the referee had at last clamped down on the scrum-feeding issues that dogged the tourists in the opening matches. From just inside the opposition half he landed a penalty to "deafening cheers" after one such misdemeanour. With the tidying up of the scrums, the NU forwards won a higher percentage of possession than before. As one NU player later outlined: "it enabled us to get our attacking machinery working". James added a second penalty before giving the Australian crowd a sample of what to expect later with a powerful break that spelt danger for the defence, who eventually grassed him through sheer weight of numbers. With the play "fast and furious" and the crowd "at fever heat", James again hit the target with a third penalty, which extended the NU's lead to 6–0.

When Jack Hickey broke for the Blues he looked a certain scorer but, as one of James's teammates told the *Oldham Evening Chronicle*: "Lomas – the ever ready – came tearing along and brought him down in great style. Our captain was playing a fine game. He was here, there and everywhere, and always where required." James continued to be a nuisance after the interval and, when a high ball bounced awkwardly for Charles Russell, he was alert to the opportunity; he grabbed hold and hurled himself over the try-line. For once he proved fallible because his goal attempt was a poor one. But, as the *Sydney Morning Herald* said, he was still proving to be "a dandy in every department of the game", with two more goals in just over a minute; from a mark and a penalty, which pushed the score to 13–0.

The NU skipper had another ace up his sleeve, and brought the house down by taking the ball from his own 25 area to score in the corner. As one of his colleagues said later, "Man after man tried to down him and I should say at least half-a-dozen grabbed him but he brushed them aside and sailed over. This solo effort fairly roused the crowd who cheered themselves hoarse, and it deserved it. It was a really magnificent effort." He missed the touchline goalkick, but the tourists led 16–0, all scored by James. Again he made a strong run which took him over the try-line, but was tackled in doing so, the try was disallowed. However, in the scrum that followed, New South Wales were penalised once more and, this time "to vary matters" Thomas landed the goal. The Australians finally found their way over the line with tries from Hickey and Messenger; the latter converted both. Their efforts, meanwhile, were dissected by a touchdown from Shugars, Leytham added the extras.

The praise for James's contribution to the 23–10 victory was as warm as the weather, the *Sydney Sun* said: "Lomas, the English captain, played the best game on the field. The sturdy Britisher proved a tower in defence; in attack he shone out above his fellows, and scored two tries, and kicked five goals. It was a wonderful performance, and was quite up to some of Dally Messenger's best. He is a hard left-footed kick, and his action appears slightly cumbersome, but his direction and elevation are splendid."

At the time, possibly influenced by the design in Australian Rules football, the Australians used a ball that was slimmer and more of an oval shape than the more rounded British version. Bill Cann had admired James's goalkicking in his aforementioned 1946 feature in the Sydney *Morning Herald*: "He was the first man to stand the ball right up, and he made a half-circle in his peculiar run to the ball." It was an interesting comment to make. Was James indeed the first player to stand the ball up – as opposed to lying it flat and pointed towards its target – or was it that he was the first player from the Mother Country to take this new art to Australia?

The following Wednesday afternoon the tourists played their fourth consecutive match at the Agricultural Ground, the opposition this time was the grandly named Metropolis select. James had his first breather, and stood down from a game that became rough at times, particularly in the latter stages. The *Sydney Sportsman* commented: "Sundry swings and uppercuts were handed out in the most generous fashion." The outcome was the late dismissal of Hickey (Metropolis) and Boylen (NU) for fighting. Watched by about 3,000, although one source suggested 5,000, the tourists won 34–25 having led 21–15 at half-time. The NU paid a price for their victory, and injuries to Young (knee – he did not play again on tour) and Bartholomew (ribs – out for six weeks) were huge blows. Having taken 26 players, their numbers were already depleted through the unavailability of Oldham's Scottish-born forward Tom Helm, who did not to play at all on tour due to a knee problem.

Meanwhile, the rest had left James fresh for the following weekend's opening test against Australia, the Agricultural Ground again provided the setting. Before the kick-off it had been arranged that James would oppose Messenger to determine the 'goalkicking championship of the Northern Union', a trophy to be presented to the winner by a Mr A. Ford. The contest must have revived memories for James of his teenage years at the Maryport club. In his memoirs, he said: "I have won a few goal kicking competitions and long kicks competitions in Cumberland." The latter discipline, presumably, related to measuring where the ball actually landed, a term referred to then as 'from place to pitch.'

In Sydney, both players were allowed six shots at goal; three from the 25 yard line – one from centre, two from each flank five yards from the touchline – with a further three from halfway in similar positions. James excelled with his kicking from the 25 yard line and landed all three, while Messenger succeeded with two. The next round of shots, from halfway, was clearly more challenging and neither player found the target although, reportedly, four of the aggregate six attempts went close. Again, writing in his memoirs, James recalled it as a 'world' title contest, which, within the context of the NU, it could be argued that it was: "I beat Messenger for the championship of the world 3–2. It has never been played for since so I must still be champion. I got a silver cup and gold medal." The whereabouts of either is now unclear. The 'silver cup' was probably the trophy presented by Mr Ford. James also received a gold watch on his return home, its inscription endorsed his memories of winning a 'world's championship', but more of that in the next chapter.

Because of the on-field incidents in the previous encounter with the Metropolis, security had been stepped up for the test match. The *Sydney Sportsman* reported that "the ground was surrounded by a small army of police. The police have finally decided on a campaign against any rough football." Apparently, they had the power to arrest and prosecute wrongdoers with a £5 fine or even 12 months in prison. There was a reported crowd of 42,000, claimed to be a record crowd despite big counter attractions. The *Sydney Sportsman* reckoned the "willing go of the previous Wednesday" had been a marvellous advertisement. England's joint manager, John Clifford, took no chances, and reportedly visited both dressing rooms before the start to emphasise that a repeat of Wednesday's altercations could prove the death-knell of the code.

The Northern Union team was: Jim Sharrock (Wigan); Billy Batten (Hunslet), Lomas, Bert Jenkins (Wigan), James Leytham (Wigan); Thomas, Tommy Newbould (Wakefield Trinity); Bert Avery (Oldham), Curzon, Jukes, Ramsdale, Billy Ward (Leeds), Webster. Mr Clifford had his fears dispelled in what was another tremendously exciting encounter, described as "one of the best exhibitions of football" seen since the NU came into existence. James's team triumphed 27–20, the *Sydney Sun* exclaimed "The suddenness with which the visitors have found true form is a shock to everyone" and noted that the tourists combined "weight and pace". The NU captain again excelled, press comments such as "Lomas generally required four opponents to bring him to earth" and "Lively Lomas did a number of solid bumping runs, and his clever foot was in evidence any time a goal looked at all likely" were typical.

The tourists did not make the best of starts and were 12–3 behind at one stage, their efforts hampered through a bad injury to Sharrock, the unfortunate Wigan full-back collapsed from concussion and was taken off. Shortly before half-time, they staged a comeback through tries from Thomas and Leytham, his second of the match – James embellished the former – to reduce the deficit to just one point. The recovery was completed in the second half with four more tries. Jukes became an unlikely star by claiming the first three. His opener, which put the NU ahead for the first time at 14–12, preceded him being injured and he was carried off which left just 11 tourists on the field. In true action hero style he returned – shortly followed by a far from healthy looking Sharrock – to complete his hat-trick with two touchdowns in quick succession. The first of these owed much to his skipper, who took the ball from one of the Australians, close to the touchline and inside his own half, and raced down the field. As he was about to be overhauled he passed to Jenkins who put Jukes in. James converted both of the Hunslet forward's latter efforts and, almost inevitably, set up the final score; he opened up the defence for a try by Batten. James missed the goal and, although they responded with eight more points, Australia were well beaten.

The *Sydney Morning Herald* lauded James's efforts: "Every time the visitors secured possession of the ball and started their passing rushes, even in their own half, there came a cry from the crowd, 'They're in', and the feeling was more pronounced when Lomas had the ball... Lomas was the best man on the ground and he was splendidly supported by the other three-quarters... The English captain is a man of many parts, of many dodges, and of great strength. With legs of great development, and with it speed, and a head for doing the right thing at the right moment, he took a power of stopping and of putting down, while his tackling was more of the wrestle, for the man tackled invariably had to go down."

On the same day as the test, the tourists' first match outside Sydney took place some 80 miles north, against a Newcastle and District XIII. Played on the Saturday evening, it goes without saying that the players who made the trip were not involved in the test but, with injuries having taken their toll, they required assistance from five outsiders. Three of them – who played in the threequarters and were 1908–09 Kangaroo tourists – had recently returned from England; Jim Devereux and Andy Morton, who had both been with Hull, and Dan Frawley who had been at Warrington. The other two – both forwards – were Alby Burge, a former Australian rugby union 'Wallaby', and Con Byrne, a member of the 1907–08 New Zealand 'All Golds'. Watched by around 3,000 people, the NU combination won 24–8.

Joined by their colleagues, a second game was played against the Newcastle and District side on the following Wednesday. According to Avery, who sent regular bulletins to the *Oldham Evening Chronicle* during the tour, the 'test' contingent – which would have included James – travelled to Newcastle on the Monday, a train journey of three and a half hours that took in some "beautiful scenery" on the way. They were officially received at the local Town Hall by the Australian Native Association and in the words of Avery: "Speeches were, of course, a prominent feature, and Mr Houghton and our worthy captain, Lomas, responded to the toasts in a very efficient manner. There is no question about it, 'our Jimmy' is becoming quite an orator, and fairly brings down the house every time."

The game took place on a dull, overcast day that threatened rain. Although some sources list the attendance as again being 3,000, the *Sydney Morning Herald* considered it a "large crowd" for that region. They saw a fast, attractive game, one that was won comfortably by the tourists, 40–20, although at one stage during the second half, they were only 15–12 in front. The British side scored 10 tries, which included three from Farrar and a couple in the first half from James's Salford colleague, Curzon. None of their five first half tries were converted but, after the break, as the *Sydney Morning Herald* explained, the tourists "swept like a tornado through the scattered defence of their opponents, and took tries whenever they desired them. Lomas also commenced to kick in the way he usually does and the five tries which the Englishmen scored in the second half were all converted [by Lomas]". James, whose first goal was a fabulous touchline effort, also scored the tourists' final try.

Following the match and "after a right good send off" according to Avery, the tourists boarded an 8.50pm train to Wallangarra on the New South Wales-Queensland state border, where they changed trains the next day to join the main Queensland line. Their destination was Brisbane, where they arrived at 10.20pm on the Thursday. They were greeted by a "deafening cheer" at the station from whence they were conveyed by 'char-a-banc' to their hotel where they were entertained by Brisbane League officials. The plan was to play three matches at Brisbane's Exhibition Ground, including the second test.

The first game, on Saturday 25 June, was against Queensland. Rain, a muddy field, and an estimated 7,000 crowd awaited them. At 3.15pm, the Queensland side, accompanied by a baby kangaroo, trooped onto the field. They were followed by the tourists who were referred to by the *Brisbane Courier* as 'Great Britain' some 37 years before that title became official. Following a Herb Brackenreg penalty, James levelled the score at 2–2 via a "beautiful left-foot place kick" from near halfway following offside at a scrum. By half-time the NU led 18–6, four tries – one converted by James, another by Thomas – were responded to by a couple more Brackenreg penalties. The tourists pulled away in the second half to win 33–9. James scored the first of the visitors' three final tries, the *Brisbane Courier* described it thus: "When the leather had gradually moved up into the corner near the dressing shed, Lomas got away and darted over." James also notched his third goal, when he converted a try by Chick Jenkins. The day ended with dinner at the North Brisbane Junior Club where 'several musical items' lightened the proceedings.

On Monday 27 June, Prince Edward, the future King Edward VIII, was created Prince of Wales on his 16th birthday, his father – the former Prince of Wales – had succeeded to the throne as George V. The day was declared a national holiday in Australia, a decision only made on 24 June. Whether the touring players were over-excited at the events that followed is not recorded. The secretary of the New South Wales Rugby League, Ted Larkin, cabled Mr Houghton, who was in Brisbane with his squad, to ask if they would send a team back to Sydney to meet a side labelled the 'Kangaroos' at the Agricultural Ground on that Monday. After consulting with the players, the offer was accepted. It led to an arduous return journey to Sydney for those selected, including James. They departed from Brisbane at 7.50am on Sunday and arrived at 11.30am the following Monday, just three hours before the scheduled 2.30pm kick-off. They could barely have had time to change after the game because their return train pulled out of Sydney at 5.10pm and it was not until 10pm the next day before they arrived back in Brisbane. A report in the *Oldham Evening Chronicle* said that the railway journey between Brisbane and Sydney covered 724 miles.

In Australian rugby league being a member of the 'Kangaroos' is an honorary position – like being a 'Lion' in Britain – and one that is reserved for those who have toured. Thus the side they met in Sydney were all members of their 1908–09 tour party which just one exception; Albert Broomham, who did tour himself in 1911–12, who deputised on the wing for an unavailable player. It was little wonder, given the haste in which they had had to shoehorn the match into their itinerary, that the tourists lost 22–10. The estimated crowd of 30,000 provided some justification for their endeavour and, no doubt, helped swell the tour coffers. The *Sydney Morning Herald* conceded that – following a hectic opening 30 minutes of play – the trip took its toll on the NU men "otherwise they would have sustained their earlier effort and rendered a better account of themselves". The Northern Union actually led 10–6 at the interval, James kicked a penalty and converted a try from Ramsdale, but, after that, they were a spent force.

The party arrived back in Brisbane late on Tuesday evening. There was no respite for them because there was another match against Queensland at the Exhibition Ground the next day. Not surprisingly, there were plenty of changes to the team that had met the Kangaroos, with just four players retained and James was not one of them. The *Brisbane Courier* reported a crowd of 1,500. On a cloudy, bleak day, the tourists, who led 12–2 at half-time, won 15–4.

Three days later, on Saturday 2 July, the second test was held at the same venue. James resumed his place in a much changed line-up. However, prior to the 3.15pm kick-off, he had another duty to perform. As with the opening test, a pre-match goalkicking contest had been organised, scheduled for 3pm. On this occasion there were to be three representatives; Messenger, for New South Wales, and James, for England, were joined by Brackenreg, who carried the hopes of Queensland in his boots. This time it was to be decided from three shots each, all from the 25-yard line. It commenced with the three players having one attempt near the touchline on the grandstand side, Brackenreg was the only player to succeed. Both Australians found the target with their second efforts, taken in the centre of the line and as James missed once more it meant he was out of the running. The final round was from the opposite flank, no one hit the mark and it left Brackenreg to receive a trophy provided by Mr R.W. Eve.

On what was a fine and warm day, the match finally got underway, 18,000 having gathered inside the enclosure. Curiously, Avery's despatches to the *Oldham Evening Chronicle* suggest James's co-centre Joe Riley of Halifax captained the team on this occasion, although this is at odds with another report that says James won the coin toss before kick-off. Avery, incidentally, had, himself, led the side against Queensland in James's absence a few days earlier, although Riley also played in that match. Australia must have

168

had their fans roaring with approval as they took an 11–0 lead in the first half thanks to three tries. It was the ever-reliable James that kick-started the revival. He got hold of the ball and, in the words of Avery, "with one of his favourite bursts, broke through the defence and gave to Leytham", the winger took possession near the Australian try-line to score. According to the *Sydney Morning Herald*, the revitalised Anglo-Welsh combination began to inject "great vim" into their game, a second try, from Thomas, followed just before the interval. James added both conversions to reduce the arrears to 11–10.

Australia threatened again after the restart but were kept at bay, and it was Wakefield Trinity forward Herbert Kershaw who claimed the next try. James's goal attempt hit the upright, but the tourists now held the lead, 13–11, and would not lose it. The match was turning into another thrilling, memorable contest, although referee Jack Fihelly cautioned the British players several times for over-exuberant play. The NU extended the lead when Leytham claimed his second try, although the tourists became increasingly frustrated with the referee's decisions and Ruddick was sent off for striking an opponent. Although down to 12 men, they retained their momentum, Leytham increased his try-count to four with two further touchdowns, Australia replied with two of their own to close the scoring. James had an off-day with his goalkicking, and compounded his disappointment in the pre-match contest with further frustration during the match. Avery commented that "Lomas seemed to have left his kicking boots at the hotel, as he only kicked two goals out of seven or eight attempts." Nonetheless, the 22–17 victory meant he could draw immense pride from becoming the first tour captain to win a test series in Australia.

With the outcome of the series already settled it was, apparently, decided to replace the 'dead' third test, at the Agricultural Ground on Saturday 9 July, with a match against Australasia. It is worth explaining that, for many years, historians in Australia argued for a different version of events in this inaugural test series in Australia. While the British maintained that the two wins in Sydney and Brisbane resulted in a 2–0 win, Australian sources claimed only the first of those was a 'test', the series being completed by two games against 'Australasia'.

It is difficult to understand how the confusion arose. Contemporary reports in the Australian press support the British argument that the initial two matches were both tests and that the meetings with Australasia were special events in their own right. One of Avery's reports in the *Oldham Evening Chronicle* also confirmed this view: "Seeing we had won the first two it was thought that the third game would not be such a good attraction. It was therefore decided to substitute a match with the Australasians." A retrospective in the *Sydney Morning Herald*, in June 1946, also agreed that "Lomas's team won both matches officially included among the tests – one in Sydney, the other in Brisbane". It is curious, though, that the initial itinerary for the matches in New South Wales, published in the *Sydney Morning Herald* on 1 June, already showed the opposition for the 9 July fixture as the Australasians. Unless there was a subsequent change of plan, it implies that the match was never intended to be against Australia.

Whatever the reality of the situation, the game against Australasia, composed of 10 New South Welshman, one Queenslander and two New Zealanders, certainly captured the public's interest and it has been claimed that as many as 50,000 attended. The *Sydney Morning Herald* reported the figure as closer to 43,000, and said it was the largest gathering since 52,000 saw New South Wales oppose New Zealand in a rugby union match on the Sydney Cricket Ground in 1907. The *Sydney Sun* claimed it was a "first in the history of Rugby [that] teams representing Australasia and England [had] met." It was certainly a successful venture, the same paper said that "as an inspiring spectacle it was splendid, there was hardly a dull moment from start to finish."

On a beautiful day, the crowd must have had their appetite for the main course well and truly whetted by the spectacular *hors d'oeuvre* provided by 100 smartly attired British sailors, otherwise known as 'blue jackets'. Using long ropes they pulled a 'drag', similar to a wagonette, containing the NU team into the enclosure and around the perimeter of the playing pitch to the huge delight of a cheering crowd. The sailors – from His Majesty's ships currently in port – hosted the tourists the previous Wednesday, when they entertained them at Royal Navy House, and said then they wanted to undertake this task. The tour managers were, apparently, not too struck with the idea, but the sailors persisted and intercepted the horse-drawn trap at the zoo situated near the ground, removed the animals and attached ropes instead. Can James and his team-mates ever have experienced a more incredible, surreal entrance to a game?

The first half was described as "wonderfully fast" although the British again got off to a slow start, as the Australasians built up an 8–2 advantage. James had made an early charge at the opposition line from Bert Jenkins's pass but "was brought down a struggling unit" before being on the mark with a penalty. A try by Leytham – James missed the goal – reduced the margin to 8–5 by half-time. After the interval, the Australasian lead stretched to 13–5 before the tourists staged a late rally. James was again at the forefront, and attempted to "bullock his way through" the defence before Avery finally got over. James missed with the kick at goal and, when Winstanley scored a further touchdown, the captain handed the ball to Thomas. It was not the easiest of chances, but the Wigan half-back's aim was true, and levelled the score at 13–13 "while his comrades turned somersaults and cheered in their joy of turning what looked like certain defeat into a draw". Excitement was at fever pitch, but no more points were added and it finished as the only draw of the tour.

In reality, James – having been the shining light on so many occasions – had what was probably his worst match of the tour. The *Sydney Morning Herald* declared that "Lomas was good but not up to the Lomas of earlier matches," while another Sydney newspaper was less kind: "Had the British captain, Lomas, been on form, his side must have won. There can be no doubt about that. Lomas' usually remarkably safe left foot was all askew on

170

Saturday... Then again Lomas once broke clean away and with only [full-back Riki] Papakura in front of him he hung on and was tackled by the Maori when there were three of his men trailing alongside waiting for a pass." Even Avery, who had played in the pack in that match, conceded: "Our backs seemed to be off, especially our centres, Lomas in particular being very much off his game. He kept dropping his passes and was very poor in kicking, which handicapped [his winger] Batten's play somewhat." However James could do no wrong as far as the blue jackets were concerned and, after the final whistle, they poured onto the ground and carried him off shoulder high.

A further match was organised against Australasia for the following Wednesday afternoon at Sydney's Wentworth Park. The problem was that the tourists were due to depart for New Zealand at midday on the S.S. Maheno. Fortunately, Mr Houghton was able to prevail upon the owners to delay the voyage for five hours. Possibly the team was preoccupied with thoughts of the impending journey across the Tasman Sea because they lost 32–15. The *Sydney Morning Herald* said they were "completely outclassed" in what was "a fast and furious contest of skill and endurance". A more poetic description was that it was "a struggle between the active athletic colonials and sturdy islanders". James did not play in this match, the paper suggested "The absence of Lomas was a handicap to the visitors, but even the presence of the redoubtable forward (sic) could not have averted defeat." The tourists were behind 17–15 at the interval, but collapsed in a second half that saw the late dismissal of Curzon for kicking Papakura on the leg. After the match – seen by 13,000 – the team left in haste on a wagonette to catch the waiting ship to Auckland.

James, at the front with the ball, and other tour party members face the lens the day after arriving in New Zealand for the second leg of their 1910 tour. (Photo: Courtesy Michael Turner)

They arrived at their destination on the following Sunday afternoon, 17 July, their first match took place at Auckland's Victoria Park on the Wednesday against the Maori. It was held on a saturated ground in heavy rain before about 5,000 spectators. The tourists continued to impress, just as in Australia, Wellington's *Evening Post* said "the showing of the Englishmen under these adverse conditions was so good that further matches are being eagerly anticipated". The Maori – who gave their traditional 'cry' before the game – finished a well beaten team, losing 29–0, much of the damage inflicted by the visiting forwards, who were just too quick for their hosts to cope with. With the ball in a very greasy state, James missed several early penalty attempts and was just off target after Riley scored the opening try. By the time the halfway mark was reached in the match, the tourists led 23–0; Bert Jenkins had claimed three tries and Smith another, James chipped in with two conversions and two penalties. Despite the fact that the sun had started to break through, it was decided to dispense with the half-time break and restart straight away. Almost immediately, Jenkins scored his fourth touchdown, James completed the scoring just before the finish with a spectacular seventh try when he raced from his own '25'.

The next day – Thursday – the touring party was treated to a day out at the expense of Mr Todd, the father of Wigan's Auckland-born threequarter Lance Todd. On Saturday 23 July, the second match took place, again at Victoria Park. On a showery day – although it cleared later – the tourists again won easily, by 52–9, watched by 10,000 spectators, a figure seen by the *Evening Post* as a "large attendance". The same paper said that "the game was fast and exciting throughout – an altogether brilliant exhibition." It got off to a good start for the home supporters when forward George Seagar scored the first try, but by half-time the British led 41–3. James ended the match with seven conversions and also scored the 10th of the Northern Union's dozen tries after he dribbled into the in-goal area. It is interesting to note the *Auckland Star* journalist's comments who observed that "English players rarely tackle low" unlike the New Zealanders, but tended to tackle around the body, enabling them to keep the player "under control" until he is released to play the ball.

Unlike later undertakings, the pioneering 1910 tour had not begun with a finalised schedule. This was amply demonstrated by the last-minute games added to the Australian leg and the proposed, but ultimately unfulfilled desire to play in America on the way home. Similarly, on arrival in New Zealand, there were only three matches so far agreed, all of them in Auckland. It had been hoped to take the NU code further afield, including New Zealand's South Island, but the logistical challenges of travelling to other areas of the country, plus the fact that the touring squad was decimated through injury, made such ambition difficult. One extra match was arranged, though, at Rotorua on Wednesday 27 July. James was not in the team that departed for the Bay of Plenty area by rail on the previous Monday, a journey of around 150 miles that took over eight hours. He was certainly not missed, his colleagues entertained a crowd that numbered about 600 with a 12-try 54–18 victory.

The last match in New Zealand was a one-off test at Auckland's Domain Cricket Ground on Saturday 30 July. It finished up as another emphatic win for the tourists, 52–20, although, according to the *Evening Post*, the crowd, estimated at 15,000 to 17,000, saw "another bright exhibition". New Zealand were not as completely outplayed as the score may suggest, and led 15–10 at the interval. For the third consecutive match the tourists registered a dozen tries, number eight was scored by James "after another brilliant passing run". His follow-up goal was one of his five successful conversions; he had begun his tally with a penalty.

The party departed from Auckland the next Monday, again aboard the Maheno, and arrived in Sydney on Friday. The fluid nature of the tour was re-emphasised through the insertion of a final match into their itinerary. It was to be a fourth meeting with New South Wales at the Agricultural Ground, arranged for Saturday 6 August. One problem to be overcome was the scheduled departure at noon that same day of the tour party back to England on the R.M.S. Otranto. Their ever-resourceful management decided those not involved in the match would climb aboard, the remainder – including James – would take a Melbourne-bound train two days later to catch up with the vessel.

The match drew a 20,000 crowd and the *Sydney Morning Herald* described the contest as a "fitting finale to a phenomenally successful tour". The game itself went in favour of the visitors, 50–12, their largest win of the tour in Australia. It was claimed, though, that it fell below expectations due its one-sided nature. It was hardly surprising! The New South Wales side was a shadow of the one that had played earlier. The cream of their crop was otherwise engaged at Brisbane Cricket Ground representing New South Wales against Queensland in the last of three interstate matches. James got the scoreboard ticking with a 25-yard penalty and added two conversions – one from a tricky angle in the face of the wind – as the tourists built up a 12–7 interval lead during a competitive opening half.

The second half – which was "full of brilliant passing by the English [who] electrified the crowd" – saw James sign off his tour in great style with a try, when he sped across the try-line at the corner, and six more goals – making it nine altogether. His performance was duly acknowledged in the *Sydney Morning Herald*: "Quite a feature of the match was the brilliant kicking of Lomas [and] the English captain kicked some wonderful goals from various angles, both with and against the wind." Of eight second half tries, James attempted to convert six; his only failure was after his own touchdown. He also landed another penalty. Having scored the opening points in the first match of the tour back in June, it seemed appropriate – as captain – that his last goal concluded the scoring in the final game.

As in club rugby, James finished top of the tourists' scoring charts; he headed the lists for goals with 53 and – with the help of 10 tries – points with 136. In a 1910 interview he gave an insight into the secret of his phenomenal success: "Well my occupation – there is nothing like work for fitness – is the main factor. In the summer I do a bit of track training, some wrestling, and never object to a good swim. I am not a teetotaller, although I take very little [alcohol], and am confident anyone who takes a lot can never be really fit. Careful living is essential to good condition. I have no regular method of training, but know what suits me and I make it my duty to be as sound as ever I can in wind and limb. I am a great believer in determination and think it was this spirit which made my reputation. I always went into a match determined to score or to know the reason why, and this, for the 13 years I have been playing football, resulted in my always being top scorer every season for whatever team I played. I was top for Maryport, top for Bramley, and top for Salford."

In the evening following the final game a farewell dinner was given for both teams at Sargents Café, situated in Sydney's Market Street. The speech makers included James, who thanked the Australians "for the fine time they had had in this country". The skipper and other remaining players boarded the train on Monday to begin their long trip home; they completed the 500-mile journey to Melbourne the following afternoon. Reunited with their colleagues on the Otranto, which had docked at Melbourne, they set off for England at 2.30pm on Wednesday 10 August.

So, the big adventure was winding down and James was, no doubt, looking forward to seeing his wife and family after almost five months away. On that voyage home his head must have been filled full of fond, wonderful memories that would remain for the rest of his life. In his 1930s memoirs he said: "We had a splendid tour but [it was] a bit rough. I believe on tours at first they [Australia] wanted to teach us the game, the same thing we went out to do to them too. I think we learned (sic) them a lesson which they are not likely to forget. They tried everything they knew. They are quite different now and play the game." James also recalled in the 'Prominent Salford Sportsmen' series, published in the *Salford Reporter* in 1926, that "it was an excellent tour, everyone was agreeable and we all enjoyed ourselves immensely, but on the field the Australians are keenness itself, and every match was a hard one, and if it was won we knew about it."

15. 1910–11: Return of the conquering hero

The tourists planted their feet firmly back on English soil on Friday 16 September 1910, but they did not alight at Tilbury – R.M.S Otranto's ultimate destination – but Plymouth. Logical thought suggests that the players would have wanted to extend their break from rugby until they regained their land legs. For James Lomas and his team there was little chance of that, and they all had to hang on a few days longer before seeing their homes and families.

While they had been sailing home, the Northern Union officials had been busy arranging fixtures for them on their arrival. The first was an exhibition match at Plymouth Argyle Football Club's Home Park. Bert Avery's brother Claude – both had played rugby union in Plymouth – had been negotiating with the NU to stage the game and, following an overnight stay at the Royal Hotel, the match took place on the Saturday. The *Western Daily Mercury* said that the players had been glad to have the chance of playing in Plymouth before they continued their journey home!

The match was styled as England versus Wales and the West (of England), the two sides were drawn from the returning tourists, although the latter was bolstered by five players, which included former Salford winger Bill Hyam who had recently joined Hull KR, all of them despatched to Plymouth for the occasion. The estimated attendance of 5,000 to 6,000 was reported to be of "ordinary dimensions" while the match itself was described as entertaining. James played in the centre for England and was credited as part of a threequarter line that "distinguished" itself. He scored three tries, England's opening two and their first after the interval, and kicked a conversion. A late Bert Avery goal from a mark gave Wales and West a 27–25 win, both teams scored seven tries.

The tourists then faced a journey of more than 200 miles to London where, on Monday 19 September, they caught a train to Leeds, and were welcomed by an enthusiastic crowd. During the afternoon, another match awaited them. At Headingley, James led a team of fellow 'Tourists' against the 'Anglo-Colonials', a side composed of England-based Australian and New Zealand players attached to NU clubs. The match – which attracted 4,000 spectators – was the focal point of an official reception for the tourists, who shared the gate money from the game with the British Playing Fields Association. The Tourists led 12–5 at half-time, but conceded 26 points in the second half to lose 31–15. The *Manchester Guardian* correspondent said that the "tourists have clearly lost condition on the long voyage and not in possession of form to do great things". As was the case on tour, James claimed the majority of his side's points, and scored nine of the 15 registered, all in the first half through two early penalties and the conversion of his own try. A post-match dinner followed, J.W. Wood, president of the Northern Union, in proposing a toast of 'The Tourists', said "every player has gone out and justified his selection". The joint tour managers, Joe Houghton and John Clifford, and James, as tour captain duly responded.

That particular Monday was to materialise into one of the most exciting and memorable of James's life. After the formalities were completed in Leeds, he caught a train to Manchester accompanied by Salford colleague Ephraim Curzon, club chairman Fred Hampson, who had travelled over the Pennines to watch the match at Headingley, and Broughton Rangers' George Ruddick. After arriving at 9pm that evening, it is unlikely – apart from after Salford triumphed at Wembley in 1938 – that any rugby players ever received such a reception on their return to the 'Royal Borough' as did Curzon and James. If Curzon was treated like a Prince, James was the undisputed King. The *Salford Reporter* said: "Remarkable scenes of enthusiasm witnessed the return home to Salford on Monday evening of James Lomas and E. Curzon [and] the occasion will no doubt be long remembered by those who took any part in it. It was never anticipated for a moment that such a crowd of people would take an interest in the proceedings. One knew that there was bound to be a goodly gathering, but it was indeed a great surprise to see the thousands that assembled at the Exchange Railway Station and in the streets along which the procession passed."

The unexpectedly large crowd had assembled at the station well before the train was due to arrive and the South Salford Silver Band "pleasantly relieved the tedium of waiting for those outside the station by playing popular airs". A few minutes before the train pulled in, a loud cheer acknowledged the arrival of the Mayor of Salford, Alderman Joseph Snape JP who, wearing his chain of office, would officially welcome the players.

The *Salford Reporter* continued to describe the scene: "Punctual to time the train steamed into the station, and there was great cheering. 'There he is. There's Jimmy' shouted several, and the popular Salford captain, much tanned and looking as fit as the proverbial fiddle, waved his straw hat to his friends. In a minute or two Lomas was introduced by Councillor Hampson to the Mayor, and Curzon, also looking in the pink of condition, next came up, but George Ruddick, the Broughton Ranger, the other representative of the borough in the NU party, was captured by his friends, and hurried out of the station, so that he missed the Mayoral welcome. There was a great crush, and it was with considerable difficulty that the police and officials were able to get the official party outside the station."

Two large horse-drawn wagonettes awaited. The first was taken up by the band, with James, Curzon and other Salford officials and friends in the second. A taxicab had been arranged for the Mayor but, such was the density of the crowd, he could not reach it and he had to join James and the rest in the wagonette. The band played *See the Conquering Hero Comes* and the procession proceeded through Salford along Chapel Street, Oldfield Road, stopped briefly outside the Derby Arms where Mr Hampson was the licensee, Regent Road, Trafford Road and, finally, Tatton Street. They were followed by a large crowd which at times slowed progress. The procession pulled up outside the Duke of Edinburgh Hotel, on the corner of Tatton Street and Oxford Street and run by Bob Walmsley, a Salford official and former player. A huge crowd of people had gathered outside the hotel. James and

Curzon received "a vociferous greeting". The party made its way to a large club room upstairs, from which speeches were made from a window overlooking Tatton Street.

Following an opening address from Mr Hampson, the Mayor said "It is a proud day for you and Salford that we have Captain Lomas back again amongst us after the great triumphs that he and his colleagues have achieved at the Antipodes." Cheering followed that grew in volume, accompanied by chants of "Jimmy". The *Salford Reporter* said that "after a little persuasion Lomas appeared at the window, and had a great reception. He said he was very pleased to be among them again. Mr Curzon and himself had done their best to uphold the reputation of Salford and the Old Country. They had to play hard and there had been some keen games. He was glad to arrive back again, and he only hoped Salford would 'pull something off' this season. He thanked them from the bottom of his heart for the splendid reception they had given them. He never expected it, and he would never forget the occasion as long as he lived." His words were greeted with more cheering.

Curzon was the next to pop his head out of the window, and said: "I have come back to play for Salford and if it is possible for us to win a cup we will win one. It is about time we did." After that, Mr Hampson closed by thanking the Mayor for being present, the band played the National Anthem and the final cheers of the night rang out as James, accompanied by his wife Annie, Curzon and Mr Hampson made one final appearance at the window. James then left the hotel, surrounded by congratulatory friends. A police escort was required to get him to his home in nearby School Street.

Prior to the start of the season and while Salford's two tourists were still as sea, it was predicted that, following their return, they would reappear for the Reds in the match at Hunslet on 1 October. But, having been back on land just eight days, during which time James (twice) and Curzon (once) had turned out in the aforementioned games in Plymouth and Leeds, both were back in the familiar red Salford jersey on Saturday 24 September to face Broughton Rangers. There were 10,000 spectators at The Willows, most of them there to welcome back the tourists, particularly their captain. James kicked off, but it was the Rangers who twice went ahead during the opening half with two unconverted tries. Each time, Salford pegged them back and James was instrumental on both occasions. The first was after the Salford forwards turned defence into attack by dribbling the ball away from the danger area. James saw his opportunity, gathered the ball in his own '25' area and ran to the opposite end where he passed to Jimmy Cook for the touchdown. The second came after he received possession in a passing move and sent Bernard Mesley over. Unfortunately, James missed both goals; the score was 6–6 at the interval. The Rangers clinched an 11–6 victory with a second half try by Jim Clampitt, Billy Barlow added the goal. It was the third defeat in four matches for the Reds who – in James's absence – had followed up a home win over Merthyr Tydfil with defeats at Halifax and St Helens.

Meanwhile, the post-tour back-slapping was still not over for James and another big moment awaited him on Friday evening, 30 September, when he received further adulation at the Regent Theatre on Cross Lane in Salford. Although the usual variety bill was taking place, the main interest for most patrons was the presentation to their hero of a £25 gold watch from the theatre management. The *Salford Reporter* described the event vividly: "There was a crowded house, and the enthusiastic scenes witnessed afforded striking evidence of the Salford player's popularity. Excellent as the entertainment programme was, the presentation was undoubtedly the star turn, and the rising of the curtain upon the great feature of the evening's proceedings was awaited with manifest impatience by the great majority of the audience. When Mr Lomas, accompanied by Councillor Frederick Hampson, of the Salford Club, and members of the management and staff of the theatre appeared on the stage, a regular storm of cheers greeted the returned hero, and it was some time before Councillor Hampson, who made the presentation, could gain a hearing."

Of course, the presentation was to recognise "the conspicuous service he rendered with the English team in the Colonies;" the watch was inscribed: "Presented by the Directors of the Regent Theatre, Salford, to Jimmy Lomas, on his successful goalkicking for the world's championship in Australia won June 18, 1910." Just as he had done from the window of the Duke of Edinburgh Hotel 11 days before, Mr Hampson spoke, although this time for slightly longer. He expressed pleasure in being invited to make the presentation. Continuously pausing for applause, he said James was a player they were all proud of, who had played first class football since he was aged 15, and had the distinction of captaining Lancashire, Cumberland and England, represented the Old Country with credit and had come out with "flying colours". He added: "It was through the means of captains and players like Jimmy Lomas that we were able to hold our own and to gain supremacy in football."

When James's turn came, he was "received with prolonged cheering". The *Salford Reporter* said: "He thanked the Directors of the Regent Theatre most heartily for their appreciation, which he would always remember with the greatest pleasure. He might say how pleased he was to be back with them in Salford after their long tour. As they doubtless knew, all the time he was away he had kept in touch with Salford by means of correspondence. They had a great time in the Colonies and though they had some very hard games he was glad to say he had come back sound, in wind and limb, and ready to do his best for the club during the present season, which he hoped would be more successful than anything they had had. Although they had enjoyed their tour he was very glad to get back home again. He had seen a good many people in different places, but he did not think he had seen any to equal Salford people. He might say he had always done his best to uphold the honour of England and the Salford club and he did not think he had done anything to disgrace them. He thanked the public of Salford for the great reception they had given them when they returned. The reception was totally unexpected, and it was something he would never forget." After he had spoken, the customary three cheers were raised for James, followed by a call for another three cheers for Annie that was "enthusiastically responded to by the audience".

178

James, sat in the cart, outside the premises of Edward Hallows, beer retailer, on Eccles New Road, Salford. The posters advertise the nearby Regent Theatre where he was presented with a gold watch following his return from the 1910 tour. (Photo: Courtesy Steve Clancy)

Salford team and officials before the match against Broughton Rangers at The Willows on 24 September 1910. Standing at back: T. Coates, A. Ellis (director); third row (standing): G. Bracegirdle (trainer), S. Morton, G. Thom, E. Curzon, H. Dawson (director), S. Warwick, C. Rees, F. Foster, F. Mattinson (director); seated: E. Morton, W. Thomas, J. Lomas, V. Hampson (chairman), B. Mesley, E. Harrison; front: E. May, J. Cook. This was James's first appearance for Salford after returning from the 1910 tour. (Photo: Courtesy Steve Haslam)

Although the adrenalin-pumping excitement of that evening was probably not the best preparation ahead of James's trip to Parkside the next day, he managed to lead his team back to winning ways with an 18–12 victory over Hunslet. The *Salford Reporter* correspondent, who took the usual parochial stance of most local journalists of the time, said: "Like some other Yorkshire crowds, the Parkside men are not the best of sportsmen, and though Lomas and Curzon were, on entering the field, received with a burst of cheering, the former was hooted whenever he placed the ball [for a kick at goal]." Watched by 7,000 on what was a beautiful sunny afternoon, Salford had already conceded four points before their recent half-back signing Edgar May was awarded an obstruction try. James missed the goal, but was handily placed to go round the opposition and score under the posts after collecting a ball kicked in his direction by Mesley. It concluded an excellent passing move near the Hunslet line; James's goal put Salford ahead, 8–4. The Salford captain seemed to be revelling in a good spell of form and, having forced a Hunslet player to touch down inside his own in-goal area, created an excellent opening for Cook. The winger outpaced the opposition to score under the posts, James's goal gave Salford a handy 13–4 lead at the interval.

To be fair, Hunslet were struggling to keep a team on the field. They lost both half-backs during the first half through injury; tourist Fred Smith before a point was scored and Sammy Brear prior to Cook's try. Shortly after the interval, further mishaps reduced their numbers to nine. One of them, full-back Herbert Place, was able to resume, but it was small wonder that winger Dai Thomas – another recent Salford signing – had space to dribble the ball across the try-line and score in the corner. Hunslet's headcount increased to 11 when winger Albert Jenkinson also returned to claim an excellent try which made the score 16–7. The points were concluded with a Mesley penalty from halfway and a converted try by another of Hunslet's four returned tourists, Billy Jukes.

The following weekend, on 8 October, James should have been playing in the Cumberland versus Lancashire fixture at Whitehaven's Recreation Ground, but it was called off. Cumberland's worst ever mining disaster had occurred earlier in the year after an explosion in Whitehaven's Wellington Pit on the evening of 11 May 1910, and claimed the lives of 136 men and boys. Because of the threat of further explosions due to methane gas, a concerted rescue attempt was considered too dangerous at the time and the pit was sealed. At the end of September, when it was thought to be safer to enter, it was opened up and the grim task of recovering bodies began, a process still ongoing on the scheduled date of the county fixture. Clearly, it was inappropriate to go ahead with the game under such circumstances.

The harsh reality of the tough, unforgiving lives endured by the communities from which the NU drew much of its popular support was again demonstrated a few months later. On the morning of 21 December another underground explosion caused the Pretoria Pit disaster at Hulton Colliery, situated on the Atherton-Westhoughton border, just a few miles north of Leigh. It claimed 344 lives and remains Lancashire's worst ever mining tragedy.

It was, in fact, Leigh that Salford met at The Willows on the date of the postponed Cumberland versus Lancashire game. The deferment of the county match allowed James to assist the Reds in their 18–8 victory, Curzon and Leigh tourist Bill Winstanley – who should both have appeared for the Red Rose – were also free to take part. There were around 6,000 spectators in the ground on another sunny afternoon. In the process of winning, Salford scored six unconverted tries, three in each half, James missed four of the goal attempts, Mesley the other two. The Cumbrian did, though, give the fans "a glimpse of his best form" during the course of the match and scored the third touchdown. Described as "one of those tries which have helped to make his name famous," he retrieved a loose ball before he pushed winger Ben Lloyd aside to go in at the corner.

Salford's form took a jolt when they visited Widnes for their next match. The damage in the abysmal 15–2 score-line was inflicted before the break when the Chemicals scored all their points. Although it seemed very "matter of fact" at the time, modern supporters may wonder why, with the match almost over, Dai John bothered to notch Salford's only points with a drop-goal. James was one of three Reds' players who were "up to their standard" although he suffered criticism for his decision, as captain, to play the first half against a strong wind after he won the toss.

League newcomers Coventry provided an easy 37–10 passage for Salford at The Willows on 22 October. James stood down from the match due to a "slight" knee strain, which also caused his late withdrawal from the Cumberland versus Yorkshire match on Tuesday at Dewsbury. He was, however, able to resume in Salford's next game at Watersheddings, a fixture that marked the start of a sticky patch for the Reds and saw them tumble down the league. The Reds endured successive away defeats at Oldham, 20–2, Warrington 14–5 – a second round Lancashire Cup tie having received a bye in the first – and Swinton, 14–3. At Oldham, with 15,000 in attendance, Salford suffered a second-half collapse. Leading 2–0 after two minutes – James nailed "a beautiful goal" from a mark he had made – they were still in touch at half-time when 5–2 down having conceded a try just before the break.

The Lancashire Cup exit at Wilderspool followed a similar pattern; drawing 0–0 at the halfway stage, but then they fell apart midway through the second half when their defence leaked three tries in a five minute spell. There was, however, a more than valid excuse in that full-back Edwin Harrison – a pre-season acquisition from Runcorn – broke his leg in attempting to tackle centre Ike Taylor when the latter crossed at the corner for the first of them. Salford pulled the score back to 9–5 after James converted Dai Thomas's obstruction try, but Taylor sealed the Wirepullers' win with his second effort. As usual, James's performance was scrutinised, the *Salford Reporter* suggested that he was "too self-reliant and did not play up to his usual standard".

He received better judgement after the defeat at Swinton when it was reported that he and Willie Thomas – who both "came in for a lot of mauling" – "were ever in the thick of the fray". Their efforts did not help their cause, however, nor did the second half dismissal of forward Charlie Rees after he struck Tommy Gartrell. The Swinton packman had to be carried off. On a damp, overcast afternoon, James had his best moments early on when he made a break, only for Cook to knock on as a try looked certain, and later fell short with a penalty attempt.

Salford's home match against Hull KR on Saturday 19 November was postponed due to the Rovers' Yorkshire Cup semi-final at Huddersfield. The next game, though, was of particular interest to James. The fixture with Warrington at The Willows on 26 November was designated as his benefit match in what was his 10th season with the Reds. He had already earned over £25 as his share of the tour profits – a figure rounded up to £30 by the NU – plus almost £9 as his portion of the payout from the Tourists versus Colonials match at Headingley. It was anticipated that a large crowd would be present at the Warrington game to honour him. In the event, the attendance numbered around 5,000, considered to be a satisfactory figure in view of Salford's recent disappointing results. It was not the most entertaining of matches, although the return of Evan Thomas for his first match of the season helped Salford's pack produce a much improved performance than of late. The result was 3–3; Warrington's first half try was matched after the interval by Cook, James was unable to land the touchline conversion.

It was said that, against Warrington, James "was not as fast as usual". Apart from the fact that he had entered what is popularly referred to now as 'the veteran stage', he was struggling with his knee, a legacy from the recent tour. It was instrumental in keeping him out of the Salford team for their next seven matches as well as the rearranged Cumberland game with Lancashire at Workington on 24 November and the England versus Wales international in Coventry on 10 December for which he had been selected. He was also a late withdrawal from the second Tourists versus Colonials match. Played at Central Park on 27 December, the proceeds were donated to the disaster fund set up after the aforementioned Pretoria Pit explosion that had occurred the previous week.

On 28 December his fourth daughter Marjory – who came to be known as 'Madge' – was born at their latest Salford residence in School Street. It was an address they were to remain at for, at least, the next five years and therefore James's home throughout his subsequent rugby career with Oldham and York. At the time of the 1911 Census, the household also contained a 16-year-old 'servant' named Leah Collinson, the young lady had been born in Hulme. The reason for her presence may well have been due to the difficulties faced by James's wife Annie when he was away on tour. Annie would have been carrying Marjory at that time, and with three other young daughters to occupy her, she would certainly have welcomed any assistance.

Three days after Marjory's birth, James reappeared in Salford's team for the home match with Barrow on 31 December. Salford won 19–9, but the encounter was described as "deadly dull", both teams "playing in a listless manner". James, too, seemed out of sorts although he did score a second half try and converted another by John. The *Salford Reporter*, however, wrote "It cannot be said that he played at the top of his form and his playing at all seemed something like an experiment". It is sad to read such a comment after all the great performances he had produced on behalf of the club, because it was his last appearance for the club – for the time being at least.

Reportedly, he was still struggling with his mobility and unable, therefore, to participate in the next two matches; on 7 January at Wigan and on 14 January, against Hunslet at home. When it came to the third fixture of 1911, at Runcorn on 28 January, there was a shock in store for the Salford supporters who had made the trip to Canal Street. News had begun filtering through that Saturday morning that their beloved captain had signed with Oldham. Salford defeated Runcorn 16–3, but it is doubtful if the Salford faithful took much comfort from it.

On the face of it, it appears that his departure had more to do with the finances of the Salford club than any desire on James's part to move on. He would almost certainly have benefitted financially from the move and, as things stood at that time, he had a better chance of securing honours, given that Oldham had just won the Lancashire Cup and were in third spot in the league, whereas the Reds were struggling in mid-table. Of course, the usual stories circulated which implied that James had become restless with his lot at Salford. On 18 February, for instance, the *Salford Reporter* included the following comment: "Several idle rumours relating to Lomas's benefit match [against Warrington] having got into circulation, much to the annoyance of the directors of the Salford club, we are asked by those gentlemen to state that so far as relates to the arrangements connected with the game and the agreement with the beneficiary, all moneys due to him up to the present time have been paid, and further, that his migration to Oldham had nothing to do with the matter above mentioned."

At their Annual General Meeting, held at Stowell Memorial School the previous June, the Salford Board reported that the 1909–10 season had not been a financial success, a small profit of just under £6 had been made. This, they reminded shareholders, was a season where they had reached the semi-final stage of the Northern League Championship and Challenge Cup. They had "provided a first class team, at great expense which, as already stated, had been within an ace of capturing honours, but the attendances had not realised their expectations." The club had attempted to cut costs, but the directors felt they had not received the support "from the large spending population of the district to which they, in their opinion, are entitled."

During September – a few days before James arrived back in England with the touring side – the club announced an issue of £2,500 in 4 per cent debentures of £1 each. The purpose was to raise funds to pay off rent arrears – Salford's ground was owned by brewers Groves and Whitnall until 1933 – and a bank overdraft that was costing the club £110 per year in interest. The seriousness of the situation was underlined by the news that a meeting was also planned for Salford Town Hall when a sub-committee will "wait upon influential gentlemen in the borough to ask for sympathy and support".

Some supporters, though, were impatient with the players and their perceived lack of commitment to the club. A letter to the *Salford Reporter* in mid-October 1910, from 'Loyalty' said: "A glance at the team sheets of the Salford Club this season has shown the absence of the names of several well-known wearers of the red jersey and I gather from information obtained in conversation that the reason is that they have a difference with the officials of a financial character – in other words, they want a rise of 'screw'. Now, it is well known that these men have done good work for the Salford club and they have helped to maintain its position in the football world, but I take it that for these services they have been well paid by wages and bonus and liberal compensation when injured. These are better terms than can be obtained by the average working man, who is of equal service to his employer as any football player. Just at a time, then, when the Salford club is not too flush of money these men, so to speak, refuse their help unless they have more wages, and yet, they call themselves members of the Salford team, and they say they have the welfare of the club at heart, only they think their services are so invaluable, that unless they are better rewarded they would sooner see it at the bottom of the table. This is a narrow-minded policy, for the welfare of the club is their welfare, insomuch as the attendances and gate money would increase, and the officials are not niggardly when they have the wherewithal. Now, I call upon these men, if they have any spark of patriotism in them, to come forward and sign on at the old terms. If they will not then their help is not worth having, and the officials would be well advised to leave them alone."

James was excluded from the above criticism because he had only just returned from overseas and was, at that stage, turning out for the team anyway. The letter did imply that a dilemma was taking place at the club which came down to the old 'chicken and egg' scenario. Does a club spend more than it can afford for players in the hope of boosting receipts sufficient to cover its outlay? Or does it campaign for better support on the premise that the extra income will subsequently enable the club to strengthen the team? Clearly Salford were not paying enough from some players' points of view. Maybe they thought they deserved more after doing so well the previous season? Several were slow to re-sign for the 1910–11 season, a factor that had contributed to their poor league position.

The Salford management had made efforts to strengthen the side; recent recruits included full-back Harrison from Runcorn, half-back May – who had represented the North of England at rugby union – from Bramley, and Bob Ritchie, a county rugby union forward from Northumberland. While Harrison had his Salford career disrupted through a bad injury in only his eighth appearance, the latter two made big contributions at Salford over the forthcoming seasons. One example, however, of the difficulties the club faced was in their efforts to sign flying Welsh wingman Dai Thomas from Hull KR. Initially it was anticipated that Salford would pay a transfer fee but, instead, an exchange deal took place that saw another winger, Bill Hyam, travel in the opposite direction. The *Salford Reporter* said "the directors are to be congratulated on their capture" but, unfortunately Thomas only made 11 appearances, although he scored 12 tries.

What had prompted Oldham's interest in James is unclear. There were two Oldham players on the tour – Bert Avery and Tom Helm – so it is possible some dialogue may have occurred then. It could also be through James's performance in the Salford team well beaten at Watersheddings on 29 October when "in one case it took about half the Oldham team to hold him up on the line." The *Oldham Evening Chronicle* in its 11 February 1911 edition – over a week after James's transfer – said "Circumstances had arisen whereby Lomas was placed on the transfer list, and Oldham was the club fortunate to secure his services." Did James ask for a transfer or did the Salford club make the decision for him? The best guess, based on contemporary evidence, is that James had not pushed for a move away from Salford, although he may well have been frustrated at the lack of success. It seems more likely that a joint decision was made that his transfer would benefit both the club and himself.

Whatever the background to the transaction, and despite the bitter disappointment felt by so many Salford supporters, it can, with hindsight, be seen as good business by the Reds' management. Reportedly, Oldham paid a record fee to obtain James who, by that stage in his career was considered to be a mature player having celebrated his 31st birthday the previous August. If nothing else, though, it showed that he still possessed great ability, even at that age, for a club of Oldham's stature to pay a high price for him.

On 4 February, the *Salford Reporter*, in covering his farewell, was full of superlatives about the departing star: "one of the most capable exponents of the rugby code... always a prolific scorer... a great individualist and it is always a real pleasure to the spectators to see him make one of his characteristic dashes which invariably spells danger to the opposing side... as a goalkicker he has few equals... he has on innumerable occasions pulled matches out of the fire." The true impact of his loss, though, would only be seen in the future, although the article probably echoed the mind of every Salford supporter when it said: "It is scarcely possible to imagine Salford without Lomas, for without doubt he has been the great mainstay of the team since his connection with the club." The same paper also spelt out how crucial the sale of James was: "What the financial future is, is in the lap of the gods, but our readers may be satisfied that there will be a Salford club next season."

The first official programme produced by Salford following James's transfer was for 4 February. Ironically, the visitors were Oldham. It included the following: "The transfer of Jimmy Lomas must have come as a great surprise to the supporters and we know they will look for an explanation through these columns. We regret we cannot go so far as to place the full facts before you but, for the present, perhaps the following will suffice. Never in the whole history of the club have we had such a desperate scrabble to make ends meet, as during the present season. The 'gates' have gone from bad to worse, and when the bank are pressing for money there comes a time when some portion of the 'stock' must go. Therefore the directors were reluctantly compelled to part with one whom they considered would bring a good price, and by so doing, help the club out of financial difficulties. We ask the supporters not to take any notice of the idle talk which is going on, but to accept these facts. We have every confidence in saying, had not circumstances absolutely compelled, they [the directors] would not have parted company with this world famous player. The best of good wishes of both directors and supporters will go with him to his new club. His deeds will live long in our memories. We raise our hats to one of the finest players who ever booted a 'rugger' ball."

James, who received £10 in debentures as a parting gift, later wrote: "When I left Salford it was to benefit the club as they were in financial difficulties, not through any ill feeling or bad play by myself. They were reluctant to sell me and I was reluctant to go although never regret going to Oldham."

16. 1911: The finest hour

James Lomas was the subject of a new world record transfer fee and the main focus of attention on Saturday afternoon, 4 February 1911. The announcement of his unexpected move to Oldham was given added spice because his debut would be at the ground of his former club, Salford. The previous day's *Oldham Evening Chronicle* said: "A great deal of interest will centre on the first appearance of the latest capture, Lomas, who will turn out for Oldham against his former colleagues Salford at The Willows. There had been much speculation during the week as to whether he would be selected for this match and also as to who would have to stand down to make a place for the international captain."

The decision as to who would play had been taken on Thursday evening, George Cook was the player to miss out. Billy Dixon – another former Maryport player – was to be James's winger. The pair had played together for Cumberland in the past. The *Chronicle* thought that the line-up was a "very strong one" and predicted "there is sure to be a large following from Oldham anxious to see how Lomas works in his new surroundings." The line-ups – old and new as far as James was concerned – were, Salford: Billy Lambert; Jimmy Cook, Bernard Mesley, Willie Thomas, D.W. Bevan; Edgar May, Dai John; Ephraim Curzon, Edgar Morton, Charlie Rees, Bob Ritchie, George Thom, Silas Warwick. Oldham: Alf Wood; George Smith, Sid Deane, Lomas, Billy Dixon; George Anlezark, Tom White; Bert Avery, Joe Ferguson, Tom Helm, Billy Jardine, Arthur Smith, Fred Wise.

The crowd at The Willows was reported as being just below 10,000, a good attendance considering over 65,000 had packed themselves into nearby Old Trafford to see Manchester United defeat Aston Villa in an FA Cup tie. The match was only confirmed as going ahead on the Friday evening due to frost and, even then, the pitch was in a treacherous state when the game began. The *Oldham Evening Chronicle* writer 'Grasshopper' said "the interest in the game was enhanced by the presence of Lomas [but] to tell the truth, he did not show anything like the football we have seen him show and he was a failure from the playing point of view, though no doubt the wish to see him play attracted a great many people who otherwise would not have gone, so that from the Salford treasurer's point of view his inclusion was a success. He made a number of costly blunders, and only once or twice, towards the end of the match, when Salford were obviously tiring, did he show anything of his real brilliance."

The *Salford Reporter*, while making a concession towards James's recent injury woes, agreed that he was not at his best: "Only once did Lomas give us a glimpse of his old form, although it was evident that his great desire was to score against his former club and he made two or three attempts from short distances. In [one] case, however, although he has been running lame, he threw discretion to the winds and from centre beat all opposition in a fine run and until faced by [Billy] Lambert at the corner flag who, whilst being handed off, detained Lomas long enough to enable Willie Thomas to come across and throw him into touch." Thomas, incidentally, had replaced James as captain, while Lambert – badly injured way back in April 1905 – had recently and surprisingly returned to the Salford side.

'Grasshopper' showed remarkable sensitivity towards James's situation: "Possibly the unique conditions under which he was playing were responsible for his failing to come off, for he could not help feeling very keenly the wrench which must be made in parting from a club which he had been with so long and so honourably associated and turning out against his old mates in the first match with his new comrades. So perhaps one need not blame him for his slips on Saturday, but look forward to the fine work he is going to do for Oldham in the near future, assisting them to retain the League [Championship] Cup and recover the Northern Union [Challenge] Cup after a lapse of a dozen years."

The same writer also gave an insight into what the Oldham public had anticipated from their new signing: "Oldham had [Tom] Fletcher at centre when they last won the Challenge Cup and Fletcher was always regarded as an individualist just as Lomas is. It was good, however, to see last Saturday that Lomas could play the combined game also, and was always ready and willing to pass the ball when it was time. The point is his play was favourably commented upon and he did not try to do all the scoring himself."

The size of the fee that Oldham paid Salford for James's signature has been listed in rugby league reference books in more recent years as £300. James wrote in his memoirs "My transfer from Salford to Oldham was a record fee up to then" but verifying the actual figure in contemporary reports is difficult because the local papers for both clubs did not disclose the amount. The *Salford Reporter* said at the time that "whilst we are not in a position to say what the transfer fee is, it is, we are officially informed, a record one for a Northern Union player," and went on to say "in regard to the transfer of Lomas to Oldham it may interest our readers to know that all figures that have been published purporting to be the transfer fee are incorrect."

The revenue accounts produced for Salford's Annual General Meeting in June 1911 revealed income from transfers as £150. When this was queried by a shareholder, club chairman Fred Hampson replied that it was a net figure covering fees paid and received. Mr Hampson was then asked the amount Oldham paid for James and he "offered to impart the information privately to any member," which was not helpful for a modern historian. If Salford did receive £300 for James then it could easily have been netted to £150 as the club had, reportedly, paid Bramley £100 for half-back Edgar May and could, quite conceivably, have parted with £50 to Runcorn for the signature of full-back Edwin Harrison. However, on at least one occasion the figure of £300 appeared in print. This occurred in April 1913 when Hunslet put a price tag of £600 on their want-away star threequarter Billy Batten, which was paid by Hull. The *Yorkshire Evening Post* reported it as "double the previous record of £300 paid by Oldham last season (sic) for the transfer of Lomas from Salford."

There is one other ingredient to put into the mix; in August 1913, when James joined York, the *Yorkshire Evening Press* quoted the fee that Oldham paid to Salford as being

£350, "regarded as exceptionally high for a Northern Union footballer."

Before leaving the subject of transfer fees, there is one other point worth expanding on relating to James. Chronological transfer fee records listed in rugby league publications usually show James's £100 Bramley to Salford move in 1901 as the first entry on the list and the £300 Salford-Oldham transfer in 1911 as the second. To many readers, that has implied the former remained as the record until the latter. While both are accepted as records at the time they occurred, there were certainly transfer fees in between them that exceeded that initial £100 figure. For instance Leeds parted with £250 to sign centre Phil Thomas from Oldham in 1904, and, of course, the £100 Salford paid for May would, at the time, have equalled that original 'record' had it still stood. Noted rugby league historian Robert Gate explained to the author some years ago that it was virtually impossible, based on the lack of reliable contemporary information, to furnish an authoritative list of transfers that occurred between James's two moves.

James made his first home appearance for Oldham on Saturday 11 February in front of 15,000 spectators. Runcorn provided the opposition. With Oldham riding high in the league and the Linnets no longer the tough adversary they once were, it should have been a canter for the hosts. The final score certainly looked comfortable at 21–10, but at one stage in the second half it had been 13–10 before Runcorn fell away. James had received "a hearty welcome" from the crowd and, as would be expected with a high profile signing, "his play was closely watched" by his new army of supporters. 'Grasshopper' said: "He did not get a great many opportunities but, as compared with the previous Saturday, his exhibition showed a great improvement and he proved that he has not yet lost all his skill". James scored two of Oldham's five tries in the space of a few minutes just before half-time, both achieved "with characteristic dash, going through a crowd of players in quite his best style." His first was in the corner from a pass by Deane after George Smith had scooped up a loose ball, the second followed a few minutes later after he received the ball from Avery who had made the initial break. Wood missed both goals and it was suggested that skipper Ferguson – a prolific goalkicker himself – should have given James an opportunity to try his luck. In fact, during his time with Oldham, James was never really considered to be first choice kicker, a duty that tended to be bestowed on Ferguson and Wood.

The following weekend brought a tough first round Challenge Cup encounter with Hull KR at Craven Street. In the event, Oldham produced the winning score six minutes from the end when a draw looked the likeliest outcome. James had booted the ball into the Rovers' '25' area and was obstructed by full-back Alf Carmichael as he followed up. Wood kicked the resultant penalty to secure a 9–7 win. Oldham were 7–2 down at half-time, a situation that would have been worse had not James pushed the Rovers winger J.C. Brain into touch as he was about to score. At 7–4 midway through the second half, James produced the equalising score after he received a wide pass. As a host of defenders raced across to cut him down, he managed to avoid the touchline – aided by Dixon who shoved him clear as he looked like being overwhelmed – before he "forced himself through by weight and dash".

James experienced a new local rivalry in his next match when Oldham entertained Rochdale Hornets at Watersheddings. Despite miserable wet weather which had turned the pitch into a mud heap, 12,000 fans were at the game to see James's continuing improvement as he adjusted to life with the Roughyeds. Oldham won 9–0. James scored the only points of the first half through a controversial try after Rochdale half-back Ernest Jones had kicked the ball clear following a scrum in his own '25' area. James attempted to catch it, but the ball went to ground although somehow he managed to propel it over the try-line with his boot. He then fell on it for the touchdown "while others were appealing" that he had knocked the ball forward.

Another dose of poor weather and muddy conditions did not deter a 16,000 crowd the following week, 4 March, when Oldham resumed their Challenge Cup quest with a second round match against Wakefield Trinity. Again it was a tough draw, Trinity were one of the leading clubs but, with home advantage, Oldham progressed with an 11–3 verdict. James played a crucial part by scoring two tries in the last 20 minutes, both of them memorable. The first followed an exchange of passes with Dixon "which completely baffled the opposition" before he raced over as Trinity centre Tommy Poynton snapped at his heels. The next came when Dixon and James again "bamboozled" the opposition after an initial break by Deane and the ball was put down in virtually the same spot as before.

It was back to the league campaign next with another home match, this time against Barrow. Having scored six tries in his last four games for Oldham, James did not cross the try-line this time although he still had the satisfaction of sharing in his sixth consecutive win, 12–0, since he had joined the club. Bitter disappointment was, however, to follow in the third round of the Challenge Cup. Fate brought them back into conflict with traditional rivals, Rochdale, with the tie taking place at Watersheddings. With Hornets languishing in mid-table, the odds were stacked in Oldham's favour but, of course, derby matches and cup ties are no respecters of the form book. The match drew an eager 20,000 crowd, but what they saw was a dour contest played out in more unfavourable conditions. James's try just before the interval – following some neat passing – had given his side an 8–3 interval advantage, but Rochdale fought back for an 8–8 draw.

The replay at Rochdale's Athletic Grounds was three days later, on Tuesday. Another excellent attendance – 18,000 – saw Hornets take a 4–0 lead in the first quarter through two Jones penalties. Not long after, James made the most of a break by Avery and Deane that began in Oldham's '25' area. Taking a pass from the latter, James raced clear but still had some distance to cover. Rochdale winger Dick Paddon made a great effort by dashing across from the opposite flank to head him off, but James flew over in the corner. The *Oldham Evening Chronicle* said "how he managed it was a wonder and shows that he is faster than he appears to be." But it was to be the last score of the match, a literally pointless second half gave the Hornets a 4–3 victory that had their supporters rushing the field with joy after the final whistle.

Oldham quickly put their blues behind them, and consolidated their league leadership position with two successes in three days; 7–0 at Coventry and 15–0 at home to Leigh. The trip to Coventry took place on Thursday, just two days after the Cup replay, and several players were rested by Oldham. James was not one of them and consequently had to endure a session of non-stop rain on a heavy pitch. A stronger XIII faced Leigh the next Saturday afternoon. James landed his first goals for Oldham; a penalty – to make it 5–0 at half-time – plus a second half conversion.

It was a battle of the big two in midweek. Oldham travelled to second placed Wigan on the Wednesday, 25,000 joined them inside Central Park for the 5.15pm start. The report by 'Grasshopper' suggested that James "was not so much in the picture as usual and had the unusual experience of going through a match without scoring a point." He was not the only Oldham player to miss out on making a contribution to the scoreboard and the Roughyeds went down 11–5. The last few minutes of the match had a sour note with an unlikely altercation between Wood and Wigan skipper James Leytham; the former was sent off and required a police escort to get him through an angry crowd to the team's wagonette. The result did not affect the league places, but Wigan, with 48 points from 29 matches for a percentage of 82.75, were now breathing down Oldham's neck, who had 51 points from 30 matches for 85.00 per cent. Both clubs had a 34-match schedule.

Oldham held Wigan at bay through winning their next three games; 16–13 at Swinton, 11–5 at home to Leeds and 5–0 at Ebbw Vale. James missed the visit to Swinton on Saturday 1 April as he was helping England defeat Wales 27–8 at Ebbw Vale. The *Athletic News* correspondent 'Forward' said the English forwards dominated possession and that "Lomas was, as usual, the handy man of the back division." He also scored a couple of goals in the latter stages; a penalty and the conversion of Harold Wagstaff's try, which was the last of England's eight touchdowns.

James got Oldham off to a rousing start against Leeds. He opened the scoring with a try after three minutes play, taking a pass off George Smith after the latter made "one of those wonderful corkscrew dodges." The Roughyeds fans probably anticipated a big win at that stage, but Leeds made them fight all the way for their victory. James faced the long trip back to Ebbw Vale a fortnight after his international call up. As the *Oldham Evening Chronicle* writer bemoaned, it was an "awkward place to get to especially at holiday time," the return journey occupied three days of the Easter weekend. The team set off from Oldham at 8.30 on Good Friday morning for an overnight stay in Newport. A Saturday morning "ramble in the woods" to unwind may have been calculated to refresh the spirit, but it was a narrow win over the Welsh side; Cook's second half try, converted by James, provided the only score. The team stayed overnight in Gloucester before they arrived home at 6.30pm on Sunday.

After the exertions of the weekend Oldham had an excuse for losing 5–0 at Broughton

191

Rangers on Easter Monday morning. The early kick-off was due to Manchester Racecourse, which was on the opposite side of the River Irwell, staging an afternoon meeting. The 12,000 crowd saw James cross the Rangers try-line in the opening half, but he was "called back" by the officials and also missed an "easy chance" for a second half penalty when the score stood at 2–0. In the end, it was an unexpected and devastating defeat against a team from the lower half of the table. Wigan demolished Hull 38–0 later that day at Central Park, so the two rivals finished joint top with identical records of 28 wins and one draw.

Wigan had a much superior point scoring record but, despite that, the two were ordered to meet in an extra match to determine the two leading places ahead of the top four play-offs. It was hastily arranged for a neutral venue two days later, although not in Lancashire as anticipated, but east of the Pennines at Wakefield Trinity's ground. It was a match neither club wanted and both decided to rest players, Wigan in particular. Oldham picked James on the left wing, where he was less involved in proceedings, save for an early run when he was halted near the Wigan try-line. He was, however, culpable when, unusually, he allowed his opposing winger Albert Renwick to slip from his grasp for a try that sealed Wigan's 11–3 win.

With Oldham now officially confirmed as occupying the second rung on the ladder they entertained third-placed Wakefield Trinity in the play-off semi-final the next Saturday, 22 April. On a wet and windy afternoon, a "disappointing" 10,000 crowd was blamed by the press on the increased admission price. James – restored to the centre – scored the first try after just two minutes when he received the ball from White. He kidded the Trinity defenders with a dummy pass to his wing and hurled himself through a gap to force his way over the try-line. Wood's goal made it 5–0. Encouraged by his success, James produced some sparkling form and, having attempted a drop-goal – which did not lift – he was in the right place to finish off a move which involved himself, Avery and Dixon. Wood added his second goal and the Roughyeds led 10–0, but Trinity replied near half-time with a try by centre Billie Lynch, Jimmy Metcalfe converted.

Both teams opened their second half account with goals; Wood, from a mark, for Oldham, Metcalfe, with a penalty, for Trinity, the score was then 12–7 to Oldham. As the rain fell in torrents, Arthur Smith claimed a third Oldham try to extend the lead to 15–7. A determined Trinity gained the upper hand in the final quarter, but their only reward was a try from forward Parkes and another penalty by Metcalfe. Oldham held out to progress to the Championship Final with a narrow 15–12 score-line. James had had an excellent game and more than justified the Roughyeds' investment in him. However, his finest day in an Oldham jersey still awaited him.

That day of glory came a fortnight later in the Championship Final with Wigan, who had despatched Widnes 16–0 at Central Park in the other semi-final. Played at Wheater's Field, Oldham retained their title by defeating the Colliers 20–7 in what was probably James's finest hour as a rugby player. He had certainly made his mark in Australia and New Zealand with some exceptional performances, but his display in the 1911 Championship Final was, arguably, the zenith of his club career. For Oldham it was their fifth consecutive appearance in the final and the third on the run against Wigan. The crowd of 15,543, while seemingly low by today's standards, set a new record for the occasion. Due to a colour clash – Oldham usually wore red and white hoops and Wigan cherry and white hoops – the Roughyeds wore all-red jerseys, their opponents blue. Oldham's team was: Birdie Dixon; George Smith, Deane, Lomas, Billy Dixon; White, Anlezark; Jim Wright, Ferguson, Arthur Smith, Avery, Tom McCabe, Joe Owens.

A determined Oldham side led after only three minutes; James was the instigator. He kicked the ball skywards into the corner. Johnny Thomas's rushed clearance kick for Wigan was caught by George Smith. The winger called for the mark and James's goal put Oldham 2–0 ahead. After 15 minutes White added a try, but James missed a fairly routine conversion and was unlucky later on when his penalty attempt hit the upright. Jim Sharrock kicked a penalty goal for Wigan and, with just over 30 minutes gone, Oldham were clinging to a 5–2 lead. James then scored a crucial try. Taking a pass off Dixon, he raced into the corner for the touchdown, Ferguson's touchline goal gave Oldham a 10–2 interval lead.

Johnny Thomas landed another Wigan penalty but, within minutes, James had again raised the siege. He received the ball from Avery on the halfway line, raced down the touchline and, when challenged by Sharrock, put White over the whitewash for the latter's second try. Ferguson missed with the conversion, but Oldham led 13–4. James was on a roll. He made another strong burst through the opposition ranks which almost put Owens in for a fourth try, and then increased the lead with a penalty, awarded for obstruction. With 15 minutes left, Leytham scored Wigan's only try, but thoughts of a revival were dashed by James five minutes later. He snatched the ball from Lance Todd and dived over Sharrock to score under the posts. He added the goal to finish a wonderful afternoon's work.

The Oldham team and officials with the Championship trophy (left) and Lancashire Cup, both won in 1910-11. James is seated second-right. (Photo: Courtesy Michael Turner)

Following the presentation of the trophy to Ferguson and medals for both teams from Mrs J.B. Cooke (wife of the Northern Union and Wakefield Trinity official), the Oldham side took the train to Manchester's Victoria Station where they had tea at the Victoria Hotel before they resumed their journey on the 7.47pm train to Hollinwood on the outskirts of Oldham. From there they took a wagonette and, preceded by a brass band in another wagonette, travelled through the streets of Oldham in triumph before they arrived at the club's headquarters, the Red Lion Hotel, for more celebrations.

Quite rightly, James was proud of his contribution to Oldham's success that day. In his memoirs he wrote: "One memorable match for Oldham stands out in my career, [the] final for the Rugby League [Championship] Cup against Wigan at Broughton which we won. I could do nothing wrong and scored the majority of points." Writing in a 1930s newspaper, Todd also recalled the event. Having referred to the 1907 match when the New Zealand tourists, including Todd, had beaten Salford, with James, he went on to say: "Jimmy got his revenge some years later when he played for Oldham against Wigan in the final of the Championship at Broughton. He played the game of his life, scored two beautiful tries, and I really think he licked us all off his own bat. I have rather good reason to remember that game, as I was to be married a few days after [he married a Wigan girl three days later on 9 May 1911] and as I collected a cut lip and nose, and a black eye, I had to work overtime to make myself presentable."

It was an occasion that brought overdue reward for James after such a wonderful career and so many near-misses in the hunt for club honours. Whatever their club loyalties, supporters are always pleased to see a veteran player finally achieve his dream. One can think of the goodwill extended towards international stars Roger Millward and Clive Sullivan when they won the Challenge Cup with Hull KR at Wembley in 1980, or the fulfilment of ambition when Blackpool beat Bolton Wanderers in the 1953 FA Cup Final, a match remembered as 'The Stanley Matthews Final'.

Perhaps the 1911 Northern Rugby League Championship Final should more properly be labelled 'The James Lomas Final' because he certainly deserved it to be. The *Oldham Evening Chronicle* reporter said: "I wonder whether the fact of Lomas being clad once again in the familiar red jersey (as worn by Salford) had anything to do with the marvellous exhibition which he gave. Whatever was the case, he played a really wonderful game, probably the greatest game he has ever played. According to the accounts which we read of his doings last summer in Australia, he must have been in just such a mood as he was in last Saturday. Todd was absolutely helpless against him, and time after time he went through the Wigan crowd [of players] like a knife through butter. He was brilliant but not selfish, and always took care when he parted with the ball, to give it to somebody with a chance. He had a hand in all the scoring, and he, even above the others, richly deserved his medal."

194

17. 1911–12: Another poor hand

James Lomas must have looked forward to the start of the 1911–12 season with greater optimism than he had over the past few years. A member of the defending champions, he had played a major role in securing the victory that had delivered him his first winner's medal at club level since his days with Maryport. Having had such success after only 17 matches for Oldham, surely more was to follow.

Oldham opened up their 1911–12 campaign with three away matches, the first of which, on 2 September, was a tough-looking trip to Hull KR who had just missed the previous season's play-offs through finishing fifth. And so it proved, the Rovers mauled the Roughyeds 22–6. James did not score either of the Roughyeds' two tries, the *Oldham Standard* writer 'Settle' said: "Lomas did well, being the best of the [threequarter] line, and his efforts should have been productive of a score or two." Overall, Oldham's performance lacked cohesion after their summer break.

The next two journeys were more rewarding with wins at Leigh, 15–12, and Bradford Northern, 22–12. On a baking hot, sunny day the Roughyeds got off to an encouraging start against Leigh when Tom White touched down after only 10 minutes. James – who also kicked a penalty – added the goal. The *Oldham Standard*, however, reckoned Oldham were lucky to secure the victory, and claimed that, for the most part "they were not in the hunt" although James and his wing partner, Billy Dixon, showed good understanding and were the best of a lack-lustre Oldham attack.

The win at Bradford Northern – one of the basement teams of that period – on Tuesday 12 September was also unconvincing. In pouring rain, Bradford took an early 10–0 lead before James – who again combined well with Dixon – put his side into a good field position with a magnificent run towards the posts. George Smith scored from the resultant scrum, James added the extra points to leave Oldham 10–5 behind at the break. A minute after the restart, Joe Owens got a second Oldham try, although Alf Wood missed the goal. As the rain came down more heavily, a Bradford penalty stretched their lead to four points. But then the Watersheddings men rallied; James scored a try and converted another by George Anlezark to go in front for the first time 16–12. Two more unconverted tries followed.

The next Saturday, Oldham had their first home fixture, against Leeds. On a fine, dry day 15,000 fans saw the Roughyeds finally reach top gear with an emphatic 27–9 victory. George Smith claimed four of Oldham's seven tries, James got in on the act in the second half "swerving in with one of those strong runs for a certain open spot which gave you the impression the instant that he starts that there is no stopping him." He also landed a conversion after the break.

The 1911–12 season was when Huddersfield's 'Team of All the Talents' came to the fore and Oldham felt the full impact of that when they visited Fartown the following weekend. James opened the scoring with a long distance penalty after half-back Tommy Grey strayed offside. But that was it for Oldham who went on to concede 24 points without adding to their own score. With Dixon selected at full-back, his vacated wing spot proved vulnerable, the *Oldham Standard* said that "Lomas had to watch that space as well as his own, and that was the sole reason why he did not make the breakaway he usually does."

An indifferent September concluded with a local derby with Rochdale Hornets. It was reckoned that the Oldham contingent in a bumper 20,000 attendance received "full value for money" as their favourites bounced back to form with a 24–6 win. In a reshuffle of the threequarter line, George Smith changed flanks to play on the wing outside of James and Dixon moved into one of the centre berths. The Roughyeds scored six tries, one of which James converted while Wood added two more goals. The pairing of James with Dixon as co-centres was hailed a success, the *Oldham Standard* said that "The Salfordian [James] was much in the picture, his running and defence being a feature of his play."

It was back to earth with an almighty thump for the next match, an 18–5 reverse in front of 12,000 at Broughton Rangers. 'Settle', writing in the *Oldham Standard*, was clearly "unsettled" by the Roughyeds' performance: "Why the team should give such crude and altogether miserable displays away from home I can't say, but it is time for an improvement." There was also mild criticism of James: "The back division requires strengthening. Lomas kicked well occasionally but for speed he and his colleagues were beaten." Was age catching up with James at last? At 32 years old it was inevitable that he would be slowing down, although he had proved he could still be a match-winner in the championship victory over Wigan just five months earlier.

James was still a hit with the Cumberland selectors and, two days later, Monday 9 October, he travelled to Warrington for the opening county fixture against Lancashire. He had plenty of familiar company in the Cumbrian side because Oldham colleagues Dixon, Joe Ferguson and Owens were also picked. Lancashire were the current champions, but were soundly beaten 28–7 by a vigorous Cumberland outfit. James scored the last of his team's eight tries and converted a second half touchdown by Ferguson.

Halifax were at Watersheddings the following Saturday and came away with a 10–10 draw under their belts. The local feeling was that Oldham was lucky to share the points having been outsmarted in their back play. James, meanwhile, was in demand again the following Wednesday when he was called upon to make the long journey to London. The Australians had begun their second tour of the Old Country and England were scheduled to meet them at Craven Cottage, the home of Fulham FC. The tourists won 11–6, James – who played in the centre – failed to score on this occasion.

Three days later he was back in an Oldham jersey for a Lancashire Cup first round game at Barrow and was also chosen to captain the side. The Roughyeds commenced the defence of their trophy with a 13–2 win; their skipper opened the score with a 16th minute penalty, and added another goal from a second half conversion. That victory was the first in a run of six successes that included two league fixtures, a match against the Australians, and three

Lancashire Cup ties that took Oldham to the final once more. The two league victories were at home to Swinton, 36–8, and at Runcorn, 14–5, both of whom were in the lower regions of the 27-team championship table.

There were 15,000 fans at Watersheddings for Swinton's visit on 28 October. Oldham's improved showing was credited to the return of Sid Deane, following 'negotiations', for his first appearance of the season. He joined James in the centre. Oldham led 15–8 at the break, James scored the first try after a move covering the length of the field that also involved Bert Avery and Deane, the latter drew Swinton full-back Eddie Griffiths before he despatched the final pass. James completed a brace in the second half when he touched down at the corner. The victory at Runcorn, 11 days later on a Wednesday, was hard earned and there were few opportunities afforded to James – who converted one of his side's two tries – and co-centre Deane to get their wingers moving.

The match against the Australians followed on Saturday 11 November and produced one of the most exciting games of the season at Watersheddings; witnessed by almost 20,000 supporters. It was felt that the crowd would have been even greater, but for political meetings being held in the town ahead of a by-election which was taking place two days later. James was the central figure in a whirlwind start. He created an opening after just three minutes for his winger George Cook who, unfortunately, knocked on, and then had a try disallowed after he dribbled the ball into the Australian in-goal near the posts. The tourists survived and went on to take an 8–4 lead into the interval, having scored two tries. Oldham, though, staged an exciting second half rally through tries by Anlezark and Cook. The latter score came with 10 minutes remaining. Cook had a simple task after James had made mincemeat of the opposition defence with a scything run. The 14–8 triumph was Oldham's second over the Australians; they had previously beaten the 1908–09 tourists.

Interspersed among these victories was their Lancashire Cup run. Following the league win over Swinton, they entertained Leigh in the second round on 4 November. It was claimed the 12,000 attendance would have been higher but for an Oldham Athletic versus Blackburn Rovers game that attracted 20,000 to Boundary Park and – as in the case of the Australia game – a political rally was also taking place. Those that did enter the ground saw a convincing 23–0 win. James scored one of Oldham's five tries. The semi-final draw took them to Central Park on 18 November although, with Wigan now a major force – a league match at Halifax was their only defeat so far – success was not expected. But, buoyed by their win over the Australians seven days earlier, Oldham's pack gave an inspirational display and stifled Wigan's attack in front of a 20,000 crowd. The deadlock was broken in the second half when Oldham forward Fred Wise scored the only try for a 3–0 victory.

James – chosen at half-back – opposed the Australian tourists for a third time on Wednesday 22 November. It was a fixture he must have been looking forward to because he was appearing for Cumberland at the Athletic Ground in Maryport. It was the third occasion since he left his local club in 1900 that he had represented the county in his hometown. The *Manchester Guardian* said it produced one of the toughest matches of the tour so far. Australia won after taking a 5–0 lead in the first five minutes, the game thereafter developed into a fierce contest. Oldham's Ferguson was the only other scorer, with a penalty from halfway 10 minutes from time.

Along with forwards Ferguson and Avery, James was rested for Oldham's next fixture – a home match against Widnes – in preparation for the Lancashire Cup Final a week later. With hindsight it appears to have been a strategy that backfired because Widnes unexpectedly won 7–2, a result that would prove costly at the end of the season. The Lancashire Cup Final was played at Wheater's Field and turned into another disaster for Oldham. Old rivals Rochdale Hornets provided the opposition and Oldham were fancied to win well against a team stuck in mid-table. The Hornets had other plans and, in front of a 20,000 gathering, reached the interval with a 4–0 lead. It got worse for Oldham at the start of the second period when they lost half-back Anlezark due to fractured ribs. Although George Smith subsequently scored a try and a goal for the Roughyeds, it was not enough. Rochdale crossed for two touchdowns of their own to claim their first ever trophy success with a 12–5 score. It was a significant loss in James's career because it was the only time that he appeared in a county cup final.

Another match against Australia took place the next Wednesday, James joined Wood and Avery in England's team at the Notts County Football Club's Meadow Lane ground. Despite good weather, only 3,000 attended. The NU used most of the tourists' matches against representative sides to try to spread the game outside its heartlands, but a midweek afternoon match in 'alien' territory was never likely to be a success. There was little in it, James converted a try by Hunslet half-back Fred Smith in the first period, Dan Frawley replied with a touchdown in the second after winger Billy Batten fluffed a pass from James. England won 5–3. James had originally been chosen as reserve back, but came into the side when Huddersfield centre Harold Wagstaff pulled out.

James played his third match in six days when he was in Oldham's team for Thursday's visit to St Helens. Picked as outside-half, with Tommy Brice as his partner, it was the first time he had appeared for Oldham in the halves. Oldham lost 21–11; James scored a second half try in the corner after excellent passing by former Leeds player Bill Biggs and Tom Llewellyn. The Roughyeds' next match in a busy schedule was a home fixture with Broughton Rangers two days later on Saturday 9 December. Oldham won 16–5, but James was not in the team because he had been selected for Cumberland's game against Yorkshire at Millom. The Cumbrians won 16–13 to claim the county title, but an ankle injury prevented James's participation. It seemed as though there was a fixture almost every other day during December and James found himself at half-back again for Oldham's Monday afternoon's game at Barrow two days afterwards. He was not originally picked to play, presumably to rest his ankle, and was a late replacement for White. Two first half penalties from Ferguson helped Oldham to a narrow 4–3 win.

Having been overlooked for the first test, which Australia had won 19–10 in Newcastle, James was included for the second meeting, at Tynecastle Park, Edinburgh – home of the Heart of Midlothian Football Club – on 16 December. The match was two days after Norwegian explorer Roald Amundsen had reached the South Pole. He had beaten the efforts of Englishman Robert Falcon Scott – 'Scott of the Antarctic' – by 35 days. The Northern Unionists appeared keen to restore lost national pride when they led 11–3 at the interval, James having scored one of their three tries. The Australians, however, pulled the score back to 11–11 to force a draw. They felt they were robbed of two points after their forward Arthur Francis – one of five New Zealanders included in the tour party – took a first half penalty. Touch judge Claude Corbett, who was actually an Australian journalist covering the tour for Sydney's *Sun* newspaper, indicated a goal, the English touch judge signalled 'no goal,' and referee Frank Renton of Hunslet took the latter view. 'Forward' of the *Athletic News* said: "In the (Northern Union) threequarter line the soundest player of the four was unquestionably Lomas. He may not be as speedy as last season, but he was clean in his work, and there was no hesitancy in anything he attempted."

His involvement in the test meant James missed Oldham's 15–0 defeat at Wigan. He was back in their side the following week to continue his new role at outside-half, a position he kept with Oldham for the rest of the season. It was the start of a run of five consecutive home fixtures, all of which were won by some distance; Leigh, 20–0, Hull KR, 37–7, Bradford Northern, 21–3, St Helens, 35–5 and Coventry, 31–10 – an aggregate of 144 points to 25. There were 12,000 inside Watersheddings on the Saturday before Christmas for the visit of Leigh. James did not appear on the scorers' list, but made up for that omission with a brace in each of the next three games.

'Settle' felt Oldham produced their best display of the season against Hull KR on Christmas Day. Their forwards dominated possession, and allowed the backs to demonstrate their passing skills to the full. The writer added that, at half-back, "They were well served by Lomas and Billy Dixon. Both played a storming game and each swung the ball about with that precision which the Oldham crowd like." On a dull, dark afternoon, James – who landed a first half conversion – scored both his tries after the interval, his first one a spectacular effort when he burst through the defence off Dixon's pass.

Oldham continued to play "with real championship form" for the Boxing Day visit of Bradford Northern. James carved his way through the Yorkshire side's defence after 10 minutes when he came away from a scrum inside their 25 area and sold a dummy before he raced over the try-line. Oldham led 5–0 at the break as an early drizzle developed into a huge downpour that made the pitch muddy. The Roughyeds added four more tries after the interval including a second from James, who also chipped in with a conversion.

The last match of 1911 was the meeting with St Helens on Saturday 30 December. On another overcast day with the playing area churned up, Oldham again excelled. The *Oldham Evening Chronicle* said James, who continued as captain, "played a great game on this occasion, being speedy and clever and making countless openings for both himself and the others behind him." He put his stamp on all three of their first half tries. He caught a difficult, high pass from Brice and sent Tom Williams and Evan Davies away on an inter-passing move that resulted in a beautifully worked opening score by the latter. He then constructed the second for Biggs with a lengthy inside pass and, just before the break, claimed one himself with a stirring individual effort. He beat off a host of defenders before he touched down near the posts. His influence continued after the break, and he raced in for another try himself.

'Grasshopper', writing in the *Oldham Evening Chronicle* was full of praise for the manner of the four recent victories, and said: "Another factor in the recent run of success has been the return of Jimmy Lomas's best form. During the last few weeks he has been playing just such brilliant football as that which went so far towards the great victory in the League final last May. He seems not only to have found his form but also his place, and he is giving a better account of himself than ever now that he has been regularly played at outside-half."

A key ingredient in Oldham's upsurge of form was the recruitment of Welsh duo Davies and Williams. The pair – who were friends – made their joint debut against Broughton Rangers on 9 December, occupying the two wing berths. After a couple of weeks Davies moved inside as centre partner to Williams and, with George Smith, Deane and Cook also in contention, the threequarter line had a potent look. One downside though was the loss of James's half-back partner Billy Dixon, who never played again after the Christmas Day fixture with Hull KR because he developed rheumatic fever.

Oldham concluded their run of home wins on New Year's Day against Coventry, although James was not present. Instead, he captained the NU side in the third and final test against Australia. As with the previous tests, the match was used for 'missionary' purposes and played at Villa Park, Birmingham, home of Aston Villa FC. The NU made a positive start and led 8–0 through two tries, the first of which was scored by James near the corner. The Australians came back strongly and scored 22 unanswered points after the interval to win 33–8 and clinch the series. The *Manchester Guardian* commented: "The less said about the last hour the better, although Lomas and [Bert] Jenkins played by no means badly." It has to be said, though, that the hosts lost Wigan forward Dick Ramsdale in the opening minute with a knee injury and, in fact James – who was playing in the centre – was also hurt midway through the first half, but continued.

He was apparently still "feeling the effects" of his injury when Oldham visited Salford the following Saturday, and did not play. It was a disappointment for both sets of fans, Salford supporters had been eager to see their former hero in action again, and Oldham missed a player who, according to the *Oldham Evening Chronicle*, "would have been a great source of strength under the muddy conditions which prevailed." Oldham still managed to win, though, 8–0.

The traditional red and white hoops of Oldham were worn
with obvious pride by James. (Photo: Courtesy Michael Turner)

Oldham 1911-12, James's first full season at Watersheddings. Back: G. Smith, E. Davies, A. Wood,
S. Deane, T. Williams; middle: A. Avery, J. Lomas, J. Ferguson, E. Anlezark, A. Smith; front:
W. Jardine, W. Biggs, J. Wright, J. Wiltshire. (Photo: Courtesy Michael Turner)

James returned to lead the team to two further home victories over Warrington, 30–10, and Barrow, 40–5, which extended Oldham's winning streak to eight matches. He scored the opening two tries against Warrington as Oldham built up a 10–0 half-time lead; the first after five minutes when he gained possession from a scrum near the visitors try-line and jumped over the opposition to touch down, the second after he broke away with the ball at his feet, dribbled through the defence and into the in-goal. 'Grasshopper' said James "had evidently quite recovered from his injury, for he played in capital form, as did his [half-back] partner Brice."

Against Barrow and leading 8–5 at the interval, Oldham exploded into points' activity in the second half, and added 32. James converted four tries during this period and could have had a fifth; he struck the post in the final minute after forward Jack Wiltshire had touched down. Barrow were handicapped through the losses of injured winger Bob Bamber and dismissed forward John 'Runcorn' Hughes. It was said that James "has been seen to better advantage, but he is always working and always useful."

The wins over Warrington and Barrow 'sandwiched' another match at Watersheddings; the England versus Wales international on Saturday 20 January, a match the home nation won 31–5. James had been selected to play at outside-half, but a shoulder injury against Warrington kept him out, he had been unable to 'follow his employment' since Tuesday.

February commenced with a postponement at Swinton. On arriving at the Chorley Road ground, James, as Oldham captain, complained the frozen playing area was unfit, referee R.H. Jackson agreed. Swinton officials had indicated earlier that it was playable after sprinkling it with salt, but in the bright sunshine it had only liquidised on top. The *Oldham Evening Chronicle* said it "felt like walking on a set-paved road after a light shower." In fact, the frosty and icy weather caused the postponement of all but one match that day.

Oldham's next match was at Headingley. They performed poorly and lost 14–3 to Leeds, a display that caused concern for their chances against high-flying Huddersfield two weeks later. Before that encounter, though, the Roughyeds had to travel to Coventry in the first round of the Challenge Cup, a match they won 21–3. A poor attendance of 1,200 was blamed on the counter attractions of a Coventry City versus Crystal Palace football match in the Southern League and a Coventry versus Bath rugby union fixture. There was also a problem with the excursion train carrying Oldham fans to the game which did not arrive until it was nearly over. Just a week earlier, 'Grasshopper' had bemoaned that the railway system had similarly let down Oldham supporters when travelling to Headingley.

The visit of Huddersfield was considered 'the match of the season' so far for Oldham. 'Thousands' were locked out after the gates had to be closed before kick-off. The reported 28,000 attendance is believed to be the largest in the history of the Watersheddings ground. For a long period, the Fartowners led by two points before Oldham emerged victorious 6–2 through tries from Avery and Williams. The *Oldham Evening Chronicle* said: "Lomas again was another whose strong point cannot be said to lie in his tackling, but he gave a great exhibition of the art in this game and was one of the main factors of the victory." While James's defence had certainly been found wanting at Headingley, possibly a legacy of his shoulder injury, it is strange to read that his tackling, so often given as one of his strengths should be referred to as not a 'strong point'. Possibly this was an indication that as he got older and less mobile his ability to be up with the defensive line was more suspect although, by many accounts, he still retained great strength.

Two more massive home games followed, both against Wigan. The first, on 2 March, was in the second round of the Challenge Cup. After the lead changed hands three times in the first half, it was Wigan who held the upper hand, 8–5, at the interval. A rib injury to Todd just before the break depleted the visitors in the second half as Oldham overhauled them. James played his part in a spectacular try by Davies to help his team progress 12–8. A disappointing 10,000 crowd was blamed on "trouble in the coal trade" due to widespread strikes, only a few fans travelled from Wigan.

Wigan took their revenge the following week, their 8–2 league victory at Watersheddings shunted Oldham outside the top-four. Oldham were poor. James, reportedly, looked slow and did not penetrate the opposition as expected and, "when he did get going, running his centres onto the wing before giving them the ball."

Oldham travelled to Widnes the next Wednesday, 13 March, a match postponed from January after a heavy snowfall. Oldham led 10–0 at half-time, the second of two tries was scored by James – his first for two months – who, accepting a return pass from Williams, raced for the try-line. Although tackled five yards short with three opponents holding on to him, he proved he was still as strong as an ox and carried them over the line with him. Frighteningly for Oldham, Widnes made a stirring comeback to take the lead 11–10, their players "doing somersaults with glee" when Bob Jones converted half-back John Noon's try five minutes from time. But Oldham were saved by an amazing last minute penalty from Ferguson who, with the wind against him, fired the ball between the uprights from near touch and close to the halfway line.

James claimed another try during the weekend visit to the Athletic Grounds. He latched onto the ball after a cross-kick from Anlezark and ran in at the corner from 25 yards out. But it was a mere consolation in the closing minutes, Rochdale Hornets, thanks to a fine display from their forwards, won 11–3.

Any worries over their waning championship play-off aspirations took a back seat the following week when the Challenge Cup came back into view. The draw was again a tough one for Oldham, Huddersfield had followed them out of the hat although it was, at least, a home tie. As with Huddersfield's league visit a month earlier there was a big crowd, reported as 25,000. The *Oldham Evening Chronicle* said "versions of club colours did a brisk business". In a tough, hard game Oldham progressed to the semi-final stage, 2–0, thanks to a Wood penalty shortly before the break. Huddersfield, though, were up against it from the 25th minute due to the dismissal of forward Fred Longstaff.

Encouraged by their victory over the code's top team in the Challenge Cup, Oldham took their improved form back into the league campaign with three successive wins; 14–10 at Swinton, 60–0 at home to Runcorn and 11–7 at Warrington. The previously postponed match at Chorley Road against Swinton took place on Wednesday, 27 March. Despite their place in the lower half of the table, the Lions gave a good account of themselves. The margin against The Linnets the following Saturday was more emphatic. The Roughyeds scored 16 tries which included five by Davies and four from Williams. James was also involved in the points' bonanza, and scored the fourth try after 25 minutes. It was a spectacular effort, he received possession from Anlezark, burst between the Runcorn centres and sprinted 50 yards to go under the posts. He also bagged six goals; two early penalties and four conversions, including the extras to his own try. He was again on target with another conversion in the close win at Warrington two days later.

Oldham entered the Easter programme vying for fourth spot with Hunslet, both had won 22 and drawn one of their 31 games, each still had three to play. The pair also had third-placed Hull KR in their sights, although the Rovers had five games remaining. Oldham's hopes took a body blow in the match at Halifax on Good Friday. The home forwards dominated, James – who was 'in good form' – scored the Roughyeds' only points with a try in their 5–3 defeat. Pride was resurrected the following day after a tight 9–5 win over Salford at Watersheddings, James scored the second of three tries following a tremendous break by half-back W. Webster as Oldham took a 9–0 lead into the half-time break.

Oldham made six changes for their last league fixture, an Easter Monday trip to Coventry. James was one of the names left off the team sheet. It was claimed that they had injuries to contend with but, despite the importance of the match for their top-four hopes, it is more likely the club had half an eye on the Challenge Cup semi-final five days later. As expected, Oldham disposed of Coventry, 23–7, a result that left the Roughyeds in fourth place. However, the threat of fifth-placed Hunslet had not gone away because the Parksiders still had two of their games left and victory in both would be 'curtains' as far as Oldham were concerned. The next day James and his colleagues nervously awaited the outcome of Hunslet's home game against basement club Bradford Northern. Hunslet won 24–12, Oldham's ambition for a possible double ended when the Parksiders secured their second win – again at home – when they beat St Helens 34–7.

James's disappointment was tempered by the fact that, on the day Hunslet trounced St Helens, he and his colleagues were doing likewise to Wakefield Trinity in the Challenge Cup semi-final. Played at Wheater's Field, Oldham began as favourites, particularly as they had disposed of the code's top two sides in Huddersfield and Wigan. They did not disappoint, and won with something to spare, 17–0. On a dull, but dry, afternoon and watched by 15,000 fans, Oldham crept towards a 7–0 lead by half-time, James – "one of the best of the backs" – scored the latter of his team's two second half tries. He took a pass from Cook and forced his way over at the corner.

While it was a day of personal joy for James in reaching another final, the following Monday was one of national sadness through a catastrophe that is still remembered today. In the early hours of 14 April the R.M.S. Titanic sank on its maiden voyage from Southampton to New York after it hit an iceberg shortly before midnight. The disaster claimed the lives of over 1,500 people. Along with its sister ship Olympic, it was the largest vessel afloat and belonged to the White Star Line, a company founded by Maryport-born Thomas Henry Ismay.

The Challenge Cup Final was played at Headingley on 27 April when an unfancied Dewsbury side surprised Oldham by winning 8–5 after a controversial finish. The Yorkshiremen did not allow Oldham the freedom to demonstrate their superior pace, and preferred to keep play tight among the forwards and deny James and his half-back partner Anlezark any opportunity to open out play. Oldham had started well enough when, at 2–2, they scored the opening try after 20 minutes; James evaded half-back Tommy Milner following a scrum before he passed the ball to the threequarters. Cook concluded the move by crossing the try-line at the corner. The goal was missed by Wood, but worse for Oldham was an injury to Cook in scoring, which inhibited his play for the remainder of the final. Leading 5–2, the Roughyeds must have still fancied their chances in the second half, especially after Dewsbury forward Joe Hammill was carried off with a knee injury.

Oldham's numerical advantage was nullified when Avery was sent off for dissent by referee Ben Ennion with 15 minutes left. Seven minutes later, Dewsbury levelled the score at 5–5 through a try from winger Billy Rhodes. A dramatic finish was in store after Wood attempted a goal following a mark by Davies. A touch judge raised his flag and the Oldham players "jumped for joy", but Ennion ruled that the ball was wide of the upright. This turn of fortune spurred Dewsbury on and Rhodes crossed the whitewash again for the winning score. There was, however, uncertainty as to whether the ball had been grounded. The referee consulted a touch judge before he awarded the try. The *Oldham Standard* reporter was in no doubt, and argued that Rhodes had been forced into touch.

There had been some pre-match debate as to whether James would appear in the final. During the week he had wrenched a knee and was only declared fit on the morning of the game. However, 'Grasshopper' wrote: "I doubt very much whether he was right for he did not show his customary brilliance at all." The *Daily Mail* said: "To James Lomas the result of the match must have been a bitter disappointment. How often in his Salford days this great and great-hearted player has had the [Challenge] Cup dashed from his lips almost at the moment of drinking? But Lomas is sportsman and footballer enough to realise that Oldham did not deserve to win, and that Dewsbury, though not to be compared with some sides that have won the Cup and some that have never won it, merited their victory for the splendid determination they showed throughout."

To say it was "a bitter disappointment" for James is probably an understatement. The result must have been a hammer blow to him because it was his fourth defeat in four

Challenge Cup Final appearances. Added to the Lancashire Cup Final loss earlier in the campaign and the fact that he had, during his career to date, been a championship runner-up on three occasions, James had been dealt yet another undeserved poor hand when it came to club honours.

After the match, the – mostly Dewsbury – supporters rushed over to the grandstand for the presentation of the trophy and medals by the Wakefield MP, Mr A.H. Marshall. At the time it was customary for both team captains to accept the medals on behalf of their players. When it came to Oldham's turn it was said that "most" of their players were still present. One of them, though, was not their skipper, Anlezark. It may well be that the Australian – whose poor kick towards the end had presented the opportunity for Billy Rhodes' winning try – and his other absent colleagues were so crestfallen that they had wanted to leave the field as soon as possible. In his absence, James, as vice-captain, accepted the runners-up medals instead. The Oldham team was: Wood; Cook, Deane, Davies, Williams; Lomas, Anlezark (captain); Ferguson, Avery, Arthur Smith, Jim Wright, Wise, Wiltshire.

Oldham had one further commitment; a friendly match against Huddersfield on 11 May. The only thing, though, was that it was to be played at South Devon Place in Plymouth. Watched by a reported 10,000 crowd, James appeared at outside-half, but was not among the scorers in a 31–26 defeat. As with James's previous appearance in the town, in 1910 with the returning Northern Union tourists, it was probably arranged by Avery, who lined up in Oldham's pack against the Fartowners. James, meanwhile, concluded his season as Oldham's leading scorer with a tally of 106 points from 20 tries and 23 goals.

18. 1912–13: One last representative match

As luck would have it, James Lomas and his Oldham colleagues met Dewsbury in the opening fixture of the 1912–13 campaign, a repeat of the previous season's Challenge Cup Final clash. Played at Watersheddings, most home supporters would have anticipated their team taking revenge for the earlier loss. Dewsbury arrived with a different plan, and shocked Oldham yet again; the score this time was 12–5. The Roughyeds had, on paper at least, strengthened their squad. Several new arrivals included brothers Viv and Bill Farnsworth – centre and outside-half respectively – who were members of the 1911–12 Kangaroos. Their introduction resulted in a reshuffled back division with James starting the season in his former position of centre.

Writing in the *Oldham Evening Chronicle*, 'Grasshopper' concluded that the Roughyeds were well beaten by Dewsbury and the threequarter line was the "weakest part of the Oldham team". The writer singled out former Leeds winger Ernest Oliver "as not a success," and added that "neither was [his centre] Lomas". He continued "the ex-Salford man [James] and the Australian [Bill Farnsworth] in front of him seemed to be, more than the others, marked and spotted all through the game, and the spotting rendered Lomas quite harmless. True, he did get in a smart dash now and then, but he was never allowed to do anything really worthwhile." It was the start of a disappointing Oldham season.

The next match lifted the darkening clouds, somewhat, with a meritorious 14–4 victory away to Hull KR. It seemed that the new combination was clicking into gear: "[Bill] Farnsworth got plenty of ball and made good use of it, and it was good to see. Lomas came out of his shell and followed him through as he did. They both played an improved game [and] particularly paid attention to sound defence." But it was followed seven days later with another let down in the match at Headingley. Oldham played well in the first half against Leeds and were level 2–2 at half-time. The second period was a different story; Oldham crumbled and eventually lost 16–2. James, meanwhile, was in pain, he missed the last 10 minutes of the game through damaged ribs.

It was an injury that sidelined him for the next two matches, although the first of them – at home to St Helens on 28 September – would have taken place without him in any case. On that day he was due to take his place in the Cumberland team that met Lancashire at Workington but, of course, he had to withdraw from that as well. In the meantime, the *Oldham Chronicle*, under its 'Watersheddings Gossip' column said: "There is no getting away from the fact Lomas is not showing his old form yet, and we want somebody as a standby for his position. [George] Cook is to have another chance today [in the centre against St Helens] and a good deal may depend upon how he comes off."

James was back in harness on 12 October for the home game with Swinton. Whether it was due to fitness or his implied indifferent form, he was selected on the left wing, a move that was thought to be "a very doubtful experiment". Bill Farnsworth was picked as his centre with Evan Davies taking up the other centre spot. Swinton won 10–6, but the blame was laid at the feet of the Oldham forwards who "had an off day". This time James was praised: "Lomas played cleverly and strongly, and made several good openings, and on the whole his performance in that [left wing] position was pretty good."

The next game saw another positional change and James took the scrum-half role – partnering George Anlezark – in the first round Lancashire Cup match at Runcorn. In heavy rain the two teams were locked 2–2 at the interval, Oldham went ahead 10–2 before James made "one wonderful run [that was] just like his very best." However, on reaching the Linnets' full-back G. Shaw, he passed the ball and it went astray. Some critics reckoned that, having beaten everyone else, he should have taken Shaw on. The general consensus, though, was that he was "in better form than he has previously shown this season."

Saturday 26 October saw a rarity for James when, despite his improved form against Runcorn, he was relegated to 'A' team rugby for the first time in his Northern Union career. While the first team lost at home to Wigan 7–3 – their fourth home match of the season, none of which had been won – James played in the centre for the reserves at Central Park. In non-stop, pouring rain, they lost 8–2 after Tom White's penalty had given them an interval lead.

James was brought out of the wilderness for the second consecutive meeting with Wigan, this time in the Lancashire Cup second round. It took James back to Central Park and again he was in the beaten team. Oldham crashed out of the competition 24–8. James – back at scrum-half and, reportedly, showing his best form of the campaign so far – scored his first points of the season when he converted a late try by Davies.

The uncertain nature of James's role at the club continued when he was restored to centre for the next match, at home to Runcorn on 9 November. From his point of view, at least, it was the start of some stability because he continued in that position for the remainder of 1912. Oldham raced to a 20–2 half-time lead with four tries. James scored the second when winger Frank Holbrook re-passed to him out of the tackle. Oldham eventually won 47–10, their first success of the season at Watersheddings. For James it was his first touchdown since last April's Challenge Cup semi-final with Wakefield Trinity. The *Oldham Evening Chronicle* commented that "he seemed speedier and more clever than [in] many of his previous matches of this season."

Oldham had a blank date on Saturday 16 November due to Ebbw Vale's withdrawal from the Northern Union in September. The next match was a home game with Salford. Despite a miserable, wet day, 8,000 saw James play "a great game" against his former club. He did not score, but received a lot of the plaudits for Oldham's second try when he broke through the Salford ranks in brilliant fashion before he put Holbrook in. Having trailed 5–3 at half-time, it put Oldham 6–5 ahead; the Roughyeds eventually won 11–5. One incident of note was a clash between James and one-time colleague Dai John who was at half-back for Salford. 'Grasshopper' wrote: "It was rather amusing to see the referee [Mr J.F. May] have to go between the burly Lomas and the diminutive John, but I understood that the latter was doing a dirty trick on his ex-captain, which got Jimmy's gander up!"

A sudden frost caused the postponement of Oldham's next fixture, at Leigh. James's next taste of action was at The Boulevard on Thursday 5 December, when he wore Cumberland's colours against Yorkshire. As always, the Cumbrians relied on their forward strength, a tactic which served them well in the opening half, and they were 3–2 in arrears at the break. The second period, however, was more one-sided and the White Rose ran out 19–5 victors. James, who played in the centre, did not figure among the scorers although he did get a favourable mention in the match summary. It was a notable occasion because, at the age of 33, it was the last time he played for Cumberland; subsequent selections were thwarted through injury. In fact, it was his last representative match of any description.

Two days later, James was back at Watersheddings and assisted Oldham to a resounding 37–5 win over Barrow. Possibly due to his slackening pace, James's point scoring was no longer coming in floods. If anything it was more of a trickle, but he did conjure up a magnificent effort during the second half against the Shipbuilders. He received the ball from a scrum and crashed through the defence in the same old irresistible way before he touched down.

Oldham travelled to Halifax next, and earned a 10–3 victory. It was claimed that the Roughyeds showed a great improvement on earlier performances with "not a weak spot in the side" and could "easily" have doubled their score to 20. The extra 10 points should, it seems, have been the product of James's efforts, but he was twice denied. The first time was during the first half when he broke away with the ball at his feet and dribbled to within 12 yards of the Halifax try-line. With the ball "well under control" he then took it past the last line of defence and towards the posts but, at that point, his jersey was grabbed from behind and he was pulled off the ball. The verdict, according to the Oldham correspondent, should have been a penalty try. His other chance came late in the match when he "missed a splendid chance of a gap" and, instead of running into the opening, passed to Holbrook who was covered by two defenders and was subsequently bundled into touch.

With the Christmas festivities rapidly approaching, Oldham had a date at Wigan on the preceding Saturday. It was not a very jolly occasion for Oldham or James, the 29–6 defeat was the biggest he suffered during his time with the Roughyeds. Christmas Day and Boxing Day brought with them two home wins against Hull KR, 13–8, and Warrington, 5–0, respectively. The visit of the Rovers was on a dull day that just got darker and darker as the match progressed, causing doubt as to whether it would finish. Oldham led 8–0 at half-time and the rain lashed down during the second half. James charged down a kick by a Rovers player, and collected the ball before running under the posts for a try. Alf Wood converted and Oldham led 13–0. Two tries from the visitors made the score look more respectable at the finish. The following day's weather was just as bad, Bill Farnsworth's early try and Joe Ferguson's goal won the points on a wet and stormy afternoon.

Back on the road, Oldham lost the ground they had recently made up in the league table by losing at Broughton Rangers, 5–3, and Dewsbury, 15–3. The visit to Wheater's Field on 28 December was not the most memorable for James. Apart from losing narrowly, his own performance was not considered to be at its best. It was suggested he neglected his winger, Oliver, who was "rather starved" and, although he tackled well, was "not conspicuous in attack." He also came in for a disagreeable time from the Rangers fans, the *Oldham Evening Chronicle* said: "It was regrettable to notice the 'dead set' which was made by the crowd against Jimmy Lomas. It was always the same on those Manchester grounds, and I suppose it is one of the penalties of greatness. Whenever he did anything of note he 'got the bird' and when three of four opponents managed to get him down the feat was applauded with derisive cheers, but Lomas could get no credit for anything." At Dewsbury's Crown Flatt, a sunny New Year's Day greeted the teams but, again, it was not so pleasant for Oldham although, with attacking opportunities limited, James did well in defence.

The start of 1913 did not bode too well for James's future with Oldham. The Roughyeds resurrected their fortunes with five straight wins, four of them at home, but James only appeared in one of them. First off, they entertained Halifax on Saturday 4 January, and won comfortably 25–3. Viv Farnsworth – making his debut – took James's place; the Cumbrian was named as one of the two reserves. Of course in those days there was no substitutes' bench and 'reserve' or not, the player was out of the team once the match had started. The following weekend's visit to Runcorn was postponed due to a snowstorm but, in any case, James had been selected as full-back for the 'A' team who entertained the Linnets second string at Watersheddings. Possibly the new role was intended as an experimental one to take account of his slower pace. He certainly fitted the bill as the last line of defence in other respects, as a sound tackler and kicker of the ball. It was reported that the weather was so bitterly cold that players struggled to hold the ball due to the numbness in their fingers. Oldham 'A' led 6–0 at the break through three penalty goals from James, but Runcorn 'A' earned a 6–6 draw with two second half tries, one in the last minute.

James must have passed his 'test' because he was selected at full-back for the following week's home first team game with Widnes. The usual custodian, Wood, had been out since a Christmas Day injury. It was the only occasion that James was ever picked in that position at senior level. Losing 10–5 at half-time, Oldham just managed to emerge on top 11–10, but it seems James did not impress as much as he may have hoped. The *Oldham Evening Chronicle* writer analysed his performance in some depth: "The experiment of trying Lomas as the last line of defence was interesting, and naturally he came in for close attention from the spectators. He gave a rather mixed display, sometimes playing brilliantly both in attack and defence, and at other times failing to come up to requirements. Some of his saves in the face of a rush were quite worthy of Wood at his best and he frequently stopped his opponents when a score seemed certain. But he was not safe and it made one always afraid he was going to put his foot in it again. Much of this was due to the fact that he could not get away from the fancy that he was a threequarter line man. Old habit is very strong and Lomas did not succeed in altogether getting out of it. The result was that he was often out of his place when he was wanted and he was too prone to let the ball bounce instead of getting to it and the result sometimes was that by the time he got hold his opponents were on him. His colleagues were frequently to blame because nobody took the precaution to drop back to his place when he had run up the field to follow up his kick."

Was this the beginning of the end for James? Was age finally catching up with the great man? It would appear so based on the fact that while Oldham continued their winning streak with a 10–6 victory at Huddersfield and home wins over Rochdale Hornets, 12–5, and Leeds, 21–8, James was on 'A' team duty. In the reverse fixtures of the aforementioned matches, his stint began at full-back against Huddersfield 'A' at Watersheddings on 25 January. Selected as captain, he led them to a 13–0 win in front of a "good crowd," and kicked two goals, a first half penalty to put his side 5–0 up at the interval, and a second half conversion. He was again at full-back at The Athletic Grounds on 1 February. He converted his team's try in a 15–5 loss to Hornets 'A'. Although he performed reasonably well at the back, he was chosen in the centre for the visit to Headingley on 8 February, where the Oldham reserves beat Leeds 'A'. James converted all three Oldham tries in a 15–5 win and made the break that produced the first by forward W. Webster. Later he supplied the "perfect" pass that enabled Oliver to score the last.

James was recalled to first team duty for the rearranged game at Runcorn the following Wednesday, 12 February, and replaced an injured Jim Wharton at scrum-half. In front of a pitiful crowd of 1,000, it began on a fine afternoon, but the weather quickly turned foggy and it was stopped after 25 minutes play. Following a 20 minute wait to see if things would improve the game was abandoned with Runcorn leading 11–7.

Three days later, Oldham returned to that vicinity, but this time to face Widnes. James was picked again although relocated to the centre. It was not a good day's work for the Roughyeds, they lost 16–0 and James did not impress. One reporter felt that James "was much below his best, and a mull of his in the second half, when he allowed himself to be robbed of the ball in midfield, gave Widnes a try and a goal."

He retained his place for the next match although that "place" was back at scrum-half, where he partnered Anlezark as Oldham took on Leigh at Watersheddings. The match was watched by 10,000 while, on the same day, almost 27,000 saw Oldham Athletic entertain Manchester United in the FA Cup. Oldham beat Leigh 13–7; James converted a try in each half and received more praise than of late. The *Oldham Evening Chronicle* said: "the surprising thing about [Oldham's] performance was the good show given by Anlezark and Lomas. They played a very successful game and Oldham have no fear as to how to fill the half-back position it we could be sure this pair would always play in this form."

The odds on Oldham finishing in the top-four of the championship were already long when they travelled to Knowsley Road on 1 March. That St Helens won 10–2 made it look impossible. A fit again Wharton resumed at half-back, but it was Anlezark who made way for him and not James, as might have been expected given recent events and comments. James scored his side's only points during the second half, when they were already 10–0 down, from a penalty after Saints' forward Jim Prescott broke away from a scrum too early. But, overall, it was another inglorious day for the struggling Cumbrian, his defence in particular caused concern as the following extract from the *Oldham Evening Chronicle* indicates: "Lomas was very prone to snapping at his opponents head instead of going for him low and many a time he was beaten with this sort of thing. He did not play nearly so well as he did on the previous Saturday [against Leigh]."

There was a change of scenery the following week when the destination was Normanton St John's in the opening round of the Challenge Cup. This time James played in the centre and gave a good account against the junior outfit. The Normanton side showed great determination throughout, but they found James sound in his defence while "his burly figure" proved a real handful for them to bring to ground. He had a part in all three of his team's tries; he scored the first off a pass from Viv Farnsworth, his run and pass put in Holbrook for the second, and then scored the third himself. But it was an unexpectedly tight match; Oldham led 12–0 at the interval before winning 17–4.

Seven days later the roller-coaster ride that James was experiencing took a huge downward dip. Playing for Oldham in a Challenge Cup tie at Dewsbury he was sent off for the third time in his career. He received little sympathy from Oldham's press which concerned itself more with his perceived poor performance while still on the field. That second round draw may well have been the tie that Oldham fans dreaded. The journey to Crown Flatt must have been undertaken with trepidation for supporters and players alike after last year's defeat in the final and Dewsbury's league double over the Roughyeds in the current campaign. They were right to show apprehension because the Yorkshire side won 10–2, and inflicted more anguish into what was turning into a woeful season for Oldham.

James had kept his place in the centre, but it was to the displeasure of 'Grasshopper' who wrote: "I do not think the best possible team was put on the field [because] on recent form G.W. [George] Smith is a better player than Lomas and it was a matter for astonishment that he was not chosen. Lomas had his strong points but when it comes to having to choose between him and Smith the latter is at present a better man, better in attack and a much better tackler, whilst he is more speedy in his running, in spite of his years. The ex-Salford man is weak in defence, chiefly through his habit of tackling his man round the ears, a sort of tackling which is of no use against a strong and burly lot of players like Dewsbury. I am not blaming only Lomas for the same criticism applies to others."

The argument for New Zealander Smith's inclusion is an interesting one. Undoubtedly an outstanding player in his day, he was actually four years older than James and had figured far less in Oldham's first team plans that season.

Debates as to whether James should play in the next game became academic after the

212

Northern Union Committee had met in Huddersfield the following Tuesday. Having been dismissed by referee Albert Hestford at Dewsbury, along with home forwards Albert Abbishaw and Fred Richardson, he was suspended. All three were dispensed with during a period of 'rough play' in the closing stages, James and Abbishaw each received four match bans while Richardson, reportedly dismissed for a seventh time, was banished until the end of September. James himself was very much on the side of officialdom when he wrote his memoirs in the late 1930s: "It has always been the League officials' aim to keep the game clean. The players realise now they are losing money when they are sent off. We used to club up in the old days and make their wages up when they were suspended, but I don't think they do it now for more than one or two matches." He consequently missed the four remaining March fixtures; a 5–3 win at Warrington, a 5–0 defeat at home to Huddersfield, another home defeat, 13–8 against Broughton Rangers and a 23–10 win at Swinton.

He returned for the match at Runcorn on Wednesday 2 April, the third attempt to get the game played. The Linnets defended well and led 7–0 at half-time. Oldham worked hard to recover in the second half, James – playing in the centre – and Danny Shannon – at half-back – in particular tried to make the vital break. At length a try came their way when James retrieved a loose ball and sent his winger Billy Young racing over. James also kicked the goal, which reduced the margin to 7–5, but that was how the score remained.

With skipper Ferguson out injured following the Runcorn game, James was made captain for the weekend's visit to Cavendish Park to meet Barrow. On a sunny, but windy day, Oldham led after four minutes when Young left the opposition in his wake after a passing move to score a try that James converted. James continually pushed Barrow back with long, raking kicks, and almost added another try before half-time, but Barrow full-back Ben Morgan kicked the ball dead before he could place a hand on it. It could have been a match winner because, by half-time, a try and goal from Barrow centre Harry Gifford had squared the match at 5–5 and there was no further score after the break. James tried to win it, but was off target with a long-range penalty in the second half after Cook was obstructed. *Oldham Evening Chronicle* writer 'Athenian' summed up James's performance: "Lomas showed that he was far from a spent force. Once he broke through and dragged three Barrow men with him some distance before a fourth came and provided the necessary weight to bring Jimmy down. Twice he was guilty of sticking to the ball too long until he was grassed, when a pass to Young would have been more affective."

It was back to familiar territory for James on the Monday with a trip to The Willows. Continuing as captain and playing once more at outside-half, James knocked on early in the game, but atoned when he tackled Edgar May after a threatening run. He later rescued a dangerous situation when he secured the ball on Oldham's line after bravely falling on it as Salford's pack mounted a fearsome looking rush. Salford scored first, but a try by Young "leaving all opponents behind," converted by James, gave Oldham a 5–3 advantage. The 'love affair' James once had with the Salford fans appeared to be well-and-truly a thing of the past based on events that unfolded at this particular game. As half-time drew near, he was barracked for lying-on former colleague Dai John for too long, which resulted in a penalty against Oldham. When the second half began, James was clearly fired up and "defied the efforts of six Salford players to get him down." 'Athenian' wrote: "This roused the crowd, who yelled vigorously and [Oldham forward Bill] Biggs went to the assistance of his captain, with the result that he and [Salford forward Harry] Goldsmith were cautioned by the referee for their part in the scramble." When James later knocked on again the Salford fans "hooted loudly". Overall, though, the home supporters must have been delighted with the result of the second half, three more tries brought Salford victory 16–5.

Oldham closed their season with a fifth consecutive away match, and visited Leigh for the fixture originally frozen off in November. James began the scoring on 30 minutes with a penalty after being obstructed by Leigh forward Albert Hurst in following up his own kick. Holbrook later added a try that proved a little too far out for James to convert and Oldham led 5–0 at half-time. James relentlessly pushed Leigh downfield with his long kicks after the interval, but unluckily hit an upright in attempting to convert a Viv Farnsworth try that concluded the scoring at 8–0 in Oldham's favour.

The Roughyeds had at least finished on a high note after one of Oldham's most disappointing campaigns to date. They finished 11th in the table and suffered early elimination in the Lancashire Cup and Challenge Cup. It was also a highpoint for James, who captained the side in what was his last match for the club. The *Oldham Evening Chronicle* said "Lomas was a glutton for work. He wanted to be everywhere and this probably accounted for his apparent selfishness." It was the kind of comment that followed him throughout his career; his high, inspirational work-rate almost precluded the idea of passing, so determined was he to break through on his own, which he so often succeeded in doing.

19. 1913–14: Into the Minster City

In the early hours of Saturday morning, 16 August 1913, the York-based *Yorkshire Evening Press* newspaper received the following telegram: "Pleased to inform you Lomas secured for York." Those eight words began a flurry of excitement and expectation in the Minster City.

It seems "it had been known for some time" that James Lomas would leave Oldham, who had placed him on the transfer list at £150. Even though he was nearly 34-years-old, several clubs had chased his signature, particularly those based in Lancashire. Among them was his former team Salford and, although he still lived in the county borough, as it was then, he evidently decided to join York. The *Yorkshire Evening Press* said: "Rumours have been rife for some weeks, not only in York but throughout the Northern Union district, as to the destination of James Lomas," and added that they "have been set at rest" through the arrival of York secretary Mr Oman's telegram.

The newspaper did not quote the amount paid to Oldham "but it may be taken for granted that so far as the York Club are concerned a record price has been paid." The 18 August edition of *The* (Oldham) *Standard* was, however, more forthcoming, and reported the fee as £100. Why James chose York ahead of one of the west Pennines outfits – who would have been more convenient in relation to where he lived – is difficult to fathom. With all due respect to York, they were one of the code's poorer performers at that time. It may be that the Minster club made him a good offer financially, or that he was influenced in some way by their club captain Frank Boylen. The former Hull forward had been signed during the previous campaign and had been a colleague of James's on the 1910 tour.

As well as James, York had recruited wing or centre Jim Batten – brother of the more famous Billy Batten – from Hunslet, and J. France, a ball-handling forward from the Purston club who would make quite an impact in the Minster Men's pack. Also, in addition to Durham-born Boylen, the club had the vastly experienced former England centre F.W. Oliver on its books.

The pre-season activity simulated interest from York's fans. 'Old Amber and Black' said in a letter published in the *Yorkshire Evening Press* on 19 August: "As a very old supporter of the [York] club, I should be delighted [to] congratulate the York Committee in securing the services of J. Lomas. It was my great pleasure to witness many of last season's matches in which he took part, and if he can produce anything near the form he then showed, we are indeed a fortunate club. He has lost none of his cunning, if he has lost anything, and I can promise his wing many more easier journeys to the line than he has had before. [Half-back George] Daniel will now undoubtedly have a pivot which should delight him. Following the securing of that dashing wing J. Batten, and a sterling forward like France, it is up to us members to show our appreciation, and take out season tickets."

Although the actual date in the players' register for the 1913–14 season shows James's transfer as being on 2 September, he was seen in action by his new fans on the last two

Saturday afternoons of August, in the final pre-season public practice games. They were held at York's Clarence Street ground, the proceeds benefitted junior rugby in the area.

York had enjoyed a reasonably good conclusion to the 1912–13 season – despite finishing 21st of the 26 clubs in the league table – and with the positivity generated through the new signings, there were high hopes of a good campaign. A lot of that optimism disappeared in the first match on Thursday evening, 4 September, at The Boulevard against Hull. They were soundly thrashed 34–3 in what was described as a "gruelling game" for the wearers of the amber and black. Half-back M. Lavelle was concussed and out of the match after the opening minutes and forward Frank Lee was carried off 15 minutes from the end. James – who had earlier covered half the length of the field when making a break – also retired for a few minutes during the second half due to a cut over an eye that required stitches. With only 11 players left and losing 34–0, York scored their three points near the end when James managed to get over at the corner in semi-darkness, although he was unable to convert. The crowd numbered around 9,000 and the York team was: A. 'Piper' Lee; G. Cowmeadow, Oliver, Lomas, Batten; M. Lavelle, Daniel; Boylen (capt), Frank Lee, G. Lupton, France, Joe Brown, E. Bloomer.

The first home match of the season was two days later but, with a lot of juice having been taken out of the pack's tank at Hull, success against Huddersfield was not expected. In front of a 6,000 crowd, forward Jack Chilcott scored an early try for the visitors, a second almost following immediately from Fred Longstaff, but James and full-back Tot Moore, who was back at York after a year in Australia, combined to stop him just short. York, though, were 24–6 down to the awesome Fartowners at the interval. James had supplied all the home points from penalties. He began the scoring after the resumption with a fourth penalty, but points were hard to come by for York. They did manage two second half tries through France, after James had recovered a loose ball, and forward George Unsworth – the recent recruit had scored against his former club. Both scores were in the corner and James was unable to add the extras. York lost 54–14. Despite the one-sided score, James made a satisfactory home debut, defended well and made several dangerous breaks. The overall view, though, was that York were far slower than Huddersfield, particularly in the forwards. One feasible excuse was the exertions of the Hull game two days earlier.

The York players were probably glad to have a fortnight's break before the next match, on Saturday 20 September against Hull KR at Clarence Street. The Rovers took an early 5–0 lead. James almost levelled immediately when he made a break down the touchline after regaining the ball from his own kick but, with the try-line in sight, he was hauled down from behind. Shortly afterwards, he just missed a penalty from near the touchline, but then landed a brilliant effort from almost halfway after a Rovers player was penalised for interfering with a play-the-ball. The visitors, though, were dominating the forward battle and York were 11–4 behind at half-time. James had added a second penalty from a similar position to his earlier success. After they fell further adrift, 14–4, the home side enjoyed a better second half, with James their inspiration. Following a try by York half-back F. Kershaw near the corner flag, the *Yorkshire Herald* said James's kick "was a beauty and fully deserved the applause which greeted his successful achievement." It encouraged York to play their best rugby of the match; James narrowed the gap further to 14–11 when he kicked his third penalty, following an obstruction. Disaster struck for York, and James in particular, near the end when he was prominent in another attack as they searched for the winning points. Striving to create an opening for Batten, he was heavily tackled 25 yards out and had to leave the field with a leg injury. It was a setback that deflated his colleagues and, with no further scoring, led to a third defeat.

James was selected in his usual centre position for the following week's visit to Wakefield Trinity, but was forced to stand down due to his damaged leg. In fact it caused him to miss the next two York matches and also cost him an appearance for Cumberland on Monday 29 September, when he pulled out of their match against Lancashire at The Cliff, Broughton Rangers' new ground. The announcement of his selection had initially prompted the *Yorkshire Evening Press* to comment: "The fact of Lomas again being chosen to appear for Cumberland is proof, if that were needed, that the York Committee did a good stroke of business in more ways than one." James missed a third consecutive game for his club on Saturday 11 October, when they were at Keighley. In this instance, though, he was not included because he was again scheduled to play for Cumberland, this time against Yorkshire in Workington, although he was thwarted a second time through his injury.

He returned to action for York's home fixture with Runcorn on 18 October, although still not fully fit, and described as one of four players in the team that were "not sound," on top of which Batten was unavailable through injury. It was a situation reflected in the score-line, Runcorn won 16–0, inflicting York's seventh defeat in a row since the season began. Their cause was not helped when Lavelle – operating as James's co-centre – dislocated a collarbone before half-time, which left them with 12 players. Although not 100 per cent, James had worked selflessly to create openings for his colleagues.

The effort James put in did not aid his recovery and he missed the next eight games; his two month absence was his longest since he took up the sport. While he was away, York extended their dismal start to the season to 12 consecutive defeats before winning twice in December; 11–3 at Bramley and 8–5 at home to Bradford Northern. When James returned – against Wakefield Trinity at Clarence Street on Saturday 20 December – the team's league record was: played 14, won two, lost 12. In addition they had gone out of the Yorkshire Cup at the first hurdle, losing 9–4 at home to Bradford Northern.

The *Yorkshire Evening Press* reporter, 'Old Hand', viewed James's reappearance against Wakefield as salvation for the York side: "With Lomas's return – and I am assured that he is as sound as ever he was – York's threequarter line will be considerably strengthened... The personality of Lomas is such an inspiring force that it is bound to tell in a close contest [and] if the two wing men will take the passes which are sure to come their way [then]

Lomas and Batten may be trusted to do the rest." On a gloomy afternoon, York got off to a positive start to lead 5–0 at half-time, forward Herbert Banks finished off a length of field rush from the pack by dribbling over the try-line to score, T. Naylor converted. In what was described as the campaign's best match so far at Clarence Street, Trinity drew level with a converted try and then crept ahead 7–5 through Tommy Newbould's penalty. It was enough to win the match for Wakefield, even though they lost their try-scorer Ernie Bennett who was sent off for kicking a York player. James, meanwhile, had played a steady game on his comeback, made several breaks and fulfilled his usual share of tackling duties.

Christmas Day brought with it another home fixture and James celebrated by winning his first match in York colours following five defeats. Their victims were Barrow who they narrowly defeated 13–10 in poor weather on a windy day. James introduced himself to the Shipbuilders' defence early on. He broke through in grand style to set up a move that had the crowd on its toes, Barrow rescued a dangerous situation by bringing down Boylen after he took a pass from fellow-forward T. Foster. It was the visitors, though, that scored first with a converted try, York came back through four goals from Naylor with three penalties and an awesome drop-goal from near halfway, to lead 8–5 at the turn around. Referee Ernie Tonge restarted the second half without a break because, due to the limitations of Christmas Day transport, Barrow had organised a motor vehicle to take them to Leeds immediately after the match in time to catch a 5 o'clock train home. James helped York stretch their lead when he completed his sudden burst through the Barrow ranks with a try-scoring pass to Foster, who scored near the posts, Naylor missed the easy goal chance due to the strong wind. Barrow came back to within one point with another try and goal, Naylor concluded the scoring with a penalty for offside.

York travelled to Halifax on Boxing Day where they suffered another heavy defeat. They lost 36–10 on an unpleasant day of driving wind and rain. James showed some good touches early on; he caught the eye with a dribbling run and later thwarted a Halifax attack by intercepting a pass. But his efforts – and that of his colleagues – were not enough to stop their hosts taking a 14–0 lead into the half-time break. However, by that stage York were down to 11 men; Brown – with a split head – and Naylor – with concussion – had left the field. Naylor resumed in the second half, but the Halifax scoring machine rolled on and they led 30–0 at one stage. The Minster Men saved face with two consolation tries, Naylor converted one, and James added a penalty. York's display was not up to scratch, but James was exonerated from any blame, his running and tackling left "nothing to be desired".

Another miserable day awaited at Swinton on Saturday 27 December, both in terms of the weather, heavy rain and hailstorms produced muddy conditions, and the score, a 19–0 defeat. York were known as the Wasps due to their amber and blacks hoops, but on this day they wore chocolate coloured jerseys, because their kit had failed to arrive with them. Amid the confusion, the match began 20 minutes late and was subsequently played in two 35 minute halves in an effort to finish in daylight. However, it did not start late enough for two of York's players; C. Burbridge and Daniel required last minute adjustments to their boots while their colleagues commenced the game with 11 men. York were only three points behind at the interval but, despite "Lomas and Batten striving hard to open out the game" for York, they were completely outplayed during the second period.

York's first match of 1914 was a visit from Dewsbury on 3 January. With more wretched weather to contend with, just 2,000 hardy souls turned up to see yet another loss for the Minster team, this time 16–0. Dewsbury adapted better to the conditions and led by six points at the break. James had an unfortunate time, and fumbled the ball during a passing move to allow Dewsbury centre George Sharples to scoop it up for a try under the posts. The subsequent conversion made it 11–0 and virtually sealed victory for their visitors.

Further defeats followed at Huddersfield, 39–9, and Leigh, 8–5. York made a promising start at Fartown and were only 8–7 adrift at half-time. All York's points came from James with a penalty and his self-converted try. The second period was very different, Huddersfield scored almost at will, York's only response was another penalty from James. The 'poor' Fartown attendance of 4,000 was said to have been influenced by Huddersfield Town entertaining London Caledonian in the first round of the FA Cup, a match that drew 6,500 fans. The game at Leigh was described as a "scrambling" and "scrappy" contest. When Brown scored a second half try – converted by Naylor – to reduce the arrears to 6–5, it gave York hope of an upset, but the only other score was a penalty from Leigh half-back Tom O'Neill, who was later dismissed for "roughness".

James's name was back on the score sheet in the following week's welcome 15–2 victory over Keighley at Clarence Street. Level 2–2 at the break, York capitalised on Keighley's loss of half-back Hilton through injury. James converted Batten's try under the posts for a 7–2 lead and was influential in two further touchdowns by wingmen Cowmeadow and F. Bell.

The next Wednesday afternoon, York entertained Leeds in a previously postponed fixture. Although only just beaten, 13–11, the *Yorkshire Post* was pessimistic over York's immediate future: "Clearly on yesterday's display there is not much hope of improvement in York's position and one can understand the disappointment felt locally that Lomas and J. Batten have failed to give the desired effectiveness to the back division. Both are lacking in that dash which they used to exhibit." Certainly it was not the best of starts for James against Leeds, his dropped pass after 15 minutes provided the opportunity for their opening try by winger S. Stacey. Shortly after the interval, and 13–3 down, James responded with a try beneath the posts, although Naylor missed the goal, and almost scored a second but the ball just rolled out of play before he could claim the touchdown. Half-back W. Boggin brought some respectability to York's score with a late consolation try, James converted.

Three more defeats followed for James and company; 3–2 at home to Rochdale Hornets, 52–8 at home to Hunslet, and 22–5 away to Bradford Northern. The loss to Rochdale was particularly frustrating for the home fans with Batten's first half drop-goal the only score until Hornets' powerful forward Walter Roman's late try. York decided to promote the visit of Hunslet, and put an advert in the *Yorkshire Evening Press* saying: "£500 Centre Three-Quarter at Clarence Street", a reference to the Parksiders' recent capture of New Zealander Edgar Wrigley from Huddersfield, and promised "The most exciting game of the season is expected on [the] Clarence Street ground tomorrow." Unfortunately, it was not too exciting for home supporters because there was simply no answer to Hunslet's power and York were beaten by a proverbial 'cricket score'. Down by 23–3 at the interval, it just got worse for the Minster Men whose only response was a try from James – which he also converted – near the end. More depression followed at Birch Lane against Bradford Northern, York's five points accrued after James and wingman Nickson broke away together, the latter was awarded an obstruction-try after being impeded; James added the extras.

However, it was not all doom and gloom at Clarence Street. On the eve of their next match the club held a meeting and, although they had only secured four victories to date, announced the receipts were up by a third on the same time last year, a situation no doubt engineered through the acquisition of star names including James Lomas. The 'feel good' factor continued the next day with an easy 45–0 win over Cumbrian junior club Glasson Rangers in the Challenge Cup first round; James scored his first trio of tries for the club.

York faced up to the long journey to Barrow on Thursday 5 March, catching an 8.25am train from York and reached their destination at 2.30pm. They were greeted at Cavendish Park by wet weather that turned the pitch into a quagmire and made the ball difficult to control. Worse still was the result, 17–0 down at half-time, the Wasps eventually lost 20–5; their points came at the end with a penalty by Naylor and try from Bell, following a sterling effort from his centre-partner James.

Two days later, York hosted Halifax and were behind 3–0 at the interval, the local paper suggested their tiring day out at Barrow as the likely reason. James did endeavour to find a way through, both for himself and wingman Bell, but to no avail, and he was also off target with a drop-goal attempt. At the start of the second half, several on-field incidents caused some spectators to get overexcited and the referee went over to warn them about their behaviour. In the meantime, James almost dribbled the ball over the Halifax try-line, but their veteran centre Joe Riley took evasive action by lying on the ball. Eventually, Naylor got through for a try near the posts, and added the goal himself to deafening cheers. York held on to win 5–3. Including the Challenge Cup tie against Glasson, it was their sixth win of the season and the *Yorkshire Herald* said that "thrills were plentiful and the spectators were kept at the utmost pitch of excitement." Despite their joy, York remained bottom of the league table with just five league wins to counter their 23 defeats.

It was back to the rigours of the Challenge Cup the following weekend with a trip to The Cliff to take on Broughton Rangers. Before the match the heavens opened, and offered the waiting spectators a cocktail of heavy rain, thunder and lightning. The *Salford Reporter* said the reappearance of James in the area had created "a lot of interest [and he was] accorded a hearty welcome on entering the field." York scored first through a drop-goal from full-back Piper Lee, but three tries from Broughton put them in control and the Wasps started the second half 13–2 down. James doubled York's score with a goal from in front of the posts from a mark made by Naylor, but the final outcome was a 24–4 reverse and they were out of the competition. Presumably James did not receive such a "hearty" accord on leaving the field because towards the end it was reported "Lomas and [Broughton Rangers centre Harry] Slater got at loggerheads and the former was cautioned by the referee."

York had just six league fixtures left in the campaign, and won just one; 17–0 on Good Friday against Batley at Clarence Street. James was not involved in any of them although no reason for his absence is given in the York papers and, unless something untoward happened at Broughton during his clash with Slater, there is no mention of his being injured during that match. The adverse results left York as the competition's basement team for the first time, a disappointing conclusion to a season that had been so eagerly awaited by the club's supporters, particularly after the news of James's capture. Ironically his former club, Salford – who had coveted him before the start of the season – finished as champions. The Wasps had suffered from injuries which made it difficult to field a settled side, particularly among the backs. James himself missed 17 of the 37 games played, his worst ever absentee count.

From the drawing board

James Lomas was often depicted in drawings or caricatures in the sports pages.

This caricature appeared in the *Daily Dispatch* in the 1930s. Drawn by 'Gannon' it is taken from a strip that claimed the Salford team had played like "thirteen Jimmy Lomases" in beating Wigan.

This image of James (right) talking to former Warrington wingman Jack Fish depicts them as spectators at a dreary Lancashire Cup Final.
It was part of a *Daily Dispatch* caricature that reflected on Salford's 5-2 victory over Wigan at Wilderspool on 17 October 1936.

20. 1914–15: A captain's tale

James Lomas reappeared in York's side for Huddersfield's visit to Clarence Street on Saturday 26 September 1914 after an absence of over six months. It was the Wasps third match of the season. James had missed two defeats, 13–5 at home to Hull and 8–3 at Bramley. He was certainly made welcome and appointed as captain of the team. But why he had not played for York since the Challenge Cup exit at Broughton Rangers the previous March is not clear. Had he missed the last six matches of 1913–14 because he was disillusioned with the team's poor performances? That appears to have been the case with the previous season's skipper Frank Boylen. He did not play for York again after the cup defeat and was transferred to Hull KR shortly afterwards. It was also possible that the long train journey from James's Salford home became wearying without the adrenalin of success.

There may well have been a perfectly innocent explanation, possibly an injury or something of a personal nature, but, whatever the answer, it seems certain York had not expected him back for the 1914–15 campaign. He was not mentioned in any of the press previews for the new term and had played no part in the pre-season practice games. In fact, his name was not mentioned anywhere in the York newspapers at this time. York had already announced that half-back George Daniel would be the new captain for the season, a decision that was evidently revoked after James materialised. James kept the captaincy throughout 1914–15 and club officials would, surely, not have bestowed that honour on a different player if they had known he was returning.

One possible reason for his delayed appearance could have been the uncertain situation that had arisen in Europe during the close season. On 14 June 1914 the Archduke Franz Ferdinand, the heir to the Austro-Hungarian Empire, and his wife were shot dead in Sarajevo by a Serbian assassin. It began a chain of events that led to the First World War. Great Britain and Belgium subsequently declared war on Germany on 4 August, and the British Expeditionary Force landed in France 13 days later.

The Northern Union Committee met in Manchester on Tuesday 8 September, and elected to go ahead with a competitive fixture list, a similar decision was made by the Football League. So as not to be perceived as blocking the war effort in any way, the NU emphasised that its clubs should encourage players to join the forces unless their occupation was of equal importance to their country. They also recommended the use of local players rather than using others who travelled from further afield. Although James was registered with York, the distance he had to cover from his Salford home for matches may have, initially, raised uncertainty as to his best course of action, and caused him to miss the opening two fixtures.

Along with other clubs, York's numbers were depleted due to players joining the armed forces. The biggest pre-season shock for supporters, though, was the tragic loss of Jim Batten who died suddenly from heart disease at the end of August. It was an infliction he was probably unaware of because he was certainly a vigorous player and regarded as a "fine specimen of manhood".

Although Huddersfield were still missing several players due to the 1914 Lions tour of Australia and New Zealand, York's feat in holding them to a 7–7 draw was considered an outstanding one. The Fartowners were the undoubted power in the land and would end the season with all four trophies available to them; Northern League Championship, Challenge Cup, Yorkshire League and Yorkshire Cup. Perhaps the Wasps were lifted by the return of James as their new captain because he certainly had an excellent game. After opening the score with a penalty he twice brought down centre Tommy Gleeson when he looked threatening. He also intercepted a pass that nearly led to a York try but his pass to J. France was not taken. Leading 2–0 at the interval, the *Yorkshire Herald* said that "every credit is due to [York] for the fine manner in which they had stood up to their powerful opponents and had Lomas, who played a sterling game, been blessed with his old-time speed, York would have had a greater lead [at half-time]."

Ben Gronow tied the scores with a goal he kicked from a mark, but the Minster Men regained their lead through a try from F. Bell that was converted by James. The new skipper continued to excel in attack and defence, but could not prevent Huddersfield squaring the match. The *Yorkshire Evening Press* commented that "it is to be hoped that Lomas will keep up this form, and in that case one of the knotty problems (the centre positions) which the committee have had to consider will have been solved."

He was again on top form for the trip to Hunslet on 3 October, although he caused the match to be delayed by 15 minutes due to his late arrival. York actually started the match without him but, having entered the field, he almost got Bell in for the first score. It was Hunslet, though, that went ahead 8–0 before James put his side on the board. He touched down near the posts after taking a pass from fellow centre F. Hughes, and added the extra points. York trailed 18–5 at the interval, after which James almost scored again before his breakaway was eventually checked. Having kicked a wonder goal against the wind off a mark made by winger Herbert Raper, he then scored his second touchdown. The *Yorkshire Evening Press* described his effort vividly: "We saw Lomas at his best; securing the ball near Hunslet's quarter line, he burst through half the home team, shook off [full-back Herbert] Place almost like a terrier would shake a rat and scored at the foot of the posts." James added the goal to claim a clean-sweep of York's points in their 20–12 defeat.

The *Yorkshire Evening Press* writer said that "since Lomas became associated with the York club I have not seen him play so well; he even surpassed his form against Huddersfield the previous week. Perhaps the greatest compliment I can pay him is to repeat the remark of a gentleman connected with ...Hunslet ... [who said] 'I wish we had a couple like him in our threequarter line, and we should have had him had [the Hunslet committee] taken my advice. He stands out by himself as the best threequarter on the field'."

James was again among the points in the following week's home game against

Wakefield Trinity with two goals. York won 7–2 to claim their first success of the campaign. Watched by their usual hardcore of 3,000 spectators, James converted Daniel's 10th minute try and added a penalty after Trinity full-back Leonard Land tripped Bell during a dribbling move; all the points were scored in the opening half. Although James stood out with his defending, it was claimed "Lomas and Raper were not so much in evidence as at Hunslet [because] they had not so many opportunities."

After the match the York players were treated to high tea by the club's committee at the Davy Hall Restaurant. During the course of events, James spoke a few words and "in a most businesslike manner gave the players some excellent advice." He concluded his short speech by saying to his team "now chaps, don't forget Huddersfield are here next week. Slip a little extra training into you." The *Yorkshire Evening Press* said "Everyone knew what Lomas meant, and by the time these notes are in print I hope the newsboys are shouting for the first time this season, 'Another victory for York!'"

As it happened, the Yorkshire Cup first round meeting with Huddersfield did not produce another victory. It was probably too much to expect anyway, the Fartowners, with their returned tourists available again, left Clarence Street after posting a 24–13 win. Huddersfield gave an excellent exhibition of rugby skills in scoring their six tries, although the York team – for whom James landed a first half conversion – was by no means disgraced. Meanwhile it was reported that York centre Harry Wright had joined "Lord Kitchener's army, making it over a dozen York players away in the forces."

James again bagged all of his side's points in a 10–10 draw at Runcorn in the next match on 24 October. The Linnets had led 10–0 at the break, the lengthy journey and "hurried dinner" were blamed for a lethargic first half effort by the Wasps. James put matters right when he touched down after a passing move and added a second following "one of his dashes" when, although tackled by "three or four" opponents, he still forced his way over the try-line. He added both goals to produce what was considered a "fair result". One of the interesting, but hardly unexpected, comments was James's "lack of dash" although at 35 years old this was entirely predictable. In all other respects; his powerful bursts and ability to hand-off opponents with his strength, his deadly tackling and kicking – both in general play and for goal – appeared to be as keen as ever.

York had a weekend off due to Batley's involvement in the Yorkshire Cup, their league meeting was rearranged for the next Wednesday, 4 November. Despite home advantage, the Wasps were no match for their visitors and the Gallant Youths scored six tries to overwhelm their hosts 24–5. York had suffered a pre-match setback through half-back W. Boggin's late withdrawal after a cut knee at Runcorn had resulted in blood poisoning. Daniel and Savage formed a hastily constructed half-back pairing, but were not successful and both took turns to work the scrum in an effort to find the right formula. The latter player was, however, responsible for providing James with the ball for his try in the second half, which he also converted to again be his team's only scorer. James did his utmost by sending Batley backwards with his long clearance kicks, but it was noted that, overall, the winners showed they knew something about "the modern game".

Three more defeats followed, all by uncomfortable margins; 30–8 at Widnes, 18–7 at home to Halifax and 40–0 away to Hull KR. After the half-back problems against Batley, James was moved to stand-off as partner to Daniel against Widnes. Although their combination worked better, the team's fortunes did not improve. On a nice afternoon James did his stint in defence and saved York from conceding an early try, but they were 16–2 down by the interval; his penalty was the last score of the half. Two of the second half tries came from A. Dennis (York) and Jack Brassington (Widnes), described as "a unique performance in class football for the full-back on either side to cross his opponents' line."

James was again the provider of all York's points in the loss to Halifax at Clarence Street. Playing at centre again – Boggin resumed his half-back position – he notched two first half penalties, both for offside, and closed the afternoon's scoring with a spectacular try described as "the finest individual performance of the afternoon". He collected a loose ball outside the Halifax 25-yard area, raced down the left flank and "handing off man after man, he at last raced over near the flag amid tumultuous applause which only died away when he failed with the goal-kick." James gave a good performance all round; typical comments were "Lomas showed himself to be in fine form by putting in a couple of great sprints which gained considerable territory," "Lomas especially distinguished himself with some lusty tackling" and "Lomas in particular was a thorn in the side of the opposition." Although their side was well beaten, it was applauded as an entertaining game for the York spectators. They would have been less enamoured with the visit to Hull KR the next week when on a misty, miserable afternoon they conceded 40 points without reply. The Wasps' forwards were too lightweight to contain a robust Rovers pack.

November closed with a refreshing win, York's biggest of the season, 21–3 against visitors Bradford Northern, having led 13–0 at the break. James scored the second of his team's five tries. Having failed to take a pass cleanly from Daniel midway between the York 25-yard line and halfway, he dribbled the ball along the ground and retained "perfect control as he bypassed one opponent after another to reach the Bradford posts, the ball bouncing up perfectly for him to collect a touchdown." It was a score that was greeted by huge cheers from an appreciative crowd. He also added the conversion, one of three he kicked in the match, and hit the crossbar with a penalty attempt in the early stages. The match was watched by a large number of soldiers from the Bradford Battalion who were stationed in York and added to the occasion by twirling their rattles. There was also a number of wounded from the Military Hospital in Fulford who were accommodated in the committee room. One was York's former full-back 'Piper' Lee who – recovering from a thigh wound – received "a sympathetic and hearty reception" as he walked to the grandstand.

York lost all four December matches; 25–11 at Dewsbury, 36–0 at Leeds, 11–2 at home to Widnes and 13–12 at home against Leigh. Crown Flatt was visited on 5 December, but the day began badly for York because centre Hughes missed the train. In heavy rain and strong winds, they played the first five minutes a man short until their trainer, A. Neale, made up the numbers and joined the pack. The Wasps scored first through a Daniels try, James – who had already come close several times – added a second just before the interval after sending out a dummy pass before touching down in the corner. Three tries from Dewsbury, however, meant that York trailed 9–6 when the half-time whistle sounded. York played uphill against the wind in the second half. James converted a try by forward G. Unsworth. However, it was only a token score; Dewsbury's forwards were well on top of York's weakened sextet.

A heavy pitch and persistent rain lay in wait at Headingley where "Lomas received a cordial reception on leading in his side." Despite the difficult underfoot conditions Leeds showed too much speed for York although James and Boggin were credited in defeat with "a really heroic game". More heavy rain and mud was on offer when Widnes travelled to Clarence Street. The groundsman had done his best by distributing bucket loads of sand over the playing area, but large pools of rainwater remained. There was also a threat of the match being stopped when a heavy mist descended. Maybe York wished it had been; their only points came from James who, having marked from long distance, scored an excellent goal to give the Minster Men a 2–0 interval advantage. The Wasps' captain made an impact in the first period with a fierce run while "bumping his way through his opponents" but, despite tackling heroically in the second half, he was powerless to stop Widnes scoring three tries.

Leigh's visit on Boxing Day produced a more competitive match than of late. Again the pitch was very wet; James kicked an early penalty and converted a try as York built a 7–2 lead only to slip 10–7 behind by half-time. Despite the muddy surface, the match kept the holiday crowd entertained, James brought respectability to the final score when, having fallen further behind at 13–7, he emerged as a try-scorer among a ruck of "half a score of players" and added the goal. Although the match was in the balance until the final whistle, York had gone down to defeat yet again, albeit by just one point. With just two wins and two draws from 15 league fixtures, they ended 1914 with only Runcorn beneath them in the 25-team league table.

There was an early opportunity for revenge when York travelled to Mather Lane on New Year's Day when another closely fought encounter ensued. Unfortunately for them, the only score came from Leigh centre George Higham, whose second half try gave the hosts a 3–0 win. On a quagmire of a pitch, James made an impression with "by far the finest piece of play in the game [when he] spread-eagled the field with a magnificent run to within ten yards of the line." Another who caught the eye was James Brown, a trialist full-back previously with Warrington. He became a regular choice for York for the rest of the season.

The *Yorkshire Herald* said he was recommended to the club by James "whose great experience… enables him to judge a good player when he sees one." His introduction was well timed because York's officials were trying to strengthen the team for the Challenge Cup competition which started in February. Forward Tom Harkness was signed from Leeds, and Welsh winger D.W. Bevan joined from Salford. The latter had made his Reds debut in 1911 in the same fixture that James had made his with Oldham.

The following day, Saturday 2 January, York travelled a few miles down the road from Leigh to take on Swinton. It was another close contest and James's penalty kept York in touch at 4–2 down when the interval was reached. He almost brought his team level after the break when he shaved the outside of the post in attempting a goal from a mark before York went further behind at 9–2. One reporter suggested that the Wasps' display was their "finest of the season" but it was not enough to bring victory, although Harkness – later sent off on his debut after kicking an opponent – claimed a try that James goaled, which left the final score a more respectable 9–7.

Having conceded over 50 points in both meetings with Hunslet the previous term, it made a nice change for the York supporters to see their favourites overcome the Parksiders 7–3 at Clarence Street on 9 January. On a soft, muddy surface, the game was played out as a power struggle between the two packs and the referee had to interrupt play several times during a stop-start confrontation. York came back from 3–0 down to lead 5–3 at the interval; James's penalty was followed by a try from Daniel. Having failed to convert the latter James claimed a second penalty after the break.

York soon returned to the losing habit and four more losses followed; 6–2 at Keighley, 11–2 at Wakefield, 23–6 at home to Leeds and 11–7 at Halifax. Keighley led 3–0 at the halfway stage, James just missed out with a first half penalty. But, when his co-centre T.J. Jones failed to take his pass after the interval, Keighley winger Wilson nipped in for their second touchdown, Daniel scored a consolation drop-goal for the Wasps. James did his best to turn things round in the second half, and made "one of his desperate dashes" that took him "clean through" the opposition before he was eventually overhauled. He was later denied when the ball was kicked from beneath him as he was about to pounce for a try.

At Wakefield, James was the lone York scorer with a penalty from near the halfway line which made it 3–2 at the break. Again, the York skipper worked hard in a game that was played at a fast pace and, reportedly "his strong rushes took a great deal of stopping as [Wakefield centre J. W.] Todd found out." An above average crowd of 5,000 was at Clarence Street to welcome Leeds for a match that began earlier than scheduled due to a threatening mist. The visitors proved too quick for York, although James, on at least three occasions, threatened their try-line. He did, however, register all his side's points with three penalties. At Thrum Hall, York got off to a fine start and led Halifax 7–0 at one point; James succeeded with a 2nd minute goal following a mark by Dennis and then threaded through a difficult conversion after a try by W. Lynch. Halifax, though, chipped away at the Wasps' lead, three tries plus a drop-goal by winger Clem Garforth saw them safely home.

With the Challenge Cup rounds looming, York's officials must have been relieved to see their charges claim a 10–4 victory when Dewsbury visited on 13 February. Rain fell heavily, and the playing surface was muddy. Joe Brown scored the opening try after just 10 minutes, James just missed the goal. By half-time though, the lead was reduced to 3–2. James had prevented their guests from going in front by bringing off a magnificent tackle on Farrar as the winger defied the sticky conditions in racing towards the York line. In the second half the soaked, unrecognisable players looked a pitiful sight as they attempted to manoeuvre around the swamp-like pitch as forward barges and hopeful kicks became the main means of offence. With less than 20 minutes to go, James increased the lead with a penalty. The *Yorkshire Herald* said "Under ordinary circumstances the place kick would have been an easy one for Lomas, and great credit is due to the home captain for successfully piloting the ball over the bar." Dewsbury claimed a second penalty before James responded in kind for a 7–4 lead, Daniel then dribbled the ball into the visitor's in-goal for a try. It concluded the scoring; referee Frank Renton ended the game eight minutes short due to the adverse state of the ground.

The following match at The Boulevard saw York come up with a tremendously gritty performance against Hull, who were one of the season's leading sides. York suffered a setback before the game started because Boggin did not travel after being taken ill, which necessitated James switching to stand-off. Despite that they began well and James gave them a 2–0 lead with a great touchline penalty, given for offside. From then on York fully contributed to a fast-paced opening 40 minutes and were only 6–4 down at the break; centre A. Wild had added a drop-goal to the Wasps tally. James made a major contribution to York's only try after Wild reached Hull's 25-yard line. With his progress stopped, Wild got the ball out to James, who evaded former Oldham colleague Sid Deane and drew Jimmy Devereux before he sent Lynch over in the corner. Unfortunately, James just missed with the goal that would, at that stage, have tied the scores. Hull edged further ahead 11–7 before Bell broke away for York but, with only former York wingman Jack Harrison barring his path, he ignored the supporting James and, caught in two minds, was tackled. Instead of the Wasps producing a possible match-winner, it was Harrison who later intercepted James's wide pass to Bevan for an unconverted touchdown just before the finish. York lost 16–7. Harrison is remembered today through the awarding of his posthumous Victoria Cross, after making the supreme sacrifice in May 1917 in the First World War.

Next up was the Challenge Cup. York had drawn Rochdale Hornets at home. It was a tough looking tie against a team who were second in the league table at the time, and a crowd of 5,700 turned up at Clarence Street to witness the outcome. The *Yorkshire Post* said it was "a long time since such a strenuous contest took place at York," a fair assessment of a war of attrition fought out on a heavy pitch, which produced no points despite an extra 30 minutes being played. Except for one change in the York pack, the same players lined up for the replay at the Athletic Grounds the following Tuesday, 2 March, the traditional half day weekly holiday in Rochdale. Whether the players were suffering the effects of their earlier confrontation is hard to judge, but thoughts of another scoreless afternoon must have been looming until Rochdale opened the score after 25 minutes play. James's penalty midway through the second half were his side's only points in a 19–2 loss.

Incredibly, York, who had won only four matches since the season began, claimed five victories from their eight concluding fixtures. They started with two home wins against Runcorn, 31–3, and Hull KR, 9–0. Bottom of the league Runcorn were hopelessly outclassed as James played a real captain's part with a hat-trick of tries. His first opened the scoring; he touched down near the corner flag after he accepted a pass from Bevan, the ball passed from one side of the field to the other following a scrum. He then scored his side's third touchdown with a neat run in near the posts after Daniel had despatched him. The Wasps reached half-time 15–3 ahead with all the points from tries; the nearest to a goal was when James shaved the outside of the post after his second try. Lynch began the second half scoring and James landed his only goal of the game – it bounced in off the crossbar – in converting the winger's try. James's third try – and his team's ninth of the afternoon – was scored close to the corner flag, the York skipper narrowly missed with the goal attempt.

James was also prominent in the success against Hull KR, firing over an early penalty from a difficult angle. It clearly lifted his team, the *Yorkshire Post* said "from this point onwards York never looked back". A try followed from Unsworth, the forward forced his way through from a scrum, James's resultant goal brought up a 7–0 half-time score. He added a further penalty during the second half, which concluded a match where "excellent work was done by the York captain."

The March fixture list ended with a trip to Mount Pleasant where York were beaten on a fine, but bitterly cold, afternoon by Batley, 10–3. James almost scored with an ambitious penalty from halfway and then came close to a touchdown. He eventually opened the scoring after a bout of passing involving Daniel and Wild; the latter gave out a dummy before he sent his skipper in at the corner. James almost got a second touchdown when, following a tremendous run in which he handed-off full-back Jimmy Lyons, he was just pushed into touch by centre Benny Laughlin. The Gallant Youths eventually clinched an entertaining contest with a converted try in each half. In the second half, James injured his knee but was able to resume and, subsequently, came close to another try when the ball was kicked out of his reach in the corner.

The Good Friday match followed on 2 April, visitors Bramley were beaten 10–5. James did not make it to the match, having, reportedly, missed his train. It was news that encouraged the Villagers, who had won 12–4 at Clarence Street the previous season. The *Yorkshire Herald* said "The opposition came with a strong side and in the absence of the York captain they fully anticipated repeating last season's victory." It was not the first time that James encountered problems with the trains, nor was he the only player to suffer through misadventure with the timetables, particularly during holiday periods. On Christmas Day 1913, team-mate Joe Brown was unable to get to York for the match with Barrow, he

230

had had to work on the previous night and he then discovered the train times were "not suitable" for him to travel to the Minster City.

When James had signed for York back in August 1913 the *Yorkshire Evening Press* had suggested "There is every reason to hope Lomas will settle in York for the remainder of his days – football and otherwise." While relocation would certainly have helped him reach Clarence Street quicker and with less hassle, it is doubtful that the thought of moving seriously entered his head. While York is, without doubt, a beautiful location to live in, with its historic buildings and the picturesque River Ouse running through its heart, he had a wife and four young daughters to consider and, like during his time with Oldham, he remained rooted in Salford, and preferred to commute to home matches. Coming from Maryport, he was not a stranger to the railway network which had enabled him to live in his birthplace for a short period while playing for Salford and had often provided the means for him to return to his home town for weekend and close season visits. In fact James was one of several York recruits who lived in other areas such as Hull or Leeds. At the time that James joined York, the *Yorkshire Evening Press* commented that such players "of course, do their training at the nearest football grounds – the general practice in Northern Union football – but in the (pre-season) practice games each man is expected to turn up at headquarters unless something untoward arises."

Thankfully, James did make it to Clarence Street for the Easter Monday clash with Swinton where 3,000 spectators witnessed another Wasps victory, 12–4. James chipped in with two early goals; his penalty from the near the centre of the field and his conversion of Daniel's try helped his team to a 7–0 lead in the first 11 minutes. A measure of how high their veteran skipper was still rated was implied by a comment in the local paper that York "still held the upper hand" despite his temporary absence on the touchline, although he was not injured on this occasion, merely changing his boots. York scored all their points before the break, James converted a further try, scored by C. Burbidge, to lead 12–0 when the half-time whistle blew.

Easter Tuesday is also considered as a holiday in many Yorkshire towns and, consequently, York made their way to Fartown the following day to take on runaway league leaders Huddersfield. James was "all present and correct" at the time of the kick-off having presumably stayed overnight in Yorkshire. York did very well in the first half and were still in touch, although 13–9 down at the interval. The Wasps had taken an unexpected 5–0 lead after only three minutes; James added the goal to W. Webster's try, the latter having intercepted Tommy Gleeson's pass. James subsequently kicked two penalties, but it was not enough to stop a razor-sharp Huddersfield side from winning, 30–11.

York's last home game – on Saturday 17 April – was against Keighley, and produced yet another success with an 18–3 win. Played on a hard pitch, it created a "lively" ball. James made the most of it with three goals as he converted three of his team's four tries. It could have been four goals because, having made a mark in front of Keighley's posts at the start of the second half, the touch judge awarded the score, but was then overruled by referee Renton. He also threatened to register a touchdown and, on at least three occasions after he had made a charge, was "quelled by force of numbers".

The season closed for James and his York colleagues in front of an estimated 3,000 spectators at Bradford Northern's Birch Lane enclosure one week later. In a splendid start for the Wasps, James scored a try which he converted, and kicked a penalty a few minutes later. When Bevan contributed a drop-goal to put York 9–0 up it looked like it was going to be a happy conclusion to the season. Bradford, though, hit back with a converted try just before half-time to set themselves up for a more comfortable ride after the break when four more tries saw York upstaged 21–9.

James ended the season as York's leading try scorer with 14 and goalkicker with 51. His time at Clarence Street had come to an abrupt halt in a rapidly changing world. The war in Europe was escalating and many men – including Northern Union players – were giving their lives in the bloody conflicts taking place. Towards the end of 1914, trench warfare had begun to dominate affairs on the Western Front. With thousands of troops being lost in infamous places like Ypres and the Somme, conscription was consequently introduced in January 1916. Two weeks after York's last match of the season, on 7 May 1915, the R.M.S. Lusitania was sunk in the Atlantic by a German submarine, drowning 1,400 passengers including 128 from the United States, ensuring the latter's entry into the war. It was inevitable that competitive rugby would cease and, from 1915–16 clubs, including York, arranged friendly matches. Any thought of James travelling across the Pennines was out of the question.

In some respects his appearance at Birch Lane could be considered to have been the final match of his professional rugby playing career. It is not strictly true because, as will be seen in the pages that follow, he had not completely finished with the game he so dearly loved. There were to be several 'comeback' appearances; a war-time stint with Salford, a brief post-war return for York and a sprinkling of outings for Salford – where he was also coaching – during the 1920s. But by that time he was every bit the veteran player and, although still more than useful, unlikely to create a queue for his signature as in those sparking earlier years of his career. The 1914–15 season was, therefore, his last full term of Northern Union rugby. He bade it farewell with his head held high; York's top point scorer for the season with 144 and joint-seventh in the Northern Union points chart – not bad for a player in his mid–30s.

21. Lacing up the boots once more

The turmoil surrounding the Great War – First World War as it is known today – meant that the composition of teams for the wartime friendly games of 1915 to 1918 was difficult to predict. Some players were able to turn out frequently through having occupations vital to the war effort that kept them at home, such as coal miners and shipbuilders. Others declared their availability during periods of leave from the armed forces. Then there were veterans who made short comebacks to help out, such as Salford forward Billy Brown, who returned after 10 years in retirement for one game in 1918, aged 41. Some appeared for their local team because regular travel to the club they were registered with was not feasible, such as Jimmy Burgess, a young forward on Runcorn's books who played for Salford throughout the war.

James Lomas laced up his rugby boots once more on 6 April 1917, the first time he had done so since appearing two years previously for York. This time, though, it was in the red jersey of Salford, he lined up at centre for the Good Friday game at Warrington. He was still registered with York but, living in Salford, he volunteered to help out the club he had last played for over six years earlier. Typical of the liquid nature of team selection were the circumstances surrounding the appearance of two Salford forwards in the same match. New Zealander Harry Goldsmith – on leave from the Royal Flying Corps – was turning out for the first time in almost a year, while George Currie – who had played for most of that season – was leaving for active service after the Easter programme; he had been called up.

James's appearance was a minor surprise for supporters because he had not been named in the selected team, although – as already outlined – that was not unusual, given the last-minute nature of the line-ups. Salford lost 17–5, the *Salford Reporter* said: "The inclusion of Lomas and Goldsmith would have produced excellent results had these players, and especially the old Salford captain, received better support." James did not get his name on the score sheet and had the same experience the following day at The Willows when he again played for Salford, against St Helens Recreation. The Reds lost 14–0 to the side that was normally referred to as the 'Recs', and "only Lomas and [his wingman R.] Burrows seemed to have any great ideas of the way to the line."

It said a lot for James's experience and know-how that he could return to the rugby field, aged 37 and after a lengthy absence, and still create a favourable impression. He played in just one more match in this period, at home to Broughton Rangers on Saturday 28 April. He helped Salford achieve their first win since Boxing Day 1916. It was almost like old times for James, he shared the centre berths with Willie Thomas, just as they had for his last match with Salford, prior to joining Oldham, in December 1910.

Burgess claimed the opening two tries for Salford, James converted the first with a difficult angled kick, but missed with his second effort. At 8-0, the Rangers were unlucky to lose skipper Jimmy Barnes through a broken collar bone after 30 minutes play and, over the next seven minutes, Salford took advantage to claim three more tries. The scorers were winger Sammy Wood, from a pass by James, Willie Thomas and James who, rolling back the years and to great acclaim, broke clear of the opposition. Almost on half time, the Rangers responded with a converted try, and Salford led 17-5. James grabbed his second touchdown in the final minutes, intercepting a pass to score beneath the posts. The result was 20-5 and James could take pride in a performance in which "Salford were all round the better side, and (full-back Harry) Launce, Thomas and Lomas the leaders."

There is evidence to suggest James served in a non-combative role during the war with the Royal Army Service Corps, who were responsible for transport and supplies. Also, Jimmy Rushby, whose grandfather knew James well, believes James had been a batman, effectively an officer's servant, to Captain Victor McLaglen, who later became a well known film actor.

Competitive rugby resumed in 1919 and James returned to Clarence Street on Saturday 26 April for York's second round Yorkshire Cup match against Bramley. Amazingly, it was the only time he ever played against the Villagers after leaving them in 1901. In a tight contest, he again captained York and was unlucky to miss with all three of his penalty attempts in a scoreless first half, including one from halfway that was diverted wide by a strong breeze. All-in-all, he gave a good account of himself and defended well, although he was unlucky when his second half clearance kick led to the winning score for Bramley. It was caught by Bramley's winger Hughes who made a mark, full-back Grayson's subsequent goal then produced the only points of the afternoon. Watched by 4,000, it was the last of a handful of games played by York that season and James's final appearance for the club.

It was around this time that James and his wife Annie made the bold decision to move to Ireland, taking their four young daughters with them. Their destination was Belfast and it is likely that James was seeking work, quite possibly in the shipyards. The famous Harland & Wolff was just one of several major shipbuilding companies based there. One of James's descendants told the author that Annie may have had two brothers already living in Belfast which would have been another reason to relocate. According to records at Belfast Central Library, James's name does not appear on the housing lists of that period. As the practice at that time was to only list the head of the house, this supports the theory that they were living with someone else.

James also took the opportunity to play rugby while he was in Ireland and turned out for one of the local rugby union clubs. It was a relationship that was curtailed when it was discovered he was a former Northern Union player. James recalled the experience in his memoirs: "I played a few rugby union matches in Belfast before they discovered me. I explained the situation to the club but [said] I would take the risk. The authorities told them what they would do [to the club] if they played me anymore and told them they would let the matter drift if they didn't play me again." Exactly what risk James felt he was taking is not explained in his notes. As a former Northern Union professional they could do no more than reinforce his lifetime ban from rugby union, the mandatory 'punishment' for any player who had played Northern Union rugby. The gamble lay with the Belfast club who possibly knew of James's credentials and had tried, but failed, to play him surreptitiously.

It seems that any aspirations James held for employment in Belfast did not materialise in a satisfactory way because, by 1922, he had returned to England and, as expanded on in the following chapter, he left his family behind in Belfast. On 19 August that year, a *Salford Reporter* headline proclaimed "Jimmy Lomas returns – to coach the 'A' team." It was an appointment ahead of its time as the majority of clubs did not employ coaches until the late 1940s, following the Second World War. Hitherto, the only individual with any direct responsibility was a trainer who took care of the players' fitness, through sprint training, etc. and, on match days came on to the field with the famed 'magic sponge' to sooth injured players or wipe a spot of mud from their eyes. Any form of coaching or tactics usually rested with the captain and other senior players while the team was usually selected by the club's committee. James's remit was to help lift the fortunes of a club that had slipped badly since the war had ended. Indeed, for Salford – who finished fourth bottom of the 26-team league in 1921–22 – the 1920s was to be the worst decade in their history as far as on-field results went.

The *Salford Reporter* went on to say: "Realising the importance of good reserves and of the value of the 'A' team as a supply for the premier thirteen, the directors are leaving no stone unturned to secure a strong reserve team. Here the value of good coaching is beyond expression and the Reds supporters will hail with delight the news that the directors have engaged 'Jimmy' Lomas to act in that capacity. To write for Salford people of the brilliance of Lomas would be equal to taking coals to Newcastle. It is sufficient to say that the engagement is a step that may have far reaching results and one on which the directors are to be congratulated."

James's thoughts on coaching received an airing in August 1924 when the New Zealand newspaper, *The* (Wellington) *Evening Post*, included a feature by 'Half-back' on the 'Essentials of Fitness' for rugby players. With James having made such an impact in that country in 1910, it pointed out that he was now coach to the Salford reserve team and was "still accomplishing good work." Asked about his approach to the job and the methods he employed, James replied: "As a result of the strenuous football played today [in 1924], if a player kept free from injuries and was out [playing] each Saturday he did not require much more training. A sprint once or twice – not more – in a week was all that was absolutely necessary for the fully developed player." James's philosophy was certainly very different to that of today's coaches, and he emphasised that a player who "over-trained" was worse off than one who "under-trained". He also said that, in his peak years as a player, he was usually at his best when, in the week, he had followed his occupation as a boilermaker.

The feature went on to quote James as follows: "In Rugby football one wants a strong body and muscular arms, in addition to speedy legs. There is nothing, in my opinion, to beat honest work for developing brain, body, and arms. This cannot, perhaps, all be achieved at once, but get the body right and then take measures to improve the pace. Perfect development cannot be accomplished in a year. It may take seasons before the perfect condition stage arrives, but I advise persistence with what I might call manual exercise to co-operate with the actual training. Pace, of course, is necessary, and my method was to take a 50 to 60 yards sprint, interspersed with a run 130 to 150 yards at half-speed, and if one's bodily health is all right pace must improve. Ball practice, with kicking and passing exchanges once a week, are all that is required."

He continued: "Today the football appears to be a bit faster than during my active connection with the game, and no doubt hard and fast methods of training would be unwise. Players are apparently trained more for pace and short dashes. In the old days they were trained for stamina. Today the forwards must, to be a success, possess pace and be able to sprint when called upon. He must not be content merely to stay the game, but should be trained sufficiently to do what the backs can do.

Dribbling and wheeling have gone in favour of quick breaking-up and handling the ball with the backs, and there can be no doubt that this style of football is far more attractive and appreciated more by the spectators than was the old tight game. Players must concentrate on their own and the brain must work with the body. They must be alert, for the modern game does not allow for recovery, and the first mistake is generally fatal. All the talking and preparation should be done on training nights. Methods of attack and how to improve the defence should all be cut and dried before the players enter the field, for the play today will not permit of talking."

James also gave his insight into tackling and kicking, skills he was renowned for as a player: "To tackle a man successfully, you must grasp him by his thighs. Body gripping is not effective enough, but only get round one thigh, and your opponent is helpless. Also get the man with the ball, and don't wait for his transfer. Put him out of the attack and a great deal has been accomplished. Another point which the student should master is the ability to kick with both feet. This is one of the first lessons a rugby pupil should learn. My kicking only came after hard persistent practice, for when I commenced my career I could only kick with my right foot." This is quite a revelation because he was known to kick goals with his left foot.

His final piece of advice concerned weighing up the opposition and keeping in good condition: "Never be too orthodox, develop a style. Watch opponents for any sign of weakness, and then play on that weak spot. Realise that what is required is to get over the line, or to make it easy for someone else to get there. Training and coaching are only secondary essentials to the youth who has natural ability for the game, but football today can only be played successfully by the careful-living man. Condition and fitness cannot be brought about solely by training, and the player must first of all look to himself. That is the great secret of fitness."

James returned to a sport that had given itself a new title, 'Rugby League' which had replaced the parochial sounding 'Northern Union' for the start of the 1922–23 season. He obviously had thoughts on taking a pro-active role on the field of play because he took part in the final trial match ahead of the 1922–23 season, played on Saturday 19 August. He appeared in the centre for the 'Whites' ('A' team backs, first team forwards) against the 'Reds' (first team backs, 'A' team forwards), implying that he was likely to operate as a player-coach. The *Salford Reporter* said James "got a special cheer of welcome when he appeared" and informed its readers that "Lomas will coach the 'A' team and may turn out for the first thirteen." The latter comment was something of a surprise. The idea of James playing the odd game with the reserves seemed just about feasible, but a return to first team action for a man well into his 40s was a tougher challenge altogether. The Whites won the trial game 20–5. James did not score but the report said "Lomas showed some of his old touches at centre threequarter and will be of great value to the Reds this season."

His first match in charge of the 'A' team was at home to Wigan 'A' on 26 August. Whether James selected the line-up for the reserve team is not known. In all probability he did not, although it may well have been his own decision to take part on a day when he also celebrated his 43rd birthday. Salford lost 31–8 and, reportedly, "Lomas did sterling work for Salford". He also played in the next match two weeks later, a whopping 42–5 away defeat at the hands of Leigh 'A'. A third reserve appearance came at Wilderspool on 23 September. James's presence in the centre and his conversion of a second-half try were insufficient to stop Warrington 'A' winning 22–8. According to the *Warrington Examiner*, his inclusion created "much interest" and he received a "hearty reception" from the home supporters.

On 9 September, the *Salford Reporter* revealed "it is the intention of the directors of the Salford Football Club to hold a benefit match in the near future for Jimmy Lomas," a game that came to be played at The Willows on Wednesday evening, 27 September. It was, of course, James's second benefit, having been the subject of such a match in 1910, shortly after returning from tour. This time it was billed as J. Lomas' XIII versus J. Ferguson's XIII. Oldham forward Joe Ferguson had a career that paralleled James's, having also been born in 1879, in Ellenborough, near Maryport, and was, amazingly, still playing. It was reported that Salford officials "are hoping that the friends and admirers of Lomas will be present in large numbers to show their appreciation of his services to the Willows club." The paying attendance on the day was actually 1,500, producing gate receipts of £22. However, tickets bought in advance added £30 plus an interval collection of £8 and donations amounted to £12, which made up a grand total for James of about £72.

James's team won 8–0 and he scored a try and goal, having received a "rousing reception by the crowd" before the game started. Apparently "Jimmy Lomas and [Willie] Thomas delighted everyone by their splendid play." James's team was mostly composed of Salford players bolstered by the notable additions of full-back Jack Pearson, winger Frank

Evans and forward Henry Blewer, all from Swinton, and Oldham half-back Ben Beynon, while Ferguson's XIII fielded mostly Oldham colleagues with the help of a few Cumbrians in Salford's threequarter Fergie Southward and forwards Jim Clampitt of Broughton Rangers and Huddersfield's Duggie Clark.

It was reported in the *Daily Chronicle* that James had taken part in eight 'A' team matches for Salford, a figure which is difficult to verify due to the scant reporting of these matches, when recalled to first team duty on 23 February 1923 for a home match against St Helens. James – a replacement for the injured Billy Anderton – played at scrum-half, his stand-off partner was team captain T.H. Smith. It was his first competitive first team game for the Reds for over 12 years and six years since his three wartime appearances. The *Salford Reporter* said: "Special interest was attached to the meeting of Salford and St Helens at The Willows on Saturday by reason of the reappearance of Jimmy Lomas, an old stalwart and one of the finest players the Northern Union had ever produced. Such was the interest it aroused in his appearance in the Salford team [that] a crowd numbering about 6,000 gathered at The Willows." Salford's team was: Walter Clegg; Clifford Hall, Chris Brockbank, Fergie Southward, Harold Norrey; T.H. Smith, Lomas; Ted Haines, Jimmy Burgess, Jack Muir, Bill Wilkinson, John Williams, Ernie Woods.

The match was played in poor conditions, but it did not detract from James receiving "a great ovation from the crowd." St Helens led 3–0 at the interval. James had made a good break in the first half before lack of pace "proved his downfall" and he was tackled. Nonetheless, it was considered "a gallant effort on the veteran's part". Salford drew level with a try by Burgess who was now a fully-fledged Salford player, having transferred from Runcorn when that club folded after the war. Salford went 6–3 ahead with eight minutes to go through "brilliant work by Lomas"; the Reds attacked on the right flank after a long pass found the ball with James "who coolly viewed the field" before he kicked to the left corner for Norrey to score. Almost on full-time, Norrey claimed his second and, with Southward and Burgess missing the first two conversions, James supplied the extra points by "adding a brilliant goal with a left foot kick." It completed the scoring at 11–3 in Salford's favour. One report said James "showed many flashes of his old form."

James retained his place for the following week's Challenge Cup second round match with Wakefield Trinity at The Willows. On a day of muddy, slippery conditions and, with the ball difficult to control, Salford won 6–0 with a try in each half. It was reported in the *Daily Chronicle* that James "put in several clever touches. His lack of speed was, however, an obvious handicap but his tackling recalled his palmiest days."

It was a return to the league competition on Saturday 10 March when Salford were again at home. The opposition looked fearsome in the shape of league leaders Wigan, who had beaten Halifax at Central Park 64–0 the previous Wednesday. Salford rose to the occasion and James had a starring role in what finished as a scoreless stalemate. Two comments from the *Salford Reporter* relating to James are worth repeating; "The subtlety of Lomas got the visitors in many tangles from which they were frequently lucky to escape" and "Lomas was full of cleverness and was a rare trouble to the visitors, who could not fathom his tactics." It was an incredible triumph for the former Salford skipper that, despite advancing years, he could more than hold his own with a Wigan team that included greats like Jim Sullivan at full-back and Johnny Ring on the wing. The meeting of James and Sullivan was historic. It was the only time that the two legends opposed each other, the Cumbrian in the twilight of his career, the young Welshman embarking on his. Maybe fate realised the significance because a photograph of the pair was taken before the match to mark the occasion.

The report by 'Free Lance' in the *Daily Chronicle* was full of admiration for the former Salford skipper: "I visited the Willows [for the match against Wigan] because of the desire to once more see 80 minutes football from Lomas – a veteran well in the forties. I believe he acknowledged to being in his 44th year, and I came away full of surprise and admiration that such an exhibition of middle-aged grit was possible. Lomas from start to finish was a force to be seriously reckoned with. He perhaps kicked over much. This natural weakness dismissed, Lomas adapted himself to the conditions in a way which savoured of his palmy days. He worked the scrimmage, and some of our younger half could well copy his methods, for there was little difficulty in getting the ball quickly into the kennel. His forwards fairly rose to the occasion, and gave their gallant veteran the ball as often as he desired. No doubt the Salford forwards felt that when Lomas was in possession Wigan would make little progress. His following up and his deadly tackle was just as sure and convincing as well. Much has happened in Rugby League football since I described Lomas as a leading genius in both attack and defence. He was the one obstacle on the Salford side that Wigan could not overcome, and on the play I thought the League leaders were fortunate to escape defeat."

For the fourth consecutive match – each taking place at The Willows – Salford fielded the same side. This time it was a third round Challenge Cup tie, the winners would progress to the semi-final stage. But what would have been a major upset was never on the cards, a powerful Hull team – who ended the season as Challenge Cup runners-up and league leaders – crushed Salford 24–0. It concluded a unique Manchester-Salford treble for Hull who had won at Broughton Rangers and Swinton in the previous two rounds. There was a crowd of 18,000 to watch a match that had few highlights for the home fans. A rare passage of excitement occurred in the first half when James and Norrey passed and re-passed the ball for 50 yards before the former was finally brought down. The *Salford Reporter* writer said: "Lomas, I thought, kicked too much and did not open out the game enough, but the veteran often showed tactical skill of a high order."

Salford travelled to Widnes the following Thursday to fulfil a previously postponed match but were again defeated, 12–5, James converted Norrey's second half try in response to the Chemics' 10-point half-time lead. James played the last of a personal sequence of six matches for the Reds at Hunslet two days later. It was an experience that must have conjured up many memories for James of his old adversary Albert Goldthorpe although the result was less memorable – a 41–2 thrashing.

James was praised for his "admirable kicking" which gave Salford good territorial position early on when Burgess put them ahead 2–0 with a penalty. But they were totally outplayed afterwards; Hunslet scored 31 points following the interval.

James had done well during his recent elevation to the first team but for the next match, at home to Oldham, younger blood was brought in, in the shape of Fred Whittle. The remainder of James's season was focused on the 'A' team and, overall, he could look back on the campaign as a satisfactory one. Apart from his personal fulfilment of working with the reserves, the first team climbed six places to finish 17th in the league and the club had made a profit, £457, one of only six to do so.

James was retained for the 1923–24 season. The *Salford Reporter* said "The players will again have the benefit of the experience and knowledge of Jimmy Lomas who will again coach the 'A' team. In addition to his valuable work for the young players, Lomas showed last season that he is still a force as a player and he is a most useful man to have available in case of emergency."

This time he took no part in the pre-season trials, but continued to keep his hand in playing-wise, and was captain of the reserve side that travelled to Central Park on 8 September to meet Wigan 'A'. He played in the centre. In front of 1,500 spectators he opened the scoring with a penalty, awarded for obstruction, but his side eventually succumbed 36–4 having trailed 10–4 at the halfway stage. He was, however, soon utilised once again in the first team. Having lost their opening four matches, Salford decided to bring James into the threequarter line at centre for the home game with Widnes on 22 September. Tom Quigley moved out to the wing to accommodate him. The *Salford Reporter* commented: "The reappearance of Jimmy Lomas should give the three-quarters a much needed steadiness." Salford won 19–6; the match report concluded that "the new combination worked quite well. Lomas had a 'bag' of four goals and his effortless methods and nonchalant air were a comparison to the methods of the younger generation who studiously place the ball in position and take a terrific lunge at it." Salford were 6–3 behind at the interval, James's four goals were all scored in the second half through two penalties and two conversions.

He kept his place for the following week's trip to play Wakefield Trinity. The date was Saturday 29 September 1923 and it was to be the final first team game of his career. The Salford team was: Walter Clegg; Tom Quigley, Lomas, Sid Boyd, Harold Norrey; Fred Whittle, Alex Hurst; Jim Burgess, Frank Butterworth, Jack Muir, George Whitney, Bill Wilkinson, Ernie Woods. The report said "Lomas revealed some clever touches and was fairly prominent" but, unfortunately, he was unable to sign off with any points. He missed two first half penalties as Trinity built an 11–0 interval lead. Burgess scored a second half try, and missed the goal, but it was a token gesture, the home side won 26–3. The following week James's place went to returning fellow Cumbrian Fergie Southward who had been on duty for the county at Whitehaven when the Reds travelled to Wakefield.

Jimmy was 44 years and 34 days old on the day of his final match. Earlier in the year, on 14 April, Joe Ferguson had played his last game for Oldham at 44 years, 48 days, just 'beating' Jimmy by 14 days. On 6 March 1995, forward Jeff Grayshon played his final professional match, for Batley, at the incredible age of 46 years, 2 days. Based on known information, the above three are the oldest to compete in the sport professionally in Britain, thereby placing James third on the all-time list.

For the remainder of the 1923–24 season, James concentrated on his role of 'A' team coach although, except for a home game against St Helens Recs on 20 October, there is no record of him playing any further matches with the reserves in that campaign. Salford lost £553 that season, their poor results – they finished three places off the bottom of the 27-team table – blamed on unemployment and bad weather. One remedy was to improve the team's performance and, to that end, James was promoted to first team coach for the following term, the first 'senior' coach to be appointed by the club.

The 1924–25 season preview in the *Salford Reporter* included the following comment: "At the Willows one finds optimism prevalent, hope being entertained that a more successful season, both from a financial and playing point of view, is about to be embarked upon... the former the club cannot overcome, but the latter they can, and those responsible are determined to do so, by all the means in their power. To this end, Jimmy Lomas, the old stalwart of the club, has been appointed official coach to all the players, and his varied experiences should serve him and the club in good stead in his new position."

James was again named among the club's threequarters in a list published in August 1924 but played only once during the season. That was on 18 October 1924 in a reserve match against Leigh 'A' at The Willows. Salford lost 23–8. James converted the second of his side's two tries, which had been scored by forward Frank Butterworth. It was his final points and his final match in a Salford jersey and over 23 years since his first. In all probability he had not originally intended playing because he was not among the 16 players initially named from which the final 13 was to be chosen. His appearance also indicates a difference in the priorities of coaches compared to the attitudes today. It would be unthinkable in the modern game for a first team coach to be elsewhere – unless due to extenuating circumstances – when his charges were in action; the first XIII were at Leigh that day and lost 26–0. Of course, the answer is that he was coach to all the club's players and could not have been present to watch both teams anyway in an era when – as regular as clockwork – first and 'A' teams alternated with home and away fixtures each Saturday.

But it also seems that the unwritten job description of a coach did not include match day duties in the way they are understood now. The players would look after their own 'game plan' and a trainer would, as always, be on hand to tend to the wounded. The real work for

James took place on Tuesday and Thursday when he managed their training sessions in preparation for the weekend.

It has been difficult to ascertain if he was still on the coaching staff in 1925–26. There is no evidence that he was not but, equally, there is no mention that he was, which seems to suggest he had stood down. The only reference to him is that he was again included in the club's register as a threequarter whereas for the season after, 1926–27, he was no longer listed. It was also announced that W. Taylor, who had been recruited from Stoke City FC, was the Reds' new coach and trainer for 1926–27. The latter was followed, in 1928, by the appointment of Lance Todd, who would lead Salford to their greatest triumphs.

In his memoirs, written when Todd was still in charge, James said "I have done a bit of coaching and spade work… to help put the Salford club in an affluent position. Prior to Mr Todd's arrival they only wanted a man in that position to make the club go and he [Todd] is the right man in the right place. I wish he would get more material to work from. It has been the fault ever since I came. You can't win cups and leagues with the bare team as has been tried long ago." He was probably harking back to his own time as player and coach when Salford's playing resources – due to poor finances – were usually stretched when injuries struck. Fortunes rose after Todd's revolution and he was able to call on some of the greatest names to be associated with the club and continued to identify and recruit outstanding talent throughout his time in office.

Although James had played his last match for Salford, his days as a rugby player were still not quite over. This was a time when it was common for the professional clubs to organise tournaments on their ground for local companies to participate in, no doubt hopeful of discovering new talent. Broughton Rangers were one such club and at the end of the 1924–25 season they staged their annual Workshops Competition at The Cliff – they had left Wheater's Field in 1913. There were 51 entries and the mammoth knock-out tournament commenced on Monday 6 April with several matches staged each day over the coming weeks.

James had found employment with the Manchester Ship Canal Company and was in the team that had entered as the Manchester Ship Canal No.9 Dock. Following a bye in the opening round they overcame four opponents, including a second round replay to eliminate Cussons Soap Works, to reach the final on Friday 8 May. Their opposition was Chloride Recreation Club and, according to the *Salford Reporter*, "both were loudly cheered for their brilliant play". Possibly their route to the final was aided by the fact that the two teams were led by distinguished captains; James mentored the Dockers side, Halifax full-back Billy Young, a former Broughton Rangers player, directed Chloride. After only five minutes play, James succeeded with a "brilliant" penalty goal to give his side a two point lead but, when the interval arrived, they were 8–2 down after conceding two tries. James's team lifted their game after the break and the sides became so well matched "that almost to the end it was a moot question as to which side would triumph." Excitement increased after J. Malone scored a try for the Dockers although James missed the goal. However, there was no more scoring and they just lost 8–5. Afterwards Broughton Rangers' long-serving chairman Fred Kennedy presented a "handsome cup" to Young who gave thanks and praised the Dock's side for their efforts. In response, and on behalf of his team, James congratulated the winners, and thanked the directors of Broughton Rangers "who had originated the competition". James's team did not go away empty-handed, however, as medals were presented to both teams.

The participation of the Docks motivated them to enter a team in the Manchester and District Rugby League for the following 1925–26 season, when they became known by the more manageable name of Manchester Ship Canal. Match reports are difficult to find and there is little evidence that James played except for one occasion at the start of the season. He was in the side that met Seedley Rangers in a home fixture at Longford Bridge in nearby Stretford on 31 October 1925. The match was lost 8–0 and, in all probability this was his last taste of rugby activity. For the record he would have been aged 46 years, 66 days.

James and Annie celebrated their Golden Wedding at their home in Byrom Street in September 1953. This family picture, taken at the event, shows them with their four daughters; from the left Olive, Madge, Evelyn and Annie. (Photo: Courtesy Rob Dellar).

James and Annie with grandchildren Brian and Pat outside their Byrom Street home in the late 1940s. (Photo: Courtesy Pat Clancy)

The respect for James in the Southern Hemisphere was shown through touring captains shaking hands with him prior to games against Salford at The Willows. When New Zealand visited on 1 December 1951 he greeted 18-year-old Bruce Robertson, the youngest ever Kiwi at that time.

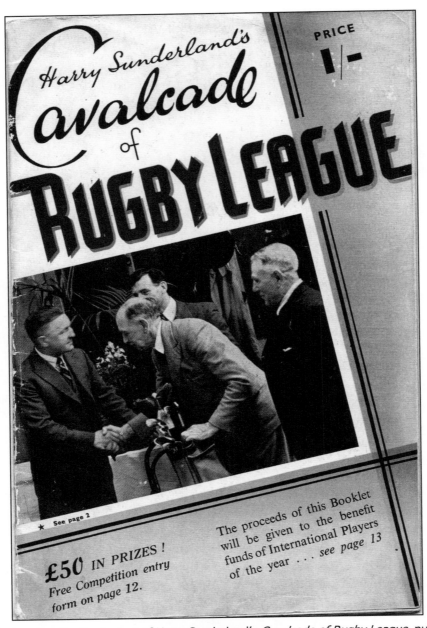

Harry Sunderland's Cavalcade of RUGBY LEAGUE

★ See page 2

£50 IN PRIZES!
Free Competition entry
form on page 12.

The proceeds of this Booklet
will be given to the benefit
funds of International Players
of the year . . . see page 13

James featured on the front cover of Harry Sunderland's *Cavalcade of Rugby League*, published in 1950. Jonty Parkin on the left (1924 and 1928 tour captain) presented a set of golf clubs to RFL secretary John Wilson when he retired in 1945. He was watched by a partially obscured Gus Risman (1946 tour captain) and James (1910).

22. A proud legacy

After James Lomas severed his active involvement with rugby in the mid–1920s, he continued to live in Salford and, indeed, regularly attended matches at The Willows. Towards the end of his playing career, and according to the Rugby League Playing Register, he had had various addresses in Salford; Elizabeth Street (1922–23), Langworthy Road South (1923–24) and Thurlow Street (1924–25). His continual movement may be because, having recently returned from Belfast, he had not established a permanent address. It is almost certain that he had returned alone to Salford, probably to search for employment and quite possibly with the offer of a coaching appointment from Salford, something he began in August 1922. The fact that he was given a benefit match just one month after taking up his new role also suggests that the club provided a 'helping hand'.

It is well documented that James spent the remainder of his working life as a casual labourer on the Manchester Docks, which were actually based in Salford off Trafford Road. Having been an apprentice riveter in Maryport in his younger days, he subsequently gave "riveter" as his profession on his 1903 wedding certificate, and later declared his occupation to be "boilermaker", followed by "journeyman" in brackets, on the birth certificates of his four daughters from 1905 to 1910. The 1911 census entry also showed his occupation as a "boilermaker" with the additional information that he was employed in the Iron Works industry. At the time of the wedding of his daughter Evelyn in 1927 he had abbreviated his occupation to "journeyman".

Whatever skills he possessed with his hands he seemed unable to find appropriate employment on his return to Salford prior to labouring on the dockside. Exactly when he began work at the docks is unclear. Workers such as labourers, dockers and stevedores were not employed by the Ship Canal Company itself, but by the National Dock Labour Board. There are no known surviving records relating to the latter's employees.

There are, however, some clues. He was featured in a newspaper series around 1934 called 'The Sportslights of Yesterday' which began as follows: "Meeting Jimmy Lomas, the one-time Salford Northern Union star, was quite an acrobatic feat – on his part as well as mine. First of all, I had to find a certain Norwegian steamship. Then I had to climb an improvised gangway on to the iron-plated deck and introduce myself to the stevedore [gang boss]. After that it was plain sailing. Jimmy was down in the hold, loading lengths of timber on to the swaying derrick, and when the stevedore's booming voice announced that he was wanted, he was on the iron ladder before one could say Jack Robinson. By the way, he is 54. You try running up one of these precarious, vertical ladders when you are 54! For 12 years now he has been employed as a casual at the Docks."

Those words reveal several things. First, his current age and length of service imply that he was 42 when he first began working on the docks and therefore it would have been around 1922. In 1920 Manchester Docks was one of the busiest in Britain, and employed over 16,000 labourers. The year 1922 was, of course, when he took up his coaching post with Salford. The fact that he was loading timber also implies he was employed on the Number Nine Dock. Opened by King Edward VII in 1905, it was the last section of the Manchester Docks complex to be completed and, by coincidence, the very reason Salford had to vacate New Barnes for The Willows in 1901. James was clearly working at that particular dock back in 1925 because, as mentioned previously, he captained the 'Manchester Ship Canal No.9 Dock' team in Broughton Rangers' workshops competition that year. Going further forward to the period after the Second World War, his granddaughter Pat Clancy remembers, as a young girl, greeting him on Broadway after he finished his day's work. Broadway ran alongside the Number Nine Dock and was the location of several timber companies that sprang up around that dockside.

At least one man was grateful that James spent time at the docks. As recorded earlier in this story, James had saved several people from drowning in the River Ellen in his younger days. Reportedly he also saved the life of a fellow docker at the Manchester Docks. Summoning his remarkable strength and a little of his old rugby skill, he succeeded in handing-off a precariously swinging bale as it headed towards his colleague.

Even in his mid–50s he was evidently still strong enough to meet the physical demands of the work, as suggested by the aforementioned article: "It is a strong man's job. Either you carry on and just grow stronger, or you look out for something more restful. Jimmy is in the first category. He is hard, tough, and very strong." But it must have become more difficult as he got older – his granddaughter Pat believes he worked there until he was about 72. On occasions James gave the impression that he would have preferred a different type of employment. One issue for him to deal with was that, as casual labour, he was not guaranteed work on a daily basis. Again, in the above mentioned feature, he concludes the interview with the confession that "for myself, I am happy enough, but you won't blame me for hoping that something better will turn up before I am too old to enjoy it."

In his memoirs, which he would have written in his late–50s, he revealed: "Money has been elusive to me. I could help make players better. I don't want a lot of money. I am just like thousands more. I only want a chance to earn some of my own. I don't want anybody else's. I was on the dole for two years prior to working on the Docks." His comments suggest he would have liked to have continued to be involved with rugby in some capacity, possibly as a coach, although he did not seem to harbour any grudge towards the Salford club: "I took some debenture shares in Salford [when leaving to join Oldham in 1911] but I have sacrificed them at various times to help the club out of a hole. I have no fault with the Salford club. They treated me alright and does yet." The above text, while reflecting the kindness and generosity of the man, also hints at the frustration of someone who was a winner at rugby league, but could never lay claim to being affluent in his later years.

It is rare to find James's words in print. There was one occasion, however, when he was prevailed upon to write a brief eulogy on Ferguson 'Fergie' Southward in Salford's official match programme for 8 April 1933. Salford's league fixture with St Helens Recreation on that date had been designated a benefit match for Southward, who had joined the Reds in 1921 and played alongside James in his final first team appearances in 1923. The skilful threequarter came from the same part of the world as James and had signed from Maryport's old foe, Brookland Rovers. Under the heading 'A Tribute from a Great Player' James wrote: "I am of the opinion that the Salford Club will never have a more loyal servant than Fergy Southward. He has been a credit to the game, and is deserving of a 'Bumper Benefit.' He bids fair to break the record for [Cumberland] County appearances held by Joe Ferguson and Douglas Clark, and will probably be playing when some of the younger ones have finished. I wish you every success, Fergy. Jimmy Lomas, ex-captain of England, Cumberland, Lancashire and Salford."

Sometimes, James's views received an airing through a feature on him in one of the newspapers. When he was included in the 'Prominent Salford Sportsmen' series in April 1926, he gave his opinion on the current state of the sport: "I think the game today is more open than it used to be. The forwards are faster and there is not as much scrimmaging as used to be the case. This is better from the spectator's point of view, but more scrimmaging would be useful at times. I think the loose forward is an impediment to the progress of the game and ought to be dispensed with. Taken as a whole, I don't think the present day backs are as fast as in former days, and they do not seem to be of the same calibre. There were as big men playing in the backs then as there are in the forwards now, and the players do not seem to take the same interest and do not seem to have the same knowledge of the game as they used to have."

A decade later, in the late 1930s, he gave an insight into his views in his memoirs: "Most players today are what I call positional players. A player who can fill any position is what I call a footballer. There are not many these days, they only come two or three in a decade but when you see one he stands alone. You want the physique combined with science, then you find the perfect player. To be an athlete it is essential to live a clean life and take everything in moderation and learn to look after your body. I don't think players are as good today as pre- [First World] War [and] I am not saying that because I am not playing."

From 1934 until 1937 James lived in Sutherland Place, and it was while there that he wrote the memoirs referred to above and in various sections throughout this book. He still retained his love affair with the Salford club and in a 1930s interview said: "I am still very keen on the Rugby League game, and there are not many Saturdays but you will find me at the match at Salford. I go away with them pretty often too."

By 1939 he had settled in Byrom Street in Salford where he remained for the next 20 years or so. Exactly when his wife Annie reunited with him is uncertain. She was certainly with him at Byrom Street from 1939, but not mentioned for Sutherland Place where James was possibly a lodger as another couple were also named on the Electoral Register as living there. As already stated, when James returned to Salford he came back alone. Annie remained in Belfast with their four daughters. To reiterate a previous suggestion, Annie possibly had relatives living in Belfast and, in 1922, when James reappeared in Salford, their eldest daughter would have been aged about 17 and the youngest 11. It would have made sense for them to remain in Belfast until James had 'found his feet.' What probably began as a temporary arrangement seems to have become semi-permanent. His two youngest daughters, Olive and Madge, spent the rest of their lives in Ireland where they both married and had children. They reached 'the age of majority' in January 1930 and December 1931 respectively, so it is feasible that his wife Annie still lived there around then.

Eldest daughter Annie eventually returned to Salford in the early 1940s while Evelyn, the second eldest, met Jim Dellar, an Englishman serving in the Army. There is evidence that they first met in Belfast although they subsequently married in Fulham in 1927 when Evelyn was 20, and settled in the south of England, raising two sons, Robin and Brian. Both boys displayed a talent for association football. Robin played for senior amateur teams Ford Sports in the Spartan League and Dagenham in the Corinthian League. His younger sibling represented Dagenham Schoolboys in the same team as future England international Jimmy Greaves and the pair subsequently signed together for Chelsea. Whereas Brian – who played for England Youth – left Stamford Bridge in 1959 and made his mark in the semi-professional Southern League with the likes of Chelmsford City, Clacton Town and Ashford Town, Greaves went on to play for Milan and – just like Tom Smith all those years earlier – Tottenham Hotspur.

Despite his absence from the rugby field, James was not forgotten. In 1936, the Courtney International Goodwill Trophy was donated by New Zealand businessman Roy Courtney. This imposing, impressive trophy stands over four feet tall with a four foot square base and is made of gold, silver and enamel. Each of its four sides depict an engraving featuring a significant individual in the history of the four major rugby league-playing nations of the time; Albert Baskerville (New Zealand), Dally Messenger (Australia), Jean Galia (France) and, of course, James Lomas (Great Britain). The trophy was initially awarded to Great Britain during their 1936 tour after defeating New Zealand in the test series and brought back to England. Subsequently it was up for grabs each time its holders took part in a test series. Due to its size and weight, transporting it became an issue and it is now housed in an Australian museum having spent many years at the New South Wales Rugby League offices at Phillip Street in Sydney.

Another accolade was bestowed upon James when the British Lions Rugby League Association was founded at Belle Vue, Manchester, on 18 November 1945. The Association – open to all former tourists including management and coaching staff – duly elected him as its first chairman, an honour he retained until Australian journalist Harry Sunderland took over the mantle in 1948. There is a photograph of that meeting that shows James seated in the centre surrounded by around 70 people, including many of the greatest names in rugby league history. Sadly, with rugby league tours down under now consigned to the sport's history and the Great Britain team rebranded as England in 2008, the Lions Association disbanded in 2010.

James was also remembered down under as journalist Tom Bergin noted in the *Salford City Reporter* in the early 1960s: "As evidence of his reputation was the practice of every visiting team of Aussies to make a point of meeting him and shaking hands with the legendary footballer." There was a nice moment when James was photographed greeting Bruce Robertson before the Salford versus New Zealand match at The Willows on 1 December 1951. The significance was that Robertson – who scored three tries from the wing in a 27–12 win over the Reds – was, at the time the youngest ever Kiwi at 18 years old. He was incidentally, the younger brother of their tour captain, Maurie Robertson.

James and Annie continued to live in Byrom Street in the years following the Second World War. They were joined there by granddaughter, Pat, who lived with them as a youngster during the late–1940s and 1950s until she was about 16, and has nothing but fond memories of James, some of which are shared in the foreword to this publication.

Another granddaughter, Carol, remembers travelling from Belfast during and after the 1940s with her mother, Madge. They stayed with her grandparents at Byrom Street and Carol recalls the visits as 'holidays'. She remembers James as a quiet man: "He used to just sit in his chair, but he came home in the evening after working at the docks all day. It must have been hard work. He always seemed exhausted. I think he was just tired." His wife Annie was more outgoing. "There were a lot of women around the house.' recalls Carol.

James relaxed by smoking a pipe, something that he must have indulged in back in 1910 when his Salford colleagues presented him with a pipe and tobacco ahead of the tour. In later years he was known to smoke cigarettes, Woodbines in particular. He also remembered his roots and returned to Maryport on occasions to visit his elder sister, Sarah.

In 1953 James and Annie celebrated their Golden Wedding at their Byrom Street home. It must have been a very proud and special occasion for the couple. They were joined by their four daughters; Annie, Evelyn, Olive and Madge. They were both still active and it was reported that Annie – a few weeks short of her 75th birthday – enjoyed "going to the pictures" while James was still a regular Salford supporter. Reportedly, the couple also had 15 grandchildren and six great-grandchildren at that time.

James and Annie both lived to be a good age. Annie – eldest by almost a year – was the first to pass away on 5 May 1959 at the age of 80. James was also 80 years old when he departed on Thursday 11 February 1960. Pat recalls that he had initially been taken ill with bronchitis which gradually got worse and he spent most of one winter at home in bed. With his health deteriorating he was admitted to the former Ladywell Hospital on Eccles New Road, Salford, and was subsequently transferred to Springfield Hospital in Crumpsall, an area now occupied by North Manchester General Hospital where he eventually died. James must have been in Springfield for a good while because Annie was still alive at the time he was first admitted and, along with Pat, used to visit him each Sunday, a journey that required two buses – changing in Manchester – each way.

Two days after he died, Salford had a first round Challenge Cup match at The Willows against Halifax. Before kick-off a two minute silence was observed in his memory. The Salford players wore a black diamond on the left hand sleeve of their all red jerseys. It must have been a very emotional moment for the club chairman who, at the time, was James's long-time playing colleague Willie Thomas.

His funeral took place on Tuesday morning, 16 February. The cortege set off from the home of daughter Annie on Goodiers Lane in Salford for a service at Stowell Memorial Church, where his wedding had taken place over 56 years earlier. This was followed by committal at Agecroft Crematorium where his ashes were subsequently scattered on the lawn. There is also a memorial stone at Glen Gormley in Belfast that bears his name. The memorial, which remembers the husband of James's daughter Olive, Thomas Patterson, who passed away in 1961, says: "Also loving memories of mother Annie Lomas died 5 May 1959, father James Lomas died 11 February 1960. Interred in Salford."

James Lomas left behind a proud legacy for rugby league in general and Salford in particular. Playing as he did in an era that produced so many of the true legends of the game, his selection as the 1910 tour captain illustrates the huge respect he commanded at that time. He was also a prolific points scorer, as this biography has already demonstrated. His final points haul from official matches was 2,312. He also scored 28 points for Maryport in competitive fixtures, including the Challenge Cup, although this is excluded from 'official' figures due to the Cumbrian club's perceived lower status at that time. James's record stood until finally overhauled by Wigan's Jim Sullivan in November 1928. At the time neither of the players – nor anyone else for that matter – would have realised the significance. Record keeping was not as meticulously undertaken then as it is today.

When writing his memoirs, James was aware of Sullivan's phenomenal point scoring: "He is a great player. Apart from anything his records will never be approached, let alone beat." The bulk of Sullivan's haul came from his boot – he kicked 2,867 goals and scored 96 tries in amassing his 6,022 career points – a skill that impressed James, who named his 'best' goalkickers as Hunslet's Albert Goldthorpe for accuracy and Oldham's Joe Ferguson, Australian Dally Messenger and Sullivan for consistency.

Tom Bergin, who covered Salford's affairs for over 50 years and was chairman of the Rugby League Writers' Association, wrote in the 1960s that "in the opinion of many of the best judges, he was the greatest individualist who ever graced the code. My memories of him were when I was a small boy [in the 1920s] and I saw him in his declining days as a player with still obvious signs of his genius." Although Bergin saw little of James's playing career he would have been well acquainted with him in later years, and commented that "Jimmy was a legend but he was always modest about his achievements, although fiercely proud of rugby football."

Alf Beecroft – Bergin's predecessor as 'Ajax' for the *Salford Reporter* – said of James in

1926: "The great work he did for the handling code cannot easily be erased from one's memory, and I must confess that I ally myself with the views of scores of Salford followers who express the opinion that he is one of the greatest if not the greatest figure in the long and honourable history of the Weaste club, to whom he rendered such faithful service for so long a period. His unorthodox style and his typically different methods of paving the way to a score soon brought him into prominence, and it is to his credit that his star never waned. In many instances one knows of players whose names were household words during their football career, but the passage of time found them comparatively unknown. Not so Lomas, whose sturdy figure is as well known to the younger generation of Rugby enthusiasts as it is to the old."

Appendices

1. Career summary

Club summary season-by-season (competitive/official matches only):

	Season	Apps	Tries	Goals	Points
Maryport	1898-99	16	0	5	10
	1899-1900	19	4	3	18
	Total	**35**	**4**	**8**	**28**
Bramley	1900-01	31	4	21	54
	Total	**31**	**4**	**21**	**54**
Salford	1901-02	31	20	52	164
	1902-03	34	19	20	97
	1903-04	38	25	57	189
	1904-05	31	20	36	132
	1905-06	32	21	34	131
	1906-07	35	33	81	261
	1907-08	30	16	51	150
	1908-09	33	28	71	226
	1909-10	31	23	57	183
	1910-11	9	3	5	19
	1922-23	6	0	2	4
	1923-24	2	0	4	8
	Total	**312**	**208**	**470**	**1564**
Oldham	1910-11	17	13	6	51
	1911-12	37	20	23	106
	1912-13	26	5	8	31
	Total	**80**	**38**	**37**	**188**
York	1913-14	20	7	17	55
	1914-15	32	14	51	144
	1918-19	1	0	0	0
	Total	**53**	**21**	**68**	**199**

	Apps	Tries	Goals	Points
Bramley	31	4	21	54
Salford	312	208	470	1564
Oldham	80	38	37	188
York	53	21	68	199
Test matches*	7	4	14	40
1910 tour**	10	9	42	111
England	13	6	21	60
Cumberland	14	6	8	34
Lancashire	9	2	6	18
Lancashire trials	4	3	9	27
Tour trial	1	2	1	8
Tourists XIII	1	1	3	9
Total	**535**	**304**	**700**	**2312**

(* includes Test matches on 1910 tour)
(** excludes Test matches)
(appearances for Maryport not included)

2. Match-by-match

First team games only, including friendly fixtures.
Club matches are all League Championship fixtures unless stated.
(Abbreviations: CC – Cumberland Cup, CPO – Championship Play-Off, CSL – Cumberland Senior League, F=Friendly, LC – Lancashire Cup, NUC – Northern Union Challenge Cup, NWL – North Western League, RLC – Rugby League Challenge Cup, SEL – South East Lancashire League, YC- Yorkshire Cup, t - try/tries, g – goal/goals, DNP – did not play, N/A – confirmation of Lomas' involvement not available, **bold** type - home matches)

Date	Opponent /competition	Result /score	Position /points
Rugby Union:			
At Maryport:			
1896-97 season:			
17 Oct	Tynedale (F)	D 8-8	N/A
24 Oct	Seaton (F) L 3-16		N/A
31 Oct	**Whitehaven Recs** (F)D 0-0		N/A
7 Nov	**Langholm** (F)	W 8-0	N/A
14 Nov	Millom (F) L 0-3		6
21 Nov	**Whitehaven** (F)	W 3-0	6
28 Nov	**Workington** (F)	W 10-3	6
5 Dec	**Aspatria** (F)	W 7-0	6
12 Dec	Barrow (F) D 3-3		N/A
25 Dec	**Brookland R** (F)	L 0-3	N/A
1 Jan	Whitehaven (F)	W 3-0	N/A
2 Jan	Langholm (F)	W 5-3	N/A
9 Jan	Barrow (F)	L 0-8	N/A
6 Feb	**Millom** (F)	L 4-9	6
13 Feb	Whitehaven Recs (F)	W 5-0	N/A
27 Feb	**Aspatria** (CC1)	L 3-22	6
3 Apr	Aspatria (F)	L 3-9	N/A
17 Apr	Workington (F)	L 7-11	N/A
1897-98 season:			
18 Sep	**Penrith** (CSL)	W 4-0	N/A
25 Sep	Whitehaven (CSL)	W 4-0	6
2 Oct	**Aspatria** (CSL)	D 3-3	6 (t)
16 Oct	Wath Brow (F)	W 5-3	6 (t, g)
30 Oct	**Aspatria** (F)	L 0-3	6
6 Nov	Wath Brow (F)	L 0-6	N/A
13 Nov	**Whitehaven R** (CSL)	L 0-4	6
20 Nov	Langholm (F)	L 3-6	6
27 Nov	**Brookland Rov** (CSL)	L 0-3	6
4 Dec	Brookland R (CSL)	D 0-0	N/A
11 Dec	**Seaton** (CSL)	L 0-9	6
25 Dec	**Brookland R** (F)	L 3-5	N/A
1 Jan	South Shields (F)	L 0-7	N/A
15 Jan	Cockermouth (CSL)	D 0-0	N/A
22 Jan	**Cockermouth** (CSL)	W 3-0	N/A
5 Feb	Whitehaven R (CSL)	W 3-0	N/A
12 Feb	Seaton (F)	L 0-13	N/A
26 Feb	**Whitehaven** (CC1)	W 11-0	6
5 Mar	**Workington** (CC2)	W 9-3	6 (t)
Northern Union:			
19 Mar	Barrow (F)	L 0-31	6
2 Apr	**Workington** (F)	L 8-13	6
9 Apr	**Millom** (F)	W 3-0	6
16 Apr	**Wath Brow** (F)	W 8-0	6 (t)
20 Apr	**Brookland R** (F)	W 2-0	6
23 Apr	Wath Brow (F)	D 0—0	6
1898-99 season:			
10 Sep	Birkenhead W (F)	L 0-3	6
17 Sep	Workington (NWL)	L 0-12	6
1 Oct	Brookland Rovers (F)	W 7-3	6
5 Oct	**Millom** (NWL)	L 0-6	6
15 Oct	**Ulverston** (NWL)	W 7-4	6
22 Oct	Askam (NWL)	W 7-6	6
29 Oct	**Lancaster** (NWL)	W 3-0	6
12 Nov	**Wath Brow** (F)	W 22-2	6 (t,2g)
19 Nov	Workington (F)	D 0-0	6
26 Nov	Dalton (NWL)	L 0-3	6
10 Dec	**Askam** (NWL)	W 21-0	6 (3g)
17 Dec	**Brookland R** (F)	D 0-0	6
24 Dec	Ulverston (NWL)	L 0-2	6
26 Dec	Workington (F)	D 0-0	6
31 Dec	**Whitehaven** (F)	W 39-0	6 (t,6g)
2 Jan	Whitehaven (F)	W 3-0	6
7 Jan	Wath Brow (F)	L 0-3	6
14 Jan	**Workington** (NWL)	D 0-0	6
21 Jan	Lancaster (NWL)	D 0-0	6
11 Feb	**Whitehaven Recs** (F)W 14-2		6 (t)
18 Feb	**Dalton** (NWL)	W 9-0	6
25 Feb	**Seaton** (F)	W 3-0	6
4 Mar	**Brookland R** (NUCQ)	W 2-0	6 (g)
11 Mar	Whitehaven (F)	W 22-0	6 (t)
18 Mar	Hunslet (NUC1)	L 2-11	6 (g)
25 Mar	**Barrow** (NWL)	L 0-12	6
29 Mar	Brookland Rovers (F)	W 6-0	6
1 Apr	Seaton (F)	L 5-8	6
8 Apr	Millom (NWL)	L 6-13	6
12 Apr	**Brookland R** (F)	W 16-6	6 (2g)
22 Apr	Barrow (NWL)	L 0-14	6
29 Apr	Whitehaven Recs (F)	W 7-5	6
1899-1900 season:			
13 Sep	**J. Elliott's Team** (F)	L 3-6	6
16 Sep	Whitehaven Rcs (CSL)	W 4-3	6 (g)
23 Sep	Workington (CSL)	L 0-5	6
30 Sep	CUMBERLAND vs Cheshire (at Whitehaven)	W 3-0	6 (t)
7 Oct	**Wath Brow** (CSL)	W 19-0	6
14 Oct	**Whitehaven R** (NWL)	W 9-5	6
21 Oct	CUMBERLAND v Lancashire (Oldham)	L 7-17	7
28 Oct	**Workington** (NWL)	D 0-0	DNP
4 Nov	**Whitehaven** (CSL)	W 29-0	DNP
25 Nov	CUMBERLAND v Yorkshire (Millom)	L 5-7	7
2 Dec	Seaton (CSL)	W 5-2	6 (g)
9 Dec	Whitehaven (CSL)	W 13-2	6
23 Dec	**Seaton** (CSL)	D 0-0	6
25 Dec	Brookland R (CSL)	W 3-0	6
30 Dec	**Whitehaven R** CSL)	W 13-0	6 (t)
1 Jan	**Brookland R** (CSL)	W 4-0	6
6 Jan	**Workington** (CSL)	D 3-3	6 (t)
13 Jan	Aspatria Hornets (F)	W 3-0	6
20 Jan	**Barrow** (NWL)	W 3-0	6 (t)
3 Feb	Seaton (F)	W 8-2	6 (t, g)
17 Feb	Whitehaven R (NWL)	L 3-5	6
24 Feb	**Seaton** (F)W 8-0		6 (2t)
3 Mar	Wath Brow (CSL)	W 12-0	6 (t, g)
17 Mar	Kendal Hornets (NUC1)W 9-0		6
24 Mar	Runcorn (NUC2)	L 0-12	6
31 Mar	**Millom** (NWL)	W 7-0	6
7 Apr	Workington (F)	L 0-3	6
14 Apr	Workington (NWL)	L 2-3	6
21 Apr	Millom (NWL)	L 0-8	6
At Bramley:			
1900-01 season:			
1 Sep	Halifax	L 5-14	6
8 Sep	**Brighouse Rangers**	L 0-5	6
15 Sep	Wakefield Trinity	L 0-10	6
22 Sep	Hunslet	L 5-10	6
29 Sep	**Liversedge**	W 10-0	6 (t,2g)

Date	Opponent	Result	Scorer
6 Oct	Huddersfield	L 2-12	6 (g)
13 Oct	**Holbeck**	W 3-0	6 (t)
20 Oct	Leeds	D 0-0	6
27 Oct	**Batley**	D 0-0	6
3 Nov	**Manningham**	L 6-8	6
10 Nov	**Castleford**	D 2-2	6
17 Nov	Keighley (F)	W 8-2	6 (g)
24 Nov	Hull Kingston Rovers	L 8-13	6 (g)
1 Dec	Hull	L 2-14	6
8 Dec	**Bradford**	W 5-3	6 (t, g)
15 Dec	Halifax	L 0-18	6
22 Dec	Brighouse Rangers	L 6-20	6
24 Dec	**Leeds Parish Church**	W 7-0	6 (2g)
26 Dec	**Wakefield Trinity**	W 7-2	6 (g)
29 Dec	**Hunslet**	W 11-3	6 (g)
5 Jan	Liversedge	L 2-3	DNP
12 Jan	**Huddersfield**	W 5-3	6 (t)
19 Jan	Holbeck	W 5-2	6 (g)
26 Jan	**Leeds**	D 0-0	6
9 Feb	Manningham	W 6-0	6
16 Feb	Castleford	W 7-5	4 (2g)
19 Feb	Leeds Parish Church	D 0-0	6
23 Feb	**York** (F)	D 0-0	4
2 Mar	Rochdale H (NUC1)	W 7-3	6 (2g)
9 Mar	**Oldham** (NUC2)	L 7-10	6 (2g)
12 Mar	Batley	L 0-4	6
16 Mar	**Hull Kingston R**	W 23-0	6 (4g)
6 Apr	**Hull**	W 8-2	6 (g)
8 Apr	Bradford	L 3-10	6

At Salford:

1901-02 season:

Date	Opponent	Result	Scorer
7 Sep	**Brighouse Rangers**	W 16-0	DNP
14 Sep	**South Shields** (F)	W 25-0	DNP
21 Sep	Leigh	L 2-11	7 (g)
28 Sep	Huddersfield	W 11-3	3 (2t,g)
5 Oct	**Bradford**	L 10-14	3 (t,2g)
12 Oct	**Halifax**	W 9-4	6 (3g)
19 Oct	Broughton Rangers	L 2-3	6 (g)
26 Oct	Hull	L 5-14	6
2 Nov	**Batley**	W 14-6	6 (t, g)
9 Nov	Brighouse Rangers	W 24-8	6 (2t,3g)
23 Nov	**Leigh**	W 11-3	6 (t, g)
30 Nov	**Hull**	W 11-5	6 (g)
7 Dec	Halifax	D 0-0	6
14 Dec	Rochdale H (SEL)	D 0-0	DNP
21 Dec	**Swinton**	W 2-0	6 (g)
25 Dec	**Broughton Rangers**	L 0-3	6
26 Dec	**Stockport** (SEL)	W 7-0	6 (2g)
28 Dec	Runcorn	L 2-6	6 (g)
1 Jan	**Hunslet**	L 0-7	DNP
4 Jan	Oldham	D 0-0	6
11 Jan	South Shields (F)	W 13-7	6 (t, g)
18 Jan	Hunslet	W 11-3	6 (t,4g)
25 Jan	**Oldham**	W 6-0	DNP
11 Feb	Bradford	W 2-0	6 (g)
22 Feb	Swinton	L 5-13	6 (g)
25 Feb	Batley	W 11-9	6 (g)
1 Mar	**Warrington**	W 16-6	6 (2t,2g)
3 Mar	**Rochdale H** (SEL)	W 19-3	6 (2t,g)
8 Mar	**Runcorn**	D 0-0	6
15 Mar	**Pontefract** (NUC1)	W 28-2	6 (t,5g)
22 Mar	Dewsbury (NUC2)	W 2-0	6 (g)
28 Mar	Stockport (SEL)	W 8-3	DNP
29 Mar	**Goole** (NUC3)	W 67-0	6(3t,11g)
31 Mar	**Huddersfield**	W 57-0	6 (2t,5g)
5 Apr	Huddersfield (NUC4)	W 9-6	6 (t)
12 Apr	Batley (NUC sf, atOldham)	W 8-0	6 (t, g)
14 Apr	Warrington	W 8-7	6 (g)
26 Apr	Broughton Rangers (NUCf at Rochdale)	L 0-25	6

Date	Opponent	Result	Scorer
29 Apr	SALFORD/SWINTON v Broughton/Oldham (F)	W 20-6	6

1902/03 season:

Date	Opponent	Result	Scorer
6 Sep	**Hunslet**	W 11-7	DNP
13 Sep	Wigan	W 5-0	DNP
20 Sep	**Widnes**	W 5-0	6 (t, g)
27 Sep	Bradford	D 2-2	6 (g)
4 Oct	**Huddersfield**	W 4-0	6 (g)
6 Oct	POSSIBLES v Probables (Lancashire trial, Widnes)	L 7-21	6 (t,2g)
11 Oct	**Warrington**	W 9-5	6 (t)
13 Oct	Brighouse Rangers	L 0-4	6
18 Oct	**Broughton Rangers**	L 0-5	6
25 Oct	St Helens	L 5-9	4 (g)
1 Nov	**Runcorn**	W 10-6	DNP
8 Nov	Batley	L 2-5	6
22 Nov	**Halifax**	W 12-0	4 (3g)
29 Nov	Leigh	W 5-0	4 (t)
6 Dec	**Hull**	D 3-3	DNP
13 Dec	Oldham	W 2-0	4
25 Dec	Broughton Rangers	D 0-0	4
27 Dec	**Hull Kingston Rovers**	W 17-0	4 (3g)
1 Jan	Swinton	D 6-6	4
3 Jan	Hunslet	W 16-2	4 (2t,g)
10 Jan	**Wigan**	L 0-13	DNP
10 Jan	LANCASHIRE v Cumberland (Millom)	W 21-3	7
24 Jan	**Bradford**	W 14-0	4 (t, g)
31 Jan	Huddersfield	W 12-6	4 (t)
5 Feb	Widnes	L 3-7	4
7 Feb	Warrington	W 11-2	6 (g)
21 Feb	**Leigh** (NUC2)	W 11-0	4 (t, g)
24 Feb	**Brighouse Rangers**	W 14-0	4 (t, g)
28 Feb	Runcorn	L 0-4	4
7 Mar	Rochdale H (NUC3)	W 15-0	4 (3t)
14 Mar	**Swinton**	W 10-0	4 (t, g)
16 Mar	**Batley**	W 28-8	4 (2t,g)
21 Mar	York (NUC4)	W 25-2	4 (t, g)
28 Mar	**Leigh**	W 14-0	4 (t, g)
4 Apr	Oldham (NUC sf at Broughton)	D 0-0	4
8 Apr	Oldham (NUC sf replay at Broughton)	W 8-0	4 (t)
11 Apr	**Oldham**	W 3-0	4 \
13 Apr	**St Helens**	W 11-3	DNP
16 Apr	Halifax	D 5-5	4 (t, g)
20 Apr	Hull	L 5-12	4 (g)
25 Apr	Halifax (NUC f at Leeds)	L 0-7	4
27 Apr	Hull Kingston Rovers	L 0-16	4

1903-04 season:

Date	Opponent	Result	Scorer
5 Sep	Batley	W 13-3	3 (2g)
12 Sep	**Keighley**	W 24-2	4 (t,2g)
19 Sep	Broughton Rangers	W 20-6	3 (2t,2g)
26 Sep	**Hunslet**	W 18-2	4 (t,2g)
3 Oct	Widnes	W 13-0	3 (t,2g)
10 Oct	**Swinton**	W 8-0	3 (g)
12 Oct	PROBABLES v Possibles (Lancashire trial, Warrington)	W 31-8	6 (t,2g)
17 Oct	Hull Kingston Rovers	D 7-7	4 (2g)
24 Oct	**Oldham**	L 2-8	4
31 Oct	Halifax	L 3-6	DNP
7 Nov	**Huddersfield**	W 16-3	4 (t,2g)
14 Nov	LANCASHIRE v Yorkshire (Leeds)	W 8-0	6 (g)
21 Nov	**Wigan**	W 5-0	4
28 Nov	Leeds	L 0-6	4
5 Dec	**Runcorn** (abandoned at 5-0)		4 (g)
9 Dec	LANCASHIRE v Durham & Northumberland (S. Shields)	W 42-0	6 (2t,2g)
12 Dec	**Hull**	W 11-0	4 (4g)
19 Dec	Leigh	W 5-0	4 (g)
25 Dec	Bradford	L 0-9	4

Date	Opponent	Result	
26 Dec	**Warrington**	L 3-11	4
28 Dec	**Runcorn**	W 19-0	3 (t, g)
2 Jan	**Batley**	W 39-0	4 (4t,6g)
9 Jan	Keighley	D 2-2	4 (g)
13 Jan	LANCASHIRE v		
	Cumberland (Wigan)	W 15-0	6 (3g)
16 Jan	**Broughton Rangers**	W 5-3	4 (t, g)
23 Jan	Hunslet	L 2-12	6 (g)
30 Jan	**Widnes**	W 17-2	3 (t, g)
6 Feb	Swinton	W 11-0	3 (t, g)
13 Feb	**Hull Kingston Rovers**	W 16-0	3 (t,2g)
20 Feb	Oldham	W 2-0	3 (g)
27 Feb	**Halifax**	W 5-0	3 (g)
5 Mar	Huddersfield	W 21-0	3 (2t,2g)
12 Mar	**Brookland R** (NUC1)	W 57-0	4 (3t,5g)
19 Mar	Hull (NUC2)	W 23-5	3 (t,4g)
26 Mar	**Leeds**	W 12-3	4
28 Mar	**Bradford**	W 4-2	3 (g)
2 Apr	**Hunslet** (NUC3)	L 2-5	3 (g)
4 Apr	Wigan	W 5-2	3 (g)
5 Apr	ENGLAND v Other		
	Nationalities (Wigan)	L 3-9	4
9 Apr	Hull	L 0-7	4
11 Apr	Runcorn	W 11-3	3 (2t)
16 Apr	**Leigh**	W 28-6	2 (t,4g)
23 Apr	Warrington	W 19-3	4 (t,2g)
28 Apr	Bradford (CPO f at Halifax)	L 0-5	3

1904-05 season:

Date	Opponent	Result	
3 Sep	Halifax	W 5-3	4 (t, g)
10 Sep	**Hull**	W 13-7	4 (2g)
17 Sep	Bradford	L 3-11	4 (t)
24 Sep	**Leeds**	L 3-9	3
1 Oct	Runcorn	L 3-10	6
8 Oct	**Oldham**	W 10-3	6 (2g)
12 Oct	PROBABLES v Possibles		
	(Lancashire trial, Wigan)	L 15-17	4 (t,3g)
15 Oct	Wigan	W 10-3	6 (2g)
22 Oct	**Swinton**	L 3-8	6
26 Oct	LANCASHIRE v Cheshire		
	(at Runcorn)	L 0-3	3
29 Oct	St Helens	L 11-13	4 (4g)
5 Nov	**Hull Kingston R**	W 15-4	3 (2g)
12 Nov	Batley	W 7-3	DNP
12 Nov	LANCASHIRE v		
	Yorkshire (Oldham)	L 5-14	6
19 Nov	**Hunslet**	W 12-6	3 (t,3g)
3 Dec	Broughton Rangers	L 5-20	4 (g)
10 Dec	**Warrington**	W 5-0	2 (t, g)
17 Dec	Wakefield Trinity	W 10-0	2 (t, g)
24 Dec	**Leigh**	L 6-11	2 (2t)
31 Dec	**Halifax**	W 7-3	2 (t, g)
2 Jan	Widnes	L 0-2	DNP
2 Jan	ENGLAND v Other		
	Nationalities (Bradford)	W 26-11	7 (t)
7 Jan	Hull	L 0-18	4
14 Jan	**Bradford**	L 3-14	DNP
21 Jan	Leeds	L 10-15	3 (t,2g)
28 Jan	**Runcorn**	W 8-0	4 (2t,g)
4 Feb	Oldham	D 0-0	2
11 Feb	**Wigan**	W 14-2	2 (t, g)
18 Feb	Swinton	W 8-3	4 (t, g)
25 Feb	**St Helens**	W 19-2	3 (t,2g)
4 Mar	Keighley (NUC1)	L 0-8	3
11 Mar	**Batley**	D 0-0	3
25 Mar	**Widnes**	W 23-2	5 (3t,4g)
8 Apr	Warrington	L 0-5	4
15 Apr	**Wakefield Trinity**	W 21-0	4 (t,2g)
21 Apr	**Broughton Rangers**	W 7-0	3 (g)
22 Apr	Leigh	W 16-2	DNP
25 Apr	Hunslet	W 16-11	4 (2t,2g)
26 Apr	Hull Kingston Rovers	L 3-14	4

1905-06 season:

Date	Opponent	Result	
2 Sep	**Hull**	W 12-3	3 (t)

Date	Opponent	Result	
9 Sep	Swinton	W 8-0	3 (t, g)
16 Sep	**Batley**	W 21-6	3 (3g)
23 Sep	Leigh	L 5-8	3 (g)
27 Sep	PROBABLES v Possibles		
	(Lancashire trial, Broughton)	W 31-15	4 (2g)
30 Sep	**St Helens**	W 25-5	3 (2t,3g)
7 Oct	Runcorn	L 3-4	DNP
7 Oct	LANCASHIRE v		
	Cumberland (Wigan)	D 3-3	3
14 Oct	**Swinton** (LC1)	W 3-0	5
21 Oct	Rochdale Hornets	W 19-0	3 (t,2g)
28 Oct	**Oldham** (LC2)	L 0-10	3
4 Nov	**Hull Kingston Rovers**	L 5-8	DNP
4 Nov	LANCASHIRE v		
	Yorkshire (Hull)	W 8-0	3
11 Nov	**Oldham**	W 2-0	3 (g)
18 Nov	Leeds (F) (abandoned at 0-5)		4
25 Nov	Barrow	W 26-5	3 (t,4g)
2 Dec	Hull Kingston Rovers	L 10-13	3 (t,2g)
9 Dec	**Widnes**	W 25-3	3 (2t,2g)
16 Dec	Batley	W 13-2	3 (2t,2g)
23 Dec	**Swinton**	W 10-0	3 (2g)
25 Dec	Broughton Rangers	L 5-11	3 (t, g)
26 Dec	Warrington	W 5-4	3 (g)
30 Dec	**Bradford**	W 13-0	3 (t,2g)
1 Jan	Leigh	L 0-9	DNP
1 Jan	ENGLAND v Other		
	Nationalities (Wigan)	D 3-3	4 (t)
6 Jan	Wigan	D 0-0	3
13 Jan	**Broughton Rangers**	D 0-0	4
20 Jan	Hunslet	L 5-9	3 (t, g)
27 Jan	**Warrington**	L 6-8	4 (2t)
3 Feb	**Rochdale Hornets**	W 8-0	DNP
10 Feb	Oldham	D 0-0	5
17 Feb	Swinton (F at Liverpool)	L 6-8	4
21 Feb	LANCASHIRE v		
	Cumberland (Wigan)	D 3-3	3
24 Feb	Hull	L 2-13	5
3 Mar	Rochdale H (NUC1)	W 6-0	4 (t)
10 Mar	Halifax	L 5-10	5 (g)
14 Mar	**Wigan**	L 6-8	5
17 Mar	**Egerton** (NUC2)	W 38-5	5 (3t,4g)
24 Mar	Bradford	L 0-33	DNP
31 Mar	**Broughton R** (NUC3)	D 2-2	4 (g)
4 Apr	Broughton R (NUC3 replay)	D 3-3	3
6 Apr	Broughton R		
	(NUC3 2nd replay, Wigan)	W 5-3	DNP
7 Apr	Barrow	L 0-24	DNP
14 Apr	Keighley		
	(NUC sf, Warrington)	W 6-3	3
16 Apr	**Runcorn**	L 0-33	DNP
19 Apr	Widnes	L 0-11	DNP
21 Apr	**Halifax**	W 21-3	DNP
23 Apr	**Hunslet**	L 12-26	DNP
28 Apr	Bradford (NUC f, Leeds)	L 0-5	3
30 Apr	St Helens	L 0-11	4

1906-07 season:

Date	Opponent	Result	
1 Sep	**Batley**	W 12-7	4 (t.3g)
8 Sep	Liverpool City	W 28-3	4 (t,4g)
15 Sep	**Leeds**	W 22-4	4 (5g)
22 Sep	Hunslet	L 5-17	4 (g)
29 Sep	Bradford	L 5-35	4 (t, g)
6 Oct	Warrington	L 3-33	DNP
6 Oct	CUMBERLAND v		
	Lancashire (Maryport)	L 4-15	3 (2g)
3 Oct	**Wigan** (LC1)	W 12-3	4 (3g)
20 Oct	Broughton Rangers	L 3-26	3
27 Oct	**Runcorn** (LC2)	L 2-3	4 (g)
31 Oct	**Warrington**	W 8-5	4 (2t,g)
3 Nov	Runcorn	L 2-17	DNP
10 Nov	**St Helens**	W 26-13	4 (4g)
17 Nov	**Leigh**	W 17-8	4 (4g)
24 Nov	Oldham	(abandoned at 7-0)	4 (2g)

257

1 Dec	**Wigan**	W 7-2	4 (2g)		12 Sep	Oldham	L 5-20	3
3 Dec	Oldham	L 6-10	4		19 Sep	**Wigan**	L 7-36	3 (t,2g)
8 Dec	**Bradford**	W 16-0	4 (t,2g)		26 Sep	Broughton Rangers	W 14-5	6 (t,3g)
15 Dec	Barrow	L 5-11	4 (t, g)		3 Oct	**Warrington**	W 14-7	DNP
22 Dec	Swinton	L 6-15	4 (3g)		3 Oct	CUMBERLAND v		
25 Dec	**Broughton Rangers**	W 7-5	4 (t,2g)			Lancashire (Workington)	L 8-15	4 (t, g)
26 Dec	Leeds	L 6-14	4 (2t)		10 Oct	Widnes	W 15-2	4 (g)
1 Jan	**Hunslet**	L 10-11	4 (g)		17 Oct	**Australia** (tour)	D 9-9	DNP
5 Jan	Swinton	W 27-0	4 (4t,3g)		24 Oct	Rochdale Hornets	W 13-2	6 (2g)
12 Jan	Oldham	W 17-15	DNP		31 Oct	St Helens	W 13-8	3 (2g)
12 Jan	CUMBERLAND v				7 Nov	Oldham (LC1)	L 5-20	6 (t, g)
	Yorkshire (Huddersfield)	L 12-15	3 (2t,2g)		14 Nov	**Leeds**	W 20-2	6 (3t,3g)
16 Jan	Leigh	W 22-4	4 (t,2g)		18 Nov	**Halifax**	L 8-11	6 (t, g)
19 Jan	Halifax	L 9-11	4 (3g)		21 Nov	Broughton Rangers (F)	21-24	6 (3g)
2 Feb	**Liverpool City**	W 78-0	4 (5t,12g)		28 Nov	Wigan	L 2-5	6 (g)
9 Feb	Batley	W 11-7	4 (2g)		5 Dec	**Swinton**	W 17-0	6 (t,4g)
13 Feb	**Barrow**	W 49-0	4 (4t,5g)		12 Dec	Runcorn	L 4-16	6 (2g)
16 Feb	**Wakefield Trinity**	W 26-2	4 (2t,4g)		16 Dec	**Hunslet**	W 17-6	6 (g)
23 Feb	**Halifax**	W 9-5	4 (3g)		19 Dec	**St Helens**	W 15-14	6 (t,3g)
2 Mar	Wigan	L 5-10	4		25 Dec	**Broughton Rangers**	W 19-10	6 (t,3g)
16 Mar	**Leigh** (NUC1)	W 10-5	DNP		26 Dec	Leigh	L 3-5	6
23 Mar	**Wigan** (NUC2)	W 18-5	4 (3t,3g)		28 Dec	ENGLAND v Wales (Broughton)	W 31-7	3 (t,5g)
29 Mar	**Runcorn**	W 5-0	4 (g)		2 Jan	Barrow	W 16-6	DNP
30 Mar	**Leeds** (NUC3)	W 12-3	4 (t,2g)		2 Jan	ENGLAND v Australia		
1 Apr	St Helens	L 5-30	4 (t, g)			(Huddersfield)	W 14-9	3 (g)
6 Apr	Wakefield Trinity	L 5-29	4 (g)		9 Jan	**Rochdale Hornets**	W 18-3	3 (2t,3g)
13 Apr	Oldham (NUC sf, Rochdale)	L 0-6	4		16 Jan	Leigh	W 27-5	6 (t,3g)
1907-08 season:					23 Jan	NORTHERN UNION v Australia		
7 Sep	**Rochdale Hornets**	W 12-8	4 (3g)			(2nd test, Newcastle)	W 15-5	4 (t,3g)
9 Sep	Halifax	L 7-12	4 (2g)		30 Jan	**Widnes**	W 14-8	6 (t, g)
14 Sep	Ebbw Vale	W 29-0	4 (3t,4g)		3 Feb	ENGLAND v Australia (Glasgow)	D 17-17	3 (4g)
21 Sep	**St Helens**	W 21-2	4 (t,3g)		4 Feb	CUMBERLAND v Australia		
28 Sep	Leeds	L 2-23	4 (g)			(Carlisle)	W 11-2	4 (t, g)
5 Oct	**Leigh**	W 16-8	DNP		6 Feb	Wakefield Trinity	W 10-7	6 (t,2g)
5 Oct	CUMBERLAND v				8 Feb	Ebbw Vale	W 20-6	6 (t,4g)
	Lancashire (Broughton)	W 7-3	6 (g)		13 Feb	**Barrow**	W 29-2	6 (t,4g)
12 Oct	Hunslet	D 12-12	6 (3g)		15 Feb	NORTHERN UNION v Australia		
19 Oct	Barrow	L 2-6	DNP			(3rd test, Birmingham)	W 6-5	4
19 Oct	CUMBERLAND v				20 Feb	Leeds	L 7-13	6 (2g)
	Yorkshire (Whitehaven)	W 7-3	6		27 Feb	**Dewsbury** (NUC1)	W 28-0	6 (2t,5g)
26 Oct	**Wigan** (LC2)	W 10-8	4 (2g)		3 Mar	ENGLAND v Australia		
2 Nov	**Warrington**	D 8-8	DNP			(Liverpool)	W 14-7	3 (3g)
9 Nov	**Broughton Rangers**	W 8-5	4 (g)		6 Mar	Swinton	W 11-6	DNP
16 Nov	**Oldham** (LC sf)	L 7-8	4 (t,2g)		13 Mar	Broughton R (NUC2)	W 4-0	6 (2g)
23 Nov	Wigan	L 10-13	4 (t,2g)		17 Mar	**Ebbw Vale**	W 19-14	3 (3t,2g)
7 Dec	St Helens	W 18-0	4 (2t,3g)		20 Mar	Halifax	L 2-22	3 (g)
11 Dec	**Widnes**	W 26-0	4 (g)		27 Mar	**Halifax** (NUC3)	L 7-12	6
14 Dec	**Swinton**	W 11-0	4 (g)		3 Apr	Hunslet	L 8-16	6 (t, g)
21 Dec	Oldham	L 5-6	DNP		9 Apr	**Wakefield Trinity**	W 53-0	6 (2t,6g)
25 Dec	Broughton Rangers	L 10-14	4 (2g)		10 Apr	Warrington	D 15-15	6 (2t,3g)
26 Dec	**Leeds**	W 20-2	4 (2t,g)		12 Apr	**Oldham**	L 13-19	6 (g)
28 Dec	**New Zealand** (tour)	L 2-9	4 (g)		13 Apr	Merthyr Tydfil (F)	D 8-8	6 (t)
1 Jan	**Wakefield Trinity**	W 18-12	4 (3g)		*1909-10 season:*			
11 Jan	**Ebbw Vale**	W 15-2	DNP		4 Sep	Runcorn	L 5-13	6 (t, g)
11 Jan	ENGLAND v New				11 Sep	**Oldham**	W 9-8	6 (3g)
	Zealand (Wigan)	W 18-16	4 (t, g)		18 Sep	Wigan	L 11-22	6 (2t,g)
15 Jan	Runcorn	W 14-6	4 (t, g)		25 Sep	**Broughton Rangers**	W 20-7	6 (3g)
18 Jan	Widnes	W 8-5	4 (g)		2 Oct	Warrington	L 5-8	6 (g)
25 Jan	**Hunslet**	W 7-6	4 (2g)		4 Oct	CUMBERLAND v Lancashire		
1 Feb	**Runcorn**	W 12-0	4 (3t)			(Barrow)	W 8-3	3
3 Feb	Warrington	D 0-0	4		9 Oct	**Hunslet**	W 17-12	6 (4g)
8 Feb	Swinton	W 2-0	4 (g)		23 Oct	**Widnes**	W 11-5	DNP
15 Feb	Leigh	W 13-5	4 (t,2g)		23 Oct	CUMBERLAND v Yorkshire		
22 Feb	**Oldham**	W 5-0	4 (g)			(Maryport) (abandoned at 3-5)		3
29 Feb	**Widnes** (NUC1)	W 15-2	4 (3g)		30 Oct	Leigh (LC2)	L 6-13	6 (2g)
7 Mar	**Halifax**	L 10-11	4 (2g)		6 Nov	**Barrow**	W 25-6	DNP
14 Mar	Hull (NUC2)	L 9-15	4 (3g)		13 Nov	Hull Kingston Rovers	W 3-2	DNP
21 Mar	Wigan	L 0-2	4		18 Nov	Treherbert	W 19-2	3 (2t,2g)
4 Apr	Rochdale Hornets	L 5-6	DNP		20 Nov	**York**	W 27-10	3 (3g)
6 Apr	**Barrow**	W 15-2	DNP		27 Nov	Swinton	W 11-3	3 (g)
11 Apr	Wakefield Trinity	L 3-11	4 (t)		4 Dec	**Leigh**	W 23-8	DNP
1908-09 season:					4 Dec	ENGLAND v Wales		
5 Sep	**Runcorn**	L 7-18	3 (t,2g)			(Wakefield)	W 19-13	3 (t,2g)

Date	Opponent	Result	Pts
11 Dec	St Helens	L 3-7	5
18 Dec	**Runcorn**	W 20-0	5 (t,4g)
25 Dec	Broughton Rangers	W 10-5	3 (2g)
27 Dec	**Swinton**	W 10-3	3 (t,2g)
1 Jan	Barrow	W 15-0	7 (t,2g)
8 Jan	**St Helens**	W 24-5	7 (3g)
15 Jan	**Warrington**	W 8-0	3 (2t,g)
5 Feb	Rochdale Hornets	W 8-3	3 (t, g)
12 Feb	**Halifax**	W 12-8	3 (2t,3g)
16 Feb	**Wigan**	L 2-12	3 (g)
19 Feb	Leigh	W 14-8	3 (t, g)
26 Feb	**York Irish NL** (NUC1)	W 64-0	4 (4t,3g)
5 Mar	Oldham	D 3-3	7
12 Mar	**Wigan** (NUC2)	W 12-5	6 (3g)
14 Mar	FIRST SELECTED v Yorkshire Probables (tour trial at Leeds)	W 27-16	3 (2t,g)
16 Mar	Widnes	L 0-8	4
19 Mar	**Ebbw Vale** (NUC3)	W 8-2	3 (g)
25 Mar	York	W 21-17	3 (t,3g)
26 Mar	**Hull Kingston Rovers**	W 19-11	3 (2t,2g)
28 Mar	**Rochdale Hornets**	W 23-12	DNP
2 Apr	Hull (NUC sf, Wakefield)	L 6-20	6 (g)
4 Apr	Halifax	W 6-0	4 (3g)
9 Apr	Hunslet	W 3-2	DNP
9 Apr	ENGLAND v Wales (Ebbw Vale)	L 18-39	3 (t,2g)
16 Apr	**Wigan** (CPO sf)	L 6-17	4 (2t)

1910 Northern Union tour:

In Australia:

Date	Opponent	Result	Pts
4 Jun	New South Wales (Sydney)	L 14-28	3 (3g)
6 Jun	New South Wales (Sydney)	L 20-27	3 (2t,3g)
11 Jun	New South Wales (Sydney)	W 23-10	3 (2t,5g)
15 Jun	The Metropolis (Sydney)	W 34-25	DNP
18 Jun	Australia (1st test, Sydney)	W 27-20	3 (3g)
18 Jun	Newcastle & District (Newcastle)	W 24-8	DNP
22 Jun	Newcastle & District (Newcastle)	W 40-20	4 (t,5g)
25 Jun	Queensland (Brisbane)	W 33-9	3 (t,3g)
27 Jun	Kangaroos (Sydney)	L 10-22	3 (2g)
29 Jun	Queensland (Brisbane)	W 15-4	DNP
2 Jul	Australia (2nd test Brisbane)	W 22-17	3 (2g)
9 Jul	Australasia (Sydney)	D 13-13	3 (g)
13 Jul	Australasia (Sydney)	L 15-32	DNP

In New Zealand:

Date	Opponent	Result	Pts
20 July	Maoris (Auckland)	W 29-0	3 (t,4g)
23 Jul	Auckland (Auckland)	W 52-9	3 (t,7g)
27 Jul	Rotorua (Rotorua)	W 54-18	DNP
30 Jul	New Zealand (Test at Auckland)	W 52-20	3 (t,6g)

In Australia:

Date	Opponent	Result	Pts
6 Aug	New South Wales (Sydney)	W 50-12	3 (t,9g)

At Salford (continued):

1910-11 season:

Date	Opponent	Result	Pts
3 Sep	**Merthyr Tydfil**	W 34-2	DNP
10 Sep	Halifax	L 8-29	DNP
17 Sep	St Helens	L 14-19	DNP
17 Sep	ENGLAND v Wales and the West (at Plymouth)	L 25-27	3 (3t,g)
19 Sep	TOURISTS vs Colonials (at Leeds)	L 15-31	3 (t,3g)
24 Sep	**Broughton Rangers**	L 6-11	3
1 Oct	Hunslet	W 18-12	3 (t,2g)
8 Oct	**Leigh**	W 18-8	3 (t)
15 Oct	Widnes	L 2-15	3
22 Oct	**Coventry**	W 37-10	DNP
29 Oct	Oldham	L 2-20	3 (g)
5 Nov	Warrington (LC2)	L 5-14	3 (g)
12 Nov	Swinton	L 3-14	3
26 Nov	**Warrington**	D 3-3	3
30 Nov	**Hull Kingston Rovers**	L 5-9	DNP
3 Dec	Merthyr Tydfil	L 2-7	DNP
10 Dec	**Runcorn**	W 19-8	DNP
17 Dec	Rochdale Hornets	L 3-15	DNP
24 Dec	Broughton Rangers	W 3-2	DNP
26 Dec	Coventry	L 5-14	DNP
27 Dec	**Swinton**	W 11-5	DNP
31 Dec	**Barrow**	W 19-9	3 (t, g)
7 Jan	Wigan	L 0-17	DNP
14 Jan	**Hunslet**	W 16-8	DNP
28 Jan	Runcorn	W 16-3	DNP

At Oldham:

1910-11 season:

Date	Opponent	Result	Pts
4 Feb	Salford	W 16-11	4
11 Feb	**Runcorn**	W 21-10	4 (2t)
18 Feb	Hull Kingston R (NUC1)	W 9-7	4 (t)
25 Feb	**Rochdale Hornets**	W 9-0	4 (t)
4 Mar	**Wakefield T** (NUC2)	W 11-3	4 (2t)
11 Mar	**Barrow**	W 12-0	4
18 Mar	**Rochdale H** (NUC3)	D 8-8	4 (t)
21 Mar	Rochdale H (NUC3 replay)	L 3-4	4 (t)
23 Mar	Coventry	W 7-0	4
25 Mar	**Leigh**	W 15-0	4 (2g)
29 Mar	Wigan	L 5-11	4
1 Apr	Swinton	W 16-13	DNP
1 Apr	ENGLAND v Wales (Ebbw Vale)	W 27-8	3 (2g)
8 Apr	**Leeds**	W 11-5	4 (t)
15 Apr	Ebbw Vale	W 5-0	4 (g)
17 Apr	Broughton Rangers	L 0-5	4
19 Apr	Wigan (CPO for 1st place at Wakefield)	L 3-11	5
22 Apr	**Wakefield T** (CPO sf)	W 15-12	4 (2t)
6 May	Wigan (CPO f, Broughton)	W 20-7	4 (2t,3g)

1911-12 season:

Date	Opponent	Result	Pts
2 Sep	Hull Kingston Rovers	L 6-22	3
9 Sep	Leigh	W 15-12	3 (2g)
12 Sep	Bradford Northern	W 22-12	3 (t,2g)
16 Sep	**Leeds**	W 27-9	3 (t, g)
23 Sep	Huddersfield	L 2-24	3 (g)
30 Sep	**Rochdale Hornets**	W 24-6	3 (g)
7 Oct	Broughton Rangers	L 5-18	3
9 Oct	CUMBERLAND v Lancashire (Warrington)	W 28-7	3 (t, g)
14 Oct	**Halifax**	D 10-10	3
18 Oct	ENGLAND v Australia (Fulham)	L 6-11	3
21 Oct	Barrow (LC1)	W 13-2	3 (2g)
28 Oct	**Swinton**	W 36-8	4 (2t)
4 Nov	**Leigh** (LC2)	W 23-0	4 (t)
8 Nov	Runcorn	W 14-5	4 (g)
11 Nov	**Australia** (tour)	W 14-8	4
18 Nov	Wigan (LC sf)	W 3-0	4
22 Nov	CUMBERLAND v Australia (Maryport)	L 2-5	7
25 Nov	**Widnes**	L 2-7	DNP
2 Dec	Rochdale Hornets (LC f, Broughton)	L 5-12	4
6 Dec	ENGLAND v Australia (Nottingham)	W 5-3	3 (g)
7 Dec	St Helens	L 11-21	6 (t)
9 Dec	**Broughton Rangers**	W 16-5	DNP
11 Dec	Barrow	W 4-3	6
16 Dec	Wigan	L 0-15	DNP
16 Dec	NORTHERN UNION v Australia (2nd test at Edinburgh)	D 11-11	3 (t)
23 Dec	**Leigh**	W 20-0	6
25 Dec	**Hull Kingston Rovers**	W 37-7	6 (2t,g)
26 Dec	**Bradford Northern**	W 21-3	6 (2t,g)
30 Dec	**St Helens**	W 35-5	6 (2t)
1 Jan	**Coventry**	W 31-10	DNP
1 Jan	NORTHERN UNION v Australia		

Date	Opponent	Result	Pts
	(3rd test at Birmingham)	L 8-33	4 (t)
6 Jan	Salford	W 8-0	DNP
13 Jan	**Warrington**	W 30-10	6 (2t)
27 Jan	**Barrow**	W 40-5	6 (4g)
10 Feb	Leeds	L 3-14	6
17 Feb	Coventry (NUC1)	W 21-3	6
24 Feb	**Huddersfield**	W 6-2	6
2 Mar	**Wigan** (NUC2)	W 12-8	6
9 Mar	**Wigan**	L 2-8	6
13 Mar	Widnes	W 12-11	6 (t)
16 Mar	Rochdale Hornets	L 3-11	6 (t)
23 Mar	**Huddersfield** (NUC3)	W 2-0	6
27 Mar	Swinton	W 14-10	6
30 Mar	**Runcorn**	W 60-0	6 (t,6g)
1 Apr	Warrington	W 11-7	6 (g)
5 Apr	Halifax	L 3-5	6 (t)
6 Apr	**Salford**	W 9-5	6 (t)
8 Apr	Coventry	W 23-9	DNP
13 Apr	Wakefield Trinity		
	(NUC sf, Broughton)	W 17-0	6 (t)
27 Apr	Dewsbury (NUC f, Leeds)	L 5-8	6
11 May	Huddersfield (F at Plymouth)	L 26-31	6

1912-13 season:

Date	Opponent	Result	Pts
7 Sep	**Dewsbury**	L 5-12	3
14 Sep	Hull Kingston Rovers	W 14-4	3
21 Sep	Leeds	L 2-16	3
28 Sep	**St Helens**	D 10-10	DNP
5 Oct	Rochdale Hornets	W 13-10	DNP
12 Oct	**Swinton**	L 6-10	5
19 Oct	Runcorn (LC1)	W 13-7	7
26 Oct	**Wigan**	L 3-7	DNP
2 Nov	Wigan (LC2)	L 8-24	7 (g)
9 Nov	**Runcorn**	W 47-10	3 (t)
23 Nov	**Salford**	W 11-5	3
5 Dec	CUMBERLAND v Yorkshire (Hull)	L 5-19	3
7 Dec	**Barrow**	W 37-5	3 (t)
14 Dec	Halifax	W 10-3	3
21 Dec	Wigan	L 6-29	3
25 Dec	**Hull Kingston Rovers**	W 13-8	3 (t)
26 Dec	**Warrington**	W 5-0	3
28 Dec	Broughton Rangers	L 3-5	3
1 Jan	Dewsbury	L 3-15	3
4 Jan	**Halifax**	W 25-3	DNP
18 Jan	**Widnes**	W 11-10	1
25 Jan	Huddersfield	W 10-6	DNP
1 Feb	**Rochdale Hornets**	W 12-5	DNP
8 Feb	**Leeds**	W 21-8	DNP
12 Feb	Runcorn (abandoned at 7-11)		7
15 Feb	Widnes	L 0-16	4
22 Feb	**Leigh**	W 13-7	7 (2g)
1 Mar	St Helens	L 2-10	6 (g)
8 Mar	Normanton St John's (NUC1)	W 17-4	3 (2t)
15 Mar	Dewsbury (NUC2)	L 2-10	3
21 Mar	Warrington	W 5-3	DNP
22 Mar	**Huddersfield**	L 0-5	DNP
24 Mar	**Broughton Rangers**	L 8-13	DNP
29 Mar	Swinton	W 23-10	DNP
2 Apr	Runcorn	L 5-7	4 (g)
5 Apr	Barrow	D 5-5	4 (g)
7 Apr	Salford	L 5-16	6 (g)
12 Apr	Leigh	W 8-0	6 (g)

At York:

1913-14 season:

Date	Opponent	Result	Pts
4 Sep	Hull	L 3-34	3 (t)
6 Sep	**Huddersfield**	L 14-54	3 (4g)
20 Sep	**Hull Kingston Rovers**	L 11-14	3 (4g)
27 Sep	Wakefield Trinity	L 7-8	DNP
4 Oct	**Bramley**	L 4-12	DNP
11 Oct	Keighley	L 6-10	DNP
18 Oct	**Runcorn**	L 0-16	4
25 Oct	Runcorn	L 0-6	DNP
1 Nov	**Bradford N** (YC2)	L 4-9	DNP
8 Nov	**Hull**	L 0-28	DNP
15 Nov	Rochdale Hornets	L 3-51	DNP
22 Nov	Hull Kingston Rovers	L 16-24	DNP
6 Dec	Bramley	W 11-3	DNP
13 Dec	Batley	L 5-43	DNP
17 Dec	**Bradford Northern**	W 8-5	DNP
20 Dec	**Wakefield Trinity**	L 5-7	4
25 Dec	**Barrow**	W 13-10	4
26 Dec	Halifax	L 10-36	4 (g)
27 Dec	Swinton	L 0-19	4
3 Jan	**Dewsbury**	L 0-16	4
10 Jan	Huddersfield	L 9-39	4 (t,3g)
17 Jan	Leigh	L 5-8	4
24 Jan	**Keighley**	W 15-2	4 (g)
28 Jan	**Leeds**	L 11-13	4 (t, g)
31 Jan	**Rochdale Hornets**	L 2-3	4
7 Feb	**Hunslet**	L 8-52	4 (t, g)
14 Feb	Bradford Northern	L 5-22	3 (g)
28 Feb	**Glasson Rangers** (NUC1)	W 45-0	3 (3t)
5 Mar	Barrow	L 5-20	3
7 Mar	**Halifax**	W 5-3	3
14 Mar	Broughton R (NUC2)	L 4-24	3 (g)
21 Mar	Hunslet	L 5-54	DNP
28 Mar	**Swinton**	L 12-13	DNP
10 Apr	**Batley**	W 17-0	DNP
11 Apr	Dewsbury	L 13-24	DNP
18 Apr	**Leigh**	L 3-12	DNP
29 Apr	Leeds	L 6-27	DNP

1914-15 season:

Date	Opponent	Result	Pts
12 Sep	**Hull**	L 5-13	DNP
19 Sep	Bramley	L 3-8	DNP
26 Sep	**Huddersfield**	D 7-7	3 (2g)
3 Oct	Hunslet	L 12-20	3 (2t,3g)
10 Oct	**Wakefield Trinity**	W 7-2	3 (2g)
17 Oct	**Huddersfield** (YC1)	L 13-24	3 (g)
24 Oct	Runcorn	D 10-10	3 (2t,2g)
4 Nov	**Batley**	L 5-24	3 (t, g)
7 Nov	Widnes	L 8-30	6 (g)
14 Nov	**Halifax**	L 7-18	3 (t,2g)
21 Nov	Hull Kingston Rovers	L 0-40	3
28 Nov	**Bradford Northern**	W 21-3	3 (t,3g)
5 Dec	Dewsbury	L 11-25	3 (t, g)
12 Dec	Leeds	L 0-36	3
19 Dec	**Widnes**	L 2-11	3 (g)
26 Dec	**Leigh**	L 12-13	3 (t,3g)
1 Jan	Leigh	L 0-3	3
2 Jan	Swinton	L 7-9	3 (2g)
9 Jan	**Hunslet**	W 7-3	3 (2g)
16 Jan	Keighley	L 2-6	3
23 Jan	Wakefield Trinity	L 2-11	3 (g)
30 Jan	**Leeds**	L 6-23	3 (3g)
6 Feb	Halifax	L 7-11	3 (2g)
13 Feb	**Dewsbury**	W 10-4	3 (2g)
20 Feb	Hull	L 7-16	6 (g)
27 Feb	**Rochdale H** (NUC1)	D 0-0	4
2 Mar	Rochdale H (NUC1 replay)	L 2-19	4 (g)
6 Mar	**Runcorn**	W 31-3	4 (3t,g)
20 Mar	**Hull Kingston Rovers**	W 9-0	3 (3g)
27 Mar	Batley	L 3-10	3 (t)
2 Apr	**Bramley**	W 10-5	DNP
5 Apr	**Swinton**	W 12-4	4 (3g)
6 Apr	Huddersfield	L 11-30	4 (3g)
17 Apr	**Keighley**	W 18-3	4 (3g)
24 Apr	Bradford Northern	L 9-21	6 (t,2g)

At Salford:
1916-17 season:

Date	Opponent	Result	Pts
6 Apr	Warrington (F)	L 5-17	4
7 Apr	**St Helens Recs** (F)	L 0-14	3
28 Apr	**Broughton R** (F)	W 20-5	3 (2t,g)

At York:
1918-19 season:

Date	Opponent	Result	Pts
26 Apr	**Bramley** (YC2)	L 0-2	4

At Salford:

1922-23 season:

24 Feb	**St Helens**	W 11-3	7 (g)	
3 Mar	**Wakefield T** (RLC2)	W 6-0	7	
10 Mar	**Wigan**	D 0-0	7	
17 Mar	**Hull** (RLC3)	L 0-24	7	

22 Mar	Widnes	L 5-12	7 (g)	
24 Mar	Hunslet	L 2-41	7	

1923-24 season:

22 Sep	**Widnes**	W 19-6	3 (4g)	
29 Sep	Wakefield Trinity	L 3-26	3	

3. Chronological honours list

Season	Team	Competition	Status
1899-1900	Maryport	Cumberland Senior League	Winners
1901-02	Salford	Northern Rugby League	Runners-up
	Salford	Northern Union Challenge Cup	Runners-up
1902-03	Lancashire County Championship		Winners
	Salford	Northern Union Challenge Cup	Runners-up
	Salford	Northern Rugby League	Runners-up
1903-04	Lancashire County Championship		Winners
	Salford	Northern Rugby League	Runners-up
1905-06	Lancashire County Championship		Winners (shared)
	Salford	Northern Union Challenge Cup	Runners-up
1907-08	Cumberland	County Championship	Winners
1909-10	Cumberland	County Championship	Winners (shared)
1910-11	Oldham	Northern Rugby League	Winners
	Oldham	Lancashire League	Runners-up
1911-12	Oldham	Lancashire Cup	Runners-up
	Oldham	Lancashire League	Runners-up
	Oldham	Northern Union Challenge Cup	Runners-up
	Cumberland	County Championship	Winners

4. Representative matches missed after being selected.

Date	Team	Opposition	Venue	Reason
28 Oct 1903	Lancashire	Cheshire	Broughton	leg injury
16 Jan 1905	Lancashire	Cumberland	Whitehaven	bereavement
8 Jan 1908	Cumberland	New Zealand	Workington	late withdrawal*
17 Oct 1908	Cumberland	Yorkshire	Huddersfield	late withdrawal*
25 Oct 1910	Cumberland	Yorkshire	Dewsbury	knee strain
24 Nov 1910	Cumberland	Lancashire	Workington	knee strain
10 Dec 1910	England	Wales	Coventry	knee strain
27 Dec 1910	Tourists	Colonials	Wigan	knee strain
9 Dec 1911	Cumberland	Yorkshire	Millom	ankle injury
20 Jan 1912	England	Wales	Oldham	shoulder injury
28 Sep 1912	Cumberland	Lancashire	Workington	damaged ribs
29 Sep 1913	Cumberland	Yorkshire	Broughton	leg injury
11 Oct 1913	Cumberland	Yorkshire	Workington	leg injury

(*no specific reason reported)

Note: He was selected for the Lancashire Probables versus Possibles trial at Broughton on 26 September 1906 but declined in favour of representing Cumberland. He was also chosen for England versus Other Nationalities at Leeds on 1 January 1907, a match that was called off due to bad weather and not subsequently rearranged.

5. Scoring corrections

Research undertaken for this book has highlighted several scoring differences compared to those of previous publications. Mostly those publications would have based their information on the excellent work of the former Rugby League Record Keepers' Club (RLRKC). Listed below are the scoring adjustments subsequently made for this book compared to those originally published by the RLRKC.

26 Oct 1901 Salford (v Hull) 1 goal subtracted
25 Feb 1902 Salford (v Batley) 1 try subtracted
31 Mar 1902 Salford (v Huddersfield) 1 try subtracted
3 Jan 1903 Salford (v Hunslet) 1 goal subtracted
21 Feb 1903 Salford (v Leigh) 1 goal subtracted
2 Jan 1904 Salford (v Batley) 1 try subtracted
12 Mar 1904 Salford (v Brookland Rovers) 1 try subtracted, 1 goal subtracted
5 Nov 1904 Salford (v Hull Kingston Rovers) 1 goal subtracted
24 Dec 1904 Salford (v Leigh) 2 tries added, 3 goals Subtracted
16 Sep 1905 Salford (v Batley) 3 goals added
13 Oct 1906 Salford (v Wigan) 1 try subtracted
24 Nov 1906 Salford (v Oldham) 1 try subtracted
1 Jan 1907 Salford (v Hunslet) 1 goal subtracted
13 Feb 1907 Salford (v Barrow) 1 try added

25 Dec 1908 Salford (v Broughton Rangers) 1 goal subtracted
16 Jan 1909 Salford (v Leigh) 2 goals added
9 Oct 1909 Salford (v Hunslet) 4 goals added
30 Oct 1909 Salford (v Leigh) 1 goal added
18 Nov 1909 Salford (v Treherbert) 1 try added
4 Jun 1910 NU (v New South Wales) 1 goal subtracted
18 Jun 1910 NU (v Australia) 2 goals added
6 Aug 1910 NU (v New South Wales) 1goal subtracted
1 Oct 1910 Salford (v Hunslet) 1 goal subtracted
6 May 1911 Oldham (v Wigan) 1 goal subtracted
30 Sep 1911 Oldham (v Rochdale Hornets) 1 goal added
7 Oct 1911 Oldham (v Broughton Rangers) 1 goal subtracted
11 Nov 1911 Oldham (v Australia) 1 try subtracted
27 Jan 1912 Oldham (v Barrow) 1 goal added
22 Sep 1923 Salford (v Widnes) 1 goal added

Best in the Northern Union

The pioneering 1910 Rugby League Lions tour of Australia and New Zealand

Tom Mather

Fascinating account of the first Great Britain Lions tour of Australia and New Zealand. Published in 2010 at £12.95, special offer £12.00 direct from London League Publications Ltd. Credit card orders via www.llpshop.co.uk , orders by cheque to LLP, PO Box 65784, London NW2 9NS